Duke Haney

Death Valley Superstars

Occasionally Fatal Adventures in Filmland

Praise for *Death Valley Superstars*

"These darkly fascinating tales are like scalpel slices during an autopsy on the corpse of the American Dream. While Hunter S. Thompson traced the scene of the crime to Las Vegas, Haney effectively counters with Hollywood and bravely guides us like Dante into the searing inferno of our collective fantasy life."

—Brin-Jonathan Butler, author of *The Domino Diaries* and *The Grandmaster*

"A smart, funny pop-culture cocktail, served straight, no chaser. Mixes smooth 100-proof prose (and research!) with the street-level buzz of a punkish homebrew."

—Paul M. Sammon, author of *Future Noir: The Making of Blade Runner*

"Duke Haney's passion-fueled love letter to the past radiates with a clear-eyed nostalgia for old-school celebrity. Like the best kind of writing, these tales, full of disarming charm and sly wit, both entertain and leave an ache in your heart."

—Mary Guterson, author of *We Are All Fine Here*

"I only have two requirements of book authors. One is that he loves his material. The second is that his sensibility yields insight. Duke Haney is one of a handful of writers I trust implicitly in both categories. In these times of lie and compromise, we need his truth all the more."

—Art Edwards, author of *Badge*

"Duke Haney tells the stories you think you've heard before but haven't, and the stories you can't believe no one else has told. He makes Hollywood more beguiling, more lurid, and more human while getting to the bottom of what it means to chase a dream."

—Jim Ruland, author of *Forest of Fortune*

"I know what you're saying. Yet *another* Hollywood book? As if. I'm on a Death Valley trip riding shotgun with Steve Cochran and Sean Flynn and I'm not giving up my seat. Even if there's no escape hatch."

—Donna Lethal, author of *Milk of Amnesia*

Also by Duke Haney

Banned for Life
Subversia

DEATH VALLEY SUPERSTARS
Occasionally Fatal Adventures in Filmland

Duke Haney

First edition

Cover and book design by
Michael Kronenberg

Delancey Street Press
1133 Venice Boulevard
Los Angeles, CA 90015

Front Cover: Anthony Steel catching the photographer, Rome 1958.
Photo by Tazio Secchiaroli ©David Secchiaroli

Back cover: Photo by the author. Inset photo: See page 240.

ISBN: 978-0-692-17239-1

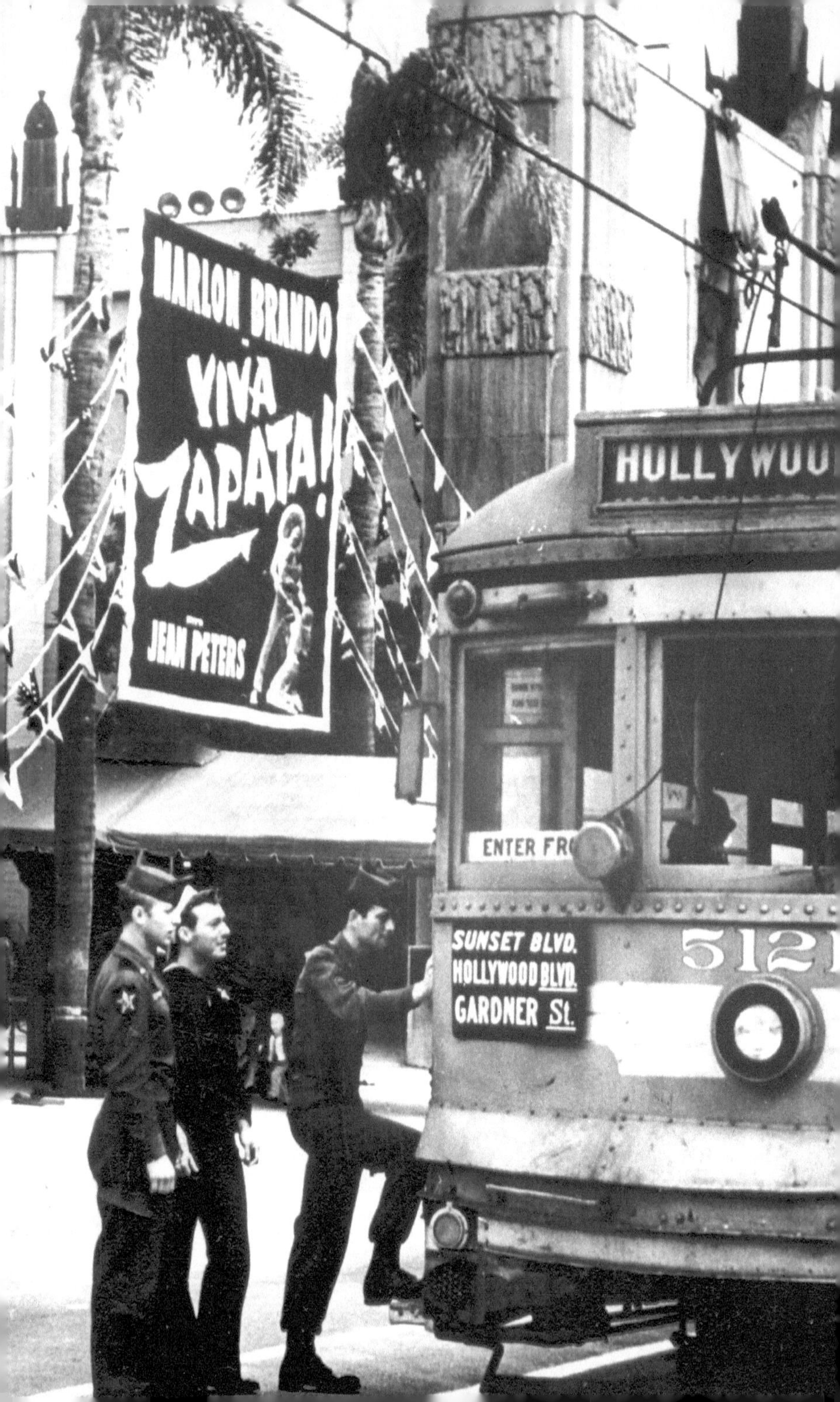
MARLON BRANDO
VIVA
ZAPATA!
JEAN PETERS
HOLLYWOO
ENTER FRO
SUNSET BLVD.
HOLLYWOOD BLVD.
GARDNER St.
5121

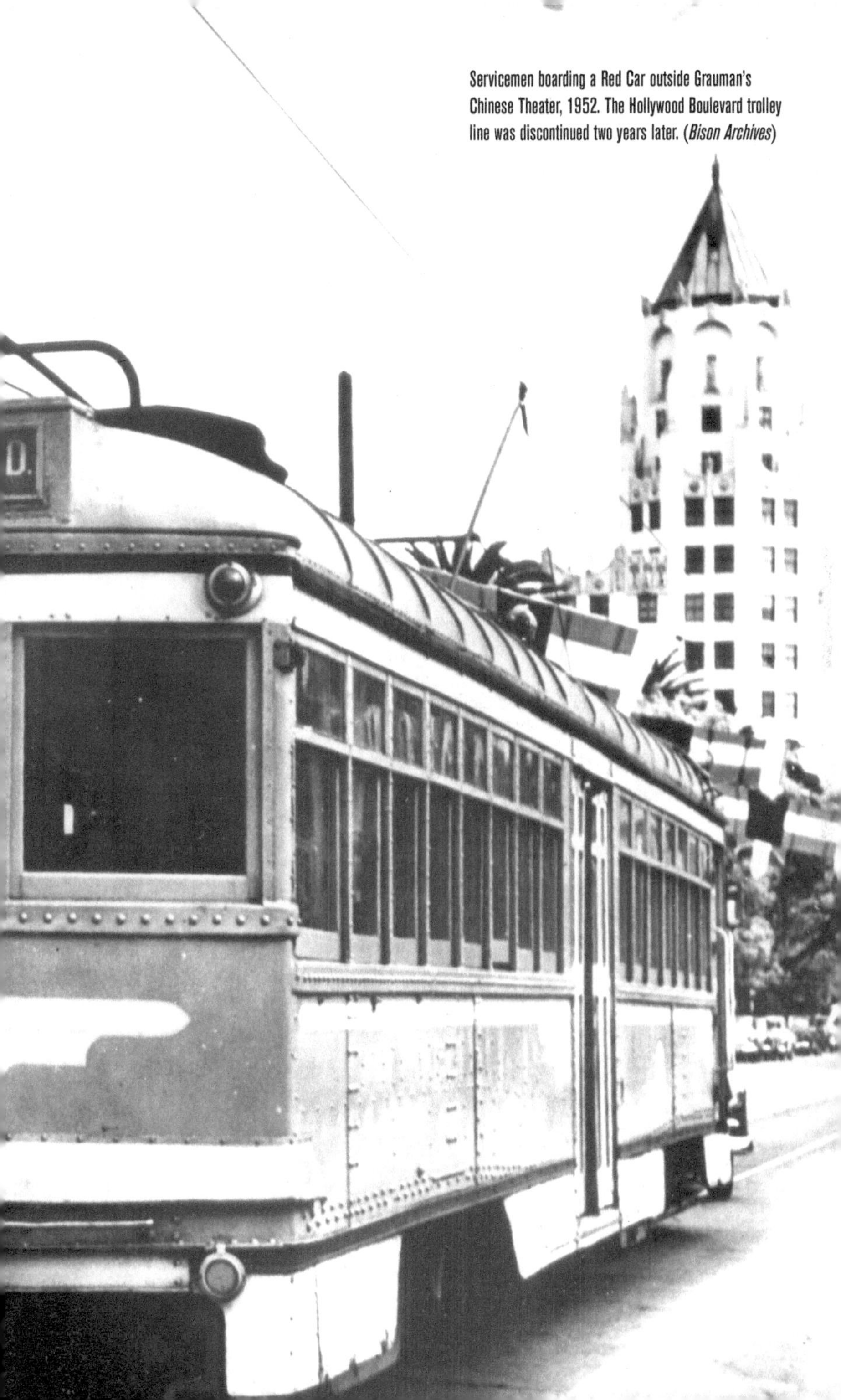

Servicemen boarding a Red Car outside Grauman's Chinese Theater, 1952. The Hollywood Boulevard trolley line was discontinued two years later. (*Bison Archives*)

For
Cynthia Bechhold Hawkins
and
Sherry Dodd

If I close my eyes and picture L.A., all I see is one big varicose vein.
Marilyn Monroe, quoted by Truman Capote

"Be of good heart," cry the dead artists out of the living past. "Our songs will all be silenced, but what of it? Go on singing."
Orson Welles in *F for Fake*

Contents

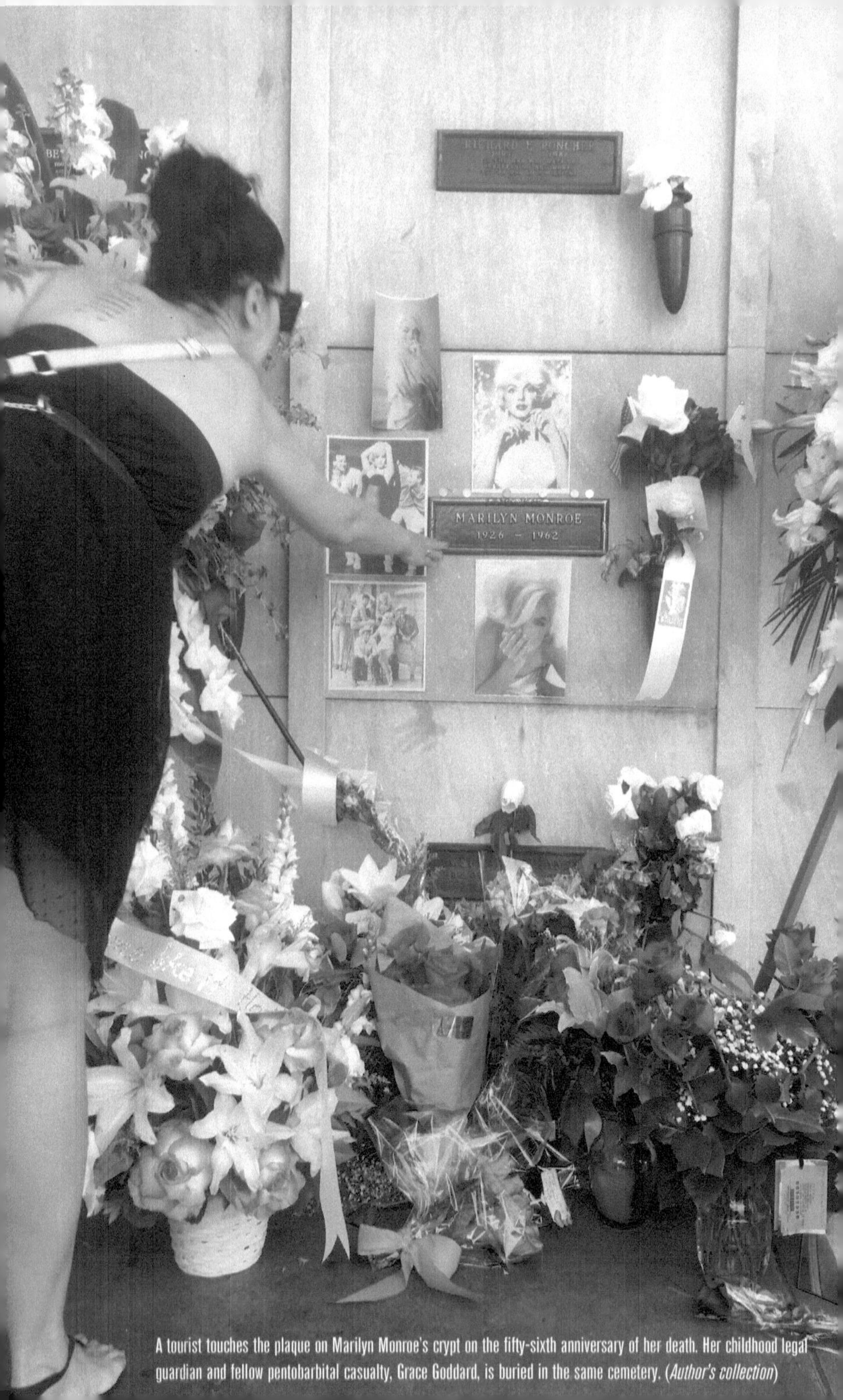

A tourist touches the plaque on Marilyn Monroe's crypt on the fifty-sixth anniversary of her death. Her childhood legal guardian and fellow pentobarbital casualty, Grace Goddard, is buried in the same cemetery. (*Author's collection*)

Introduction

I FIRST MET DUKE HANEY AS AN AVATAR.

We both belonged to an online writers' collective called The Nervous Breakdown, which was everything a community should be: supportive, honest, encouraging, and eclectic.

Duke first appeared on the site as if in shadow. One couldn't help but notice him: first, his name, as if straight out of a western, and then his avatar image of a bruised and bloody face with a wary smile gazing out from a hospital bed. Many of us found ourselves wondering just who this Duke Haney character was.

It turned out the image was taken after Duke had been hit by a car on Sunset Boulevard—an accident that, while serious and debilitating, was in keeping with his backstory. Even his traumas were cinematic.

It took some time for him to reveal that he had been a Roger Corman darling, a young scene stealer before he turned his hand to writing. It took even more time for him to reveal that he had written one of the cultish *Friday the 13th* scripts. But even before I knew this, he had the scent of Hollywood on him.

On my first visit to L.A., he took me to the cemetery where some of Hollywood's most famous bones lie, Westwood Village Memorial Park. It's a small patch of green grass and granite, surrounded by concrete block towers just off the busy Wilshire Boulevard. We stumbled first upon Farrah Fawcett's newly minted grave (and of course he had a story about Farrah), and then we made a pilgrimage to Marilyn Monroe's crypt, festooned with a dozen lipstick marks of fans still grieving the loss of the silver screen's most celebrated blonde.

His role of tour guide didn't stop there. As we drove across the city, down the wide boulevards, Duke would point out places where Jim Morrison used to drink, the seedy motel where Janis Joplin breathed her last, and where the Manson Family parked their car before murdering the tragic LaBiancas. Although a native of Virginia, he seemed somehow to be of the streets of L.A. The dust from the nearby desert seemed to leave its mark on him, and he appeared as if from some other time.

As a radio producer in my homeland of New Zealand, I commissioned Duke to read a series of his short pieces from his book *Subversia*—we called it "Tales from Hollywood." The stories, although set firmly in America, crossed the Pacific with ease. The audience loved his drawl; and they loved the timelessness of his stories.

Death Valley Superstars is a little like a guided tour. Duke takes us to Virginia, where he meets Elizabeth Taylor, married at that time to the local senator. He writes about Marilyn with the eye of a smitten director and casts her in a role that she never had in real life, that of thinking, breathing, powerful woman. There are stories that are not, at first glance, related to the movie industry, stories concerning gentrification and the vanishing of eccentric locals, the lasting impact of the Kennedy assassination, and an hilarious account of a séance in which the spirit of Jim Morrison comes to visit.

Duke has the feel of a gumshoe detective, looking for clues to where the bodies are buried and the secrets are kept. Having known him as both as a writer and a friend for nearly a decade, I know the price he pays for his writing. He sweats over each word, every comma placement. But his perfectionism never tilts to pedantry, and he manages to interlock facts with his own life story. His is a shadowy pen, which writes from an observational seat: the bus window, the corner of the bar, or the table across the room.

What makes these stories truly memorable is not just the fascinating subject matter, and what differentiates Duke from other writers is a trifecta of talent: meticulous research, photographic memory, and a deep understanding of and compassion for fallen idols and human frailty. These stories may be about celebrity, but they're also a reminder of the luck and chance and fate that can befall us all, and they don't look away when the car crash happens or the lights go down.

For me, Duke Haney is inextricably linked to the movies, and this collection deserves a front-row seat in any library.

Zara Potts
Auckland
May 2018

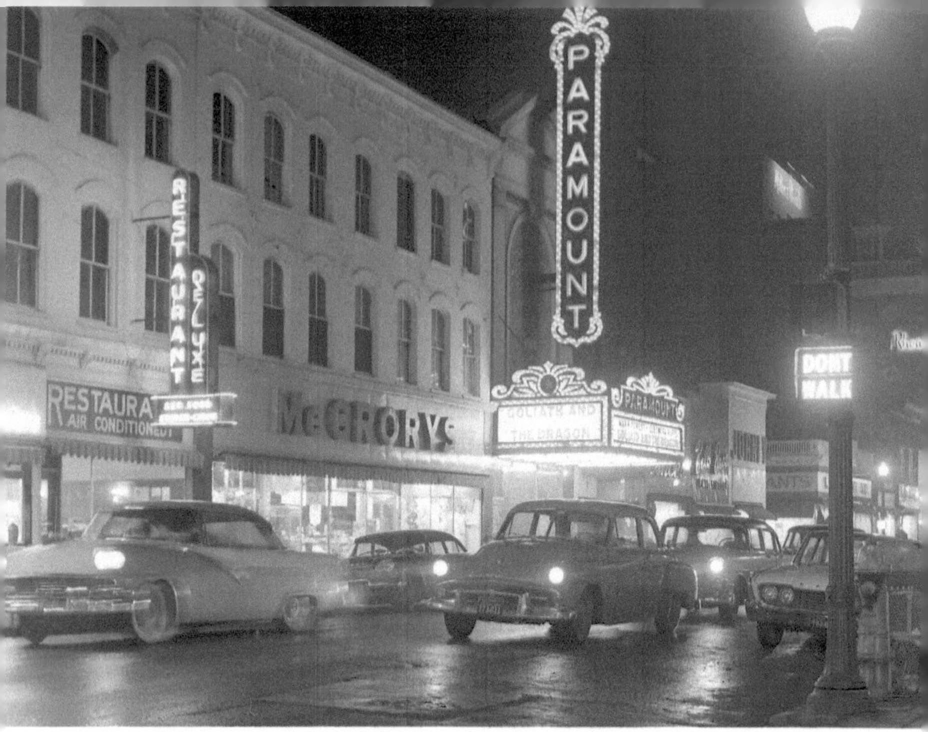

The Paramount Theater in Charlottesville, Virginia, an oasis of light in 1961 (top) and scuffed and forlorn in 1974 (bottom). The year before it closed, the town's first television station opened next door, as if to symbolize a larger cultural shift. (*Ed Roseberry, C'ville Images*)

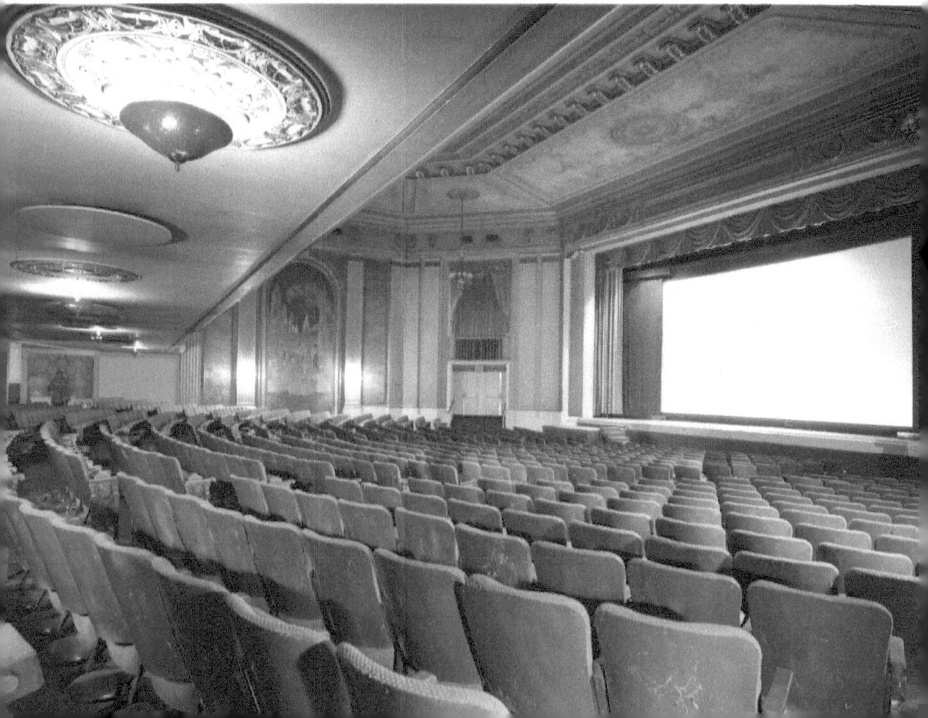

WHEN DINOSAURS RULED THE EARTH

MY CHILDHOOD EXCITEMENT about movies was inextricable from my excitement about the Paramount Theater, the jewel of Main Street in my hometown in Virginia. It was a movie palace, not a movie theater—there were four of the latter in town—and owned originally by Paramount Pictures, part of a nationwide chain. Other Hollywood studios owned theater chains, which they, like Paramount, were forced to sell after the Supreme Court decided a historic antitrust case in 1948, but new ownership didn't mean new names for most or all movie palaces. The one in my town was among the last built. The Great Depression was on and worsening when it opened in 1931, and it must have warmed its earliest patrons even more than it did me as a child in the late sixties, with PARAMOUNT glowing vertically in green light on a three-story sign above the marquee and horizontally in red light on the marquee itself, framed in both cases by flickering constellations of yellow bulbs. Only in Elvis Presley movies had I seen anything comparable, quick shots of nightclub signs that cut to Elvis performing for girls who go-go danced at the foot of the stage and guys who trashed the place during the compulsory brawl. I found that kind of indulgence terribly, if furtively, attractive, and the marquee of the Paramount seemed to promise it, while the interior prompted respect. A long, wide corridor, carpeted in red, sloped to the lobby from the ticket booth beneath the marquee. Colonial chandeliers lit the way and flanked the panoramic screen. The proscenium, crown moldings, and ceiling medallions were painted in gold leaf, and on the left and right walls of the auditorium, there were silk murals, twenty feet high, of rococo aristocrats in chateau-garden settings. In later years, before the Paramount went out of business, tickets were sold at the concession stand, where posters of movie stars were also sold: Brigitte Bardot in black leather on a chopper, Raquel Welch in the fur bikini she wore as a cavewoman in *One Million Years B.C.* Victoria Vetri, a *Playboy* Playmate of the Year, likewise wore a fur bikini in *When Dinosaurs Ruled the Earth*, the first movie I saw alone at the Paramount; and Vetri and Welch stirred things in me that, as a Christian child, I was afraid were unacceptable to God.

It was the outing, the moviegoing experience, that used to thrill me more than the movie itself, unless it somehow pertained to one of my fascinations: dinosaurs, snakes, hawks, pirates, tornadoes, the Civil War, the American Revolution, American Indians, the Renaissance, and ancient Egypt. I became interested in the last because of a coffee-table book, *The Epic of Man*, that belonged to my grandparents, and in the Renaissance because I painted and drew. In the fifth grade I wrote and starred in a play about an Indian massacre, and as a sixth-grade charity project, I wrote another play, *Santa's Elves and the Stolen Toys*, which was performed just once, with me as the head elf, at a pediatric hospital. The performance made for a two-paragraph item in the local newspaper, and later that year I was mentioned again in the paper when one of my paintings (it was of a tornado) placed ahead of work by adults in an art show. I thought I might be an illustrator one day, or a historian, or a herpetologist. I was, my parents were convinced, a brilliant boy. "He can name all the presidents in order," they would boast when I was seven, my cue to recite the list. Belated apologies to those on whom I inflicted it.

My classmates may always have considered me a little eccentric, but they liked me well enough until the seventh grade. If there was a precipitating event or a shift in my behavior, I was unaware of it; suddenly and officially I was "weird," and since to associate with me was also to be weird, I was shunned. Kids moved to other tables when I sat beside them at lunch. They sat beside me on the bus as a last resort. I started to skip school. My grades sank. I failed history, my expert subject. My parents, naturally, were aghast. What was happening to me? But it was too painful to confide, so I became belligerent at home, hurting the people who could be hurt. I flirted with delinquency, detained but never charged for stealing and vandalizing. I refused to attend church. I no longer believed in God, I said, a fainting-couch announcement in a family like mine. I had cousins who were missionaries. My grandfather was a deacon. My great-grandfather had been a preacher. My parents threatened to enroll me in military school or commit me to a reformatory, and so it went for the next few years.

I can't entirely blame my classmates. On some level I was looking for an excuse to revolt. I felt understimulated in class, certainly in church, and even by most pop culture, the disaffected kid's usual consolation. Covers of golden oldies were trending on Top Forty radio: Johnny Burnette's "You're Sixteen," Roy Orbison's "Blue Bayou," and Little Eva's "The Loco-motion" were big hits for Ringo Starr, Linda Ronstadt, and Grand Funk Railroad, respectively. The originals were released before America was rattled by assassination, Vietnam, race riots, campus radicalism, and the sexual revolution. The covers mirrored the widespread nostalgia for pre-sixties "innocence," as did, on television, *Happy Days* and its spinoff *Laverne & Shirley*, sitcoms set in the fifties, though you would never guess it by the feather-haired actors in bellbottoms. I hated those shows. I hated television in general. The idiot box, it used to be called accurately. Even so, I watched it for hours every day, a childhood habit I couldn't break.

I could sense, as a child, the audacity of the sixties. That's what I missed in the mellow seventies. Punk rock, a late arrival, appeared to be a solution, even if punk was arguably another fifties retread: early rock & roll with an accelerated tempo and apocalyptic lyrics, played by short-haired hoods (pseudohoods, really) in black leather jackets. To me that was the best of the fifties, so I welcomed the resurgence. It was a disappointing resurgence. The press dismissed punk as a British fad soon to implode, and when its standard-bearers, the Sex Pistols, disbanded and ostensibly affirmed the press, punk went underground, submerged where no small-town kid in Virginia had a prayer of finding it—not without guidance. I lacked that guidance. I lacked it with books also. There were writers, such as Jack Kerouac, who might have appealed to me, but no one ever spoke of them, and by middle school I had the same complaints about books that many (or most) kids have now: *They're so dull, so boring; I can't concentrate.* My attention span had been fried by television.

But movies could sustain my attention, and the seventies were an outstanding period for American movies, as we all know now. Few thought so at the time. The quality of movies had deteriorated since the golden age of Hollywood: that was the consensus view. A revival house had opened in my town, and it was within walking distance of my address, but so was the Paramount and so was the Jefferson, and they showed new movies, the ones I wanted to see. I would see almost any new movie for the escape it offered, though I preferred horror movies in my early teens. Monsters are freaks. I was a freak, evidently. Even socially deft kids can feel freakish in puberty, with their new emissions (menses, semen, musky sweat) and mutations (pimples, braces, growth spurts), and empathize with monsters. Then too horror movies provide boys with the chance to test their bravery by facing scenes that would have caused nightmares a few years earlier. In a strange way, horror movies are a preparation for manhood, if manhood is measured by fearlessness, as I believe remains the case. Boys recognize innately that they may be called upon to act one day in emergency situations where strength is required and timidity can cause fatalities, and that can't be willed away by progressive doctrine. Not all sex differences are inculcated.

This is not to say that women are timid or that men can't be emotionally complex. In fact, men in movies of the seventies were a complex breed, and while I didn't know it at thirteen, they were following the precedent set in 1951 by Marlon Brando in *A Streetcar Named Desire*. Brando, as Stanley Kowalski, was crude yet canny. He exploded in rages, yet he openly wept. He was domineering, yet childishly dependent on his wife, whom he swept off to bed after bellowing "Hey, Stella!" in *Streetcar*'s most indelible scene, and when Stella was seen waking in the morning, it was clear that she and Stanley had rocked the bedsprings hard. Brando was carnal in a way that no film star had ever quite been, a pagan in a world of Christians, an animal and proud of it. He popularized "Method" acting, a Russian import that prized genuine emotion, and his progeny included Al Pacino, Robert De Niro, Jack Nicholson, Paul Newman, Warren Beatty, Dustin Hoffman, Nick Nolte, and James Caan. These were the actors, among others, who made moviegoing more than a mere escape, I decided by fifteen. I had outgrown horror movies. An oft-quoted verse from the Apostle Paul's letter to the Corinthians seems apropos: "When I was a child, I spoke like a child, thought like a child, and reasoned like a child. When I became a man, I gave up my childish ways."

And so I gave up childish movies. I was hardly a man, but manhood was imminent, and I was trying to develop a winning persona. Weird boy, weird man. Complex man was better. Complex was as good as it would ever get, and that could be good indeed, judging by my screen models. I became more adventurous, seeing movies at the revival house, especially those from earlier in the seventies, and since the program changed every three or four days, I might see an instant favorite three or four times before it disappeared. Robert Altman's *The Long Goodbye* was one of those favorites: I was so enamored of Elliott Gould's disheveled performance as Philip Marlowe, the iconic detective of pulp fiction, that I wore a hand-me-down suit for a week in homage. Peter Bogdanovich's *The Last Picture Show* was another movie I saw repeatedly at the revival house: I identified acutely with Jeff Bridges and Timothy Bottoms, provincial boys smitten with Cybill Shepherd, the breathtaking classmate who spurned them, just as I had been spurned by a breathtaking classmate. Shepherd went on to spurn Robert De Niro in Martin Scorsese's *Taxi Driver*, a movie I saw when it was first released after asking an adult stranger to accompany me inside the theater: *Taxi Driver* was rated R and my parents disapproved of R-rated movies. There was no carding at the revival house, so when Hal Ashby's *Shampoo* was shown there, I would dash to the theater, night after night, and walk home feeling shattered for Warren Beatty as the swinging-sixties hairdresser jilted by Julie Christie in the final scene. It took a long time for me to puzzle out the point of the movie: much like America at the end of the sixties, Christie's character pined for stability, and pressed to choose between a charming but erratic playboy (Beatty was legendarily a playboy in life) and an old-school Republican businessman, she opted for the businessman. As if the point could be overlooked, *Shampoo* was set predominately on November 5, 1968, the day that Richard Nixon, vice president for most of the fifties, was voted into the White House.

All of these movies had a keen sense of place: Beverly Hills in *Shampoo*, Manhattan in *Taxi Driver*, the Texas panhandle in *The Last Picture Show*, and post-hippie Hollywood in *The Long Goodbye*. They were filmed on location, not, as with so many television shows, on prefab sets, and they broadened a boy who had barely been out of Virginia. All of them dealt with recent history, directly or indirectly, though I didn't regard recent history as true history and only in retrospect do I realize that I preferred it as a subject; and they all dealt candidly with sex, a subject I preferred indubitably. I could find nudity at any newsstand (or hidden under my mattress), so I looked to movies less for titillation and more for education. Even *American Graffiti*, George Lucas's innocuous sleeper hit about hot-rodding teenagers of the fifties (or, technically, 1962), had something to impart about sexual behavior. Kids groped in cars and hunted for hookups while cruising the streets. A peripheral character was sleeping with her teacher, it was hinted. A dated hint I didn't catch: the teacher was named Mr. Wolfe.

American Graffiti started the wave of nostalgia that spawned *Happy Days*, which borrowed and gelded some of its elements; and for his next movie, George Lucas reached beyond the fifties for inspiration, basing Star Wars on Saturday-matinee serials of the thirties and forties: *Flash Gordon*, *Buck Rogers*, *King of the Rocket Men*, and so on. I learned that from news stories when *Star Wars* was declared a cultural phenomenon in the summer of 1977. I knew little about it otherwise. I saw Steven Spielberg's *Jaws*, the highest-grossing movie made before *Star Wars*, on the day it opened in hundreds of theaters across the country in 1975. There was a lot of advance publicity for *Jaws*, and none that I recalled for *Star Wars*, though I watched for news of forthcoming releases. I was at the head of the line to see *Star Wars* on the day it opened in my town. It had already broken box-office records in major cities, and in such a climate I didn't have the temerity to admit my dissatisfaction with it. I liked the crisp design of the indoor sets, but they were *sets*, and I would rather have spent more time outdoors in Tunisia, filling in here for Tatooine, or whatever the planet was named. I felt badgered by the rollicking score, the swashbuckling action left me cold, and I was impatient with the movie's nebulous religiosity. I had rejected religion as Luke Skywalker embraced it, and he annoyed me in any case; he was too puppyish, too earnest, too wholesome. The movie itself was earnest and wholesome, almost defiantly so. The only history in it was the make-believe history of its fairy-tale universe, and sex didn't figure at all, except perhaps for the quick kiss Luke Skywalker received "for luck" from Princess Leia. *Flash Gordon* and the rest seemed lewd compared to *Star Wars*; where they featured unwittingly kinky bondage scenes and suggestively attired women, Princess Leia was covered in loose-fitting white from neck to toe, while her breasts were bound and moved symbolically to the mounds of hair that framed her face—look here, not there! Meanwhile, among the scores of young actresses who might have played Princess Leia, George Lucas chose a real-life Hollywood princess who had been victimized as a child (or so many believed) by her pop-star father's marriage-ending affair with the oft-married Elizabeth Taylor, and who, at seventeen in *Shampoo*, had (successfully) propositioned Warren Beatty with "You wanna fuck?" Did George Lucas take none of that into account when he cast Carrie Fisher? Either way it informed the reactionary subtext of his simpleminded "space opera." Behold, in white befitting a nun, a girl whose father slept with a slut, a girl who became an onscreen slut when she slept with that celebrated slut Warren Beatty in another movie. There *are* no sluts in *this* movie, not even the pirate Han Solo or the soldiers of the black-masked, black-caped, black-gloved villain voiced by a black man. He may be evil incarnate but he isn't motivated by sex, and this all happened *a long time ago, in a galaxy far, far away*, so relax, it isn't *your* universe that he proposes to annihilate, and evil can always be defeated anyway if you're innocent and you believe in God. Weren't you happier as an innocent child? Of course you were, and you can be a child again! It's as easy as cheering for the good guys!

And adults cheered. Adults swarmed to see *Star Wars*, as I'm certain they didn't swarm to see Saturday-matinee serials in the thirties and forties. They ignored William Friedkin's *Sorcerer*, an existential thriller that was supposed to be one of the big summer movies of 1977. *Sorcerer* ran in my town for a week or two. *Star Wars* lingered for months: I took my ten-year-old brother to see it that fall. It was perfect for someone my brother's age. I preferred *Sorcerer*, a movie for adults, who preferred *Star Wars*. I didn't get it, but then, I didn't yet get the larger point of *Star Wars*: per *Shampoo*, it came to me slowly.

I saw *Star Wars*, incidentally, at the town's first two-plex, a utilitarian red-brick box that opened at the approximate moment that the Paramount, splendor gone to seed, was shuttered. Years later, refurbished with minor changes, it became a special-event venue; but it was a relic when I left Virginia at eighteen to study acting, first in Washington, D.C., then in New York City. It was no longer enough to watch movies; I wanted to make movies, to follow in the footsteps of Brando and his lineage, to go from fan to fellow.

MIRA ROSTOVA, one of my teachers in New York, had coached Montgomery Clift, who was nearly as venerated in the fifties as Brando. Another of my teachers, Frank Corsaro, succeeded Lee Strasberg as the artistic director of the Actors Studio, the Method mecca where I attended sessions every Friday. I appeared in numerous fringe-theater productions and student films, and debuted professionally as one of the leads in a low-budget thriller shot in Nova Scotia. Every audition, rehearsal, and gig was a lesson, and when I was idle, I tried to train in other ways for the challenging roles that were surely forthcoming. Actors should know literature, I was told, so I read without skimming for the first time since childhood, and I furthered my film education at Manhattan revival houses, discovering the work of European masters like Antonioni, Herzog, Buñuel, and Godard. The VHS player, a household staple by the mid-eighties, caused most revival houses to close, however, so that after I moved to Los Angeles, I became a regular at Jerry's Reruns, a video store with an inimitable inventory. It wasn't uncommon for me to rent half a dozen movies at Jerry's and watch them in a single sitting, some for pleasure and some for research, since I was now being paid to write screenplays. Roger Corman, the so-called King of the Bs, was the first producer to hire me. I wrote nine movies for Roger and acted in three of them. Other producers declined to cast me in the parts I wrote for myself, as if they had adopted a child—my script—and wanted the biological father literally out of the picture. Thanks, but no thanks, for the DNA. Here's a check. Now scram.

I expected a rough ride in the movie business before I left Virginia, so my growing disenchantment with it was unrelated to ego. Rather, adult-minded, character-driven movies, always a minority, were going the way of the palatial theater. The success of *sex, lies and videotape* had initiated an independent-film boom at the start of the nineties, but the new generation of "serious" filmmakers was unable to sustain it. Talk is cheap as style is expensive, so there was an abundance of talk and an absence of style in "independent film," a genre unto itself within a few years. It throve on the festival circuit, where its flaws were considered assets, and it floundered in the real world, where its gaudy nemesis, the effects-driven franchise movie, was popular even with industry professionals. This surprised me. Somehow I thought I would meet a more sophisticated class of people in Hollywood, despite its philistine reputation. Roger Corman was sophisticated. He distributed films by Fellini, Kurosawa, and Bergman, whose medieval magnum opus, *The Seventh Seal*, influenced *The Masque of the Red Death*, one of several Edgar Allan Poe adaptations that Roger directed in the sixties. In the industry of the nineties and later, many had never heard of Bergman. They had scarcely ever seen a foreign film. Old Hollywood classics bored them, unless *Alien*, say, counted as an old Hollywood classic. They had the taste and interests of middle-school nerds, a sensibility that, incubated by the industry, had spread like a pandemic, infecting the population at large with a talismanic attachment to fantasy and science fiction, comic books and superheroes, and gadgetry and electronic candy of any kind. Driving to Jerry's video store in Los Feliz, I would pass the quasi-palatial Vista Theater and ticket lines that stretched around the block for *Spider-Man*, *X-Men*, *Batman Begins*, for green-screen versions of the Harry Potter books and the Pirates of the Caribbean ride at Disneyland, for feature-length cartoons. The adults in those lines outnumbered the children by twenty to one, anecdotal proof, as if I needed it, that adult children were killing the adult-minded movie by voting with their wallets for childish blockbusters.

But criticism was unwelcome, as I learned awkwardly at a party where *Iron Man* was being discussed by people in their thirties and forties. Those who hadn't seen *Iron Man*, released a few days earlier, queried those who had. Oh, it was great, they were told; it was *fantastic*. Somebody asked if I intended to see it, and I said simply, testing the waters, "I don't see movies made for children." Silence. Frozen looks of horror. One person laughed nervously. Except for that laughter, it was a bit like repudiating religion to my family at thirteen. I didn't rebuke anyone for seeing *Iron Man*, but the effect was the same, and it's the same, I've noticed, when technology is criticized. Nobody wants to be a party pooper, a dinosaur, so that misgivings are typically voiced after a preamble that, as I'll burlesque it, goes something like: "Now, I don't want you to get the wrong idea. I think computers and cellphones are just wonderful. I couldn't live without them! But don't you think maybe, possibly, we're all a little alienated? Probably not, I know! But maybe, possibly, if I can go on for a minute without giving you the impression that I'm against those things, which I'm definitely not..." Adults weren't so timid in the past, but the children of the past didn't hold the cultural power that children do now. I'm reminded of "It's a Good Life," a 1961 episode of *The Twilight Zone*, in which a despotic boy with godlike powers, including the ability to read minds, threatens to banish to "the cornfield" any grown-up with insubordinate thoughts. (Interestingly, save for television, which he programs telepathically, the boy prefers the natural world to the world of machines, and the episode concludes with a man being turned into a jack-in-the-box after an attempted insurrection.)

The Twilight Zone is fantasy, of course. I'm not unilaterally opposed to fantasy, or comic books or science fiction and so on, though I can't help but wish for equally popular alternatives. Latter-day television shows like *Mad Men* are often said to compensate for the dearth of adult-minded movies, but I can't agree. I've never watched a television show as stunning visually as *Days of Heaven*, another of those instant favorites that I was compelled to see night after night in the seventies. I've never been as devastated by a television show as I was by *Chinatown*, *The Deer Hunter*, and *Who'll Stop the Rain*, three more teenage favorites; and I've never identified with a television actor as I identified with Jack Nicholson in *Five Easy Pieces*, Al Pacino in *Serpico*, and Sam Bottoms in *Apocalypse Now*. (I envisioned myself going native in any primitive setting, as did Bottoms's surfer character on reaching the jungle enclave of Brando's Colonel Kurtz.) My teens would have been intolerable without movies, and I hoped to inspire others as I had been inspired, but I sailed too late to find the Hollywood I sought. It was a desperate Hollywood that produced art accidentally. Studios like Paramount had struggled since they were forced to sell their theater chains and a rival medium arrived simultaneously in the late forties, and by the seventies they were betting blindly on unproven filmmakers: Altman, Ashby, Scorsese, Friedkin, Bogdanovich, Spielberg, Lucas. Maybe *they* knew how to pack theaters. The last two knew exceptionally well; but while *Jaws* changed the Hollywood business model, its cultural impact was slight compared to that of *Star Wars*. Anticipating the age of algorithms, Lucas "had done sociological research on what makes hit films," he said in 1977, and "saw that kids today don't have any fantasy life the way we had," *we* being the generation of the sixties, which understood, "as every movie made in the last ten years points out, how terrible we are, how we have ruined the world and what schmucks we are and how rotten everything is." His nostalgic antidote, a "vision about the way you want the world to be," might have been praised sheepishly by adults *a long time ago, in a galaxy far, far away* as a fun but silly thing their kids dragged them to see. *Star Wars* removed the qualifiers and launched the era of the puerile epic that continues to this day. People are "terrible." The world is "ruined." Everything is "rotten." Yes, that's what audiences really meant when they complained that movies had gone downhill since the golden age of Hollywood: reality wasn't handled with kid gloves as it used to be when Hollywood adhered to the Hays Code, its in-house censorship system that was abandoned in the late sixties. Lucas acted as his own Hays Code in directing *Star Wars*.

In its sobering epilogue, *American Graffiti* allowed that the innocence of the fifties was precarious, touching a nerve that its small-screen counterpart, *Happy Days*, avoided like the third rail. I admire the Lucas of *American Graffiti*, and whatever else I may say of *Star Wars*, I admire Lucas's uphill battle to realize it. Few thought it would prove profitable. The joke was on them. The joke was on me too: the triumph of *Star Wars* marked the beginning of the end of a teenage dream.

But countless others lost something as well, including those yet to be born when *Star Wars* premiered, and a telling, if digressive, example of what I mean can be found in an anecdote in *The Armies of the Night*, Norman Mailer's Pulitzer Prize-winning account of the October 1967 March on the Pentagon. Organized by the National Mobilization Committee to End the War in Vietnam, the event drew some 70,000 demonstrators, with Mailer among the hundreds arrested by MPs. He spent the night in jail, where he dispersed cash to "a dozen young men who were probably without money, who had hitched to Washington and slept on a floor" the night before the march. One of them, "small, lithe, with the body moves of a superb athlete and the small bright snubbed features of a cat," had "the most spectacular arrest," as elaborated by Mailer, who writes of himself in the third person, a signature device:

> Breaking through the line of MPs near to where Mailer had been arrested, [the cellmate] had dodged back and forth among the Marshals for many minutes, outrunning them, crossing field on them, doubling back, stopping short, sprinting, loping, teasing them, then outrunning them again—they had been too fatigued to hurt him when finally, fox to their hounds, he was caught by the [Potomac] river. He spoke with a stammer, great intensity behind his words, much intelligence. He gave Mailer a critique of the staging of *The Deer Park* which was about as incisive as his own. A remarkable boy, Mailer had decided—just the sort to have in your army.

The Deer Park is a novel by Mailer—about Hollywood, incidentally—that he adapted for the New York stage. It wasn't the sort of production that would have interested many tourists, so Mailer's cellmate was likely from the New York area and had indeed hitched to Washington and slept on a floor. That's commendable, but indigent protesters have hoboed to Washington before and since, and a purse snatcher can spectacularly resist arrest. The pluck of this boy with the "features of a cat" doesn't, by itself, render him remarkable.

But consider this: Mailer was perhaps *the* most important American writer of the sixties, a celebrity intellectual with no modern equivalent. He can be said rightly to have invented New Journalism with "Superman Comes to the Supermarket," his 1960 essay about John F. Kennedy, and magazines like *Harper's* and *Life* paid him unparalleled sums for his insights into current events. Joan Didion and Hunter S. Thompson, both influenced by Mailer, are better known now, and where Mailer is known, it's less for his writing and more for his image as an obnoxious, violent egotist. He cultivated that image, but however authentic it was or wasn't, his ego is key to my point: here, in *The Armies of the Night*, he praises a critique that's "about as incisive as his own" from a stranger of "much intelligence" and "great intensity" who was probably in his late teens or early twenties.

That, to me, *is* remarkable, particularly when I wonder if someone of comparable age could engage a writer on a par with Mailer today. But I don't believe there are such writers, and I don't believe there are such kids. I can imagine a kid asking a fantasy writer—or George Lucas, for that matter—about sorcerers and robots and clones and elves, or better yet, how to break into the business of writing fantasy. But a kid with a mind nuanced enough to critique a literary lion so perceptively that it's mentioned for posterity—no, I sadly can't conceive of such a kid. Mailer's "army," long gone, has been replaced by a hive mind stuck in chrysalis.

WHEN I SAID I don't believe there are any writers on a par with Mailer, I didn't mean to suggest that good writers are a thing of the past; I meant that no writer now is the luminary that Mailer once was, and even he wasn't compared to movie stars, unlike his contemporary, Jack Kerouac. What Brando was to film, Kerouac was to letters, and *On the Road*, his best-known book, ultimately changed my life, with its casually rebellious characters, young guys who, while crisscrossing America in pursuit of "kicks," had manic exchanges about books and ideas. They were pagan intellectuals, a combination I hadn't thought possible, and I envied not only their devil-may-care coolness but their knowledge of literature and, more than that, their *excitement* about it. *On the Road*, overrated in hindsight, was my gateway book; I read more Kerouac, and from him I moved on to a long list of writers—poets, playwrights, essayists, philosophers—though I favored novelists, or rather, the novel as a form. Its effect on me was cinematic, and gradually a Plan B cohered: if movies finally failed me, if I couldn't play the kind of characters I set out to play because I wasn't allowed to play those I had written for myself and they didn't exist in scripts written by others, I could channel and, in a sense, play them as a novelist. Eventually I acted on Plan B, even if the timing was unfortunate, with the audience for print in decline. "Just as long as people are still reading," I've said dutifully when asked about e-books, tech's solution to the problem it created, its bandage for a beheading. I try to keep an open mind, but "electronic book" to me is as incongruous as seeing Frank Sinatra in love beads as he covers the latest hit by—what's their name again? You know, those kids from England—the ones with the long hair?

A friend of mine, applying the cyclical view of history to reading, believes that revival is inevitable; but vaudeville was never revived after it was phased out by movies, and movies were nearly as marginalized as books by television, and virtual reality may abolish every narrative medium. The sort of movies I loved are effectively extinct already, though every so often I'll catch a new one—the last was *The Assassination of Jesse James by the Coward Robert Ford*—and for a couple of hours I'm furloughed from the incessant pop culture of the twenty-first century, which I can never escape entirely; I glance up and there it is, a clown making balloon animals and "knock, knock" jokes that slay the people around me, people of every age, while I sit and wonder what the fuck they're *laughing* about. Have they lost their minds? Is there a boy who's threatened to send them to the cornfield if they don't respond as he does?

But that boy is all of them, it seems to me, and nothing like the boy I was, even before he was asking adult strangers if they would accompany him to an R-rated movie. I can picture him now, about to see a movie alone for the first time. He walks up the long corridor, carpeted in red, of the Paramount Theater, pausing at the concession stand to gawk at thumbnail photos of the posters for sale, and a voice in his head says, *Don't look. God doesn't want you to look.* But the voice is quiet in the darkness of the auditorium, where the boy watches a girl in a fur bikini cavort anachronistically with a dinosaur, and the boy thinks, *Man, I would love to be that dinosaur*, never dreaming that, when he's a man, a dinosaur is just what he'll be.

2011

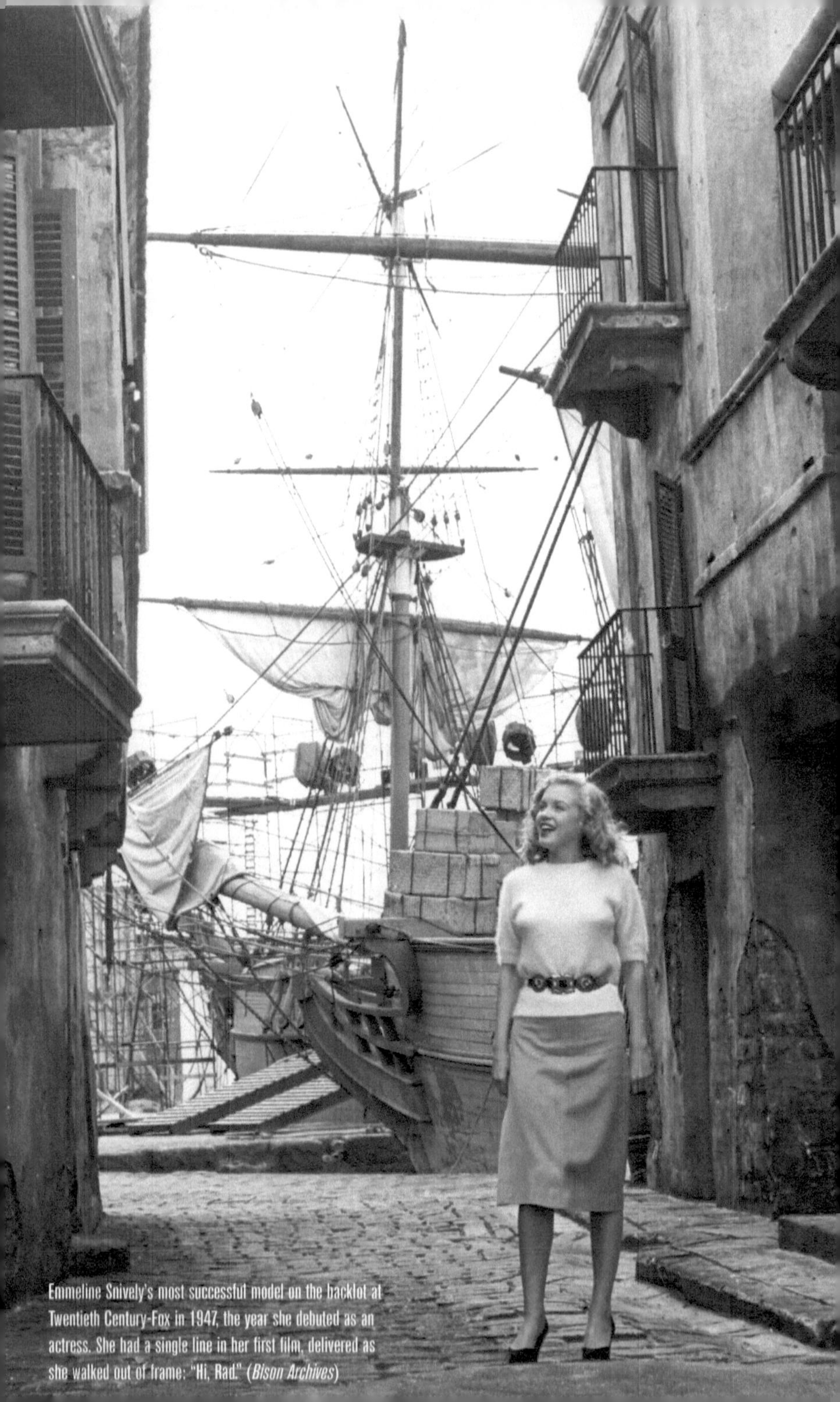

Emmeline Snively's most successful model on the backlot at Twentieth Century-Fox in 1947, the year she debuted as an actress. She had a single line in her first film, delivered as she walked out of frame: "Hi, Rad." (*Bison Archives*)

GOLDEN STATE GIRL

FIFTY YEARS AGO today in Los Angeles, where I'm writing these words while facing a screen of a kind that didn't exist in 1962, a thirty-six-year-old woman fatally overdosed on Nembutal and chloral hydrate, sedatives she used to sleep. She had a documented history of insomnia and attempted suicide, but there's no conclusive proof that she killed herself intentionally or accidentally or that someone else administered the drugs. Her housekeeper, whom the LAPD thought "vague" and "possibly evasive in answering questions," reported finding her dead at around three a.m. in the master bedroom of the Spanish Revival hacienda she had bought six months earlier on the advice of her psychiatrist, who supposed it would give her a sense of stability. She lacked that sense, having lived since childhood like a nomad, for the most part in California, where flux was and is the norm.

She was a product of California both spiritually and factually, born in the charity ward of Los Angeles General Hospital to an emotionally disturbed mother who worked as a negative cutter at Consolidated Film Industries, a processing lab for Hollywood studios. Her father, also employed by Consolidated, refused to acknowledge her, and after her mother was institutionalized, she went from a Hollywood orphanage to a series of foster homes in a demoralizing trajectory made bearable by her love of movies. She dreamed of being an actress, a common dream for a girl of her time and ours, in California and elsewhere, but this girl could, and no doubt did, fantasize of discovery by a talent scout, per the local myth.

When she was eighteen, a variation on this myth was realized. By then she was married to a merchant seaman and holding a Rosie-the-Riveter job at an aircraft factory in Burbank, where a photographer with the Army's First Motion Picture Unit, impressed by the way she photographed, encouraged her to model professionally. She applied to an agency owned by the wonderfully named Emmeline Snively, who was initially underwhelmed: the girl was "too plump," though "cute-looking," and "knew nothing about carriage, posture, walking, sitting or posing. She was a California blonde—dark in winter, light in summer."

Most of the "cheesecake" photos of the day were taken in Los Angeles, and, tutored by Emmeline Snively, the girl soon became a favorite of cheesecake photographers. She bleached and straightened her kinky hair, and slimmed by jogging and lifting weights. She corrected a slight overbite with braces, and improved her nose and chin with cosmetic surgery. She scrutinized every frame on every contact sheet of her photo sessions, a lifelong policy, and devised makeup tricks to tweak remnant flaws. For instance, her lips were "really very flat," a friend remembered, so she "painted them with about five shades of lipstick, to get the right curves, the right shadows to bring out the lips." She further highlighted her lips by darkening a pale mole just above them. As a California girl, let alone a working model and aspiring actress, she was alert to the importance of surfaces, and she was searching for a look, *the* look, that would captivate the world. And bit by bit, from her first modeling job in 1945 to her first starring role in Technicolor in 1953, she achieved it, and so invented one of the most famous entertainers of the twentieth century, now more famous than any other, still instantly identifiable as Marilyn Monroe, even to twenty-first-century children who might be pressed to name the dead president on the dime they see daily without seeing it.

THE NOTION THAT CALIFORNIA is a place where people reinvent themselves is older than Hollywood, though it was bolstered by the Hollywood star system, which amended the features and biographies of unknown novices and seasoned performers alike, often recalibrating the initial image if it failed to click. Lucille Ball, now maybe the second most famous entertainer of Marilyn Monroe's era, underwent a series of image overhauls at RKO and MGM, where her brown hair was dyed its trademark red, the star system's only significant contribution to her later success in television. It could claim even less for Marilyn's success in movies. She was dropped by the first studio to sign her, Twentieth Century-Fox, apparently because, as California girls are wont to do, she was dating a surfer, another Fox discovery likewise desired by the daughter of Darryl Zanuck, chief of production at Fox. A contract with Columbia wasn't renewed after, supposedly, Harry Cohn, the Columbia chief, watched rushes of *Ladies of the Chorus,* a backstage musical featuring Marilyn, and snarled to an assistant, "What did you put that fat pig in the picture for?" Finally, despite Zanuck's dislike of her, she was signed again by Fox, where Zanuck was inclined to ignore her. But Marilyn wouldn't let him ignore her. She courted journalists who published stories that stressed her desolate childhood, with Dickensian embellishments provided by Marilyn. Meanwhile, she haunted the Fox publicity department so that whenever a starlet was needed for a photo, there was Marilyn, who played "the camera the way a virtuoso plays an instrument," in the words of *Life* magazine photographer Philippe Halsman. Numerous photographers concurred, including Richard Avedon, who raved that Marilyn "gave more to the still camera than any actress—any woman—I've ever photographed," and Eve Arnold, who marveled at a photogenic quirk: the "very fine golden hairs" that covered Marilyn's face and "trapped the light. It was extraordinary; I've never seen it before. It acted as a nimbus so that she looked almost angelic."

Marilyn's self-promotion campaign generated mail from people who had never seen her onscreen. It made fans of film exhibitors and theater owners, and at a Fox party where established stars were on hand to meet them, they instead mobbed Marilyn, asking, "What pictures are you going to be in, Miss Monroe?" Marilyn replied coyly that such questions should be directed to Darryl Zanuck, who, at last forced to recognize her potential, mandated her use in any production that suited the image that, over his head and through the chinks of the system, she had peddled directly to the public: an orphaned bombshell, sweetly oblivious to her beauty and sex appeal.

In reality, of course, beauty and sex appeal were Marilyn's currency. A classic Hollywood climber, she slept her way to the middle, which is still as far as the casting couch, in its manifold forms, can take anyone. "It wasn't any big dramatic deal," she later told a friend. "Nobody ever got cancer from sex." She told other friends that, at especially fraught moments, she scraped by as a call girl. Would the public have forgiven her, had it known? Possibly. It forgave her when she copped to posing nude in desperation, a startling mea culpa for 1952, just as it forgave her incorrigible unprofessionalism, her oft-reported tardiness on the set. That was viewed then as an impish foible of the waifish Marilyn and not as passive aggression, a concept decades from popularization, even in Hollywood, which led the world in passive aggression, the "Good to see you!" followed by an unctuous retreat and an unspecific invitation to get together soon.

But Marilyn wasn't just passive-aggressive; at times she was frankly hateful. Her occasional hairdresser, George Masters, recalled that if he was "two minutes late, she was furious, though she thought nothing of keeping others waiting for hours or days." Masters considered her the coldest person he ever knew, while Billy Wilder, the director of two of her best films, once said that he had "never met anybody as mean as Marilyn Monroe," perhaps thinking of her tirade after seeing rushes of *Some Like It Hot*—"I'm not going back into that fucking film until Wilder reshoots my opening"—

or her response to an assistant director's knock on her dressing-room door: "Go fuck yourself."

But such accounts are usually overlooked, or anyway rationalized, by those acquainted with them. There's no pathos in the image they propose; but there's pathos aplenty in the image of Marilyn as a wounded stray, as the candle in the wind of Elton John song, as a martyr of celebrity, of Hollywood, of men and patriarchy and the male gaze. This image—and it's finally a single image—excludes those traits it can't, and doesn't want to, accommodate: opportunism, toughness, willfulness, petulance, all of which, and then some, can be found in a convoluted woman with a genius for appearing the opposite.

IN DECEMBER 1954, wearing a brunette wig, Marilyn flew to New York with a ticket she had bought under the name Zelda Zonk—even her protopunk alias was alliterative, with the *Z*s suggesting sleep—and, lest somebody recognize her, was driven in the trunk of a car to a hideout in Connecticut. Typecast and underpaid, she disappeared to force Fox to renegotiate her contract, and after she emerged from hiding to hold a press conference, she took an apartment in New York, where she would live, on and off, to the end. New York was thought to be cultured as California was not, a belief that persists, so that many Californians have entertained ideas of moving to New York. It has also worked the other way, of course. There may be more expatriate New Yorkers living in California than anywhere else in the world, but they, as well as transplants from elsewhere, often speak of leaving once they've gotten what they came to get, and that's sometimes fame and wealth, though it used to be wealth alone, per the 49ers who panned for gold in the Sierra Nevada and another wave of gold seekers who in 1848 descended on the San Gabriel Mountains north of L.A. This earlier gold rush is all but forgotten, but so much is forgotten in California, a place with a scant sense of history, at least compared to my native Virginia. Flux is a foe of memory.

But Marilyn—an anomalous Californian in this way, among others—was versed enough in history that she would cite Eleonora Duse, a legendary Italian actress who died two years before Marilyn was born, as her role model. Duse was known for "living" her parts with a technique so subtle it didn't seem to be a technique at all, inspiring the Stanislavski Method and its various interpreters, among them Lee Strasberg, Marilyn's mentor in New York. She wanted to be a serious actress, she announced, not an "erotic freak," and to that end, she formed her own production company, which would create projects of a kind that she knew she would never be offered by Fox. Long interested in literature, she befriended poets and novelists, marrying one of America's two best-known playwrights, Arthur Miller, while the second, Tennessee Williams, looked on and, after her death, weighed in:

> People praised Marilyn because she read books, because, I think, we couldn't conceive that an ambulatory bowl of rich vanilla ice cream needed to think or to grow a mind. Marilyn sought and developed her identity as a sex symbol; she wiggled and cooed for the camera, but, incapable of satisfaction or understanding, she fought this image, so she would read Joyce and Schopenhauer and Woolf and Jung. Of course she understood none of it, because there was no fertile ground in which any of this could take hold: You can throw a multitude of seeds into the desert sands, but there will never be fruitage. Marilyn's mind was a desert, a drought, with tiny compartments devoted to clothes, makeup, stardom, and fucking. That is all. That is absolutely all.

This blistering assessment might sadly have rung true to Marilyn at her most insecure, and nothing made her more insecure than acting. A dream she noted helps to explain the crippling stage fright that worsened as her career progressed. In the dream Lee Strasberg was a surgeon who opened her with a scalpel, "deeply disappointed" when he discovered "absolutely nothing there." Acting, then, may have terrified Marilyn because it could expose her as the hollow shell—her mind "a desert," a metaphor that recalls Southern California—she suspected herself to be.

Williams's attack on Marilyn was also an attack on the "gnomish" Strasberg, who "lied to her and told her she was the new Duse," making her believe "that she might become the great actress Strasberg told her she could and should be," though "we never did and never will look at her and admire her acting—we will admire her bust and butt and her giggling stupidity." Many thought the same. Far from being praised for reading books, Marilyn was widely mocked for it, and even her advocates, with the customary exceptions, admitted her limitations as an actress. Laurence Olivier, her co-star in *The Prince and the Showgirl,* which he also directed, decided she was really a model after she followed his instructions perfectly, as she had never done before, during a scene without dialogue. To call an actress a model is a degradation for a classical actor like Olivier, but where Marilyn is concerned, I think, in a way, he was onto something.

A few years ago, I watched Marilyn's first collaboration with Billy

Wilder, *The Seven Year Itch*. I had seen it before, just because it happened to be on television, when I was a kid with no interest in old movies or the people in them, and I liked it to the extent that I could like any old movie, but seeing it again years later, what struck me, as it hadn't when I was a kid, was the ineffable magnetism of Marilyn Monroe. Every time she was offscreen, I wanted her back, and every time she was onscreen, I couldn't take my eyes off her. It was, I slowly realized, partly because she was posing in ways that command attention, just as cats command attention with their poses, though I wouldn't say that Marilyn otherwise reminds me of a cat. I wondered if she had been directed to pose as she did, but she did it so often and so well that it had to be her doing alone.

Marilyn's difficulty with dialogue was as irritating to her colleagues as her habitual tardiness. Multiple takes were sometimes necessary—the record may have been forty-seven—to get a single usable shot, even if her line was one word long. Yes, she was frightened. Yes, she was passive-aggressive. Yes, she was hazy from insomnia and the drugs she took to sleep. But her background as a model had prepared her to pose, not act, just as she was used to still photographers talking her through a shoot, which no movie director would do unless the shot was silent. Also, as a model, she was used to photographers pausing between frames to make small adjustments, as would she, with her preternatural sense of what did and didn't look good to the camera. Those pauses were standard when she was working as a model, but she was expected to keep going as an actress, even as the model in her head, concerned with lighting and angles, found it natural to stop. Meanwhile, the actress in her head must have resented the intrusion of the model. She was there to act, not pose, and if Marilyn the model wouldn't insist that every moment be "real" in the Method way, Marilyn the actress was determined to have an equal say. Am I feeling this? Am I really *feeling* it? Wait, I forgot my line. Can we do another? Damn, I'm getting a shadow on my face. Another, please. Is this real? Am I faking it? What's my line again?

And so on. As much as she tortured her colleagues, Marilyn tortured herself most of all. Yet the result is that she almost always, in the slang of her day, looks like dynamite, since the model in her wouldn't settle for less, while there's a rawness, a freshness, a subtle spontaneity that comes through even when she's posing. Then too the camera likes fear, which is why some directors prefer first takes, the ones in which the player we're likeliest to watch is the least comfortable. All of Marilyn's takes were first takes. Her terror of acting was an asset.

Of course, none of this qualifies her as a great actress as Tennessee Williams or Laurence Olivier would define greatness, with her slender range and dicey technique. But Marilyn the actress is roughly equivalent, I would argue, to singers like Bob Dylan or Mick Jagger, who are far less versatile and skilled than any contestant who ever made the first cut on *American Idol,* while even the winners of *American Idol* are as immediately forgettable as Dylan and Jagger were memorable from the gate. As for Marilyn, I can hardly point to anyone else I find more enjoyable to watch onscreen, and by that measure, not only do I think she's a great actress, I think she's a great artist.

MARILYN THE ARTIST is the Marilyn we always heard the least about, and we hear almost nothing about her now. The mysterious death of Marilyn the victim is making a few headlines again—is it proper to speak of this as the golden anniversary of her death?—and, over the years, there has been considerable talk of the alleged affairs of Marilyn the temptress—or is that again the victim?—with John and Robert Kennedy, though it's unmistakably Marilyn the retro sex goddess who has materialized recently on Facebook to provide an authoritative example of an outstanding body versus the contemporary body ideal. Her films? How many now watch them, aside from old-movie buffs? They're too slow for most of us. We want nonstop action and special effects, not dated bedroom comedies featuring dead people, including Marilyn Monroe.

In fact, the only Marilyn Monroe movie most people have seen, if they've seen one at all, wasn't made in Hollywood; it was made at Madison Square Garden three months before Marilyn died, when she sang "Happy Birthday" for John Kennedy after being introduced—a gag about her tardiness—as "the late Marilyn Monroe." Two clips of Kennedy's forty-fifth birthday celebration were the first to come up when, researching Marilyn before writing about her, I checked YouTube for clips, with the shorter version of her brief performance at the top of the list. The quality is poor, but she can be heard and seen in action, as she can't be, of course, in her many still photos.

But those photos are the key to her durability. Unlike most entertainers of her day and before, she doesn't have to be heard or seen in action for someone unfamiliar with her—are there such people?—to glance at an image of her decked out and dolled up as "Marilyn Monroe" and grasp her essence reflexively: *Hot blonde! Bimbo! Bombshell!* Her makeup tricks, her tireless self-inventory, her scrutiny of every picture taken of her: all have paid off in a future world she could never have anticipated, and her acting has paid off too, since it's her alter ego, not her, that we observe in most of her photos. She no longer needs her auxiliary alter ego, the ragsto-riches waif, to help put her across. That's for people curious enough to read a little about the overwrought inventor of Marilyn Monroe, and most people aren't that curious, and why should they be regarding a woman who's been dead for fifty years? She's history, and now it seems that all of us are inventing alter egos through the photos and clips and updates we post online, peddling ourselves to "friends" we never met or barely know in a world that reduces everybody to driveway neighbors, people we wave to as we exit or enter our cars and dash off, on foot or behind the wheel, hoping never to be trapped in a complicated exchange.

I recognize this fast, simple, self-absorbed world, a simulacrum of suburban California produced by Silicon Valley, in my offline life. For better or worse, it's the life I've always known here in Los Angeles, where I moved in search of fame and fortune, though, really, if I had been made immortal by fame, I would gladly have forgone the fortune, or so I used to tell myself. I didn't understand then that fame is ephemeral for the few who achieve it by will or by luck or by fuck. I wasn't one of them, and even if I left California after failing to get what I came to get, I could never leave it altogether. California is everywhere now, and its most famous daughter, as immortal as any dead celebrity can be, is everywhere known, and everywhere invisible in the way she most wanted to be seen.

2012

Sean Flynn at his Hollywood apartment in 1961, appearing as uneasy as he felt about his acting career and California. "I had to get out," he told a friend later. "Out of the smog and away from those freeways." (*Photographer unknown*)

NOWHERE MEN

I WAS IN THE BASEMENT of the downtown Los Angeles courthouse, where I was researching a possible nonfiction book about a film-noir actor whose offscreen brawling and balling led to trouble with the law. The basement is where old case files are stored on microfiche, and one of the files I needed was lost, so I kept returning to the courthouse to see if it had been found. I was out of luck again that day and headed to the elevator when I was stopped by a nondescript man of sixty or so. He couldn't find his way out of the basement, he said. I told him to follow me. He did, talking as we walked.

"I used to know somebody who wore a hat just like that," he said, referring to my flat cap. "She was a big racing-car driver back in the thirties. She was friends with my family."

He repeated that. He repeated everything he said. Something was clearly wrong with him, though whatever it was, he posed no threat. Evidently obsessed with height, he informed me, apropos of nothing, that he was six feet tall. Then he asked how tall I was, and before I could answer, he said, "Six-one, right? You're six-one."

"Very good. People usually think I'm taller."

"No, you're six-one. I used to know somebody who was taller than you. He disappeared in Vietnam."

That was all he said, but I blurted instantly, "Sean Flynn?" I had once considered collaborating on a screenplay about Sean Flynn, who disappeared during the Vietnam War and was, I remembered, tall. It was a guess that felt more like telepathy, and I could tell by the man's spooked expression that, yes, he had been speaking of Sean Flynn.

"How did you *know* that?" he said.

"I don't know how I knew. I just knew."

LIKE MOST MOVIE LEGENDS of his day, Errol Flynn, Sean's father, fades from collective memory a little more each year, but he was once so famous that "in like Flynn" was wink-nudge slang for sexual success. He claimed that he never chased women, they chased him, and that was certainly true of Sean's mother, Lili Damita, an actress who met Errol aboard the ship that was carrying him from England, where he performed in regional theater, to America, where, on the strength of a screen test, Warner Bros. had placed him under contract. Already a movie star known behind the scenes for her incendiary temper, Lili campaigned for marriage and threatened to kill herself when Errol balked. They wed in Yuma, Arizona, an incongruous setting for an international pair—she was French and he was Australian—and, back in Hollywood, she used her influence to win him the title role in *Captain Blood*, the pirate movie that established him as the heir of Douglas Fairbanks, the recently retired king of screen swashbucklers.

Naturally, Errol's new celebrity attracted other women. "Sometimes," he said, "they come into my dressing room at the studio and shut the door and do it to me. I just let them, that's all." Lili retaliated with tantrums and trysts of her own, and the couple separated and reconciled with tidal regularity before Lili became pregnant with Sean. Then thirty-six, five years older than Errol, she wanted a child and he didn't, and after they split irrevocably, she "devoted many years of her life to pursuing him through the divorce courts and trying to destroy him," to quote Flynn's biographer Jeffrey Meyers. Finished with acting, she put distance literally between Sean and his father, moving to Palm Beach, Florida. It was just as well, since Errol had become addicted to heroin and cocaine, to say nothing of his outstanding addiction to alcohol, which he regarded as the deadliest drug—a seasoned opinion that should give us all pause. His roller-coaster marriage to Lili seems to have soured him permanently on older women; his second wife was nineteen to his thirty-three when they met at the courthouse where he was being tried for statutory rape. (Though technically guilty, he was acquitted.) His third wife was two years younger than his second, and his final flame was fifteen, a year younger than Sean, when she started dating forty-seven-year-old Errol. "This little girl could well become your mother someday!" he would razz Sean on the rare occasions they saw each other. "Don't talk to your mother that way!" Meanwhile, he provided Sean with hookers.

But Sean was never the womanizer his father was, probably because of his close relationship with Lili—too close, at times, for Sean. He was her only child—Errol went on to have three daughters—and she fussed over him, polishing his manners and overseeing his education at an elite prep school. He was a senior at that school when his father died of a heart attack at fifty, so decayed by years of debauchery that he could have been taken for seventy. Sean flew to L.A. for the funeral, where mourners gaped at his blond good looks. His future agent recalled him as "maybe the most beautiful boy I had ever seen." *Beautiful* is a recurring word in eulogies of Sean, most notably in a passage from *Dispatches*, his friend Michael Herr's justly acclaimed memoir of the Vietnam War: "Sean Flynn could look more incredibly beautiful than even his father, Errol, had thirty years before as Captain Blood, but sometimes he looked more like Artaud coming out of some heavy heart-of-darkness trip..." The Conrad allusion anticipated Herr's screenplay work on *Apocalypse Now*. He also co-wrote Stanley Kubrick's *Full Metal Jacket*.

As a child, Sean had a few small parts in productions featuring his father, and at home in Florida, three months before he entered Duke University, he had another small part in *Where the Boys Are*, arranged by its male lead, George Hamilton, who grew up with Sean in Palm Beach. A photo of them on the set of *Where the Boys Are* was seen by the producer of *Captain Blood*, stirring memories of Sean at Errol's funeral and sparking a brainstorm: *The Son of Captain Blood*, starring the son of Errol Flynn. Sean had only been at Duke for three months when the producer contacted him.

Sean was an apathetic student with little interest in acting. He liked cars, guns, boats, travel, and here was an offer that might subsidize all that, Lili being something of a tightwad. Torn about the offer, Sean discussed it with a Duke classmate who gave an account of their talk to Jeffrey Meyers. If he did this movie, Sean projected in what Meyers characterizes as "a shocking (and surprisingly prescient) forecast," he would end up moving to Hollywood and "getting into that whole moviemaking scene," though he would "probably get very bored with it."

"After that?" asked the classmate.

"I'll go sailing around for a little while."

"After that?"

"I'll go to Africa and do some hunting."

"Then what?"

"Then, I'll probably find some way to get myself killed."

SEAN DIDN'T TAKE to Hollywood, as predicted. There was an embarrassing attempt at pop stardom, undoubtedly orchestrated by his management, but he wasn't much of a singer, and he wasn't much of an actor either. Errol could deliver a line almost as gracefully as he could ride a horse or fence, and though Sean was equally athletic, he seemed self-conscious in dialogue scenes. He was sensitive to comparisons to his father and wary of the inevitable questions about him, telling reporters they were practically strangers, or as he said to one, "He sired me, that's all." Errol's absence from Sean's childhood, Lili's bitterness toward him, the shadow cast by his notoriety: all guaranteed Sean's ambivalence about Errol; but he wasn't ambivalent about Hollywood. "Everyone I met [there]," he remarked in Vietnam to his friend Zalin Grant, "was extremely cynical and knew everything. To them, screwing a girl had nothing to do with love. Even liking a girl was a kind of therapy. Life just didn't have much meaning." It's striking that he emphasized sex in his condemnation of Hollywood, as if to contrast, in code, his film-star father's treatment of women and his own.

He moved to Paris, living in his deceased grandmother's apartment in the 17th arrondissement, and continued, without much enthusiasm, to act in movies, including three spaghetti westerns. Between movies, he satisfied his taste for sport and travel, at one point working as a safari guide in Tanzania, another fulfillment of his prophecy at Duke. Again in Paris, he dabbled as a fashion photographer and petitioned *Paris Match* to send him to Vietnam as a war correspondent. His surname overrode his inexperience: *Paris Match* complied.

During the Spanish Civil War, Errol had likewise tried his hand at journalism, one of several efforts, foreshadowing Sean, to prove that he was more than a mere actor. He funded and documented a science project for his father, a professor of biology, and wrote a play and three books: a novel, a nonfiction account of his sailing expeditions, and *My Wicked, Wicked Ways*, his autobiography. The first two are out of print, but the third, often cited as the gold standard of movie-star memoirs, has been in print since its publication two months after Errol's death in 1959. He had help with *My Wicked, Wicked Ways*, but he could turn a phrase, as when he summarized his marriage to Lili as an "impossible snarl of two volatile people" from which "there came something good anyway." The something good was Sean.

Errol's career as a war correspondent was a short-lived fiasco. Wounded and reported dead in Spain, his hasty retreat to Hollywood prompted derision and accusations of cowardice, which Jeffrey Meyers believes unfair. In any case, just as Sean had followed his father onto the screen, he now followed his father into battle. Impeccably polite, reserved but approachable, humble despite his glamorous background and appearance, he "blew minds all over Vietnam," Herr writes in *Dispatches*. GIs loved him, and while some journalists dismissed him as a slumming dilettante, he bonded with others: Herr; Zalin Grant; the English photographer Tim Page; Anthony Strickland, another Englishman; and John Steinbeck IV, who, as the son of a prominent author, could empathize with the son of a prominent actor. Sean shared a flat in Saigon with Steinbeck, Strickland, and Page, describing it in a letter to Lili as "a lovely place" with "good company when I come back from the field. We have a houseboy and his wife, stereo music, PX cards to get food & liquor from the Army. I enjoy myself very much here." The flat was called Frankie's house after the houseboy, and Tim Page, the inspiration for Dennis Hopper's feral character in *Apocalypse Now*, set the tone. A lot of women came and went. A lot of pot was smoked. Opium wasn't uncommon either.

War photography is risky business to say the least, but Page took more risks than most, and Sean did as Page did and, like Page, he was injured, though not as routinely or seriously. He parachuted into combat and walked point on patrol missions in areas filled with booby traps and snipers. He carried arms and sometimes participated in firefights. "Mud and fear, blood and death, where no films exist, is where my life is," he told a reporter who surely enhanced the quote. Either way, low on money, Sean left Vietnam for a few weeks to make a movie, his last, *Five Ashore in Singapore*. It was filmed, of course, in Singapore, and when it premiered in Vietnam, it was billed as starring "Saigon's own Sean Flynn."

He left Vietnam again during this period to cover a conflict in Borneo, and the following year, interrupting a visit to the States, he flew to Israel for the Six-Day War. There were more travels: to New Guinea, where he introduced aboriginals to pot; to Laos, where he shacked up with a local girl; to Bali, where he fell in love with another local girl and was jailed for assaulting a taxi driver who insulted her. It's said that he planned to marry the girl in Bali and settle there with her, but that may have been a pipe dream, since her parents disapproved of him and he felt that, for "some incredible reason," he belonged in Vietnam. The Frankie's-house crew had scattered, save for Page, and he and Sean found a new flat and new flatmates: the writer Perry Deane Young and the photographer Dana Stone. Young would publish *Two of the Missing*, a book about Sean and Dana, who vanished together. To see pictures of Dana, short and spectacled, you would never think that he once worked as a stripper; but you would also never think that the movie-star offspring of two movie stars could reinvent himself as a war correspondent, or that another war correspondent was a former model for Coco Chanel. Michèle Ray had been a Chanel model, and her capture and release by the Vietcong, the South Vietnamese insurgents, may have factored in the fate of Sean and Dana.

If Sean wished to become something other than Errol Flynn's son by going to Vietnam, the wish had been realized: Herr notes in *Dispatches* that people who "had barely ever heard of Errol Flynn" were impressed by Sean. He had also found his calling. Apolitical and vaguely patriotic prior to seeing firsthand the toll of American intervention, he spoke against the war in images, which suited him better than words. He admitted that he "may not have been as good a photographer as some of the other newsmen in [Vietnam], but I went into some places and got into some situations which they did not. This was the difference. I took some idiotic chances—but here I am."

He said that in March 1967. He disappeared in April 1970. Famous last words are seldom said last.

FOR TWENTY YEARS after Sean's disappearance, no one set foot in his apartment in Paris, as if he still had use for it, per *The Year of Magical Thinking*. The apartment, then, except for the dust and cobwebs, remained exactly as Sean left it when he last locked the door in 1969, and when the door was finally unlocked, pictures were taken and published in a tabloid. A book on the kitchen counter, letters sealed in envelopes, ties and jackets hanging in a wardrobe, professionally laundered shirts: such shots litter social media now, and the ones snapped at Sean's place are just as unremarkable unless you're acquainted with their backstory.

But other shots are remarkable without the backstory. Sean's apartment looks almost like a page from the collage diaries of the photographer Peter Beard, like Hemingway's den if Hemingway had been twenty-eight, Sean's age, in 1969. Animal heads and hides are mounted on the walls, as is a human skull with antelope horns arranged like tusks on either side of it. Beads circle the skull and dangle from its teeth, while nearby peacock feathers graze a poster of Che Guevara, blending with his beard so that the feathers, which stand in a white urn, look like the stems of an uprooted flower, the urn its bulb, the head of Che Guevara its blossom. There are psychedelic posters, one that reads HAIGHT-ASHBURY, as well as posters of Jimi Hendrix and Ho Chi Minh, and glossy photo prints, including a self-portrait of Sean taken while parachuting, and Chinese lanterns, and stacked poker chips, and a decorated scabbard, and a turntable on the dining table, which suggests that Sean usually ate at restaurants and not at home.

Of course he did.

This trippy bachelor pad, so specific to its time and occupant that it could never be recreated now, by itself demonstrates Sean's transformation from a clean-cut preppy to the stylishly shaggy globetrotter who died somehow in Cambodia, where the war had spread. The Vietcong and their confederates, the North Vietnamese, had installed bases in the Cambodian jungle, which the U.S. was bombing, driving the communist Vietnamese deeper into the country and closer to its capital, Phnom Penh. Cambodia had its own communist insurgency, the Khmer Rouge, and a flimsy government, led by Prince Sihanouk, under mounting pressure from without and within. When Sihanouk was deposed by his prime minister, the result was chaos: some reports had Phnom Penh about to fall to the Vietcong and the North Vietnamese. This is what Sean and Dana, on assignment for *Time* and CBS News respectively, had come to document.

Phnom Penh didn't fall, not yet, but two days after their arrival, Sean and Dana learned that the Vietcong had attacked Chi Phou, a town ten miles from the Vietnam border, and they set out for it on rented motorcycles. Another journalist told them they looked like characters in *Easy Rider*. "Queasy riders is more like it," Sean quipped. He was hoping to be captured by the Vietcong.

So it's conjectured, based on his overheard quarrel with Dana at a café in Chi Phou hours before they were in fact captured. Or maybe they didn't quarrel. Dan Southerland, a *Christian Science Monitor* reporter at the café that morning, has written that they "seemed to be in a light-hearted mood" and that Dana was "joking" when he said of Sean: "This guy wants us to get captured." If that was the plan, Sean must have been thinking of the "war from the other side" stories filed by Michèle Ray and a few other journalists following their release by the Vietcong. Ray played cards with her detainers, who clothed her in customized pajamas and composed poems about her. Vietcong troops "had explicit orders to handle all journalists correctly," according to Tim Page, since their superiors "knew the value of the press and the persuasive power of propaganda." Even so, they refused to cooperate with foreign media, and Sean may have been trying to convince Dana that they would return from captivity with the photos that eluded their colleagues.

The last known images of Sean were shot by a French news crew that showed up later that day on a stretch of National Road 1, almost four miles from Chi Phou, where a white car had been abandoned in the middle of the road and villagers told of seeing four men being marched at gunpoint by the Vietcong into the nearby woods. Three of the men were French and Japanese journalists—the fourth was their Cambodian driver-interpreter—and the same villagers were to witness Sean and Dana being forced off their motorcycles and led away.

Though the abandoned white car is in the French news footage, Dana is strangely absent as Sean advises the crew that Laotian guerrillas are in the woods. How did he know the guerrillas were Laotian? And did he spook the crew because he was concerned for their safety or anxious that they might scoop him? Whatever his intention, they credited him with saving their lives: still more journalists would vanish in the same area over the next week or so, and none of them were ever seen by Western eyes again.

"This will be the end, I know," Lili had sobbed to a friend on hearing that Sean was headed again to Vietnam that March. Interviewed by the *Palm Beach Daily News* the day after her only child and living blood relative was reported missing, she read the close of the letter he had written in Saigon minutes before he boarded a plane to Phnom Penh. As if he shared Lili's foreboding and was bracing her for the anguish to come, he encouraged her to take comfort in "this idea that all things here in the world are God's toys, you, me, Cambodia. Make peace with Him and your heart is still. Do you know how to do it? Watch the plants, rains, sunsets, bugs, the changes in the wind, sea and clouds. Watch them and relax in peace. There is a place for all us.

"Must go,
Love, Sean"

I ONCE BOUGHT car insurance from a Cambodian man who escaped from a Khmer Rouge prison camp. He was tortured for the slightest infraction, he told me as I signed papers at his office on Sunset Boulevard, and not only did he see his entire family murdered, he was forced to help bury their corpses in a mass grave. The Khmer Rouge were monsters, and if they're referenced rarely now, it's partly because, except for *The Killing Fields*, released in 1984, their atrocities have never been dramatized by the world's most popular historian, Hollywood, which continues to dramatize the atrocities of the Nazis, cueing the uneducated to conclude that mass extermination was practiced by the Nazis alone. Yet from 1975, when the Khmer Rouge took control of Cambodia, to 1979, when Cambodia was invaded by Vietnam, by then a united communist state, as many as three and a half million people were annihilated by the Khmer Rouge. The exact number is disputed—the Khmer Rouge claimed it was two million—though it's widely agreed that half the victims were executed and the other half died of starvation and disease. The Khmer Rouge sought a perfect society of godless and purely Cambodian peasants so that Christians, Muslims, and Buddhist monks had to be eliminated, as did professionals, intellectuals, and the various ethnic groups, Thai, Chinese, and Vietnamese, who called Cambodia home.

All things here in the world are God's toys, you, me, Cambodia. There is a place for all of us.

Sean and Dana, along with the other journalists taken prisoner near Chi Phou, were turned over to the Khmer Rouge by the Vietcong at some point in 1970 or early 1971. Few Westerners knew much about the Khmer Rouge at the time, so the journalists probably supposed that they would be treated by their new jailers as they'd been treated initially by the Vietcong, and that wasn't altogether bad, according to an American intelligence report. The journalists were able to bathe and move freely about the house where they were kept, only losing such privileges shortly before they were sent first to a Khmer Rouge POW camp and then to a Cambodian rubber plantation. There, surprisingly, the Khmer Rouge restored their privileges, allowing them to roam the plantation in black pajamas and sandals fashioned from rubber tires, or so Cambodian informants told Tim Page. However, Page was told, the journalists went on a hunger strike, demanding their release, and in June 1971 they were beheaded with a sharpened hoe because the Khmer Rouge reserved bullets for combat.

Jeffrey Meyers has likewise dated Sean's death to June 1971, though under different circumstances. In a magazine article titled "The Nowhere Man" and again in *Inherited Risk*, his dual biography of Errol and Sean, Meyers cited a Cambodian report of a malaria-stricken man who was euthanized with Thorazine at a field hospital and may have been in a coma when his burial finished the job. The report stated that this luckless man, despite "a large beard that made it difficult to recognize his face," was "physically similar to Mr. Sean Flynn," and Meyers is certain the man was Sean, while Tim Page is equally certain that his version of Sean's end is the correct one.

Other versions have surfaced over the years: Sean was burned alive; he was shot accidentally or deliberately; he was beaten to death with clubs and shovels. Zalin Grant, who, like Page, has spent decades searching for the remains of Sean and Dana, believes that Sean, at least, wasn't executed by the Khmer Rouge until late 1973 or early 1974. A former Army Intelligence officer, Grant first investigated the case at the behest of CBS News anchorman Walter Cronkite, and he was friendly with Louise Stone, Dana's wife, who conducted her own investigation and became "an accomplished intelligence agent," in the qualified view of Grant. She followed case updates even as she was increasingly debilitated by multiple sclerosis, dying in Kentucky in March 2000, a month shy of the thirtieth anniversary of her husband's disappearance.

Lili died in March 1994, four months shy of her ninetieth birthday. In her later years, remarried to a wealthy dairyman and dividing her time between Palm Beach and Fort Dodge, Iowa, she was known as Lillian Loomis, and she spent a sizable chunk of Mr. Loomis's millions on missions to find her son, hiring soldiers of fortune who journeyed to Cambodia and returned with nothing. She had Sean declared legally dead in 1984 and, in the hope that his remains would materialize one day, she left behind a sample of her blood to help identify them.

Sean's half-sister Rory Flynn sanctioned a search in 2010 with promising results that forensic tests negated: no, these were the bones of somebody else. With an estimated 20,000 mass graves in Cambodia, courtesy of the Khmer Rouge, it's "like [trying to find] a needle in a haystack," Rory has said of the hunt for Sean's remains, but she has vowed to continue it, determined to give her brother the proper burial he deserves.

Not everyone agrees. Some say that Sean got exactly what he deserved by taking the risk he did in April 1970, but he might have died in a war zone any number of ways even if he had never been captured. The great photojournalist Robert Capa was killed in Vietnam by a landmine while covering the First Indochina War in 1954. His photojournalist lover, Gerda Taro, who worked alongside him during the Spanish Civil War, did not survive it: she was crushed by a tank in 1937. Larry Burrows, maybe the best Vietnam War photographer, died in a helicopter crash caused by enemy fire in 1971. Twenty-two-year-old Dan Eldon was stoned and beaten to death by a mob in Somalia in 1993. Chris Hondros and Tim Hetherington, on assignment in Libya in 2011, were fatally injured in a mortar shelling.

The death of Tim Hetherington rattled me. A couple of months earlier, when he was in Los Angeles, a friend of mine had interviewed him about *Restrepo*, his Oscar-nominated war documentary, and I had watched *Restrepo* only days before I heard the news from Libya. Even Barack Obama acknowledged the news, issuing a statement in which, "saddened," he reminded us that journalists "risk their lives each day to keep us informed, demand accountability from world leaders and give a voice to those who would not otherwise be heard." Oh, I thought, *that's* what they do. I was disgusted by the gung-ho attitude of American journalists when George W. Bush initiated the invasion of Iraq on a blatantly false pretext, but I was then and still am concerned about the decline of journalism as a paid profession and unpersuaded by the fashionable notion that, in a world where everyone carries surveillance equipment, we can rely on "citizen journalists" to keep us informed. I'm far more skeptical of citizen journalists than I am of paid ones. I've never seen, and I'm sure I'll never see, an Instagram photo as powerful as *Reaching Out*, Larry Burrows's shot of a wounded soldier rushing to check on another, just as I'm sure I'll never read a book as durable as *Dispatches* patched together from tweets. Beware the milk when the cow is free.

Dispatches and Sean figure in a 2011 piece by Gary Brecher, a.k.a. "the War Nerd," about Hetherington's death. "Somebody with a face finally died in Libya," the piece begins, and not only did Hetherington "have an Oscar-nominated face, it was a real good-looking face, too, which all the tributes to him seem to repeat over and over." For Brecher, one such tribute recalls the "ridiculous" description of Sean in *Dispatches*—"incredibly beautiful" and so on—and Sean and Hetherington, an Englishman educated at Oxford, are "the same breed," children of privilege who "soak up the blood and the cool of a war zone without getting any of it on their hands: they take pictures of it instead of getting dirty shooting people."

Gary Brecher is the alter ego of John Dolan, who, under his own name, was the first critic to challenge the veracity of James Frey's bestselling rehab memoir, *A Million Little Pieces*, and its sequel, *My Friend Leonard*, both later revealed to be fiction sold cynically as fact. In "A Million Pieces of Shit," Dolan's opening fusillade against Frey, he writes in terms that evoke his later take on Sean and Hetherington: "Rehab stories provide a way for pampered trust-fund brats like Frey to claim victim status. These swine already have money, security and position and now want to corner the market in suffering and scars, the consolation prizes of the truly lost." But Sean and Hetherington *were* truly lost, and while I concur with Dolan about James Frey, his general loathing of "pampered trust-fund brats" may have hindered his judgment of Sean and Hetherington, whom he scorned further as "decadent freaks, no-touch perverts who want to roll in the gore without getting dirty"—that word again. In fact, Sean did get "dirty" in Vietnam: he shot and killed an enemy soldier. That likely isn't dirty enough for Dolan, whose work I usually enjoy for its black humor and flippant insight, and there was insight when he concluded that Hetherington's death was a publicity coup for the rebels fighting Muammar Gaddafi in Libya, since none of the other victims of the conflict there had "got an Oscar nomination in their lives" and they "weren't all that good-looking, either." They were, to add to Dolan's point, as faceless to the world at large as the victims of the Khmer Rouge, with two exceptions if I count Dana, who might be faceless also but for his capture alongside Sean.

Meanwhile, a glance online tells me that 1,655 Americans who served in the Vietnam War, the majority not by choice, are still "unaccounted for," a number down from the 2,646 it was in 1973. How many of those Americans were pictured on matchbooks, buttons, and bumper stickers by way of calling attention to all prisoners of war and the missing in action? How many inspired songs like "Sean Flynn" by the Clash?

As far as I know, just one.

So, yes, even in matters of war, it pays to have a good-looking face and Hollywood credentials, even if they couldn't prevent the death of the one in question.

I HAD NO DOUBT that the man at the courthouse had known Sean: he corrected me on details that I remembered dimly from the reading I had done years earlier for my discussed but never-written screenplay about Sean. When I mentioned, for instance, that Sean had grown up in Miami Beach, the man said, "No, it was Palm Beach. Sean grew up in Palm Beach. That's where I met him." His family used to spend a few months in Palm Beach every year, he explained as we spoke outside the courthouse for fifteen minutes or so, and one day, at a swimming pool, he very nearly drowned and Sean dove into the pool and saved him. Afterward he met Lili, who, by coincidence, had been friendly with his mother in L.A. His mother and Lili reconnected, and Sean became an older brother to him. They stayed in touch for years, even after Sean went to Vietnam. But Sean changed, he said.

"What do you mean?"

"He was moody. You couldn't talk to him anymore. He stopped calling me. He didn't write. Why did he change?"

"Well," I fumbled, not sure that he expected an answer, "I guess war will do that to you."

He would call Lili every so often, he said, after Sean was taken prisoner and Lili was spending most of her time in Iowa, and every time they spoke, she would say, "Why did Sean break my heart?" He repeated that more than once. He also repeated, again and again, "Why did Sean change?"

I had to go, but before I did, I asked for his e-mail address. Meeting him hadn't reactivated the screenplay idea; rather, it seemed significant, somehow, that I had guessed the name of his tall friend as we waited inside for the elevator, and I was curious about him and wanted a way to reach him if I ever had cause. But he didn't have an e-mail address, he said, and he wasn't on Facebook, and he didn't have a cellphone. I believed him. There was a sense of the otherworldly about him, like a man out of time, and I'm at a loss to describe him otherwise, except to say that he was six feet tall, as he had apprised me out of nowhere, and he was balding and dressed blandly and twenty pounds overweight, so that he looked like any sixty-year-old white man, invisible to the world. But so am I. So are most of us, once we're robbed of any beauty we may have possessed in youth. I walked away and turned for a moment to watch as he grew smaller and smaller until, the fate of us all, he disappeared.

2013

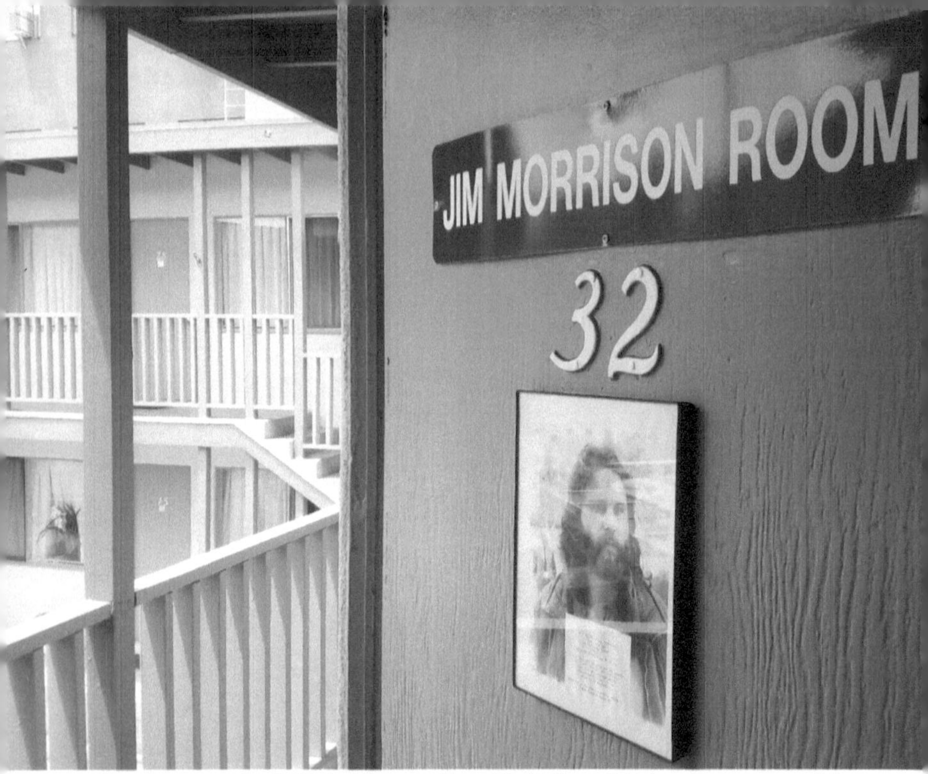

No one here gets out alive: Jim Morrison's frequent residence at the Alta Cienega Motel. Among the messages scrawled above the bed: "Jim, come back from Africa," where some contend he fled after faking his death. (*Author's collection*)

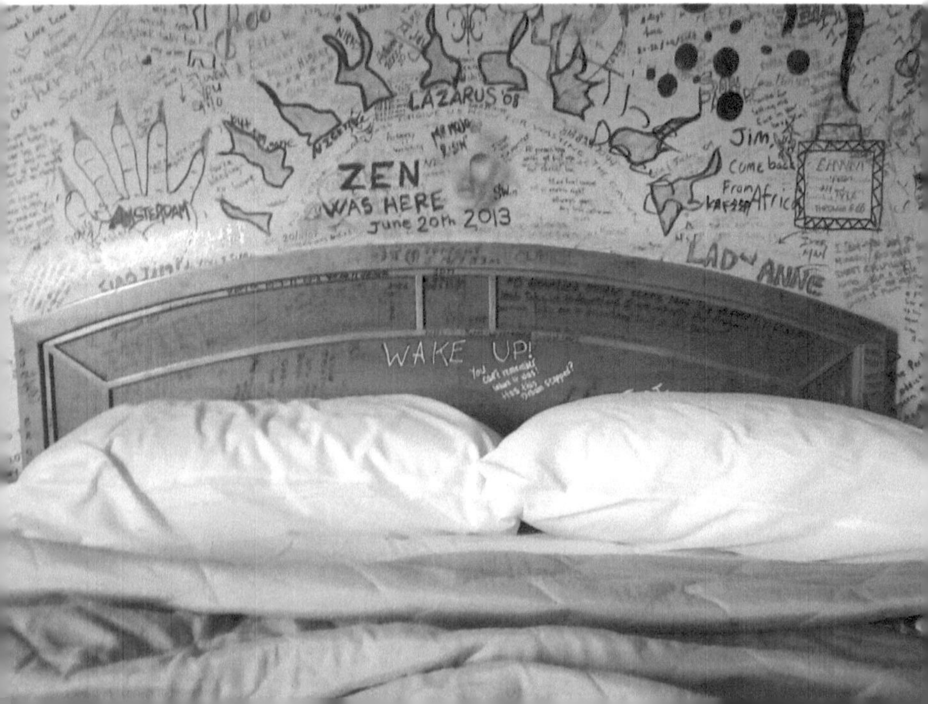

ROOM 32

THE IDEA, I THOUGHT, was a simple one: rent for a night the West Hollywood motel room where Jim Morrison lived on and off for three years, hold a séance with a few friends, and afterward throw a party. It seemed a fitting homage to Morrison, a party-hardy mystic who believed himself possessed by the spirit of a Pueblo Indian he had seen as a boy while traveling through New Mexico and happening upon the aftermath of a deadly accident. *Indians scattered on dawn's highway bleeding,* he wrote famously of the incident in "Newborn Awakening," his poem set to music by his band, the Doors, seven years after he died. *Ghosts crowd the young child's fragile eggshell mind.*

Originally I planned to host the séance in late May or early June, before summer travel had truncated the guest list. On the other hand, I knew that the motel room was a "tiny little monk's cell," per an interview with Morrison's bandmate Ray Manzarek, so the guest list had to be brief anyway. Some declined the invitation. "I don't mess with stuff like that," a woman friend told me during supper one night. "I don't even know if I believe in ghosts, but I'm not taking any chances."

"I don't know if I believe, either," I said. "I mean, I really *don't* believe, but I try to keep an open mind because I know people who claim they've seen ghosts, and they were sort of incredulous themselves. But, you know, this isn't going to be a *real* séance. I'm just going to buy a Ouija board and we can all kind of play around with it."

"That's worse than having a real psychic. Who *knows* what you could dredge up."

I heard the same, or similar, from others, giving me pause. Why was I treating the séance flippantly, and what would I gain from it that way? At best, a few cheap laughs. But there was, potentially, something to be learned here, something about spiritualism and the atavistic streak in us all, so that rather than proceed like a kid at a sleepover, I should hire a psychic known, or anyway believed, to have contacted the dead. Finding one should be effortless. As Farnworth Crowder, a journalist whose name evokes the wealthy villains and waspish columnists of old Hollywood movies, wrote circa 1931: "In the South of California has gathered the largest and most miscellaneous assortment of Messiahs, Sorcerers, Saints and Seers known to the history of aberrations." Surely that was still the case in 2013.

It was, Google confirmed, directing me to a long list of area psychics on Yelp. Since even matters of spirit are now subject to customer reviews, I weeded from the list those psychics unable to contact the dead, either because that wasn't a service they provided or, as indicated by their low star ratings, they were poor psychics.

Then I read a review by a customer greatly pleased with her experience at a place called House of Intuition. Through one of the staff psychics at House of Intuition, this customer had contacted her dead father, and he had made "the same comments he always did, jokes, etc." while settling lingering mysteries of his passing. "It was the best money I ever spent," the customer summed up, awarding House of Intuition five out of five stars.

House of Intuition is in my neighborhood. I had passed it many times, put off by the crude paintings of tarot cards on the cement wall at the mouth of the property. But that was before I started searching for a psychic, and it seemed fortuitous that I had located one in my backyard, as it were. I called House of Intuition immediately and explained what I had in mind to the woman who answered the phone.

"Let me get this straight, honey," she said. "You're a writer, and you want to interview Jim *Morrison*?" At least she had heard of Jim Morrison. I take nothing for granted these days.

"I don't want to *interview* him," I told her. "I don't even have anything I particularly want to say to him. I just want to see what happens if a psychic comes to this room and tries to contact him. Maybe nothing will happen. Maybe the psychic will pick up on other people who've been in the room. I really don't care what happens. I have no expectations. It's just a kind of experiment."

"And you're going to write about it? I don't know, sweetie."

She clearly feared a hatchet piece, but I promised that if I wrote about the séance, I would render it fairly and faithfully, and at last she offered to set me up with a psychic named Bianca who could phone me in a couple of hours. However, Bianca's fee was $225 an hour, sweetie, and Bianca had a two-hour minimum for special events like this one, honey, so I was looking at $450, and that didn't include travel time to and from the motel—I would have to pay for that too. Did I still want Bianca to phone? Sure, I said, though I felt like I was hiring a hooker, not a psychic, and I had set aside $300 for the motel, the psychic, and the liquor for the post-séance party. But maybe a budget of $300 was naïve, and if Bianca impressed me enough when she called, I would consider meeting her price.

Bianca called two days, not two hours, later. That may have been the fault of Sweetie Honey, not Bianca, but it didn't produce confidence either way. Nor, I decided, did starred reviews written by strangers produce much confidence. Maybe a friend, or a friend of a friend, could vouch for a reasonably priced psychic medium who promptly returned phone calls and would welcome the chance to channel Jim Morrison. That wasn't too much to ask, was it?

So it would soon appear.

NO BAND IS LOVED universally, of course, but few bands are as loved and hated in even measure as the Doors. Ray Manzarek's fairground keyboards are usually cited by those who hate the Doors for their music alone. Others, mostly in middle age, regard the Doors as an embarrassing phase they went through when they were too young to know any better, while today's young are apt to sneer at the Doors as a "boomer" band, per this muddled comment posted online following Manzarek's death: "the importance of pop music from the 60's to now is way out of proportion to it's [*sic*] actual relevance." People began to speak of "relevance," as applied here, in the irrelevant sixties, but never mind; the Doors have always been hated most for their pretentiousness, and Jim Morrison has drawn more complaint in that sense than Manzarek, guitarist Robby Krieger, and drummer John Densmore combined. Morrison was inscrutable, writing enigmatic lyrics like *The blue bus is calling us / Driver, where you taking us?* ("Santa Monica," the driver of the blue bus, which still runs in Santa Monica, might have answered.) Morrison was ethereal, characterizing Doors shows as religious experiences akin to "purification ritual[s] in an alchemical sense." (His informal study of religion, especially pagan religion, began in high school, when he also began his precocious reading of such writers as Plutarch, Nietzsche, Rimbaud, and Joyce.) He pompously instructed celebrity hairstylist (and eventual Manson Family victim) Jay Sebring to "make me look like Alexander the Great." (He looked better than Alexander the Great; he looked like Antinous, the beautiful youth memorialized throughout the ancient world in statues and busts commissioned by the Roman emperor Hadrian.) He inflicted his beatnik poetry on audiences who had paid only to watch the Doors play their hit singles, particularly "Light My Fire." (He lived near San Francisco in 1956–58, when the San Francisco Beat scene was at its peak and he was a teenager who once braved a few words to Lawrence Ferlinghetti at City Lights bookstore.) Rock stardom wasn't enough for bratty, arty, pseudointellectual Jim Morrison, with his parallel ambitions as a writer and filmmaker. (He moved to Los Angeles to study film at UCLA, where he met Ray Manzarek, as well as Francis Ford Coppola, who would open and close *Apocalypse Now*, arguably his greatest film, with "The End," arguably the Doors' greatest song.) Even the name of the Doors, chosen by Morrison, has been mocked by those detractors acquainted with William Blake's *The Marriage of Heaven and Hell*, which inspired it. (*If the doors of perception were cleansed every thing would appear to man as it is, infinite. For man has closed himself up, till he sees all things through narrow chinks of his cavern.*) How pretentious!

The Doors are loved for some of the same reasons they're loathed, though of course not by the same people; but I was unaware of both camps when, as a teenager in Virginia, I bought my first Doors record. It was the late seventies, a period of relative obscurity for the Doors, who were rarely noted on television or played on the radio, aside from "Light My Fire" on Golden Oldie weekends. "Light My Fire" was the only Doors song I knew, and whenever I came upon a photo of Jim Morrison, as I did occasionally in record stores and magazines like *Creem*, I wondered why he wasn't as famous as other sixties rockers whose music I preferred to contemporary music. Finally, to satisfy my curiosity about the Doors, I bought *13*, a best-of compilation, but the only song on it that excited me was "The Crystal Ship," which I would play again and again, usually at night, like a bedtime ritual practiced, I was sure, by no one but me.

Then *Apocalypse Now* was released, introducing "The End" to a new generation, and the publication of *No One Here Gets Out Alive*, the first of several Morrison biographies, soon followed, and the Doors have never been obscure since. *No One Here Gets Out Alive* presented Morrison as reckless hedonism personified, the definitive *enfant terrible*, and kids from across the rock & roll spectrum—metalheads, punks, neo-hippie jam-band fans—claimed him and deified him. I was past the stage of deifying rock stars, though I increasingly warmed to the Doors, starting with my move to Los Angeles, where their eclectic, eerie, carny sound clicked as it could never have clicked in Virginia or New York City, where I spent my early twenties. Meanwhile, reading about Jim Morrison, I learned that we shared key influences: Nietzsche, Frazer, Rimbaud, Céline, Kerouac, Mailer (Morrison's favorite writer at thirteen and one of mine still), and even James Dean (*Rebel Without a Cause* sparked Morrison's interest in film, while I idiotically imitated Dean in my formative days as a New York actor). As far as I knew, Morrison was the only public figure, living or dead, equally devoted to literature, music, and film—the same three subjects that preoccupied me—and if he was sometimes trite or bombastic, he was only twenty-seven when he died, and how many writers are fully formed at twenty-seven? How many filmmakers?

But he was certainly fully formed as a frontman, which I didn't realize until I saw *When You're Strange*, Tom DiCillo's 2009 Doors documentary. *When You're Strange* incorporates scenes and outtakes from *Feast of Friends*, a 1970 documentary sanctioned by the Doors and never officially released, though it's long been cannibalized in other films. I had already seen some of the footage included in *When You're Strange*, but I had never seen it like this, gloriously restored and magnified on a big screen, where Jim Morrison in performance belongs, leaping like a rock & roll Nijinsky and crashing to the floor of the venue, or nonchalantly lighting a cigarette in the middle of a song, or lying as if dead or asleep while the band played on. He gave everything he had, and when he had nothing left to give, he made that part of the performance, which is how I think it should be after watching countless musicians fake or force passion. Besides, even inert, Morrison was magnetic, at least to me, because he was private in public, while most of us aren't private in private.

This is the sense of danger I've always sought in performers, actors as well as musicians, and I've rarely found. It's what made me the sort of stone Jim Morrison fan who would attempt something as preposterous as hosting a séance in his erstwhile motel room, pending the participation of a referred psychic.

GET IN TOUCH with Ivory, more than one friend told me. I was dubious. I had known Ivory for years, and she had never said anything about being psychic, just as she had never spoken my thoughts aloud or announced the presence of invisible people. She was a well-meaning but flighty girl, who, whenever I saw her, would rush up to hug me and peck me on the cheek, then quickly alight to hug, and peck the cheek of, someone else. Still, I phoned her and left a message about the séance, and she called back a day later and said, "Duke! This is a great idea! I want to do it!"

I asked her how much she charged, referencing the House of Intuition rate of $225 per hour, and she said, "Oh, those fakes. Forget those fakes; they don't know what they're doing. You know, I don't even know if it's *possible* to contact the dead, but I would love to try, and I won't charge you anything."

I liked her price. I liked her enthusiasm. I liked that she was forthrightly skeptical about contacting the dead. Yes, I decided, I'll go with Ivory. Then I phoned a mutual friend to invite him to the séance, and he said, "*Ivory?*

She's about as psychic as my shoe, and you *know* how flighty she is." I knew, indeed. I pictured myself at the motel, texting no-show Ivory, who, busy hugging people and pecking their cheeks, would fail to respond until hours after the séance, if then.

I took the search to Facebook, asking, without mention of Jim Morrison, if anyone knew of a psychic medium who charged less than $225 per hour. A couple of respondents recommended Ivory. Others made jokes, like a friend who lives in Tennessee: "The one down the street here charges twenty-five bucks. I think you get a back rub with that though." Still other out-of towners cited out-of-town psychics, including a friend in upstate New York: "Duke, did you ever hear of Lily Dale? It's a community of psychics & mediums about an hour south of Buffalo in Chautauqua County." I phoned Lily Dale repeatedly, hoping somebody there might be able, or kind enough, to refer me to a psychic in L.A., but I never got through or heard back.

Meanwhile, my friend Rachel, far more popular on Facebook than I, posted a query on Facebook at my request and was apprised of an "amazing," "fabulous" psychic named Rebecca. This sounded promising. I waited for Rachel to hear from Rebecca, and while I waited, Ray Manzarek died. The timing, from my perspective, was curious; here I was, trying to arrange a séance for Jim Morrison, and now I wondered briefly if I should hold a séance for Ray Manzarek instead. As the oldest member of the Doors and an Army veteran married for forty-five years to Dorothy Fujikawa, whom he met at UCLA, Manzarek had always seemed the band's superego, the father figure who held the Doors together, even subbing on vocals when errant-child Morrison, the band's id, was too smashed to perform. Because we somehow expect stabilizing forces to endure, Manzarek's death was a jolt for anyone who read the psychodynamics of the Doors as I read them. Still, I never seriously thought of holding a séance for anyone other than Morrison.

One night I had dinner with my friends Sean and Sanja, who were both on the séance guest list. As hard as it was to believe, I complained, I couldn't find a psychic in L.A. Sure, there were plenty of psychics of the storefront sort, but they were notoriously grifters, and I didn't trust the word of strangers online, and appeals to friends had led only to flighty Ivory, while Facebook had led only to amazing, fabulous Rebecca, who was apparently playing hard to get. I didn't know where to look next.

Sean knew where, having heard of a psychic who had once channeled Albert Einstein. The idea of channeling Albert Einstein was no more ridiculous than the idea of channeling Jim Morrison, of course, but I snickered nonetheless. Had the psychic spoken with a German accent while channeling Einstein? Had channeling him made her smarter? Still, I was certainly appreciative when Sean offered to dig up her number and call her.

A week passed, maybe two. "Just left her another MSG," Sean texted at one point. "Maybe I shall try telepathically." "Yes," I texted back, "we might have better results that way." Why were psychics so goddamn flaky? But they're really no different than most people nowadays. Technology has inculcated wariness of any communication except the remote, superficial kind.

Finally, one night, Sean phoned to say that he had just spoken with the psychic, who didn't want to do the séance. "I told her we want to party with Jim Morrison," he elaborated, "and she said he's the kind of entity that other entities try to impersonate. She said you can always tell it's an impersonator because when you ask a question, the impersonator will ask a question back, turning the tables, so you never get an answer. But sometimes these impersonators are evil, and they might attach themselves to somebody who's there, and the psychic doesn't want to be responsible for that."

Great, I thought. The afterlife is just like Hollywood, with nobodies passing themselves off as somebodies. My ongoing strategy of postponing death had been vindicated.

I asked Sean if he would call the psychic again, or let me call her, and present the séance in a different light. "I mean," I said, "if you tell her we want to party with Jim Morrison, she's going to imagine a bunch of drunk people, and maybe that's exactly the situation that's going to attract these evil impersonators. I mean, originally, the idea was to party with Jim Morrison, sort of, but I want to approach this thing respectfully, and maybe if she knows that, she'll reconsider."

Sean said he would phone the psychic the next day. A week later, still waiting to hear from Sean, who was still waiting to hear from the psychic, I invited friends visiting from New Zealand to meet me at Barney's Beanery, a storied pub on Santa Monica Boulevard in West Hollywood. Jim Morrison was a regular at Barney's Beanery, and there's a plaque on the bar to commemorate the spot where he once drunkenly pissed. Meanwhile, the Alta Cienega Motel, where Morrison lived for three years in room 32, is a block and a half from Barney's Beanery, on La Cienega Boulevard.

None of this was on my mind, consciously anyway, when I proposed Barney's Beanery as a place to meet my Kiwi friends. But they were too fatigued to join me, they called to say after I arrived, and by way of justifying the drive, I decided I would walk to the Alta Cienega and book room 32 for the séance. I had delayed booking the room, thinking I should first hire a psychic, but maybe it would be better if I booked the room first and so had a definite date. Yes, I thought, maybe I should book the room for my birthday, which was two weeks off in late June. Then I remembered that Jim Morrison died on July 3, 1971, and what better date for a séance than July 3 forty-two years later?

The Alta Cienega is so inconspicuous that, for years, whenever I craned for a glimpse of it while driving through West Hollywood, I would overlook it. A lesser example of Mid-Century Modern, a popular style in post-war California, it has two floors and thirty-two rooms exactly, though I was unaware of the precise location of room 32 until I walked over from Barney's Beanery that night, just as I was unaware that, to the left of the motel driveway, a storefront psychic did business, the window lit by multicolored neon signs: ESP, PALM & TAROT CARD READINGS, OPEN. The driveway is a kind of underpass, and, on the other side of it in the motel parking lot, I turned to see that room 32 capped the driveway like a bridge. A sign that read JIM MORRISON'S ROOM was posted above the white 32 on the olive-green door, and a photo of Morrison was framed below the 32. The parking lot was all but empty. I smelled fried food.

The smell came from the manager's office. I tried the door. It was locked, but, peering through the window, I saw an East Indian woman standing at a stove in a narrow kitchen adjoining the office. Asian tchotchkes garnished the office counter—a green ceramic elephant, two-inch Buddhas painted gold—while on the wall behind them, a homemade poster declared that NO ONE HERE GETS OUT ALIVE—a touch of noir humor? Whatever it was, I rang the office bell, and the woman turned and stepped to the window, stooping so that she could hear and be heard through the slot at the bottom of it. I want to reserve room 32 for July 3rd, I told her, and she reached for a spiral notebook with a handwritten date on the top line of every page, flipping through the notebook until she came to the page with *July 3* on the top line, followed by a handwritten name and phone number. No explanation was necessary, but I wasn't disappointed, since I now remembered (inaccurately, I would learn) that Morrison died at around two a.m. in Paris, and Paris is nine hours ahead of L.A., so that if I made a reservation for July 2 and checked in before seven that evening, I would still have the room on the anniversary of Morrison's death.

The room was available for July 2, and the woman wrote my name and number below that date in the notebook. Then, as I walked toward the driveway, I glanced again at the olive-green door of room 32 and thought of Morrison's best known poem, "The Celebration of the Lizard," and specifically of a few lines supposedly inspired by the Alta Cienega:

One morning he awoke in a green hotel
With a strange creature groaning beside him.
Sweat oozed from its shining skin.

Is everybody in?
The ceremony is about to begin.

The ceremony will begin soon enough, I thought, forgetting for the moment that not everybody was in.

IN SOME INTERVIEWS, Ray Manzarek has placed Jim Morrison at the Alta Cienega around the time the Doors signed a deal with Elektra Records in 1966, but most sources say that Morrison's residence at the motel began in early 1968, shortly after he shot to fame. Prior to that, he had split an apartment with roommates in Westwood, crashed with friends (among them Manzarek and Dorothy Fujikawa) in Venice Beach, and lived with his girlfriend, Pamela Courson, in Laurel Canyon.

Pamela's spritelike beauty masked a formidable will and a wild streak that even Jim Morrison was pressed to match. She collected pistols. She did heroin. She would punch Morrison in the face when he disappointed her, as he often did, disappearing for weeks with other lovers. She did the same to spite him. But they invariably reconciled, and though he spent almost nothing on himself—his luxuries were mostly confined to books and booze—he indulged Pamela, paying her rent and funding her rich-hippie boutique, Themis, where she delighted in overcharging the wives and girlfriends of the other Doors. She was easily the most influential of the original Doors haters, prodding Morrison to quit the band, despite the perks it afforded her, and devote himself to writing poetry.

Themis was on La Cienega Boulevard in the same building as Morrison's film-production company—*HWY: An American Pastoral*, the fifty-minute film he codirected in 1969, was edited there—and a few blocks from the Alta Cienega. So was Pamela's apartment on Norton Avenue. So were the offices and recording studio of Elektra, while Morrison's three favorite bars, including Barney's Beanery, were closer still, as were the Doors' office and Monaco Liquor, across the street and around the block respectively, so that Morrison could walk to business meetings, walk to pick up liquor, walk to piss on the bar of Barney's Beanery. He seldom drove in any case, with his driver's license typically suspended following his latest drunken smashup.

For Ray Manzarek, the Alta Cienega was Morrison's "escape hatch," the place he went to think. For Tony Funches, Morrison's bodyguard, it provided the "kind of Beat Generation atmosphere" that Morrison craved as a writer. But he was peripatetic by nature, perhaps because of his Navy-brat upbringing, and he sometimes opted for other motels and hotels: the Tropicana, the Chateau Marmont, the Continental Hyatt House (known to rockers of the day as the Continental Riot House). He's said to have chosen motels for their neon signs. The Alta Cienega used to have a neon sign, as seen in *HWY*, which shows Morrison checking into the motel at night, making a call from a pay phone—now gone—in the parking lot, and pissing in the bathroom of room 32. (At least, on this occasion, he pissed in a designated spot.) The rest of room 32 is too murky to make out, and Morrison quickly leaves it anyway, passing the neon sign as he walks outside to a terrace—now closed to guests—where he gazes down at traffic and the twinkling lights of bar signs. That he had a similar view from room 32 probably explains his preference for it.

There are stories of slapstick bravado associated with Morrison's stays at the Tropicana (he set fire to his bed), the Chateau Marmont (he fell while trying to enter his room from the roof), and the Continental Hyatt House (he hung from an upper-floor window by his hands), but there are no such stories set at the Alta Cienega. Once, hours before the Doors' momentous Hollywood Bowl show, Mick Jagger visited room 32 to talk shop with Morrison, rock star to rock star, but they were both well behaved, sadly, just as Morrison seems always to have been well behaved at the Alta Cienega, aside from boozing and cheating on Pamela, who naturally exacted revenge. Morrison's motel days were ended, in fact, by Pamela's December 1970 return from Paris, where she had pursued another lover: a drug dealer suspected of supplying Janis Joplin with the heroin that killed her. Morrison moved into Pamela's apartment on Norton Avenue, and she badgered him anew to quit the Doors, this time adding a twist: she was relocating to Paris with or without him. She left on Valentine's Day 1971, and he followed a month later and remained in Paris permanently, though maybe not in spirit.

LATE ONE NIGHT, I met my friend Damon Packard at a diner in Burbank. Damon is a filmmaker, and we usually talk about movies when we get together, but tonight I whined, as I had weeks earlier to Sean and Sanja, about failing to find a psychic. A family crisis had claimed Sean's attention, so that I never heard more about the psychic reputed to have channeled Einstein. I was back at the starting gate, and turned again to the

Internet, which led me to call a couple of psychics with high customer ratings. One never called back. The other wasn't available on July 2nd, but that didn't prevent him from lecturing me about metaphysics. "It's like opening a door," he said of contacting the dead, with startling originality and no evident clue that "door" plus Jim Morrison equals pun. I was really coming to hate psychics.

Still, I needed one if I was going to keep my date at the Alta Cienega, and Damon now mentioned Psychic Eye, an occult bookstore where psychics held readings. It was in the San Fernando Valley, Damon said, but, checking the store's Web site the next day, I learned that there was another branch elsewhere in Southern California and several branches in Nevada, suggesting the answer to a question I would never have thought to ask: who requires occult assistance more, grasping dreamers or desperate gamblers?

The Psychic Eye Web site made shopping for a psychic easy. A click on a name called forth a photo, a concise bio, and a one-minute clip in which the psychic, dimly lit in what looked to be a hookah lounge, solicited patronage, sometimes handling tools of the trade—tarot cards, pendulums, crystals, magick candles—while announcing areas of specialization: "I find missing people," "I'm good with relationships," "I can teach you the new spiritual laws." Most clips had spooky or spacy soundtracks of canned electronica. Floral patterns were popular. So was the color black. A lot of pendants were worn.

But style and personality were irrelevant. I cared about one thing: that the psychic purported to speak with the dead. As many as ten out of forty-five did, and all of them, according to the Web site, were available for special events, and all of them had the same low rate of $50 per hour. Finally, I thought, I'm going to make this thing happen. It was supposed to be an experiment, an adventure, an anecdote for my dotage, but it was victory that mainly mattered now, and victory, after so many false leads and dead ends, meant making this thing happen.

I couldn't book a psychic directly. I had to go through the store. I phoned the store and was told I would have to speak with Chris, the manager, who wasn't there. I left a message, and when Chris phoned back a day later, I told him I wanted to hire a psychic for a séance at the former residence of a deceased (and unspecified) celebrity, reading aloud my list of ten or so candidates. A few, for arbitrary reasons, interested me more than others, but I welcomed the input of Chris, who said he would help me to choose, though there was a special rate for special events—$125 per hour—with a two-hour minimum. That was fine by me. I would gladly pay $250 for victory. Chris was about to leave for a weekend business trip, he said, but he would call me when he returned, instructing me to remind him by e-mail.

Chris didn't acknowledge my e-mail. He didn't call. I sent him another e-mail. He didn't respond to that one either. I called the store and was told that, yes, Chris was back in town. I left a voice-mail message. I left a second voice-mail message. Finally I called the store and asked when Chris would be around. From seven to ten in the evening, I was told. All right, I thought, tonight I am going to drive out to that goddamn bookstore in the goddamn Valley, and if I haven't hired a goddamn psychic for this goddamn séance after booking that goddamn motel room for July 2nd, which is only two goddamn weeks away, I am going to know the goddamn reason why.

I arrived at the store at nine-thirty. There weren't many books for sale. The décor reminded me of a sex shop for couples, so that I half expected to see lingerie, handcuffs, vibrators, French ticklers, and tubes or bottles of scented lubricant—all displayed as "tastefully" as possible—instead of incense, pentagrams, crystal balls, talismanic jewelry, and figurines of deities and demigods. A scowling, thirtyish, longhaired man, presumably Chris, was behind the counter. It wasn't Chris. Chris wasn't there, the scowling man scowled. I was too incensed to speak. I turned and fairly stomped out of the store, passing, in the foyer, a bulletin board with photos and bios of psychics pinned to it. These were the psychics available for readings that night, and one of them, Rachel, was at the top of my list, since, according to her bio, she was part Ojibwa Indian, which jibed with Jim Morrison's account of possession by an Indian spirit. Of course I knew that Indian blood was a selling point for those who believe Indians are more spiritual than prosaic Caucasians; but whether Rachel was or wasn't part Indian—her photo was inconclusive—I may as well meet her, if I could.

I approached the scowling man, who reached for a wall phone and pressed a button on it. "Rachel," he said, "you got somebody." He hung up. "Twenty dollars for fifteen minutes," he scowled. "Cash only." I had no cash on me, and he pointed to an ATM in the rear of the store. A short corridor led to the ATM, with closet-sized rooms on one side of the corridor, each door covered by a burgundy curtain. I heard murmurs. I was in the psychic hub. I returned to the scowling man and presented him with a twenty-dollar bill, and he said, "Don't pay me, pay *her*," recoiling like a pimp avoiding entrapment and sealing my new impression of the store as a bordello with a Wiccan theme.

A burgundy curtain opened and Rachel emerged. She was petite, five-three or less, with dyed-black hair and a frank manner certified by her unfussy clothes. It was instantly clear that she was in fact part Indian—she reminded me of a half-Iroquois acquaintance—and I guessed her age as fifty, though most would probably guess younger. I trailed her back to her room and said, "I've never done anything like this before"—what a bordello line!—and she smiled the smile of a seasoned pro and said, "Oh? Are you a skeptic?"

"I'm definitely an agnostic. But I'm here for a very specific reason."

The walls of her room were draped with Persian carpets. I sat, facing her, at a bridge table with tarot cards stacked in the center of it, and spoke with barely a pause for maybe ten minutes, explaining what I wanted to do and all I'd been through, hoping my letdowns would put her on my side so that when I finally posed the crucial question—"Would you please come to the motel and do the séance?"—she would agree. She did agree. Victory was mine. I had an urge to hug her.

"Now, I want to be really clear," I said. "I'm fine with whatever happens. It would be nice if Jim Morrison came through, but I don't expect it."

"He'll be there. My spirit guides just told me."

Spirit guides. Wow. Okay.

"But he's not in that motel room," Rachel went on. "He's someplace else, the place where he first started to play music. I see stairs, a building with a lot of stairs."

I knew that psychics "fish" with vague and leading remarks—"Her name starts with an *A*"—fleshed out by gullible clients—"It's my cousin Anne." If Rachel was fishing, I would play along. It felt rude to do otherwise, and besides, I didn't want to risk losing her and so spoil my victory.

"Well," I said, "he lived on the roof of a building in Venice and that's where the idea of the Doors came to him. He did a lot of LSD up there and it spawned this vision of a band."

"He was psychic; he didn't need LSD. But it was the sixties, I guess. I don't really know anything about him—I was always into dance music, not rock & roll—but there are a lot of tears associated with his spirit. Everyone thought about Jim, not James. That's what I'm picking up: James. He got lost, and he wants to talk about his life, not his music."

She laid down some rules for the séance: I could record it and invite a couple of friends, but more would be disruptive, and nobody could drink until afterward. Then she wrote down her phone number and e-mail address and gave them to me, mentioning chattily, as she walked me out, that she had worked for the police on a few murder cases, which helped to legitimize her, as she knew. But we all tout our credentials, and even if she had fished a little, I decided I would advance her $125 in cash—half her fee for the séance—to ensure that she didn't flake.

But she had already begun to flake when I dropped by the store one night a week later. She greeted me coolly and refused my cash advance, saying she couldn't do the séance unless I cleared it with Chris, who was still ignoring my calls. Maybe, I thought, she doesn't want to do the séance and Chris is her excuse. Maybe she's decided I'm a psychopath trying to lure her to his flophouse of horrors. And yet, as we spoke, she broke off and said she could see Jim Morrison, who was in the room with us and laughing, not at me or her but at those who had mourned or were mourning something that wasn't and never was; they never knew James, and they didn't care to know him, but he would show me James at the Alta Cienega on July 2nd if Rachel was permitted to meet me there. We even set a time to meet: six p.m., the approximate hour of Morrison's death forty-two years earlier, or so I believed.

But Chris continued to ignore my calls. I e-mailed Rachel. She needed Chris's approval, she reiterated. In the interest of victory, I phoned flighty Ivory and left a message, asking if she still wanted to do the séance, but I was sure she wouldn't respond and she didn't disappoint me. That was it. There was no more time, and there would be no séance, though I could always visit the storefront psychic at the Alta Cienega to purchase luck or have a family curse removed.

My party in room 32 had also fallen apart; many of the guests had forgotten about it and now had other plans. I invited new guests, but I doubted that I would see them or hear from them when I headed to the Alta Cienega on the morning of July 2nd. I would write, I thought. That's all I would do: I would write at the same table where Jim Morrison used to write, back when people could not possibly have been as flaky as they are now.

SOME BELIEVE Jim Morrison faked his death as a prank, a permanent escape from celebrity, or both. Others believe he died from natural causes, an accidental combination of alcohol and prescription medication, or a combination of alcohol and heroin that he mistook drunkenly for cocaine. Still others believe he was killed deliberately by—take your pick—himself, the CIA, French intelligence agents, radical Zionists, the Illuminati, occultists, the Indian spirit that possessed him, Pamela Courson, or Pamela's on-off lover, Jean de Breteuil, the drug dealer linked to Janis Joplin's death in L.A. It's folly to consider motive, except in two instances: Pamela, who is said to have wanted Morrison's money, and de Breteuil, who is said to have wanted Pamela.

But Pamela was already subsidized by Morrison, and de Breteuil was more interested in Marianne Faithfull, authentic rock & roll royalty, though he continued to supply Pamela with heroin: the unintended means of Jim Morrison's death. So de Breteuil told Marianne Faithfull. So Pamela told Alain Ronay, Morrison's classmate at UCLA, and Agnès Varda, the noted Left Bank filmmaker, hours after Morrison died.

Ronay, a Parisian expat on holiday from L.A., was staying at Varda's house when Pamela phoned at seven-thirty that July morning to say that she couldn't rouse Jim or, with her nominal French, call for an ambulance. Ronay woke Varda, who alerted the fire department and raced in her Volkswagen Beetle to Morrison's flat at 17 rue Beautrellis. Ronay accompanied her, and by the time they arrived, a rescue team had lifted Morrison from the bathtub where he was lying in pinkish water, tried in vain to revive him on the bathroom floor, and moved his body to his bedroom to await examination by a physician. Pamela would deal with two physicians that day, as well as two police inspectors, but she naturally omitted mention of drugs to them all.

In fact, once he soured on LSD, Morrison largely abstained from drugs, with the obvious exception of alcohol. He derided the other Doors as potheads, and he hated that Pamela did heroin, but Ronay observed that he seemed apathetic to Pamela's habit in his final days. Meanwhile, he was known to try anything once, so it's perfectly in character for him to have snorted heroin on the night he died, as claimed by Pamela to Ronay and Varda. She likewise indulged, she told them, until three a.m., when she and Jim went to bed. An hour later she woke to find Jim struggling to breathe, and though it was hard to wake him, she did eventually, helping him into the bathroom. Then she nodded off and came to and went to check on Jim, who was vomiting blood, and she ran to the kitchen and came back with a saucepan to catch the blood and returned to the kitchen to clean the saucepan. She did this three times, she said, before she nodded off again, and when she last came to, nothing she did could wake Jim.

According to his death certificate, Morrison died at five a.m. of heart failure. Hypovolemic shock, which occurs with severe blood loss, can result in heart failure. There were garish bruises on Morrison's torso. A hemorrhage in the abdominal cavity can produce such bruises. The question that can never be answered, since no autopsy was performed, is what exactly caused Morrison to hemorrhage until his heart stopped beating. Was it heroin alone? Heroin mixed with alcohol? Or was the heroin a catalyst for a preexisting condition?

Of course, the secondhand word of Pamela and Jean de Breteuil hardly counts as categorical proof that heroin was involved in the first place. Pamela gave numerous versions of Morrison's death after she buried him surreptitiously at Père Lachaise Cemetery and returned to California, where, despite her burgeoning lunacy, she warred in court for recognition as Morrison's common-law wife and sole heir. She won and, as if to celebrate, died posthaste of a heroin overdose.

Jean de Breteuil also died of a heroin overdose, but investigators never determined if it was suicide or homicide. He had a lot of enemies, as one would surmise of a man suspected of killing Janis Joplin and Jim Morrison, however inadvertently, and he may have become an enemy to himself.

That would almost recommend him.

EARLY DEATH INSPIRES cultishness as ripe death does rarely, and Jim Morrison not only died early, he died mysteriously. Add to that his posthumous image—a pagan saint of chaos, equal parts eros and thanatos—and it's no surprise that his grave became a shrine even before it was finally marked well into the eighties. Pilgrims from around the world flocked to Père Lachaise to sing and jam and drink and get stoned, leaving reefers and bottles of booze and candles and lighters and so on at Morrison's grave. They defaced his grave and others at Père Lachaise. New graffiti appeared after the graves were cleaned. So it still goes.

The Alta Cienega is the rough American equivalent of Père Lachaise. Ever since it was put on the map by *No One Here Gets Out Alive*, fans have been checking into room 32 to sleep where Morrison slept and tag the walls. Repainting the walls has proved a temporary solution, and by now the graffiti is a star attraction, as the motel management must know.

I had seen many photos of room 32 before I turned the key in the door, but no photo could do the room justice. The ceiling, the furniture, the shower stall, the medicine cabinet, the fire alarm: all were covered with crude scribbling, like a guestbook at a biker wedding. Fans had framed and hung photos of Morrison, and they drew his portrait and quoted his lyrics and addressed him in messages:

You're still alive
in my ♥
Rest in peace My Lizard King
I'll finally slep with you today
Love you A lot

In This ROOM I FUCKED A HOOKER WITHout A CONDOM,
JiM PROTECTED ME. THANKS JiM

I leave in this room babe a piece of my soul
to make love with yours in this bed
till the end Found us together again, a life is not such a long time.
wait x me. promise it won't take long. infinite nights together

Other fans advised and mused:

DON'T FIND THE NEXT WHiskey BAR

existance is just a state of mind.
Is this a dream or are we really alive?

55% of smart is understanding what we don't know

They mourned and celebrated:

My mother was one of Jim's good friends. Donna Port.
She met at the wisky agogo where she was a booker and head waitress.
She lived with him for a year or two. Robbie Kriger caused Her car
accident witch broke her back, she could not walk after that.
She died 39 yrs. Later from pressure Sores. Thanks Robbie!

A plaboy Party wouldn't be the same w/out staying here!
2004 $1mill couples Fear Factor champs Jackson and Monica

They wrote in terms understood only by them:

I would HAVE NEver Shared MY crAyons with You If I Knew
you were going to break them, melt them, Or otherwise Destroy them,.
I Will No LongeR be SHARIng them with you or ANY one else
for mAtter becAuse They ARE precious And neatly SHaRPEnED.
So please go buy Your own Crayons They
only cost $12.49 For a box of 120 plUs they come with a ShArpener

The way I see it according to Mrs. Loretta Lyn, another famous Amous,
Salmon are the canaries of the colemines in our minds or the world.
thnx Jim for a wonder-ful out of body experience,
because of you I have dedicated my life
to saving the world one squirl at a time.

With so much digital-age English on display, one foolhardy soul assumed the role of schoolmarm:

You know, for JM fans you all seem to be pretty damn illiterate.
You need some serious "boning-up" on grammer,
word usage, sentence structure and…oh, yes—SPELLING.
Also, if you're going to quote lyrics, how about getting them RIGHT?

This message was crossed out with "SUCK A DICK FAGIT" scrawled over it, while someone else had written "NICE SPELLING" and an arrow aimed at "grammer," and so the schoolmarm was schooled.

I spent a couple of hours reading the walls and taking photos. A week-long heat wave hadn't fully broken, and the air conditioner buzzed to no effect. Did the air conditioner date to Jim Morrison's day? So it seemed. I set up a workspace on the small table that faced the intersection of La Cienega and Santa Monica, startled when I opened my computer to see an e-mail from Rachel, sent early that morning:

hi duke,
just confirming tonight at six…
how is the traffic at five…
chris tried calling you yesterday as well.
do you know the best way to avoid traffic going from chatsworth to the motel? i do not have a/c in my car…

I hadn't received any calls or messages from Chris, but no matter; I confirmed immediately, deferring to others about the traffic. An hour passed without a reply. I texted Rachel. She didn't text back. Had she already changed her mind? But if she hadn't, if she showed, I would need cash, so I walked to Monaco Liquor and took as much cash as I could from the ATM there, buying a bottle of Jameson for the party, if there was a party, and noticed that the battery on my phone was all but dead. I would need the phone to record the séance, if there was a séance, but I had forgotten to pack my charger that morning and didn't have time to drive home and fetch it. I would have to buy a new charger, but I couldn't find the model I needed at any store on Santa Monica, so I walked back to the motel and drove to the Sunset Strip, where I finally found a store that sold the correct model, drove back to the motel, plugged in my phone, and called Rachel, who—hail Zeus—answered to say that, yes, she was coming, and she was bringing a friend whose car had air conditioning.

I met them on the balcony when they arrived just before six: Rachel in a black sundress, and her older, taller, heavier friend Dee Dee in tight jeans, a low-cut top, flashy necklaces, and lines of kohl that crossed at the far corners of her eyes, forming tiny *X*s. She might have worked as a snake charmer in Vegas, I thought, though Rachel introduced her as another medium. Also present was a third party, invisible to me but seen, or anyway heard, by the women.

"He's been with me for the last couple of days," Rachel said. "He's so *funny*."

They followed me into the room, and after a brief look around, Rachel said, "He's saying it's really changed. The bed was over here"—she motioned toward the south wall—"and the headboard faced this way."

"I'm picking up on others," Dee Dee announced. "Runaways. Young girls."

"Boys too," Rachel concurred.

She sat on the bed, where, according to her, Jim had stationed himself, while Dee Dee sat at the table next to the window. I was concerned about the sound of rush-hour traffic, which might interfere with the recording, but since the air conditioner was useless, I kept the window as well as the door open. An Indian man, one of the Alta Cienega managers, stood in the parking lot, staring up at the room. What did he think was going on in there?

Whatever he thought, the ceremony—unexpectedly, at long last—was about to begin.

OVER THE NEXT TWO HOURS, I checked my phone repeatedly to make sure it was recording. Rachel checked it too, and I remember saving the file and seeing it listed on my recorder app, yet it was missing a day later. I took the phone to three data-recovery specialists and none of them could find a trace of the file, which they all thought strange. This is undoubtedly a technological, not a supernatural, mystery, but in any case, I jotted down everything I recalled of those two hours as soon as I saw that the file had vanished, and what follows is based on those notes.

There were no incantations or lit candles or joined hands. I leaned against the low chest of drawers next to the television, which is mounted on the east wall, while Rachel, on the bed, spoke with her eyes shut tight and her arms moving occasionally as if trying to read a sign in braille.

"He's showing me a car," she said. "It's an old-fashioned car, from the forties or something like that. I think the seats are red, and he's sitting in the back, and there are people in the front seats. I think it's his mother and father."

My God, I thought, we're starting with the *Indians scattered on dawn's highway* incident of Jim's childhood. But Dee Dee, who was mumbling to herself or to ghosts in her corner of the room, abruptly stood and said, "I have to leave. Somebody died in here." She was gone before I could think of a reason to stop her. I felt like a bad host.

"I guess you'll need a ride home," I said to Rachel.

"No, she'll come back. Don't worry about it."

For now, Rachel dropped the crash incident. She moved on to Jim's death, which of course I had hoped to cover.

"I see a white shirt and jeans," she said, "and he's stretched out like this." She leaned back on the bed and spread her arms in a Christ pose. "I hear sirens, the kind that sound like this"—she made the *wah-wah* sound of a European ambulance—"and someone is trying to revive him. They don't know what they're doing, and he's already dead and looking down at his body and this person trying to revive him, and he's thinking, *Why are you even bothering?* It was a good death. When it came, he embraced it. He died with a smile on his face, kind of a little half smile."

Pamela mentioned such a smile to Alain Ronay and Agnès Varda, just as she mentioned slapping Jim repeatedly while trying to revive him. But how, in a bathtub, could he die in a Christ pose? In fact, the tub had armrests, but that was a detail I had forgotten. As for the white shirt and jeans, he could have been wearing them before he slipped into the tub, or maybe he didn't die in the tub; some believe his body was moved to his flat after he died elsewhere, though Rachel was adamant that he died at home. She saw him lying on a bed—in fact, the rescue team placed him on his bed after pronouncing him dead—and while she initially ascribed the cause of death to an injection of a green or greenish liquid, she suddenly, as if stuck by a pin, opened her eyes and said, "Oh, his heart stopped." It wasn't a planned death. Rachel saw a note mistaken for a suicide note—possibly the entry in Jim's Paris journal that reads *Last words, last words—out*—but, as she described it, his death was more a semiwitting suicide.

"He was playing Russian roulette with drugs and all that," she said, "because he wanted to pass. He sees his life as 'Jim Morrison' as a failure. He never did anything he considers truly worthy. He was very unhappy. Well, there were *pockets* of happiness. But he was very alone. He had no friends."

"*No* friends?"

"He's saying that if he'd had friends, he wouldn't have died when he did. I'm seeing one friend when he was very young—I want to say between first and fifth grades—and they're going to creeks and collecting tadpoles and that kind of kid stuff. Then he moved and never saw that boy again.

Oh, and his dog—his dog was his friend."

In fact, Jim owned, or co-owned with Pamela, a dog named Sage. He also had a childhood friend named Jeff Morehouse, who has spoken of them collecting frogs and snakes and so on, but Jim and Jeff were reunited in their teens when their Navy families relocated to northern Virginia.

"There were people who would come up and give him drugs," Rachel continued. "They wanted to get him high, and he let them. He doesn't blame them for what happened to him—he did plenty of stuff on his own—but nobody really had his welfare in mind. I see people tugging on him, pulling on him, trying to bend him to their will. So, yeah, dying was the happiest moment of his life. It's sad. I feel like I want to cry."

She teared up a little. Then she lunged for her purse and extracted a notebook and pen, writing something hurriedly and ripping it out of the notebook. "This is him," she said, handing the page to me.

No more tears to cry
no more lips to kiss
soft, Gentle Man
with a heart of Gold
Give love Give love

For all the stories of depravity concerning Jim, Francis Ford Coppola thought him "very sweet," while Tony Funches considered him "the nicest guy on the planet," unless he was dealing with authority figures or Pamela. I asked about Pamela, and Rachel pointed to a photo of Jim and Pamela on the wall.

"You mean her?" she said. I nodded, and she swatted at the air dismissively. "That's what he's doing," she said, repeating the gesture. "She didn't love him. It was all for show. He says he doesn't miss women. If you've had one gash, you've had them all. *I* didn't say that; *he* said it. He never found his great love, not in that lifetime."

We talked for a while about reincarnation. Rachel saw Jim meeting his great love in Italy during one of his previous lives. He loved Europe, she said. He didn't think there was any reason for the rest of the world to exist.

"Including California?"

"He's saying it's full of idiots. Look at this room. He would come here to think, and look at it now. This has nothing to do with him. That's what he's saying: 'This has nothing to do with me. These people didn't know me and they don't want to know me.' Look at this art. Look at how ugly it is." She motioned toward a fan's portrait of Jim on the wall. "He hates that.

He's saying, 'That's not me.'" As conveyed by Rachel, that was his feeling about almost every photo and drawing in the room.

Nature was a constant theme. Over and over, Rachel reported that Jim was showing her forests. He loved forests, she said, and animals and the ocean. He loved the ocean *too* much; he could easily have let it carry him away. This jibed with his song "Moonlight Drive," with its lyrics about drowning, and the overall talk of nature jibed with "When the Music's Over," the first rock song about environmental destruction. Rachel was again compelled to take dictation.

Who am I
I'm a dream
Floating on a cloud
when lightning strikes
hiding hiding
Gliding in the mud,
Seeing faces in the mud
Who are they
But they are me
Holding onto the tree
Looking up at the rain
Save me
Save me
Please.
It's too hard
Crying, stumped down,
Holding onto a tree.
My lovely tree,
Holding me with its branches
Leaves on My face caressing,
like a Mother's love
Loving Me
Loving Me.
I hide, the earth envelopes me
And so my face is coming out of the mud
Eyes closed to the world
Eyes open to God's love.
Take me, I'm yours
Now you see me.

Rachel signed this note *JM*, she said, because Jim had told her to sign it that way. He offered no help in interpreting the note.

There were several odd detours. Through Rachel, Jim spoke of his love of the comedian George Carlin. He said that he would rather have been a mailman than a rock star. He said that after he died, he sought out mediums who ignored him. (Rachel referenced the Patrick Swayze character in *Ghost* by way of clarification.) That was why he was willing to talk to Rachel: because she would listen, and so would I. Plus, people took me seriously as they never did him, and he wanted to advise me to stay true to myself.

That was the only eerie moment of the session: when Jim Morrison allegedly spoke to me personally. It was ludicrous to think that people took me seriously, compared to him or otherwise, but was part of me, deep down, flattered? Yes. Was I moved? No. I never, for a moment, lost my skepticism, but I *wanted* to lose it, I *wanted* to believe, and I believe this much: that Rachel didn't research Jim Morrison. Research would have made her more accurate, though maybe mistakes are part of the psychic con, scripted stumbles to build suspense. On the other hand, I had recently researched Jim Morrison and forgotten or misremembered details.

So I suppose it's a matter of faith, and as such, I should say that I *choose* to believe in Rachel's sincerity, even with her generalizations of the *people didn't really know him* sort, which could apply to any celebrity. I would have liked some specific but obscure item—a childhood address, the name of a distant relative—that I could verify. There wasn't one, but there was this: Rachel returned eventually to the old car with red seats, and when I asked about an accident, she said that Jim was showing her a white girl of six or so in a white nightgown.

"No Indians?"

"No, that's what I'm getting: a little white girl in a white nightgown."

Every account I've read of that accident has been sketchy—a truck full of Pueblo Indians overturned on the highway—though one account mentioned a head-on collision. If that's so, could there have been a little white girl in the second vehicle? Maybe the answer exists somewhere on microfilm, but whether it does or doesn't, it wouldn't prove what we can only learn by dying, and I'm content to remain unenlightened.

RACHEL WAS INDISPUTABLY PSYCHIC in the matter of Dee Dee, who texted shortly before eight to say that she was waiting in the parking lot. I walked Rachel to the car, paid her, and wondered aloud if tipping was protocol. It was up to me, she said. I gave her my last ten dollars in cash.

We hugged. I had had my victory, and I was simultaneously elated and exhausted.

My friend James and his girlfriend arrived minutes after Rachel and Dee Dee drove away. We opened the bottle of Jameson. I hadn't eaten since morning, so I was drunk by the second drink. More guests arrived, more than I had anticipated, since some of them hadn't replied to the invitation, and the room was filled with smoke and overlapping voices. James sent out for pizza. My friend Pete and I walked to Monaco Liquor to buy more whiskey. A girl who was staying downstairs knocked on the door and asked if she could check out Jim Morrison's room. She turned out to be a hooker, but she wasn't seeking business so much as attention, which my friends gave her, listening as she prattled at length about her true vocation as a poet, among other subjects.

So I'm told. I had passed out on the floor by the time the hooker-poet showed up, and my last distinct memory of that night is of waking briefly to see that everyone had left except for Pete and his roommate John, who were trying to get me to move from the floor to the bed. When I woke again, it was daylight and I was still on the floor. Empty bottles were everywhere, and I was wet, front and back. The floor beneath me was likewise wet. Had someone doused me with beer or water?

But it was urine. In my long history of hard drinking, I had, more than once, vomited in my sleep, but I had never, until now, pissed on myself. There was no denying it, yet for just a second, I wondered if someone else had pissed on me, someone who lived in this room more than forty years ago.

But why blame him? I was lucky if anyone, friend or stranger, answered the phone or responded to the simplest message. He, on the other hand, despite being dead, had responded immediately when Rachel reached out to him, and he promised to be present in room 32 at a specified time, and he did as he said he would do. Was that not proof of integrity?

Either way, Jim Morrison was no flake.

2013

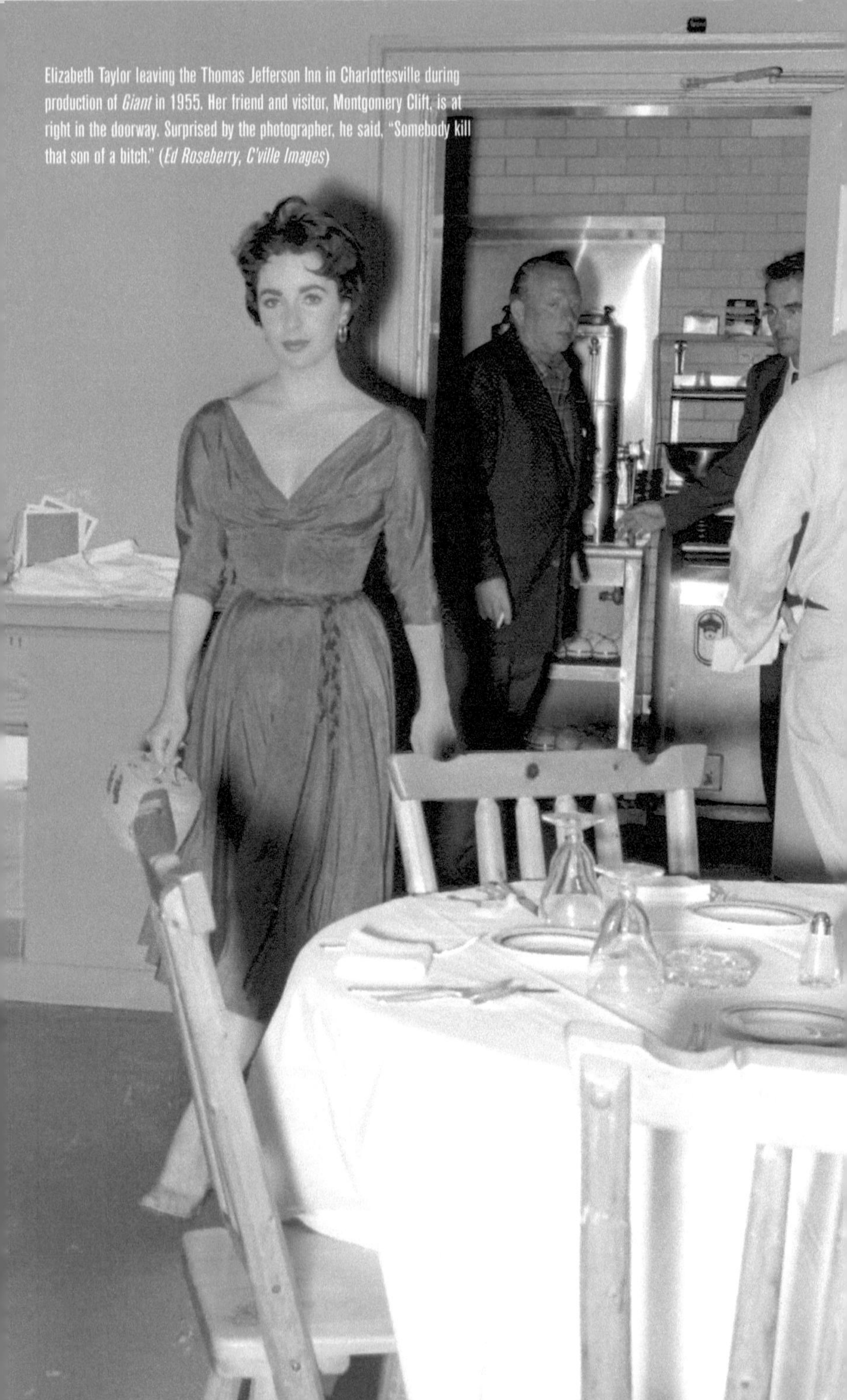

Elizabeth Taylor leaving the Thomas Jefferson Inn in Charlottesville during production of *Giant* in 1955. Her friend and visitor, Montgomery Clift, is at right in the doorway. Surprised by the photographer, he said, "Somebody kill that son of a bitch." (*Ed Roseberry, C'ville Images*)

LIFE IN ELIZABETHAN VIRGINIA

AT SOME POINT when I was a teenager, Elizabeth Taylor of Hollywood married John Warner of Virginia, my home state. Warner had served as secretary of the Navy in the Nixon administration, and around the time he became the sixth (or seventh) Mr. Elizabeth Taylor, he sought a seat in the U.S. Senate. Victory seemed a foregone conclusion. Warner's new wife was worth millions in unpaid advertising, though some regarded her as a liability. Once, in a panic after oversleeping, I called for a taxi to drive me to school and the middle-aged cabbie became apoplectic when Elizabeth Taylor Warner was mentioned on the radio.

"That goddamn whore!" he ranted. "She stole Eddie Fisher from sweet little Debbie Reynolds! That goddamn whore ought to burn in hell!"

To the cabbie's generation, Eddie Fisher would always be the faithless ex-husband of Debbie Reynolds, while my generation knew him as the real-life father of Princess Leia, if at all. Most of us were ignorant of his affair with Elizabeth Taylor, a major scandal of the late fifties, but we were certainly aware of Taylor's romance with Richard Burton, the fifth (and sixth) Mr. Elizabeth Taylor who cuckolded the fourth, Eddie Fisher, on the set of *Cleopatra* in the early sixties, the affair that launched a thousand magazine covers and enshrined Taylor as a tabloid eminence until her death half a century later. The children of the nineties and noughties may have been baffled—who *was* that batty old lady with Michael Jackson?—but anyone with vision in the seventies and before was bound to have seen pictures of Taylor at the peak of her of startling beauty, when she was wrecking homes and razing men.

Yet, overwhelmingly, she was loved for it, even in conservative Virginia, where she had filmed part of *Giant* in horse country not far from my hometown, as people of the cabbie's age and older had never forgotten. Because of her childhood role as the incognito jockey of *National Velvet*, she was still associated with horses, and because of her adult roles as Southern belles, most vividly in *Cat on a Hot Tin Roof*, she was a kind of honorary Southerner. Her American parents were living in England when she was born, and Virginia too was, in a sense, born in England, colonized by and named for Elizabeth Tudor, the virgin queen. Elizabeth Taylor, a movie queen and demonstrably no virgin, colonized Virginia on behalf of John Warner, drawing crowds wherever she went, and that was seemingly every town in the state but mine. Locals griped. "Why doesn't she come here?" they said.

Then it was announced that the Warners would be the grand marshals of the Dogwood Festival parade, an annual event in my hometown, concluding a week of concerts, picnics, carnivals, air shows, and beauty pageants scheduled to coincide with the spring flowering of the town's abundant dogwood trees, which emblazoned streets and lawns with their cross-shaped white or pink blossoms. They almost made the town tolerable for a couple of weeks, or so I thought as a restless kid who wanted to move to New York and act in the kind of gritty movies that starred Al Pacino, Robert De Niro, and Jack Nicholson, brooding, rebellious types a breed apart from the glitzy, ditzy Elizabeth Taylor. Who fucking cared if she came to my town? Not me.

ONE NIGHT I watched *Life Goes to the Movies*, a three-hour television documentary about American film as covered by *Life* magazine before its demise as a weekly in the early seventies. As much as I loved movies, I had never paid much attention to film history. I knew Marlon Brando from *The Godfather*, but here, in *Life Goes to the Movies*, were clips of Brando as the young firebrand who had virtually invented the style of acting that I revered. And here were clips of James Dean, another early avatar of that style, whom I knew only from still shots; and here was Montgomery Clift, whom I didn't know at all, eerily intense in a clip from *A Place in the Sun* with eighteen-year-old Elizabeth Taylor, a photogenic prodigy, with her raven hair and gemstone eyes, supposedly violet; though she was plainly out of her depth with an actor as powerful as Clift.

I wanted to learn more about Brando, Dean, and Clift, so I bought the book version of *Life Goes to the Movies*, but I found it less instructive than the television version, which had also introduced me to film noir. I could tell from the clips of film noir that it was the classic-Hollywood genre for me, but there was no reference to it in the book. There was a surfeit of Elizabeth Taylor, however, since she had been featured on the cover of *Life* more than any other actress. Not that she was really an actress; if not for her spectacular looks, she would never have starred opposite Brando, Dean, and Clift. Yes, she had worked with all three, study revealed, and now I decided that I would like very much to meet her. I wanted to ask her about Brando, Dean, and Clift, and the opportunity was there, if I could devise a way to engage her. On the eve of the parade it came to me: I would ask her to autograph one of her several photos in *Life Goes to the Movies.* I wouldn't select a photo; I would leave the selection to her, and hopefully that would buy a moment of conversation.

Having marched in the parade as a Cub Scout, I knew the spot where the participants queued beforehand—an uphill thoroughfare that intersected with the downtown parade route—and I set out for it, book underarm, glancing around for classmates. I was not a theater kid. My plan to become an actor was a poorly kept secret, and I had been taunted about it already, so *Life Goes to the Movies* was not the sort of coffee-table book that I wanted to be seen carrying. Still, the entire town seemed to have turned out for the parade and, as dreaded, I crossed paths with a group of kids from school. One of them asked about the book. I lied that it belonged to my sister, who wanted Elizabeth Taylor's autograph.

"Yeah, right, fag. You're the one that wants it."

I was so unhappy in that town. I continued uphill, passing idle fire engines, Shriner go-karts, floats attached to tractors. Marching bands, with bursts of brass, were warming up. Beauty queens, in sequined gowns and rhinestone tiaras, were perched in open convertibles with signs on either side that read MISS FLUVANNA COUNTY, MISS BUCKINGHAM COUNTY, and so on. The grand marshals would also ride in an open convertible, I knew, with similar signs to identify them, but this year, for once, the signs would be unnecessary. I kept walking until, at the top of the hill, I saw a roped-off crowd and cops next to the convertible I sought. It was empty, and many in the crowd held instamatic cameras, anticipating the arrival of Mrs. Warner and the spouse of little or no interest.

I waited beside the convertible. A cop told me to get behind the rope with everybody else. I complied, but I was again beside the convertible when the Warners somehow appeared. She wasn't especially charismatic, I thought, despite her regal posture. She wore a white turban and a green dress with a white floral pattern, and there was a hawkishness about her face that photos hadn't led me to expect, but she smiled easily and naturally, unlike her husband, whose smile was as forced as the jokes he made while he strolled down the length of the roped-off area, shaking hands. She followed him, and she was tailed by a mustached man in a suit and tie. She didn't shake hands, and she didn't speak. Every time someone in the crowd addressed her, it was the mustached man, presumably a bodyguard, who answered.

It was obvious that my imaginary exchange would remain just that, but I still wanted to say something, anything, if only to justify the effort I had spent on it. But what could I say? She was Elizabeth fucking Taylor! She'd won Oscars and shit! Yes, I was starstruck, to my surprise, and even more to my surprise, I wanted her autograph in earnest. I didn't know why I wanted it—as proof that I'd met her, a kind of receipt?—but I approached her meekly from behind and said, "Could you please sign this for me?" She turned, and I held out the book.

"I can't," she said in a half-whisper, and the mustached man likewise turned and said, "She can't sign anything. She hurt her hand."

"I fell," she half-whispered again, and she raised her hand as if to prove it was injured, though it wasn't bruised or bandaged.

"She fell," the mustached man repeated officiously. "She hurt her throat too. Sorry, no autographs today."

I was sure that this business of falling was a ruse to avoid talking and signing, and that was my thought when I realized that Elizabeth Taylor had paused to stare at me, her eyes locked on mine. She seemed to be trying to read me—for credulity? disappointment? a potential threat?—just as I was trying to read her, and though her face was expressionless, I thought I detected something warm, something maternal and sympathetic, in her eyes. And what color were her eyes? That was my next thought as I stood for what seemed like a very long time and gazed into those legendary eyes said to be violet. Was it true?

To me, they looked like the darkest, deepest blue with hints of maroon and brown. There's no precise word for the color I saw, or the different colors that combined to make one.

Then Elizabeth Taylor Warner, soon to be the wife of a U.S. senator, unfastened her eyes from mine and moved on.

WE BOTH MOVED ON. She left Warner and Virginia shortly after I left for New York, where I studied acting with Mira Rostova, Montgomery Clift's Russian coach, who, in all our hours together, never raised his name, as if to do so would cost her a little piece of him; but once, indirectly, she referred to Elizabeth Taylor, asking another student for her opinion of "the leading lady" in a Broadway play and smiling enigmatically when the student panned Taylor's performance. I, on the other hand, had reevaluated Taylor's acting after finally seeing *A Place in the Sun* in its entirety. It couldn't be coincidence that Clift's scenes with her were his best in the film. If he brought out something good in her, she clearly did the same for him.

I moved on again, to Los Angeles, where I worked as a movie actor, as I had long hoped to do; but the kind of gritty drama I loved as a teenager was out of fashion, and so was the style of acting pioneered by Brando,

Dean, and Clift. What use was primal emotion in fantasy movies designed for kids younger than I was when I dreamed of escaping Virginia? I thought I was glimpsing my future when I watched *Life Goes to the Movies* that night, but I was seeing a past that didn't and would never include me. The world of Brando, Dean, and Clift was done, except in documentation, and no one, of course, was documented more in the book version of *Life Goes to the Movies* than Elizabeth Taylor. I used to cringe whenever I thought of asking her to sign that book, but then I started to understand that I wasn't really looking for her autograph. Rather, she represented the world of the past, which I had mistaken for the world of the future, and her signature amounted to an ex-cathedra stamp of welcome. Yes, I think I was looking for a kind of visa.

She didn't give it to me. Nobody could give it to me. But she gave me something better, which I can only appreciate fully now that documentation is all that exists of those ineffable eyes.

2011

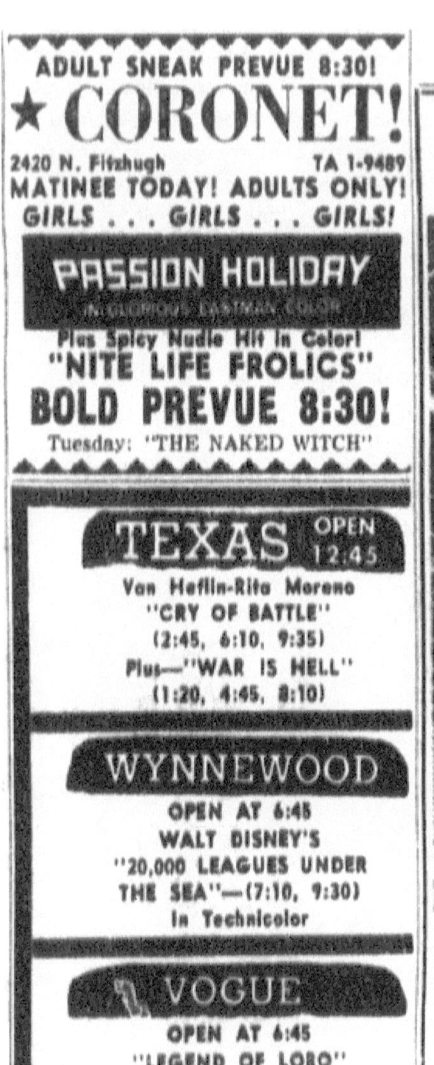

ADULT SNEAK PREVUE 8:30!
★ CORONET!
2420 N. Fitzhugh TA 1-9489
MATINEE TODAY! ADULTS ONLY!
GIRLS . . . GIRLS . . . GIRLS!
PASSION HOLIDAY
IN GLORIOUS EASTMAN COLOR
Plus Spicy Nudie Hit In Color!
"NITE LIFE FROLICS"
BOLD PREVUE 8:30!
Tuesday: "THE NAKED WITCH"

TEXAS OPEN 12:45
Van Heflin-Rita Moreno
"CRY OF BATTLE"
(2:45, 6:10, 9:35)
Plus—"WAR IS HELL"
(1:20, 4:45, 8:10)

WYNNEWOOD
OPEN AT 6:45
WALT DISNEY'S
"20,000 LEAGUES UNDER THE SEA"—(7:10, 9:30)
In Technicolor

VOGUE
OPEN AT 6:45
"LEGEND OF LOBO"
(7:00, 10:10)
Plus—"SAVAGE SAM"
(8:25)

HELD OVER!
DALLAS WILL NOT LET IT GO!
YOU SAW HER IN A NATIONAL MAGAZINE
NOW SEE ALL OF HER!
JAYNE MANSFIELD
Uncut . . . Uncensored
European Version of—
ADULTS
"PROMISES! PROMISES!"
Starring
JAYNE MANSFIELD • MARIE McDONALD
TOMMY NOONAN
1st RUN DALLAS • NOW SHOWING
LONE STAR

Cry of Battle and *War Is Hell* as listed in the November 22, 1963, edition of the *Dallas Morning News*. Lee Oswald would attend the 1:20 screening of the latter film after vanishing from his workplace amid the chaos in downtown Dallas. (*Author's collection*)

OSWALD HAS BEEN SHOT

THE MOST ICONIC MOVIE in American, if not world, history was shot on November 22, 1963, with an 8-millimeter Bell & Howell camera owned and operated by the cofounder of Jennifer Juniors, a Dallas womenswear company. The movie—which soon became known as the Zapruder film, so called after its maker—is silent and less than thirty seconds long, yet it was effectively squelched for more than a decade. Select frames from the film were published in such magazines as *Life*—Abraham Zapruder sold the copyright to Time Life the day after the assassination of John F. Kennedy, the film's subject—just as frames were published in the Warren Commission's voluminous report on the Kennedy assassination, but, except for bootleg copies, the film itself was unavailable to the public. The Warren Commission had concluded that Lee Harvey Oswald, an avowed Marxist and repatriated defector to the Soviet Union, was solely responsible for the death of Kennedy, firing three shots at the presidential limousine from the Texas School Book Depository, where Oswald worked for $1.25 per hour as a stock boy. The FBI had likewise concluded that Oswald acted alone, and many assumed that Kennedy's successor, Lyndon Johnson, had established the Warren Commission precisely to corroborate the FBI's finding and to quiet talk of conspiracy. The scarcity of the Zapruder film had the opposite effect.

Oswald's own death at the hands of Jacob Rubenstein, a strip-club owner with the appropriately seedy alias of Jack Ruby, was and is the cornerstone of conspiracy talk. This murder, which occurred in the basement garage of Dallas City Hall two days after the Kennedy assassination, was broadcast live on national television, but the footage of it, including NBC News correspondent Tom Pettit's stunned narration—"He's been shot. He's been shot. Lee Oswald has been shot"—has been largely eclipsed by the photograph snapped at the moment of impact by Bob Jackson of the late *Dallas Times-Herald*. In fact, excluding the Zapruder film, the Jackson photo may be the most famous image ever made of murder underway, more famous than any image from the Hollywood gangster movies called to mind by the familiar scene in that basement garage: Jack Ruby's hit man sent to silence Oswald's self-described patsy. The boss, offscreen, was waiting for the phone to ring with confirmation that the patsy was dead.

I was a preschooler when I first saw the Jackson photo. The home encyclopedia was a must for pre-Internet American families, and I would scrutinize the Jackson photo in ours, trying to make sense of the pain inflicted on this pitiful boy. That's what I took Oswald to be: a boy, possibly a teenager (he had recently turned twenty-four), smaller than the men who circled him, dressed informally while the men all wore suits and ties, his forehead bruised, his eye blackened. I could tell he had a black eye, despite his squint that, together with his open mouth, made him look like a baby crying for milk or affection. But he was right to cry, I thought, since he had obviously been beaten, and now he was being shot by a man in a dark suit while a man in a light suit restrained him and the other men watched blankly, as if they deeply approved. What had this boy done to deserve such treatment? He killed the president, my parents explained, but to me that didn't justify the beating and the shooting. I empathized with Oswald as a fellow child who was sometimes punished in error, and I wanted to believe that was true of him.

Then I saw the Zapruder film. I don't remember the year, but I was in middle school, and a visiting lecturer—it may have been Mark Lane, the author of three books critical of the Warren Commission—screened a bootleg copy of the film at the University of Virginia in my hometown. The film was shown again that night on the local news. Here, said the anchorman, is proof that John F. Kennedy was shot from more than one direction, and sure enough, the fatal bullet caused Kennedy's head to snap backward, not forward as it should have done if the bullet had come from the Texas School Book Depository. The official story was a lie: that disturbed me more than the sight of Kennedy's brain exploding out of his skull. Oswald may have shot at the president, but he hadn't killed him. The real killer was someone else, someone across the street from the Book Depository on the so-called grassy knoll, and he was still at large, if he hadn't been silenced like Oswald. Who was he? Were there other gunmen besides? The government knew. The government had to know. The government was part of the conspiracy, and if it had lied about the source of the fatal bullet, it might have lied about Oswald altogether. Maybe he was as innocent as I had once wanted to believe, with no involvement in the Kennedy case aside from his role as the patsy.

The Zapruder film had a similar effect on millions of Americans when it eventually aired on national television, making conspiratorialists of many who had previously accepted the official story. Fantastic theories proliferated. Kennedy was shot with a gun disguised as an umbrella. He was shot by his limousine driver. There were two Oswalds: the real one and a Soviet doppelgänger. Ruth Paine, the Quaker friend of Oswald's Russian wife, Marina, was a CIA operative who helped to frame Oswald. J.D. Tippit, the patrolman gunned down by Oswald (or his doppelgänger) forty-five minutes after he gunned down Kennedy, was an underworld hit man, like his accomplice, Jack Ruby.

But sight is one thing and interpretation another. In 1986, London Weekend Television staged a mock trial of Oswald in which forensic pathologist Charles Petty testified that the backward snap of Kennedy's head could not have been caused by a strike from the front because "the head is too heavy; there is too much muscular resistance to movement."

"So," asked prosecutor Vincent Bugliosi, "the killings that people see on television and in the movies, which is the only type of killings most people ever see, where the person struck by the bullet very frequently, visibly, and dramatically is propelled backward by the force of the bullets—that's not what actually happens in life when a bullet hits a human being?"

"No, of course not," answered Petty. "No" would have been sufficient. The additional words imply exasperation or amusement with "common sense" derived from Hollywood.

Petty was the medical examiner of Dallas County and an adviser to the House of Representatives Select Committee on Assassinations (HSCA), which reinvestigated the Kennedy case partly in response to the questions raised by the Zapruder film. Based on acoustical evidence since discredited, the HSCA decided that there was "a high probability" that a second gunman on the grassy knoll had fired one of four, not three, shots at Kennedy. But the second gunman missed. The fatal head shot was fired by Oswald from the sixth floor of the Book Depository, the HSCA echoed the Warren Commission. Computer recreations of the assassination, using the Zapruder film as a model, have verified that Kennedy was struck from that sixth-floor window, but was it Oswald who fired from it? Norman Mailer's words in the matter could as well be mine: "If one's personal inclinations would find Oswald innocent, or at least part of a conspiracy, one's gloomy verdict, nonetheless, is that Lee had the character to kill Kennedy, and that he probably did it alone." However: "The odds in favor of one's personal conclusion can be no better than, let us say, 3 out of 4 that [Oswald] was not only the killer but was alone. Too much is still unknown about CIA and FBI involvement with Oswald to offer any greater conviction."

So Mailer writes near the end of *Oswald's Tale: An American Mystery*, the 800-page tome that he moved to Minsk, Belarus, to research in the early nineties. Oswald met and married Marina in Minsk, and he was constantly watched there by the KGB, his apartment bugged, his conversations recorded. Mailer had unprecedented access to Oswald's KGB files, and he interviewed at length the KGB agents assigned to Oswald, whose mediocrity puzzled them. Could the CIA have sent this lightweight to the U.S.S.R.? No, the KGB decided ultimately, and he was of no use to them, either. It's difficult to imagine American intelligence agencies—or the Mob or Lyndon Johnson or Fidel Castro or any of the other stock players of conspiracy theories—appraising him differently. Gauche and recalcitrant, with self-regard disproportionate to his modest gifts, he could *only* have been a patsy in a conspiracy of any kind. Jack Ruby, meanwhile, mocked by those who knew him as "Sparky" for his short fuse, is another poor fit in a scheme orchestrated by professional assassins to execute the president of the United States. Rather, Sparky seems to have ignited at the sight of Oswald's smirk—Oswald appeared always to be smirking—exactly as he told the Dallas police and, later, the Warren Commission. Plot determines character in conspiracy theories, as it does in Hollywood movies. People are what the set pieces require them to be: spies, patsies, doppelgängers, accomplices, or hit men armed with fatal umbrellas.

I HAD A DISTURBING DREAM about Oswald when I was in my early twenties. I *was* Oswald in the dream, and I was standing on the roof of a tenement building on New York's Lower East Side—I was then living in such a building—while a crowd on the street cheered Kennedy's approaching motorcade. Manhattan had morphed into Dallas on November 22, 1963, and there was a rifle, leaning against the parapet, that I was compelled to pick up and fire. I had no choice. It was like the butterfly effect in reverse: I would nullify everything that had happened since the assassination—every birth, marriage, discovery, invention—if I didn't go through with it. I fired a single shot while averting my eyes, but I knew from the uproar below, a great collective cry, that I had struck Kennedy, and a second later I heard heavy footsteps inside the building on the stairs. A vigilante mob was coming for me and, trapped on the roof, my only escape was to leap over the parapet to certain death. I woke just as the door to the roof crashed open.

Clearly, my empathy with Oswald had survived childhood. I had read about him since and recognized some overlap. We both came from fractured families, though my parents divorced when I was ten and his father died before he was born. We had both been indifferent students considered odd by peers, though I wasn't as socially inept as he was. And we were both ambitious, though the mark I hoped to make on the world was a scratch compared to his chasm. But first I had to escape from Virginia, and escape is a persistent theme in Oswald's life, if we can agree that not every fact of his life is a "fact."

It begins early. Lillian Murret, Oswald's aunt, told the Warren Commission that, when she cared for him as a toddler, Lee "started slipping out of the house in his nightclothes and going down the block and sitting down in somebody's kitchen. He could slip in and out like nobody's business. You could have everything locked in the house, and he would still get out."

That was in New Orleans, where Oswald was born. He started school in Dallas, and at twelve, he and his garrulous mother, Marguerite, moved to New York, where he became a chronic truant, spending his days riding the subway or haunting the Bronx Zoo. He loved animals, Marguerite recalled for the Warren Commission, but the captivity of the zoo animals may have mirrored the captivity that he felt at school or at home with Marguerite. Her two older sons left home as soon as they were able, and one of them, Robert, has said that, despite Marguerite's "tremendous" influence on Lee, he, like his brothers, "always was trying to get away from her."

At sixteen, back in New Orleans, Oswald tried to enlist in the Marine Corps and was rejected as too young. His second effort, at seventeen, was successful, but if he was seeking more than just an escape from home, he was evidently disappointed; in Moscow in 1959, while his bid for Soviet citizenship was being weighed, he said that he had "been waiting [to defect] for two years, saving my money, just waiting until I got out of the Marine Corps, like waiting to get out of prison." So he was quoted in a United Press International story by Aline Mosby, one of two journalists to interview him in Moscow. Oswald spouted Marx to Mosby—he became a Marxist, he claimed, after a stranger in New York handed him a leaflet about Ethel and Julius Rosenberg, executed by the U.S. government as Soviet spies—and he hinted at classified information gleaned in the Marine Corps. Mosby was incredulous:

> He struck me as being a rather mixed-up young man of not great intellectual capacity or training, and somebody that the Soviet Union wouldn't certainly be much interested in. But he had this cover of conceit that—oh, that they were just going to welcome him and welcome him into the hierarchy, that he'd be having lunch with all the top leaders, Khrushchev or whoever was in power then, and would be given a *dacha* and a big apartment and a car or something.

Instead, he was given a mundane job at an electronics factory in Minsk, the capital not only of Belarus but of boredom. There, as a kind of unicorn, he was popular for the first time ever. He had a steady girlfriend, another first, but she declined his marriage proposal, and five months later he proposed to Marina Prusakova, a comely nineteen-year-old he had known for two weeks. This rush to marry is a classic rebound move, the vengeance of the spurned, but Oswald had already queried the American Embassy in Moscow about returning to the U.S., and Marguerite would have to accept reduced stature in his life if he returned with a wife, he may have reasoned. He was "completely relieved of his illusions about the Soviet Union," an embassy official wrote on Oswald's behalf to the State Department in Washington. The official, Richard Snyder, has been linked by conspiratorialists to the CIA, but Oswald noted his dissatisfaction with Minsk in his "Historic Diary," and it was further confirmed by his Soviet friends to Norman Mailer.

By the time Marina's U.S. visa had been approved, she and Oswald were the parents of a daughter, June. He expected media interest when he arrived back in Texas. There was none. He got a job as thankless as the one he had held in Minsk, and he and Marina fought and separated, as they would do again and again, but they were living together in the Dallas district of Oak Cliff when Oswald took a shot at Major General Edwin Walker with the same Carcano rifle found in the School Book Depository after the Kennedy assassination. That Oswald took a shot at Walker with any rifle is disputed, of course, but the HSCA concluded that "the evidence strongly suggested that Oswald attempted to murder General Walker." The rifle and a Smith & Wesson revolver were ordered by mail from Klein's Sporting Goods in Chicago and Seaport Traders in Los Angeles, respectively, by an "A. Hidell" of Dallas, and Oswald's handwriting matches the handwriting on the order forms, though that too is disputed, of course. What isn't disputed is that someone fired a single bullet through the window of Walker's study and narrowly missed his head as he was figuring his taxes at nine p.m. on Wednesday, April 10, 1963. But for that bullet, Walker would be forgotten to all but a handful of scholars, and were he still alive, he might prefer to be forgotten as the segregationist who incited a deadly riot at the University of Mississippi when a black student, James Meredith, enrolled there. Walker also incited an appalling attack on U.N. Ambassador Adlai Stevenson, a crypto-communist in the minds of Walker and his fellow patriots of the hilariously named National Indignation Committee, when Stevenson spoke in Dallas a month ahead of Kennedy's disastrous visit there. One wonders how Walker squared his politics with his secret homosexuality; in the late seventies he was twice arrested for "public lewdness" in restrooms.

In any case, Walker was the "fascist" cobra to Oswald's Marxist mongoose, and an assassinated cobra would have been a significant boost to Oswald's spirit at that point: he had recently lost his latest job at a graphics firm. But though he believed he had killed Walker when he fled into the night, he had failed, and two weeks later he moved to New Orleans, boarding initially with Lillian Murret, the aunt whose house he could always escape as a toddler. This period of his life would lead, after his death, to an investigation by Jim Garrison, the district attorney of Orleans Parish, and the trial of a local businessman, Clay Shaw, accused of plotting with Oswald to assassinate Kennedy. Shaw was acquitted, as anyone who has seen Oliver Stone's 1991 movie *JFK* knows. Nevertheless, *JFK* spawned, possibly, as many conspiratorialists as the Zapruder film, which was subpoenaed by Garrison and copied and leaked by his associates: the original bootleg version.

Oswald now became an activist for the Fair Play for Cuba Committee, a pro-Castro organization with a New Orleans chapter started by its sole member: Oswald. Nor did he try to recruit new members. This smacks of conspiracy to some—the chapter was Oswald's CIA or FBI cover—but it's just another escape to me: Oswald was again hoping to defect, this time to Cuba. However, since "it was illegal at the time for a United States citizen to travel to Cuba," writes Edward Jay Epstein in *Legend: The Secret World of Lee Harvey Oswald*, "he would have to obtain his visa at a Cuban Embassy outside the country, and to do that, he would need some credentials to prove that he was a supporter of the Cuban government." Hence the Fair Play for Cuba Committee and Oswald's attempted infiltration of an anti-Castro group: if he could somehow subvert the group or, at least, learn of its plans, that too would look good in Havana.

But he couldn't get a visa when he applied for one at the Cuban Embassy in Mexico City. Some insist that an Oswald impostor made this trip to Mexico City to lay a foundation for Oswald's impending frame-up, but "the majority of the evidence tends to indicate that this individual was Lee Harvey Oswald," the HSCA determined. Either way, Oswald returned to Texas, where Marina and June were now living in the Dallas suburb of Irving with Ruth Paine, a schoolteacher who wanted to better her college Russian and was, like Marina, separated from her husband. Oswald badly needed a job—Marina was pregnant with their second daughter, Rachel—and one morning, at a neighborhood coffee klatch, someone mentioned a relative who worked as a stock boy at the Texas School Book Depository. At Marina's urging, Ruth phoned the Book Depository and asked the manager there about job openings. The manager's trusty name, Roy Truly, hasn't altogether precluded him from the suspicion of conspiratorialists. He hired Oswald the next day.

Oswald's final residence was an Oak Cliff boarding house where he registered as "O. H. Lee." An alias serves a practical purpose, of course, for someone with real or imagined cause for anonymity, but it can also serve as a fantasy escape from a fixed identity, and this one is key to the Kennedy assassination: when Ruth, again at Marina's urging, phoned the boarding house five days before the assassination and asked for Lee Oswald, she was told that no such person lived there. Oswald confessed to the alias when he called Marina during his lunch break the following day. She was all too aware of his aborted defection to Cuba and his attempt on Walker's life, and that he was renting a room under an assumed name was, to her, vexing evidence of new intrigue. They didn't speak again until the evening before the assassination, when he showed up at the Paine house. He wasn't expected. It was a Thursday, and he usually came on Friday after work and stayed through the weekend, but he told Marina that "he was lonely because he hadn't come the preceding weekend, and he wanted to make his peace with me," as she related to J. Lee Rankin, chief consul of the Warren Commission.

Mr. RANKIN. Were you upset with him?

Mrs. OSWALD. I was angry, of course. He was not angry—he was upset. I was angry. He tried very hard to please me. He spent quite a bit of time putting away diapers and played with the children on the street.

Mr. RANKIN. How did you indicate to him that you were angry with him?

Mrs. OSWALD. By not talking to him.

Mr. RANKIN. And how did he show that he was upset?

Mrs. OSWALD. He was upset over the fact that I would not answer him. He tried to start a conversation with me several times, but I would not answer. And he said that he didn't want me to be angry at him because this upsets him.

On that day, he suggested that we rent an apartment in Dallas. He said that he was tired of living alone and perhaps the reason for my being so angry was the fact that we were not living together. That if I want to he would rent an apartment in Dallas tomorrow—that he didn't want me to remain with Ruth any longer, but wanted me to live with him in Dallas.

This is bizarre behavior for a man in a conspiracy to assassinate the president. Why is he offering to rent an apartment in Dallas on the day that he knows he'll be shooting at Kennedy—he's locked into place by others who will kill him, we can be sure, if he tries to back out—and presumably going on the lam afterward? Meanwhile, if he's a clueless patsy, why has he parted with routine, turning up on a Thursday night after telling his ride to Irving—Oswald didn't own a car—that he needs to pick up curtain rods for his room in Oak Cliff? There are indeed curtain rods in Ruth Paine's garage, but they'll still be there in the morning, while Oswald's rifle—it's stored in the garage, as Marina knows but Ruth doesn't—will be missing.

No, there's only one way that I can read Marina's account of that night: Oswald has a choice to make. He has planned the assassination, on his own, but he's conflicted about whether to go through with it, and he has placed the final decision in his unwitting wife's lap. If she will forgive him and come back to him, he won't sneak into the garage and wrap the rifle in brown paper and, so disguised as curtain rods, smuggle it into the Book Depository in the morning. He doesn't hate Kennedy as he hated and undoubtedly still hates Walker, but he will try to kill him because the opportunity is there, and to quote Mailer: "The assassination of a President would be seismographic in its effect. For Americans, the aftershocks would not cease for the rest of the century or more."

But Marina is ambivalent about reconciling. She wants to remain at Ruth's house through the holidays, she tells Oswald, and he finally gives up and goes into the living room, where he watches television.

Mr. RANKIN. Did he say anything at all that would indicate he was contemplating the assassination?

Mrs. OSWALD. No.

Mr. RANKIN. Did he discuss the television programs he saw that evening with you?

Mrs. OSWALD. He was looking at TV by himself. I was busy in the kitchen. At one time when we were—when I was together with him they showed some sort of war films, from World War II. And he watched them with interest.

The subject of movies will come up again in Marina's Warren Commission testimony, and it suggests a question: if our perceptions of the Kennedy assassination have been influenced by movies, what influence did movies, and pop culture generally, have on Kennedy's presumed assassin?

WHEN OSWALD WAS A TRUANT in New York, his brother Robert has said, he would "do the things he always liked to do—got [*sic*] to the movies if he had the money, go to the library and read if he didn't have it." This is a rare reference to Oswald's interest in movies, but no titles are specified, and we don't know what sort of movies he preferred as a child. What we do know is that he was arrested for truancy at the Bronx Zoo and sent by a judge to a reformatory where he was evaluated, on separate occasions, by a psychiatrist, Renatus Hartogs, and a social worker, Evelyn Strickman, whose reports are, in certain respects, almost identical.

Hartogs: "Lee has a vivid fantasy life, turning around the topics of omnipotence and power, through which he tries to compensate for his present shortcomings and frustration... Lee limits his interests to reading magazines and looking at the television all day long."

Strickman: "He acknowledged fantasies about being all-powerful and being able to do anything he wanted... it was finally learned that Lee spent all of his time looking at television and reading various magazines."

It's easy, if not safe, to guess that young Oswald's fantasy life was fed by television and magazines, though, again, no titles are specified. Marguerite Oswald told the Warren Commission that her son "loved comics, read comic books," and she was confirmed by the testimony of Edward Voebel, Oswald's sole friend in New Orleans after he and Marguerite returned there. "I can say for certain that the only thing that Lee would be reading when I was at his home would be comic books and the normal things that kids read," Voebel responded to a question about rumors of Oswald's familiarity with Marx at fourteen. Voebel dismissed those rumors as "a lot of baloney," yet in October 1956, days before he turned seventeen and joined the Marine Corps, Oswald mailed a handwritten letter to the Socialist Party of America in which he identified himself as a Marxist and said that he had "been studying socialist principles for well over fifteen months." What got him started? The leaflet about the Rosenbergs that he mentioned to Aline Mosby in Moscow? Possibly. But he may have been trying to impress Mosby with his early interest in causes and current events while concealing his true inspiration: *I Led 3 Lives*, a television series based on the "true story" of an advertising executive who spied on communists for the FBI and vice versa. The series ran from 1953-1956, which times perfectly with Oswald's remarks in his Socialist Party letter, and he was a devoted viewer, according to his brother Robert, who has Lee "still watching [the show] when I left [home] in 1952." That would be impossible, obviously, so we can't be sure that he's misremembering more than just the year. But if Lee was nevertheless a fan of *I Led 3 Lives*, its inevitably villainous communists may have appealed to him in the same way that some prefer the vampire to the vampire slayer, just as the protagonist's clandestine life may have appealed to him as a particularly secretive teenager of the fifties, when the spy was emerging as a pop-culture ideal. Ian Fleming's *Casino Royale*, the first James Bond novel, was published in 1953, and Oswald borrowed four subsequent Bond novels—*Moonraker*, *Goldfinger*, *Thunderball*, and *From Russia, with Love*—from the New Orleans Public Library in the early fall of 1963. (John Kennedy was another avid reader of Fleming's Bond novels.) Meanwhile, in her book *Marina and Lee*, Priscilla Johnson McMillan recounts a night in Minsk when the Oswalds saw a movie about a Nazi spy "who got off scot-free, unlike Soviet movies in which the enemy spy always got caught," and as they walked out of the theater, Lee told his wife, "I'd love a life like that… I'd love the danger."

McMillan was the second journalist to file a story about Oswald in Moscow. In a coincidence that wouldn't manifest as one until November 1963, she had worked as a researcher for John Kennedy when he was in the U.S. Senate, and after he was assassinated, she interviewed Marina exhaustively for the book she spent twelve years writing. It will come as no surprise that McMillan has been tied by conspiratorialists to the CIA, but hopefully we can trust what she has to say on small matters like movies, beginning in Minsk, where Oswald seems to have gone to the movies quite a bit. Of course he did. There was nothing else to do. In his apartment, he would sit by the window and, with binoculars, "scan the horizon and in particular, the main street of Minsk to his left, to see what was playing at the movies." He often went to the movies alone, Marina told McMillan, leaving her behind with June, and he did the same in Dallas, Marina told the Warren Commission: "He wanted to take me but I didn't understand English." As for New Orleans, McMillan writes that "Marina sent [Lee] to the movies so she could catch up on housework or have a little time for himself."

Oswald had fairly eclectic taste in movies, if we can judge by those he saw in Minsk, as listed by McMillan and the KGB. There's *Lili*, an MGM release about a provincial girl who joins a circus. There's Roman Tikhomirov's adaption of the Tchaikovsky opera *Queen of Spades*, which Oswald saw repeatedly. There's the Bulgarian war movie *Komandirat na otryada*, and there's a French comedy, *Babette s'en va-t-en guerre*, co-starring Brigitte Bardot and her then-husband, Jacques Charrier. *Babette* is set during World War II, like the Bulgarian movie; Oswald saw them, and three other movies, two of them dealing with war, over the course of five days in September 1960, and immediately afterward he went on a hunting trip with a shotgun that he had bought in August but hadn't yet used. In *Oswald's Tale*, Mailer connects the dots: Oswald was "filled by now, one may assume, with images of himself as a participant in war movies." McMillan, in her book, assigns significance to the song that Lee would sing in Minsk—"always, it seemed, when [he] was working on his diary"—to the irritation of Marina:

> It was not until years later that she found out it was the title song of the movie *High Noon*, the story of the sheriff of a small Western town who, against the wishes of his wife and without any help from the townspeople, is brave enough to stand up to a band of outlaws who are out to take over the town. [Oswald] saw the movie in Fort Worth in 1956 on the enthusiastic urging of his brother, Robert, and they loved to sing the song together. He may also have seen it again when he was in the Marine Corps, and it is apparent that the theme of the movie and its title song, the conflict between love and duty, made a deep impression on him.

McMillan speculates that Oswald was similarly torn between love and—as he regarded it—duty at Ruth Paine's house the night before the Kennedy assassination, and afterward he may have "expected his personal drama to end the way *High Noon* does. [The sheriff] not only earns the thanks of the townspeople, he also wins back the love of his wife."

Researcher John Loken draws a much more direct line between movies and the assassination; in his book *Oswald's Trigger Films*, Loken argues that Oswald was inspired to buy the Carcano rifle after seeing *The Manchurian Candidate* in late 1962 or early 1963, when it played at the Texas Theater in Oak Cliff, where Oswald was living at the time (and would live again), and the Palace Theater in downtown Dallas, where he was then working (and would work again). *The Manchurian Candidate*, directed by John Frankenheimer in a style that owes much to Alfred Hitchcock, is about a former prisoner of war programmed by his captors to assassinate a presidential nominee, only to gun down his virago mother and buffoonish stepfather, a U.S. senator modeled after Joseph McCarthy, in the film's climactic scene. Loken points out that the Carcano's "short length, its scope, and its military origin made it…very similar to the 'Soviet Army sniper's rifle' featured in *The Manchurian Candidate*." Loken further believes that Oswald might have conflated the stepfather character with General Walker, and as a bonus, Angela Lansbury, stellar as the assassin's mother, would have evoked Marguerite.

There's no record of Oswald having seen *The Manchurian Candidate*, though Loken devotes pages in his book, footnotes and maps and newspaper clippings, to establishing its likelihood. But *The Manchurian Candidate* is only one of Loken's three possible "trigger films," and the other two were mentioned by Marina to the Secret Service, which led to a brief discussion of them during Marina's Warren Commission testimony.

Mr. RANKIN. Do you recall films that [Oswald] saw called "Suddenly" and "We Were Strangers" that involved assassinations?

Mrs. OSWALD. I don't remember the names of those films. If you would remind me of the contents, perhaps I would know.

Mr. RANKIN. Well, "Suddenly" was about the assassination of a president, and the other was about the assassination of a Cuban dictator.

Mrs. OSWALD. Yes, Lee saw those films.

Mr. RANKIN. Did he tell you that he watched them?

Mrs. OSWALD. I was with him when he watched them.

Oswald was visiting Ruth Paine's house for the weekend. Marina was then pregnant with Rachel, and she estimates that they watched *Suddenly* and *We Were Strangers*, back to back on television, "some five days" before Rachel was born on October 20, 1963.

Mr. RANKIN. Did you discuss the films after you watched them with your husband?

Mrs. OSWALD. One film about the assassination of the president in Cuba which I had seen together with him, he said that this was a fictitious situation, but that the content of the film was similar to the actual situation which existed in Cuba, meaning the revolution in Cuba.

Mr. RANKIN. Did either of you comment on either film being like the attempt on Walker's life?

Mrs. OSWALD. No. I didn't watch the other film.

Loken doesn't believe that Oswald watched it either, at least that night. *Suddenly*—which, like *The Manchurian Candidate*, starred John Kennedy's friend Frank Sinatra—is a hostage drama about an ill-fated plan to shoot the unnamed president from the window of a house commandeered by hoods. They're contract killers, without valor or ideals, and the movie is dull, though it may not have been dull to audiences when it was released in 1954. Even so, I can't see it having much or any emotional resonance with Oswald, who was nothing if not idealistic and—in his own mind, we can surmise—valorous. Meanwhile, *Suddenly* doesn't appear in the television listings of either major Dallas newspaper in October 1963. Loken theorizes that Marina, who told McMillan that she "dozed through the first movie" and most of the second watched by Lee that night, in fact caught glimpses of *The Asphalt Jungle*, which aired just before a ten p.m. broadcast of *We Were Strangers* on Saturday, October 12, and "a Secret Service agent...trying to help Marina recall...'prompted' her with the misinformation that Lee had seen *Suddenly.*" Whatever the case, as Marina dozed, she felt Lee, beside her on Ruth Paine's sofa, "sit up straight and strain toward the television, greatly excited," McMillan writes, continuing with a synopsis of *We Were Strangers*:

> Based on the actual overthrow of the Machado dictatorship in Cuba in 1933, the movie stars John Garfield as an American who has come to help the cause of revolution. He and a tiny band of cohorts plot to blow up the whole cabinet, including the president, at a single stroke. The plot fails and Garfield dies, but the people rise up in small groups all over Cuba and overthrow the dictatorship.
>
> Marina remembers the movie's end—people were dancing in the streets, screaming with happiness because the president had been overthrown. Lee said it was exactly the way it had once happened in Cuba. It was the only time he showed any interest in Cuba after his return from Mexico.

We Were Strangers was directed by John Huston (who also directed *The Asphalt Jungle*) on location in Havana in 1948. I saw it for the first time after reading Loken's book, and while it's dated, with the usual Hollywood corniness and contrivances, it holds up better, in my view, than *The Manchurian Candidate.* I can easily imagine Oswald being galvanized by it. Marina told the Secret Service that "Lee did not like the picture as he said that was the way they did in [*sic*] in the old days"—she seems to be referring to the assassination method—but she also said he watched the movie twice, and sure enough, it had a repeat showing at one p.m. on Sunday, October 13, according to the *Dallas Morning News.* If Oswald didn't like *We Were Strangers*, why, Loken asks with italics I'll duplicate here, did he watch it *twice*? And what does it prove either way? Loken supports his "copycat" theory of the Kennedy assassination with the documented influence of Martin Scorsese's *Taxi Driver* on John Hinckley, the would-be assassin of Ronald Reagan. But Hinckley is a simpleton compared to Oswald, who has been dead for fifty years exactly as I write these words, yet remains enigmatic to all except those who would convict him without the trial he never had or exonerate him on the basis of intuition and innuendo, quack scholarship and flaky evidence, and a paranoid and adolescent mistrust of perceived authority of any kind.

He escapes us.

FEW HAVE EVER escaped to the movies as literally as Oswald did on November 22, 1963. He disappeared from the Texas School Book Depository minutes after the shooting in downtown Dallas, where a steamfitter named Howard Brennan, standing on the street below the Book Depository, saw him, or someone who resembled him, in a window of the sixth floor, withdrawing a rifle and watching the departing limousine "as though to assure himself that he hit his mark." If this was Oswald, he may have been thinking of the Walker shooting, when he fled before he finished the job. But that was at night, with no one around, and now, at half past noon, he was probably counting on the bedlam below to obscure his exit from the building, which he knew would be quickly sealed. He caught a city bus, and when it stalled in traffic, he disembarked and took a cab to the boarding house in Oak Cliff: the housekeeper, Earlene Roberts, saw him there, rushing to his room and, a minute later, rushing out the front door. But Howard Brennan's description of the gunman had been dispatched to cops all over Dallas, and one of them, J.D. Tippit, stopped Oswald—he would soon be identified in a police lineup by a waitress named Helen Markham—as he walked along an Oak Cliff street. Oswald and Tippit talked for a moment, and after Tippit stepped out of his car, Oswald removed a revolver from the pocket of his "Eisenhower" jacket and opened fire, shooting Tippit four times and turning to go before turning back to deliver the coup de grâce, a bullet to the head. Then, emptying the shells from his revolver, he took off on foot. We don't know if he was already headed to the Texas Theater, where conspiratorialists have him trysting with confederates, but that's where he would spend his final moments as a free man, watching *War Is Hell*, which was playing with another war movie, *Cry of Battle*. Oswald liked war movies, as we know.

Norman Mailer once said that while he largely dismissed the Warren Commission's investigation, there was nevertheless a wealth of detail in its report, so that "historians in two hundred years will be going through it to get an idea of what life was like in America in that period." He meant the sort of everyday detail that's rarely of interest to conspiratorialists. We learn from the report, for instance, that tickets at the Texas Theater cost ninety cents for adults, fifty cents for teenagers, and thirty-five cents for children; and when Julia Postal, the ticket seller, is asked if matinees are cheaper than evening shows, she replies in charming Texanese, "No, sir; we don't change prices. Used to, but we don't." We learn that she kept a transistor radio in the box office, and she turned it on after her daughter called to say that the president had been shot; and she tells us a little about her background: "Was born here in Dallas and...went to California and finished up [school] out there...I worked at the Paramount Theatre, and Graumans, and R.K.O. Used to work for the Pantages." Mrs. Postal made a career of working in movie theaters, not only in Dallas but, we discover with a touch of surprise, in Hollywood, and November 24, 1963, the day that Oswald died, marked the eleventh anniversary of her employment at the Texas. She had probably sold a ninety-cent ticket to Oswald more than once in the past, though she doesn't say she did in the Warren Commission report; but Oswald didn't buy a ticket for the double feature of war movies; he ducked inside the theater while Mrs. Postal was distracted by the commotion caused by the Tippit shooting, squad cars racing past the Texas with shrieking sirens. However, Oswald had been followed by a shoe salesman named Johnny Brewer, who worked nearby and thought Oswald was behaving suspiciously. "Well," says Mrs. Postal, "just as I turned around then Johnny Brewer was standing there and he asked me if the fellow that ducked in bought a ticket, and I said, 'No; by golly, he didn't.'" She too thought Oswald had been behaving suspiciously—she noticed him just before he vanished mysteriously—and she called the police and "seemed like I hung up the intercom phone when here all of a sudden, police cars, policemen, plainclothesmen, I never saw so many people in my life." There would be more: the police attracted a growing crowd of civilians who quickly decided that the president's assassin was inside the theater and called for his blood. "That is when I really started shaking," Mrs. Postal says. "I had never seen a live mob scene." This means, of course, that she had seen mob scenes in movies.

But I can't find any mention in the Warren Commission report of the last movie seen by Oswald. It was written, directed, and produced by Burt Topper, who also has a supporting role as an actor, and while the film is set in Korea during the Korean War, it was shot in Southern California, where Topper worked for American International Pictures, which specialized in the kind of exploitation movies that Topper made not only for AIP but as an independent: *Devil's Angels*, *Thunder Alley*, *The Diary of a High School Bride*. Going by what remains of it, *War Is Hell* isn't, strictly speaking, an exploitation movie, but only the first thirty minutes or so have survived with the soundtrack intact, and the soundtrack is damaged, so that the actors speak at a speed that deepens and distorts their voices. This includes Audie Murphy, the most decorated American serviceman of World War II and a native Texan who appeared mostly in low-budget westerns, and Murphy doesn't act in *War Is Hell* so much as legitimize it with his presence, introducing the movie with a brief sermon about combat psychology. "A man will not be strong enough to face any really critical situation unless he has the right equipment," he says, looking squarely at the camera and the audience, "and the most modern weapons are not enough; he must be armed with moral strength as well." Is this what Oswald saw when he entered the theater? Did the words have any effect on him? And what did he think of the battle scene that followed Audie Murphy's speech? Did the screen violence seem ridiculous compared to the real thing? Did the heads of the actors snap in the right direction?

But he probably looked at the screen without really seeing it, preoccupied with more pressing matters. Soon the house lights would rise and the police would step from behind the curtain, interrupting *War Is Hell* a half-hour after it started, and now that half-hour is all that's left, the movie cutting off at the approximate moment that its most notorious viewer was apprehended. Oswald would say, as the police approached him, "Well, it's all over now," and reach for his revolver, and in the ensuing struggle he would receive the bruises and the black eye that distressed me as a child when I stared at the Bob Jackson photo. The police would lead him in cuffs outside, and he would scream about police brutality when the police were his only protection from the mob that wanted to lynch him, just as there was a mob that wanted to lynch me in the dream I had about Oswald, the dream in which *I* was Oswald and killed Kennedy without trying and could only escape by leaping to certain death. Or maybe it wasn't certain. Dreams are like movies, where anything can happen. Arms can become wings. Asphalt can become feathers. A lynch mob can back down, no longer sure of the truth, and a bullet to the head or the gut can be reversed, and the dead can live again.

2013

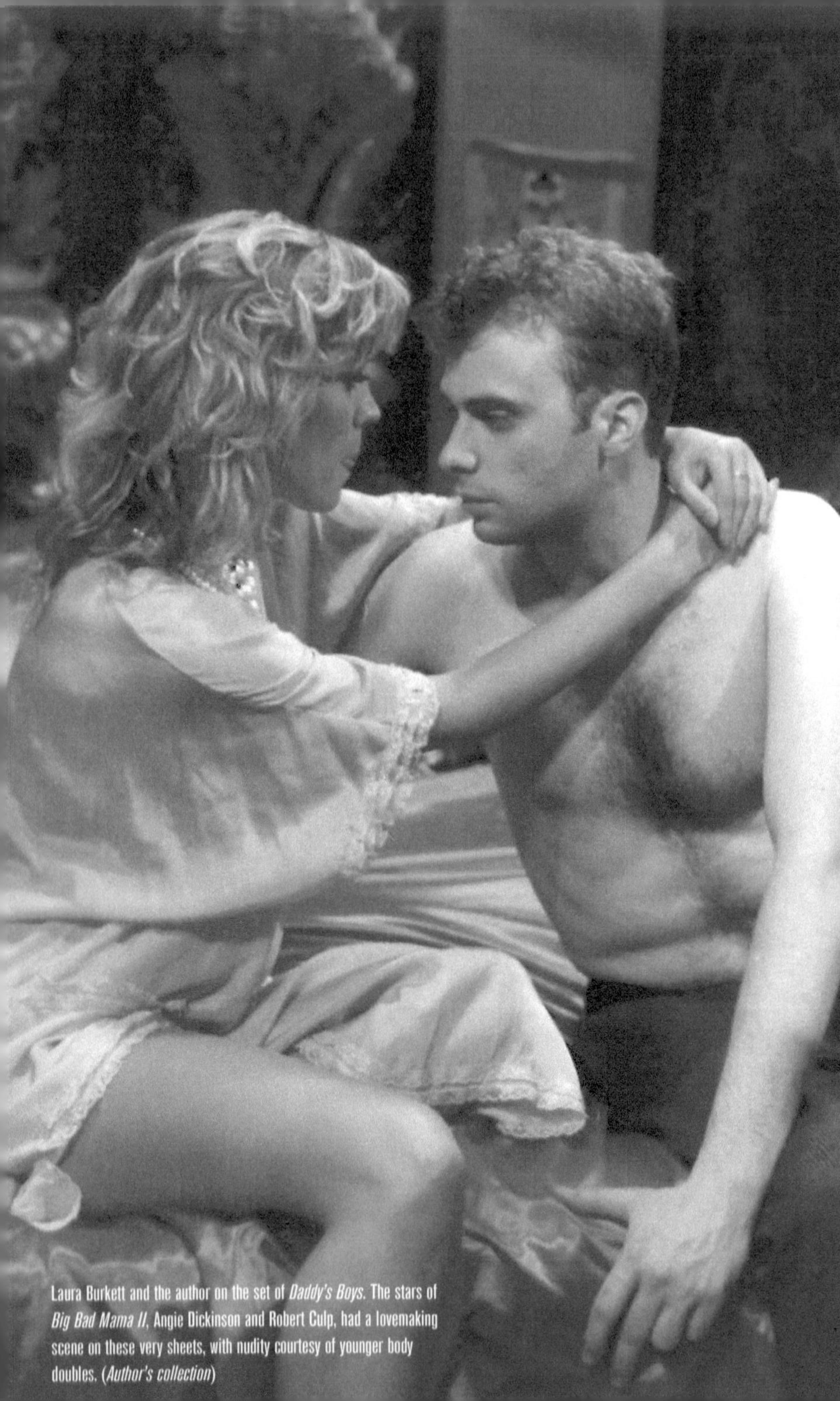

Laura Burkett and the author on the set of *Daddy's Boys*. The stars of *Big Bad Mama II*, Angie Dickinson and Robert Culp, had a lovemaking scene on these very sheets, with nudity courtesy of younger body doubles. (*Author's collection*)

YOU WILL BECOME SHORT OF BREATH

THE LAST TIME I CHECKED, my nude photos were still online. "Click to watch Daryl Haney exposed!" one site urged. "Hot Daryl Haney is sexy boy!" A second site declared that "lustful Daryl is able to turn every action into the really magic one, are you ready for that?" and the same foreign carnival barker must have co-authored this with a translation bot for a third site: "Nude Daryl will show you his wonderful body's most delicious spots without any doubts, because he likes it. Daryl's ass is so attractive and sexy that you would lose your mind. It's one of the main reasons why you got to take a glance at passionate Daryl right now. Handsome Daryl Haney needs your attention and he knows for real that you will become short of breath on seeing his pose in the altogether for you."

That wasn't composed about me exclusively, of course. Dado Ruspoli will show you his own wonderful body's most delicious spots without any doubts, and Dafydd Emyr's ass is so attractive and sexy that you would lose your mind, and you got to take a look at passionate Daishi Hori right now. Dado Ruspoli, Dafydd Emyr, and Daishi Hori are among the names listed near mine at the gay porn site where I know for real that you will become short of breath on seeing my pose in the altogether for you. In fact, my "poses" were lifted from *Daddy's Boys*, a weird little crime movie produced by Roger Corman and directed by Joseph Minion, however much the title may suggest gay porn.

Joe had directed me once before, in a Kafkaesque short when he was a student at NYU Film School. He was smitten with one of the actresses in that short, a girl who lived in a Soho loft with a roommate named Kiki Bridges, and later, after he transferred to Columbia University, Joe wrote a screenplay about a girl who was staying at a Soho loft with a friend named Kiki Bridges. The screenplay, originally titled *Lies*, somehow found its way to Martin Scorsese, who directed it with a title change: *After Hours*. By then the actress in the Kafkaesque short had become my ex-girlfriend, so for me *After Hours* was a reminder of the recent past: the keys she would toss from her fourth-floor window when I rang her doorbell, the late-night talks at the Moondance Diner. Kiki Bridges had long since moved from the loft, though I met her once at a wedding. She signed off on the use of her name in the movie.

But, in a roundabout way, *After Hours* also foreshadowed the imminent future. In his salad days, Martin Scorsese had directed *Boxcar Bertha*, one of several Depression-era crime movies produced by Roger Corman in the mold of *Bonnie and Clyde. Big Bad Mama* was another, and now, nearly thirteen years after its release, Roger was preparing a sequel at his studio in Venice Beach, building sets that included a bank and a bordello. The sets proved extravagant by Roger's miserly standards, and to maximize his investment, he decided to produce a second movie that would follow *Big Bad Mama II* from set to set, shooting on them as they became available. *Big Bad Mama II* was then days from starting production, and since there wasn't a script for the piggyback movie, Roger would have to commission one and hire a director—immediately. Anna Roth, Roger's assistant and Joe's classmate at Columbia, recommended Joe to write *and* direct the movie. The Scorsese connection was further endorsement.

And so, on a Friday, Joe flew from New York to L.A. and spent the weekend devising a story about a bank robber and a prostitute, the only conceivable characters, given the bank and bordello sets. Then, on Sunday night, he phoned me at my apartment in Brooklyn to offer me the part of the bank robber, pending Roger's approval and the money I would have to somehow borrow for a flight. The movie's beggarly budget precluded expenses like air fare and housing for imported talent. Joe was crashing on the dining-room floor of Anna Roth's bungalow in Hollywood, and I would do the same when I arrived in L.A. on Tuesday afternoon. Shooting began on the bordello set on Thursday morning, and we had a sketchy outline and a tentative title—*God's Own Mad Lover*, a phrase Joe recalled from a Jack London novel—but, apart from a couple of dashed-off scenes, no script. Joe mentioned *Gun Crazy* and *They Live by Night*, film-noir classics, as templates for *God's Own Mad Lover*, but he knew that beans don't make for a banquet. He had taken this job for the adventure, he said. He welcomed my help with the script.

Like *Bonnie and Clyde*, their progeny, *Gun Crazy* and *They Live by Night* are about sweethearts fleeing the law. Our sweethearts, Jimmy the bank robber and Christie the prostitute, were originally meant to flee the law, but as Joe and I reconfigured the story on Tuesday night, the law became incidental: it was Jimmy's family, the Haggard gang, he was desperate to escape. The Haggards were demented Okie farmers on an interstate crime spree after losing their land in the Dust Bowl, and they wanted runaway Jimmy back in the fold and Christie, his partner in both larceny and love, to replace their late matriarch. They had already sought to replace her with hostages who received, in one case, the family insignia: an ear-of-corn tattoo. Jimmy tried to remove his own ear-of-corn tattoo with a straight razor. His father, the gang leader called Daddy even by strangers, condemned Jimmy to death by crucifixion because "God killed Jesus and He didn't just shoot Him." Others were shot to death and remained standing, frozen like sculpture, rather than dropping to the ground.

The tone of the movie had obviously, drastically changed. It was now a surreal dark comedy influenced by writers like Flannery O'Connor and Sam Shepard, and a much better match for the nutty circumstances and Joe's absurdist sensibility. This sort of movie, as opposed to a forthright neo-noir, might develop legs, I thought. Roger loved it. He chuckled at our proposed title—*Be My Mama*, a cheeky nod to *Big Bad Mama II*—and asked for twelve pages of scenes, at least, to be shot the following day. Twelve pages in a single day? Well, okay, but they would have to be written out of sequence while Joe, aided by Anna Roth, urgently organized a cast and crew. Aside from me and non-speaking extras, we needed just three actors for the bordello set. Our next set, a bedroom in the bordello, wouldn't become available for a week or so, and during the lull we would finish the script, expand the cast, and tweak the crew.

I spent much of that Wednesday banging out pages in a storage room at Roger's company, New Horizons, in Brentwood. Joe was down the hall with Roger and Anna, and every so often he would walk back with an update. He had hired the first person to audition for Madame Wang, who ran the bordello, and Anna had asked a friend of hers, Raymond J. Barry, to play Daddy. There was time enough only to meet three actresses for Christie. I read with them. All had been told by their handlers that the role required nudity. Bare breasts were integral to the Corman formula for success, a guarantee of sales, and our movie wasn't exempt from the formula, absurdist approach or not. Roger had mandated a minimum of six nude scenes for Christie, Joe said, and I knew that some of them would necessarily be love scenes, which meant that nude Daryl would have to show his wonderful body's most delicious spots without any doubts.

But I did have doubts. I was a lapsed Southern Baptist with a residual streak of modesty, and an ectomorph who could only tone up, not beef up, by working out and so lacked the V-shaped torso of heroic male imagery from antiquity to Hollywood. I wasn't designed for nude scenes, in other words, either physically or psychologically, yet for that reason I should do one, I had long ago decided. Acting, for me, wasn't an art of disguise but of revelation. The character's soul was the actor's soul, loaned for the occasion, and the performance was as gripping as the actor was brave. I considered myself brave emotionally, even as I hid my narrow neck and slender arms and shoulders under bulky shirts and bomber jackets, and I saw a possible fix for that in exposure therapy of the most literal sort. Not that I was in a rush. It would happen when—or if—it happened, and here I was on the brink of it after weeks of eating pizza and deli sandwiches chased down with beer, all of which had thickened my waist and padded my ass, while the rest of me was tubercular, as always. I was a skinny fat man. Trick or treat!

But I couldn't think about that now. I had some say in the casting of Christie, and I opted for the only actress of three who remotely resembled my notion of the character, despite her feathered, beach-bunny hair. Surely the makeup department would make it less contemporary, but no, she was still Malibu Christie on the set the next day; and Ray Barry, as Daddy, was a Dogpatch moonshiner in denim overalls and a frayed straw hat. Why hadn't the wardrobe department dressed him like I had been dressed, in a wool suit and felt fedora? The hillbilly look was kitschy overkill, and the set was kitsch also: with swinging doors and a bigger bar, it might have been a saloon in a drive-in western of the Eisenhower era. Extras in vintage lingerie were positioned here and there on Victorian furniture. Laura Burkett, the actress playing Christie, likewise wore lingerie, and most of the extras had feathered hair similar to hers. One of them provided some unscripted nudity. Roger, who was on the set to supervise, offered bonus pay to any extra who appeared topless in the foreground of a shot of Laura, and off came a bra without a trace of the apprehension I felt about shedding my shirt and pants. But that would come later. No nude scenes were scheduled for me or Laura on that first day of production, thank Zeus.

We did not shoot twelve pages. I believe we shot as many as eight, which was still considerable and satisfied Roger. Again, he was a fan of the material, and after seeing it on its feet, as it were, he reorganized the *Big Bad Mama II* schedule so that Joe and I would have a little more time to complete the script. We divided the labor: I was to write the first half of the script while, simultaneously, Joe wrote the second half; but once he read my progress and I read his, it was clear that our styles didn't mesh. The script needed a unified voice, and since Joe was stealing time from directorial tasks to work on it, I took over the writing, revising his scenes to make them consistent with mine. I continued to have input in the casting, though it was Anna Roth who set up a meeting with Steve Buscemi and somebody else who recommended Johnny Depp. Both were unavailable—Depp, I remember, was busy with a new television series, *21 Jump Street*—

but an actor high on my wish list, Dan Shor, agreed to play Hawk Haggard, one of Jimmy's lunatic brothers. Dan had impressed me in John Huston's adaptation of *Wise Blood*, the Flannery O'Connor novel, and he proved a valuable casting consultant, introducing us to actors with credentials like his own, friends and former co-stars who weren't the Corman norm. And that, of course, was exactly what we wanted.

The dreaded day dawned. My gallows, the bordello bedroom set, awaited. It seemed to have been built for a *Playboy* pictorial with an Asian theme: silk sheets, hanging lanterns, Chinese scrolls on the walls. Joe and I knew about the Asian theme before we started the script, hence Madame Wang, our name for the bordello's proprietress. Madame Wang would make a brief appearance in the first scene we shot, and later, in a different scene, we would see Christie with a disgruntled customer; otherwise Laura and I were the only actors working that day, and it would be another long one, since Roger had again demanded that we shoot a dozen or so pages. He wasn't around. Anna and another of his assistants were the on-set producers, shepherding me and Laura to makeup and wardrobe while Joe and the director of photography oversaw the lighting. There was some discussion of body makeup, but it might rub off on the bedding and show up in the footage, so it was best avoided, Laura and I were told. As a local with a tan, she didn't really need body makeup anyway. I, on the other hand, had a New York pallor. Skinny, yet fat, and pale: if I didn't remove my socks, I would look like a time traveler from an early stag movie.

In our first shot of the day, Jimmy and Christie were strangers stripping down for their initial tryst. The intent of the scene was comic: Jimmy, as a fugitive, had wanted for female company, and the sight of this hooker undressing was almost enough to spill his seed before he slipped into bed. The focus of the shot was Laura, who, like me, had never done a nude scene. I was in the foreground and the camera would catch my backside, which was all the crew would likewise see, and as soon as Joe called cut I would grab a robe and cover up. Laura also had a robe on standby. Poor Laura. She alone would be subjected to a frontal view of me, but, distracted by her own anxiety, she might emerge with her sight intact. The camera began to roll. Clothes were discarded, one garment at a time. Laura was allowed to keep her underpants for this shot, but I had to shed mine, so that I was altogether naked except for, yes, my socks. I had done it. The take was over. But before I could even reach for my robe, crew members walked past me, responding to calls to adjust this or that on the other side of the set, and I suddenly felt like Adam after a bite of the apple. Nobody was unprofessional. Nobody appeared to notice me and Laura, let alone make jokes, but I was reminded of that common nightmare of being trapped naked at school or the office or wherever everybody else is clothed. In males this dream may be related to the inborn fear of castration, and my body was responding as if a knife were threateningly near, or to put it bluntly, my dick was retracting. An oft-quoted episode of *Seinfeld* would later coin the term *shrinkage* for the kind of retreat I saw down there.

At least one more take was necessary before we moved on to the next shot, in which Laura was to mime putting a condom on me while making small talk: "Where are you from?" and so on. Again, the intent was comic, a protraction of my character's overaroused agony, but there was also a practical motive for the way the scene was written: the more the characters talked, the higher the page count. The condom bit was covered in two angles, not including the close-up of my face while the condom went on. The close-up was a cakewalk: I didn't have to be fully naked as I did for the other two shots, one from the side and one from the front. My groin was just below the frame line in the side angle, I was told, and Laura hid it when the camera faced me, but the camera didn't concern me so much as the crew. They could see everything, and again I flashed on the nightmare of schoolyard nudity and, to my horror, the shrinkage worsened. I was a grown man with the penis of a ten-year-old, a happy-hour weenie without a toothpick, a mushroom minus the stem. Meanwhile, because of nerves or the heat of the lights or both, my scrotum had expanded and my balls were drooping, one significantly lower than the other, as if to distract from the miniaturization occurring above, when in fact it drew attention to the freakish configuration as a whole. Some decoy! But what could I do about it? Knead my member to a respectable size? That was suited to a hardcore porn set, not a set like this one, and an announcement seemed nearly as inappropriate. Hey, everybody, just in case you're wondering, I'm not really deformed; I'm just nervous, and I've never seen my balls do this before. Honest!

So I toughed it out, and Laura did the same, rubbing ice on her wrists between takes, a calming technique she recommended. It worked, but not as well as my robe. Then, at last, the condom bit was done, and now Jimmy and Christie had a quickie—a quickie was all Jimmy could manage—and Madame Wang was summoned to negotiate a fee for another round. I wore pants for the Madame Wang exchange, and Laura wore underpants for the quickie, since she wasn't shown below the waist, but we would both have to be completely naked for the longer love scene that followed Madame Wang's exit. We rehearsed in robes, working out the choreography—you'll be here for this part, and then I'll move there—and just before we shot the scene, Laura called for some sort of special patch, invisible to the camera, that was standard for such scenes and used as a kind of prophylactic, covering the crotch. This was news to me, but since no one had thought to bring the patch, we improvised with a silk teddy, which I folded and placed on top of my prepubescent penis and bizarre hanging balls. Then Laura dropped her robe and climbed aboard. She had the figure of a centerfold model, but it was wasted on me. I was looking at a lifetime of impotence after the humiliation I had suffered.

But, wonder of wonders, once the camera started rolling and we thrashed around, something stirred below. Yes, by God, I was getting hard. Was that going to freak out Laura? And should I feel relief or embarrassment? I felt both, and even if I could now prove that I wasn't abnormally sized, I wasn't eager to share the proof with the crew, and glanced around for my underwear when the scene was over. It seemed to have disappeared, and I asked if anyone knew where it was, and the production manager ran off and returned with my boxer shorts, which he handed to me. There was a faint skid mark on them. In a day of lows, including a pair of literal lows, the skid mark on my boxers may have been the lowest. I pictured the production manager at home with his wife or girlfriend: "Yeah, and not only did he have the tiniest dick you ever saw, he shit on himself. I saw it. I *touched* it. I touched the guy's shit!"

At least we made the day. We shot all twelve pages, if memory serves, including a long dialogue scene in which I struggled with the lines, even though I was fully dressed. I was a fool to have thought that my acting would be improved by doing a nude scene. I felt braver in one way only: exhibiting my pitiful torso was nothing to me now. I was shirtless in the last shot of the day, in fact, and there would be more such shots in the weeks to come, but it was one thing for me to be shirtless and another, of course, for Laura, who started to grumble. "I have to be nude *again*?" Not that I blamed her. I grumbled, and occasionally exploded, about other matters. The sets were consistently shabby—"It's just a Roger Corman movie," I once overheard the production designer say—and Ray Barry wasn't the only actor costumed like a hayseed, and there was talk of a country-style score, fiddle and banjo, which would fortify the *Li'l Abner* effect. Yet, somehow, I remained optimistic, if not delusional, that the movie would turn out well. I remember musing aloud to Dan Shor about its reception. "I hope," I said, "people don't think I ripped off Sam Shepard too much in the writing."

"Nobody's going to compare this movie to Sam Shepard," Dan scoffed. "They'll compare it to *Big Bad Mama II*."

We wrapped production at Newhall Ranch in the Santa Clarita Valley, a favorite location of western directors as far back as the silent era. Most of our driving scenes were shot at Newhall, as well as my final nude scene. Yes, I had one more nude scene, in which Laura and I were to run from a car parked on the edge of a lake, tear off our clothes, and dive into the water. The distance of the camera and speed of the action made it all easier, and the water covered our bodies in a second, tighter shot, but it also made for shrinkage, as I realized when the scene was over, and a young female production assistant was waiting beside the lake with towels in hand. "I'll be out in a minute," I told her. "Just leave a towel there on the bank; I'll get it." But she rolled her eyes to telegraph her indifference and went on holding a towel out to me, refusing to toss it or leave it behind, so that finally I had to wade out of the water with my withered dick and reverse weeks of psychic repair.

Joe was barely speaking to me by then because of my complaints and explosions, which led Dan to give me a nickname: John McEnroe. It was Anna who kept me updated during postproduction. The movie needed a more marketable title, she said, and Roger had decided on *Daddy's Boys* and matched it with a tagline: "Your daughters will never be safe again!" The writing credit was another issue. Roger's company wasn't affiliated with the Writers Guild, and Joe, as a member of the Guild, was prohibited from working for such companies, so even he encouraged me to take full credit for the script. I was reluctant. I wanted to be known as an actor, not as a writer, but I agreed in the end, and within weeks I was hired to write another script for Roger—"*Bonnie and Clyde* in the future" was his concept for it—and *Friday the 13th Part VII* at Paramount. Anna was instrumental in the latter: she talked me up to a friend of hers, someone with connections at Paramount, and the script for *Daddy's Boys* was forwarded as a writing sample. I had never seen a *Friday the 13th* movie when I was suggested for that job. Roger's futuristic *Bonnie and Clyde* was called *Crime Zone*, and naturally I was instructed to equip the "Bonnie" character with ample excuses for nudity. Sorry, sister. I may cook the *spécialité de la maison*, but the recipe isn't mine.

All of this occurred before I saw *Daddy's Boys* at a cast-and-crew screening at a mall in Sherman Oaks. I had recently attended a screening of *Big Bad Mama II* at the same multiplex theater—Roger often previewed movies there—and for *Daddy's Boys* I invited the musicians and film students with whom I was now sharing a house in Silver Lake. I regretted inviting them minutes into the first reel. The rinky-dink sets, the anachronistic hair, the hillbilly costumes, the hootenanny score: it all came across as kitschy as I had feared, and as good as some of our actors were, they couldn't perform miracles. It was a miracle that this crazy quilt of "absurdist" comedy and grindhouse schlock even existed! But it flopped at both; I winced more at the callow jokes in the bedroom scenes than I did at the sight of my bare ass, and the movie lacked the gung-ho conviction of *Big Bad Mama II* in the exploitation department. *Big Bad Mama II* also looked better, since it cost more. It's difficult to pinpoint the most painful moment of that screening, but it certainly chafed when the audience guffawed at my dive into the lake. It was an awkward dive because I was racing to hide in the water, but I didn't recognize that until much later. At the time I thought people were laughing at my body.

I headed to my rental car as soon as the end credits started to roll and drove first to a liquor store and then to the house in Silver Lake, where I drunkenly phoned a friend in New York and described this Nagasaki of a screening. How could I have deceived myself so utterly? But I knew how: I thought the script would salvage the movie. I was convinced it had merit, if only because of its literary influences, which nobody would ever notice, exactly as Dan Shor had said, and the script was awful anyway, and I *looked* awful, and I was *nude* in this goddamn thing. I didn't want to make another movie as long as I lived, and I would never get the chance after people saw this one. They wouldn't even have to see it; they would hear about it or detect its scent on me, the pheromone of failure. Finally, exhausted from venting and boozing, I hung up and passed out, and a few hours later I stumbled into the living room, where one of my housemates gave me a doleful look and said, "You must feel terrible after what they did to your movie." Thanks. I had woken thinking I might have overreacted, but that clearly wasn't the case, and while it was gracious of my housemate to fault others, I was too self-reproaching to concur.

Roger wasn't at the screening in Sherman Oaks, I suppose because the reaction of a partisan audience was irrelevant to him, and Joe wasn't present, either, having already returned to New York. He would later dismiss *Daddy's Boys* to an interviewer as "a piece of shit, but I still have a fond spot in my heart for it." He arranged for it to be shown as a midnight movie at the Bleecker Street Cinema, and Laura and I were pictured on the front page of the Arts & Leisure section of the *New York Times*, with a sneering review inside. The kickoff line is carved into my memory: "The muse visits in many forms, but the desire to reuse a brothel set left over from *Big Bad Mama II* isn't one of them." Witty? No doubt. True? Sure. But it was also cruel for a powerhouse like the *Times* to excoriate an impoverished movie like *Daddy's Boys*, and I wasn't much heartened by the favorable review in the *New York Post*, the *Post* being a tabloid owned by Rupert Murdoch.

Meanwhile, pulling strings on the other coast, Roger placed *Daddy's Boys* in the AFI Film Festival, prompting another nasty review from another powerhouse, the *Los Angeles Times*, and a mixed but sympathetic review in *Variety* that cited "those preexisting sets, which look phony and freshly painted" as "perhaps the worst element of the production." However, "[the] script by Daryl Haney, who also plays Jimmy, is several notches above the norm for such fare and provides quite a few sharp lines for Daddy, which Raymond J. Barry delivers very entertainingly." Finally I felt a little better about the movie. I never warmed to it so much as I forgave it as juvenilia, and because of it, because of Roger and especially Joe, I was now paying the rent as a screenwriter and not as the waiter I had been when I got that fateful call from Joe to ask if I could board the next available flight to L.A. I was supposed to begin a new restaurant job, in fact, the day after Joe called, and I never waited tables, or bused them or tended bar, again.

The screening at the AFI Festival was attended by as many as five people, including me, a woman I was seeing, and Roger, who introduced it; but his affection for *Daddy's Boys* was undiminished. He went out of his way to mention it in *How I Made a Hundred Movies in Hollywood and Never Lost a Dime*, his autobiography. The title is inaccurate. At the time he wrote the book, he had produced more than three hundred movies and directed over fifty of them, and he was rumored to have lost money on *Daddy's Boys*. There was a plan for nominal theatrical distribution to avoid the "straight to video" stigma, but that was scrapped following a screening for theater owners who sensibly revolted, and the movie was sold to cable television and released on VHS in a sleeve that featured two models, a muscular male and a buxom female, with "DADDY'S BOYS" tattooed on the male's bicep. The faces of the models were cropped out of the image, and none of the cast or crew were billed on it, though Ray Barry had some cachet at that point, having gone from playing my father to playing the father of Tom Cruise in *Born on the Fourth of July*. That made Tom Cruise my movie half-brother, I used to joke.

My real father happened upon *Daddy's Boys* while channel-surfing, and when he called to tell me, I half expected him to ask if Daddy was based on him. Instead, sounding a bit envious, he asked if that was really me rolling around naked with the blonde. Yes, Dad, there was no trick photography involved. My mother, as far as I know, never saw the movie, but the devoutly Catholic mother of a friend caught it on television and floored my friend with her only comment: "Nice ass." Another friend told me that, while driving from coast to coast, he stopped to refuel at a rural store where videos could be rented, and there on the shelf, one of maybe ten titles, was *Daddy's Boys*. That was my favorite anecdote about the movie's scant afterlife. I was familiar with such stores in my native Virginia, and I was usually struck by the odd choices on their video shelves, but I never encountered *Daddy's Boys* in Virginia or even at video stores in Los Angeles that prided themselves on their racks of rare and eccentric movies. Once it had dumbfounded the rustics who rented it because they had run out of options and the insomniacs who watched it on television because they couldn't bear another infomercial, *Daddy's Boys* disappeared.

But nude stills from it lingered. Nude pictures always linger, often to the chagrin of their subjects. There's no such thing as a former porn star, especially in the Internet era. *Daddy's Boys* predated the Internet era, and in the early days of it, I would get e-mails from acquaintances who had done a search on me, and whoa, look what I found; do you know about this? Of course I fucking knew. Did they really think I had never done a search on myself? Couldn't they tell it was from a movie? What, did they imagine that someone had broken into my apartment and installed a hidden camera to photograph me naked? I wondered if Warren Beatty, for instance, received such e-mails, though Warren Beatty could at least take pride in having dropped his drawers in a worthy movie. That's the hope of every green actor when a nude scene is an abstraction. It was my hope anyway, and if *Daddy's Boys* was a disappointment, I had learned from it what I should never have needed to learn in the first place: I couldn't undo my modesty by disrobing on a set full of clothed strangers, even if I had prepared at the gym for a year. I was not my own lab rat to be shocked in the course of a behavior-modification study. I respected that now. I had a better sense of my limitations.

So I didn't regret doing those scenes, and since they had already been seen on television and VHS, the pictures online didn't bother me. I was bothered by the "Whoa!" alerts sent by presumably well-meaning people, but the alerts stopped after search engines improved and the bounty of free Internet porn eclipsed the sites that require a fee to access nude photos of Dado Ruspoli, Dafydd Emyr, Daishi Hori and hundreds, if not thousands, of others who know for real that you will become short of breath on seeing their poses in the altogether for you. I had become short of breath for a different reason, of course, and I came to regard my pictures as a document of it, nothing more, just as I saw *Daddy's Boys* as a document in the way that all movies finally are, telling us more about the times and conditions in which they were made than those they purport to portray. Possibly there's some charm now in the late-eighties styles that informed *Daddy's Boys* and irked me at the time, to say nothing of those cheesy sets on Roger's lot in Venice Beach, which no longer exists. Almost nothing of the movie exists. Everyone associated with it has moved on and gotten older, so they're effectively different people, and no scenes from it or even the trailer have ever been uploaded to YouTube or similar sites, and eventually the negative will be lost—who would care enough to save *Daddy's Boys*? By now you have to dig to find what remains of it, and there isn't much reward: a few frames of a frightened boy and a nervous girl doing the best they could do within the constraints of budget and nature.

2017

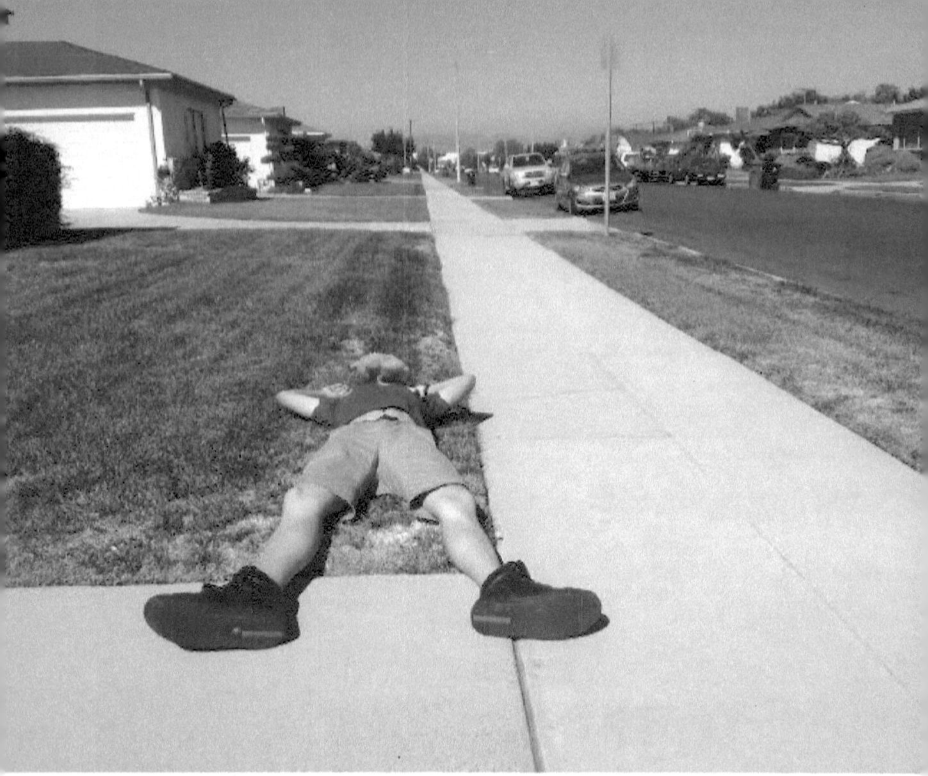

Top: The position of Elizabeth Short's body as recreated by Marcus at the site of its discovery. Bottom: The entrance of the Flying Fox, described by *Jet* magazine in 1965 as "a favorite spot of Los Angeles' burgeoning Negro bourgeoisie." (*Author's collection*)

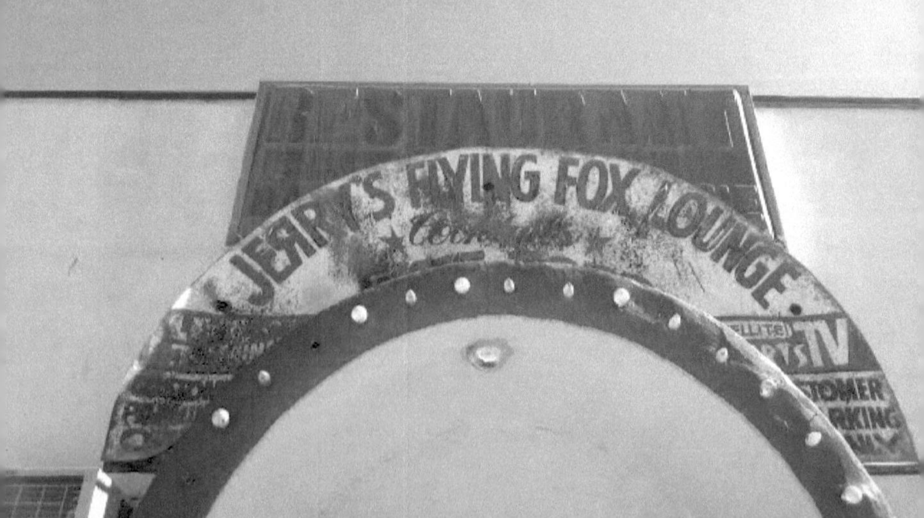

I WANT TO TAKE YOU HIGHER

JOE PASQUALE CALLED TO SAY that he and his girlfriend were going to drive around and look for Sly Stone, who was broke and living in a van. Joe invited me to tag along. Sure, I said. Then I spoke to a friend from my moviemaking days, Billy Maddox, who said, "They're going to drive around looking for Sly *Stone*? *Why?* What's the point?"

"I don't know."

"Well, what are they going to do if they find him?"

"I don't know."

"Well, why are *you* going? Are you a big Sly and the Family Stone fan?"

"Not a *crazy* fan. It sounded like an adventure, and it reminded me of my novel, so I said yes."

I was referring to *Banned for Life*, my novel about the search for an elusive singer with a rumored history of drug abuse; and drugs had surely factored in Sly Stone's retreat from the spotlight, ending a brilliant run as a funk trailblazer who arguably peaked in 1969, the year he solidified his fame with a number-one single, "Everyday People," and performed at Woodstock with his mélange of male and female, black and white musicians. The Revolution, Prince's similarly blended band of the eighties, was indebted to Sly and the Family Stone, and Sly's psychedelic peacockery influenced Prince's fashion sense, even if Prince changed his hairstyle early in his career from an afro, Sly's signature nimbus, to the curly pompadour of the *Purple Rain* period. Prince had yet to fatally overdose when Joe called me, and Barack Obama was president. Nobody anticipated the blacklash election results on the horizon, or nobody of my acquaintance.

I knew Joe, a writer and real-estate agent, from poorly attended readings at bookstores that sell more coffee than books and serve as offices to would-be screenwriters pecking out their latest on laptops. Maggie Arana, Joe's girlfriend, was in a goth band before she got a real-estate license and persuaded him to do the same. At his suggestion they once toured Jack Kerouac's haunts in Florida and Massachusetts; but the hunt for Sly Stone was Maggie's idea, I learned after they arrived to pick me up. She had been listening to his records on repeat, she said, and her curiosity about his whereabouts led her to a 2011 *New York Post* story, which I now read on my phone. A few paragraphs recapped the rise and decline of Sly and the Family Stone, who "managed to turn what should have been a snoozy middle-of-the-night slot at Woodstock into one of the highlights of the festival. As the band began to play, tens of thousands of people creeped out of their sleeping bags to watch. They left the stage with the audience still roaring, 'Higher!'" This performance of "I Want to Take You Higher" is in the landmark documentary about Woodstock, and the studio version kicked off the band's quintuple-platinum *Greatest Hits* album. Sly was living then in "a four-bedroom, 5,432-square-foot Beverly Hills mansion," but at age sixty-eight, "his fortune stolen by a lethal combination of excess, substance abuse and financial mismanagement," he "lays his head inside a white camper van...parked on a residential street in Crenshaw, the rough Los Angeles neighborhood where 'Boyz n the Hood' was set. A retired couple makes sure he eats once a day, and Stone showers at their house." He was "disheveled, paranoid—the FBI is after him; his enemies have hired hit men." Still, "ever the showman," he posed "flamboyantly with a silver military helmet and a Taser in front of his Studebaker." He had "dropped tens of thousands of dollars" on cars, but apparently the copper-colored Studebaker was all that remained of his fleet, and Maggie had bookmarked photos of it and the larger van that he had bought since the *Post* story, this one white like the first, with SOUTHWIND written inside the pale-blue stripe that wrapped around it. We should be able to spot the van or the Studebaker parked outside the craftsman house of Sly's retired benefactors, Maggie said. Meanwhile, we could gather intelligence at local bars and liquor stores, though cocaine, not liquor, had been his Achilles heel: Maggie knew someone who attended a party at his house in the seventies and his ashtrays were filled like guacamole bowls with coke. I knew someone who once rented a room in the Crenshaw area, but most white people, unlike him, avoided Crenshaw as they would Dracula's castle, and I wondered at the sort of reception that we were apt to receive from leery bartenders and liquor-store clerks, to say nothing of our "paranoid" quarry. Might he not take us for FBI agents or assassins sent by his enemies and defend himself with his Taser gun or worse?

But there was a good mood in Maggie's car and I didn't want to spoil it by raising such questions. I did, however, raise the question that Billy Maddox had raised with me—what would Joe and Maggie do if they found Sly Stone?—and I scribbled their answers in the spiral notebook that I had brought out of habit.

Joe: "Talk."

Maggie: "Say hi."

WE STOPPED FOR BREAKFAST at Canter's, one of the oldest delicatessens in Los Angeles, and were seated in a booth with photos of Guns N' Roses, former patrons, framed on the wall above us. Elsewhere on the walls there were photos of President Obama smiling alongside staff and customers, and I asked our Samoan waitress about him, and she indicated another booth and said, "He sat right there. He was fundraising in Hancock Park."

"Was he charismatic?"

"He was okay. He had hot tea and went around and shook hands."

Canter's is in the Fairfax District, just west of Hollywood, and after breakfast, we headed south, passing copious construction sites. "That's the future of L.A.," Maggie said, meaning that, like New York and San Francisco, L.A. was fated to become a city of the wealthy only. Even Crenshaw was a hub of construction, so that the businesses I glimpsed from the backseat of the car—a porn shop, a Christian bookstore, a 99 Cents Only Store—would surely be replaced in time by gelato shops, organic groceries, thin-crust pizzerias. The *Post* had reported that Sly Stone was still composing music, and rather than inquire at bars and liquor stores, I proposed that we look for places frequented by musicians: clubs with live acts, for instance. Then we passed, in a strip mall, the field office of Bernard Parks, formerly the chief of the LAPD, now a city councilmember. Maybe someone there would know something, I said.

There were two people in the office: a man and a woman, both young and facing desktop computers. Aside from their desks, there was scarcely any furniture, and aside from a map of Los Angeles, the walls were blank. The Eighth District was highlighted in yellow on the map. Bernard Parks represented the Eighth District, obviously, and the young man was his "Integrated Media Manager." Since it was my idea to intrude here, I took the lead, waving my notebook and inventing a piece that I was researching about Sly Stone.

"Sly Jones?" said the man. The woman never said a word, though I had the sense that she considered us, vaguely and not unreasonably, amusing. We referred the man to the *Post* article, and he referred us to a couple of live-music venues, the Flying Fox and the Cork, where possibly the staff or clientele could direct us to this person. Then, with the air of a docent, he lectured about the area. Prior to the Rodney King riots in 1992, he said, people didn't speak of "the Crenshaw district," an umbrella term for several neighborhoods, one of which, Baldwin Hills, sounded from his description like the African-American counterpart of Beverly Hills in the days of compulsory segregation. Celebrities such as Ray Charles and Marvin Gaye used to live in Baldwin Hills, he said; in fact, Marvin Gaye was murdered at his house there. Also, the body of the Black Dahlia was discovered in Leimert Park, if we were interested in that sort of thing. We were, of course: nobody joins a goth band by chance.

The unsolved murder of Elizabeth Short, nicknamed the Black Dahlia for her dark hair, is the archetypal crime of noir-era Los Angeles. A flirtatious drifter with a yen for servicemen, Elizabeth Short disappeared one night in 1947, and her nude corpse, bisected at the waist and otherwise mutilated, turned up a week later in a vacant lot, the legs and arms arranged in a psychopathic parody of sexual afterglow. I had read two books about the case, including *Black Dahlia Avenger* by Steve Hodel, a retired homicide detective who fingered his late father as the killer. I was skeptical. Maggie was skeptical. She had also read *Black Dahlia Avenger*, she said, and the last time she visited the spot on Norton Avenue where the body was dumped, Steve Hodel was being interviewed at the curb by a European television crew. Joe and I had never been to the spot, so we may as well make a detour. The vacant lot was vacant no longer. Cookie-cutter houses, white or beige or both, lined Norton Avenue, but Maggie could find the address we sought without googling it—there was a fire hydrant next to the driveway, she said.

A young Asian man was standing on the lawn, and he laughed when we emerged from Maggie's car, identifying us on sight as fellow ghouls. He looked to be in his early twenties, and he wore the traditional costume of Southern California—T-shirt, shorts, and baseball cap—but he was a tourist from Nanjing, China, he told us in charmingly hesitant English. He called himself Marcus, and he seemed to be documenting his stop here for a horror-themed Web site, which he showed us on his phone. We offered to take pictures of him, and he flung himself backward onto the lawn, recreating the position of Elizabeth Short's body. He asked about our interest in the case. We were just passing by, I said, while seeking a famous musician, the man who wrote this, and I sang a few bars of "Everyday People." "Ah, that one," Marcus said. Foreigners often have a better appreciation of American culture than do Americans. Our tenuous sense of the exotic doesn't extend to ourselves.

Marvin Gaye, four years older than Sly Stone, shared some of his afflictions—cocaine, paranoia, prodigious debt—and identical musical beginnings: both performed in Pentecostal churches as children. Gaye's father, a cross-dressing preacher, shot him to death following a quarrel on April Fools' Day 1984. That was as much as any of us knew about this case, but we made another detour while pursuing white vans that, as we saw on finally catching up to them, were minus the markings of the one driven by Sly. The detour was an excuse for a breather; we strolled around the crime scene, a Tudor-style mansion enclosed by a wrought-iron fence with fleur-de-lis spikes. The house stood above the Santa Monica Freeway and beside an overpass where a parking official was inspecting an abandoned car. There were holes in the windshield, as if it had been struck with a sledgehammer, and the hood had been removed, exposing the looted guts. The parking official might have ticketed Sly's van at some point, Joe and I reasoned, and we described it to him while marveling at the dystopian car. He had seen such a van repeatedly, he said, on Adams between Arlington and Western, so that was now our destination, and there we followed what turned out to be a shuttle van, not a camper van, with WILLING WORKERS, not SOUTHWIND, labeled on its side and several passengers, presumably willing workers, silhouetted in its windows.

We were in need of a different approach.

THE FLYING FOX was a small place, oblong and white with red trim, on Martin Luther King Jr. Boulevard. It had a fascinating history, I learned later. Earl Bostic, its original owner, was a saxophonist who first played on New Orleans riverboats, then with Thelonious Monk and Cab Calloway, among others, before starting his own band. John Coltrane was in Bostic's band during the early fifties. He opened the Flying Fox in 1961, but his wife, Hildegard, was the force behind its success, and she refused to leave it when, panicked by a predicted earthquake that would cause all of California to fall into the Pacific, her husband moved east, where he promptly died of a heart attack. Hildegard Bostic found love again a few years later and sold the club, which was renamed Jerry's Flying Fox after the new owner. It was closed when we arrived, and possibly shuttered, the rear windows smeared with soapy paint, the marquees the color of neglected teeth. There were two marquees, and one of them advertised an upcoming anniversary party with FOOD and FUN, the other a LIVE BAND on FRIDAY and SAT, so we might return, we decided, if we were stonewalled at the Cork, the second venue mentioned by the Integrated Media Manager.

The Cork was two miles from the Flying Fox and heralded by a neon sign shaped like an arrowhead. The sign dated from the fifties at least. The interior reminded me of the eighties. Strings of blue holiday lights were fastened here and there to the ceiling and walls, and ten or so customers, mostly male, were clustered around the square bar, watching a baseball game on overhead screens. "I figure if we sit for a while, we can ask," Maggie said, and so we sat and ordered beers and talked among ourselves and also a little with the bartender, a handsome kid who was originally from

Mississippi, he told us. Some of the customers thawed after eavesdropping, the one to my right introducing himself as a record producer. He had worked with Dr. Dre, he said, and I realized that I was in Hollywood even though I wasn't in Hollywood, that there are show-business veterans and pretenders and novices in every patch and margin of Greater Los Angeles, from blue-collar San Pedro to barren Antelope Valley, and probably the bartender here was an actor hoping that his face would be his fortune. We were writers preparing a story about Sly Stone, Maggie announced, taking the leap and lifting my lie, and we understood that he lived in the neighborhood—had anybody here seen him?

"Victoria used to come in here with her boyfriend," someone responded mysteriously.

"He's supposed to live in a motel around here," someone else offered.

But the record producer knew the score. He was friendly with Sly's nephew, he said, and he would give Jeremiah, the nephew, a call and ask him where Sly's van was parked. Sly moved around a lot, the producer continued; people would house him and feed him and supply him with drugs for a couple of months, then put him back in his van. He was broke because he sold his catalog to Michael Jackson, who was murdered, you know. Yes, Michael Jackson was murdered for his catalog. Finally, after more in this vein, the producer called Jeremiah. It was a quick call. Jeremiah believed that Sly was parked by a beach in Ventura County, the producer said, and we were welcome to call Jeremiah toward the end of the day, when he could confirm or deny. Maggie took the number. The Cork had treated us well. Would black people be treated so well if they entered a white bar and spoke of wishing to meet a white celebrity who lived nearby? On the other hand, the producer may have been a prankster.

It was now around three o'clock, too late to drive to Ventura County, and since we weren't certain that Sly was there, we might as well go on searching for him here. Throughout the day I had observed lamppost ads for Taste of Soul, a neighborhood music festival, and its organizers struck me as a fair bet for a new lead. Taste of Soul was headquartered at the office of a weekly newspaper, the *Los Angeles Sentinel*, I discovered on my phone, and the *Sentinel*'s logo, a map of Africa superimposed on a map of the United States, was atop a sign on the roof of the building and a beacon in traffic. The reception area was decorated with African art, and the receptionist was amenable, punching a button on her desk phone and saying into the receiver, "Do we have a location on Sly of Sly and the Family Stone?" The answer was no, but then she googled the *New York Post* story and said, while scrutinizing a photo with the craftsman house in it, "I can tell that's on the avenues between Vernon and Slauson." Locals referred to the grid of numbered streets near Crenshaw High School as "the avenues," the receptionist apprised us, and if we didn't find Sly there, she advised us to try Skid Row.

"I think he's living this way because he wants to be free," she added.

We covered a dozen streets, each approximately a mile long and some breaking at Crenshaw High, frustratingly, and resuming on the other side of it. There were countless craftsman houses, several with white vans parked outside them, and we would slow and sometimes backtrack, only to determine that the stripe on a van wasn't blue as it appeared from a distance, and so on. The copper-colored Studebaker, distinctive as the house and van were not, was the logical object of the search, but we never saw a Studebaker of any color, and the pedestrians weren't all black; we passed Asians and Latinos and even a few whites—the first, I was sure, of invaders to come. Maybe we were viewed as invaders by the people who glared at us from the staircase where they were lounging and, the instant before they noticed us, socializing. We were about to ask if they had ever seen a Studebaker on their block. We didn't ask.

The sun was starting to set. It was time to call Jeremiah. With Maggie behind the wheel, I volunteered to make the call, despite feeling awkward about it. I needn't have felt awkward. There really was a Jeremiah, and he said that he had tried and failed to reach Sly and he was now waiting to hear from someone else, someone who would definitely know where Sly was parked, and he would get back to us as soon as this person called him. I relayed the message to Maggie and Joe as we drove by a post office, closed for the day, and a man sitting behind it on what I took to be an upside-down mail tub. He was around thirty and Latino and wearing a short-sleeved postal uniform, and he could conceivably have delivered mail to Sly, so Maggie pulled over and Joe and I hopped out to have a word with him. The mail tub was in fact an ice chest, and the man's arms were black and blue with tattoos. He was staring at his phone, but he slowly lifted his eyes from it and coldly, without blinking, watched us walk toward him. I've been robbed by people with such eyes. I've lived in gangland, and this man had been in a gang if he wasn't in one now. You don't have to be a soldier to wear a flak jacket.

But we had created this situation, which required an explanation, and he listened without warming or moving even slightly and said in a voice as baleful as his eyes that I was "correct to insinuate" that he was a mailman and he "never heard that name before," meaning Sly Stone, and "a lot of people here live in cars," meaning, I reckoned, that Sly Stone was unexceptional in this underprivileged world that was nothing like ours.

We thanked him and walked back to Maggie's car. It felt like a long walk. Goodwill had been the rule of the day, and as the day ended, it seemed to be taking goodwill with it.

"We need to powder our noses," Maggie said.

THE FLYING FOX was open now, a handful of customers seated at the bar. The bar was orange, as were the scalloped booths and the crepe-paper tablecloths, and there were plume-shaped swirls of orange and olive on the faded carpeting. Olive was the dominant color in the darkened backroom, where the tables were bare and the walls were mirrored. Some of the walls in the main room were similarly mirrored, and a jazzed-up blues number was playing on the jukebox.

This would probably be our final stop unless we heard from Jeremiah, but whether he did or didn't call, Maggie and Joe seemed as weary of the chase as I was. I didn't regard the day as a failure. I had hoped for an adventure, and an adventure it had been; now I was content to sit and absorb the ambiance of this place, my favorite of all we had visited. The sense of goodwill was palpable here; when I glanced across the bar, a woman, still lovely in her sixties or older, smiled sweetly at me. Unfortunately the Flying Fox was set to close permanently in a few weeks, the bartender told us, while the singer on the jukebox complained in a resilient voice that contradicted the forlorn lyric.

I got up this morning
I got a jug and laid back down
I was searching for the future
But the blues is all I found

We were impressed by the voice. One of us checked the jukebox for the name of the singer: Ernie Andrews. Who, we wondered aloud, was Ernie Andrews? "That's him," the bartender said, and he pointed to a man sitting beside the sweet-faced woman. Of course we had to meet him. He was eighty-six, I learned later, but he looked ten years younger, and he had the clarity and energy of a younger man also. He introduced the woman as his girlfriend, Bernice, interrupting their tête-à-tête to answer our questions. Was he still performing? As a matter of fact, he was flying any day now to Boston for a concert there. Would he perform at the Flying Fox before it closed? L.A. was his backyard, and he didn't sing in his backyard. Las Vegas was likewise off-limits; he spent ten years there, 1959-69, singing in Harry James's band.

"I did my time in Vegas," he said. "I don't need to see it again." His voice had the grain of an instrument even when he was talking.

Another of his records, "How About Me," followed the first we heard, "The Jug and I," on the jukebox. He didn't strike me as a conceited man, so it must have been Bernice or the bartender who played those records and still another, "The Great City," on which he was accompanied by the great saxophonist Cannonball Adderley. Maggie and Joe wanted a photo with Ernie. I obliged them and took some photos of the place itself. We weren't told why it was about to close, but I chose to blame the construction boom and all it portended. To the extent that ambiance is valued in Los Angeles, the prevailing view is that it can be manufactured as movie sets are manufactured—and destroyed, incidentally, to build new sets on the same sites. But ambiance is too idiosyncratic to manufacture, and it isn't instantaneous; it accrues as it had here, decades of patrons in the styles of their day, beehives and afros and leisure suits and harem pants, who had sat in these orange and olive booths, laughing and flirting and rising to dance or settle a dispute in the parking lot. Now I sat in a booth and opened my notebook. Eventually I might write an amended version of my apocryphal story about Sly Stone, and I wanted to record everything that had happened since breakfast at Canter's, every detail that I hadn't already forgotten. In fact, I thought, I should start before the breakfast; I should start with Billy Maddox and his questions about the point of what must have seemed to him a silly waste of time and gas. I was scribbling away when Maggie walked toward me and effectively confirmed that the search was over, gesturing to the bar, where Joe was still talking to Ernie Andrews, and pitching her voice so that I could hear it above "The Great City."

"You look for something," she said, "and you find something else."

That was the point, Billy.

2018

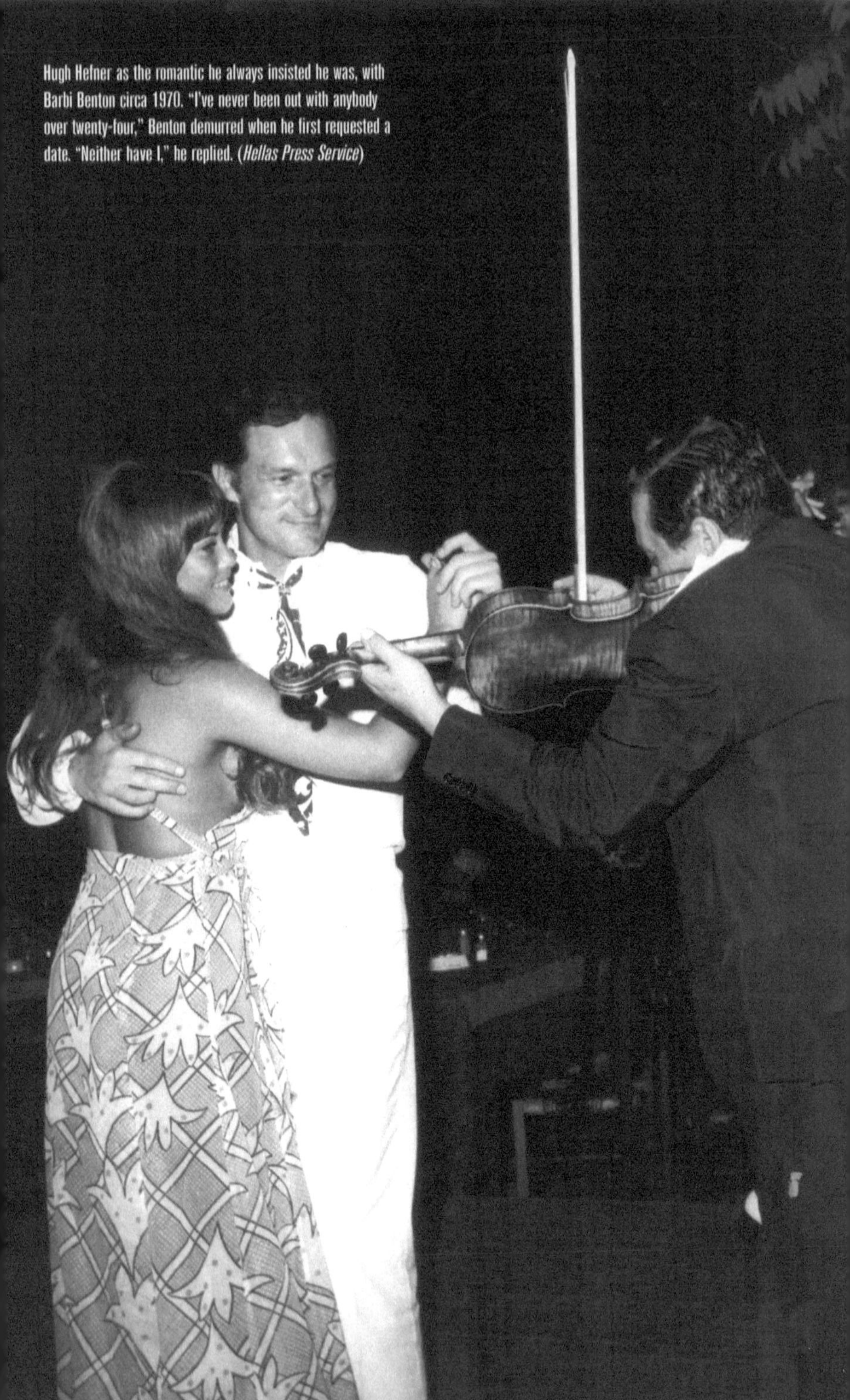

Hugh Hefner as the romantic he always insisted he was, with Barbi Benton circa 1970. "I've never been out with anybody over twenty-four," Benton demurred when he first requested a date. "Neither have I," he replied. (*Hellas Press Service*)

PLAYBOY IN THE DARK

IN 1949, MARILYN MONROE, then an obscure starlet, posed for a beer ad at Tom Kelley's commercial photography studio in Hollywood. According to some accounts, a Chicago-based calendar manufacturer, John Baumgarth, saw the ad while visiting Los Angeles and inquired about the model: would she pose nude for a calendar? In other accounts, Tom Kelley recruited Monroe for the calendar job on the day he shot the beer ad, knowing that Baumgarth was shopping for nudes. Either way, nude photos could wreck a Hollywood career at the time, as Monroe was keenly aware, so she only accepted the job after being persuaded that nobody would recognize her. To further protect her anonymity, she asked Kelley to schedule the session for night, with no assistants save for his wife. Kelley agreed, and Monroe arrived at the studio at seven p.m. and posed for two hours on a red velvet theater curtain that covered the floor and complemented the color of her hair, then a reddish blonde. Twenty-four shots were taken, and Baumgarth chose one of them for the calendar he marketed as *Golden Dreams*, a name suggested by Monroe's blondness, though it also referenced inadvertently the nighttime shoot.

Four years after the shoot, Hugh Hefner, a twenty-seven-year-old native Chicagoan, learned from an article in *Advertising Age* magazine that Baumgarth owned the *Golden Dreams* photo, which seemed perfect for *Stag Party*, the magazine that Hefner was starting with an investment of $8,000, enough to publish the first issue but not enough to promote it. He was looking for a feature that would promote the magazine for him, and while Marilyn Monroe's nude photos had been widely reported—her fortunes had since risen—few had actually seen them. Hefner drove impulsively to Baumgarth's office in a Chicago suburb and, without an appointment, met with Baumgarth, who sold him *Golden Dreams* for $500. Then, in the living room of his South Side apartment, Hefner sat at a card table and wrote the copy for the Monroe feature. At the same table, Hefner wrote a sketch of his target reader, the sort of young urban bachelor who enjoyed "mixing up cocktails and an *hors d'oeuvre* or two, putting a little mood music on the phonograph, and inviting in a female acquaintance for a quiet discussion on Picasso, Nietzsche, jazz, sex." This fantasy figure had been a stock character of Hollywood movies since the silent era: the aristocratic rake often found in drawing rooms, where he wore a smoking jacket, or exclusive nightspots, where he wore a tuxedo. His wealth and wit made him irresistible to naïve young women and shady at best to audiences enamored of the hardworking, plainspoken, outdoorsy type; but in *Stag Party*, Hefner, a movie fan since childhood, would rescue the rake from villainy as the male counterpart of the femme fatale and position him as a hero. A cartoonist drew an anthropomorphic stag to serve as the magazine's mascot, and when *Stag Party* became *Playboy,* the stag became a rabbit still dressed in the stag's smoking jacket and raising his fizzy drink in a firelit den. The rabbit would sport a tuxedo on many early *Playboy* covers and an implied tuxedo in the stylized silhouette designed by Art Paul, a graphic artist and the first addition to the magazine's editorial staff. Otherwise, Hefner worked alone on *Playboy* in his apartment while his wife and infant daughter slept. He was a night person.

The premiere issue of *Playboy*, which hit newsstands in late 1953, was a virtual sellout, thanks to Marilyn Monroe, who was billed as Sweetheart of the Month, not Playmate of the Month or Miss December. That tradition started with the second issue, derived from a movie, Hefner recollected: "In MGM's 1943 musical *Du Barry Was a Lady,* Red Skelton referred to the models in a calendar sequence as 'Miss January, Miss February' and so on." The musical, upbeat and sentimental, was Hefner's favorite Hollywood genre, and ideally, his Playmates would resemble the ingénues of musicals, though he had to settle initially for what he could afford, buying more nudes from Baumgarth and other calendar publishers and printing them in *Playboy* without naming the models. Hefner usually didn't know their names, so that decades passed before he realized that Miss February 1954, Miss April 1954, and Miss April 1955 had all been the same girl. She was a seasoned model, like most early Playmates, including Bettie Page, Miss January 1955; but Hefner wanted novices, "real" girls who had never been photographed nude before he discovered them, à la Hollywood, and masterminded the images that presented them to the public. Terry Ryan, Miss December 1954, was a step in this direction. The first Playmate shot directly for the magazine, Ryan's behind-the-scenes pictorial showed her entering a photo studio in a white dress and matching gloves, disrobing as assistants set up lights, and arranging herself against a monochromatic paper backdrop—a convention of glamour photos of the period—while Art Paul supervised. *Playboy* not only printed Ryan's name, it provided a thumbnail bio—"She's twenty-one years old, single, and plans on making modelling a career"—but the true Playmate prototype was the pseudonymous Miss July 1955, Janet Pilgrim, a Monroesque employee in the magazine's circulation department.

Janet Pilgrim's real name was Charlaine Karalus. She and Hefner were dating when he asked her to pose for the magazine—he and his wife were living apart—and she consented on being assured that she and her mother would both have photo approval. *Playboy* juxtaposed the two sides of Karalus, daytime and nighttime, public and private, in black-and-white "candid" shots of Karalus working at the office, suitably dressed, and the color, semi-nude centerfold of Karalus primping at her vanity for an evening out with a tuxedoed escort. The escort was Hefner, blurry in the background, but the presence of a man insinuated that, despite her wholesome looks, Karalus was sexually active. "I was trying to get across the message that good girls liked sex, too," Hefner would say; and since Karalus was precisely the sort of good girl whose nude photos called for an alias, Hefner decided on "Janet Pilgrim" because he "liked the puritanical connotations." America was stymied by its puritan past, he believed, and he wanted to help it to a healthy view of sex, so that just as he had reclaimed the aristocratic rake, he was now reclaiming the ingénue, the rake's staple victim. But why did there have to be victims if the parties were consenting adults? Why couldn't Americans have sex free of shame and a binding contract? He would eventually develop his ideas in the so-called Playboy Philosophy, but for now he let his pinups preach by example for him, beginning with Janet Pilgrim, who proved so popular that Hefner brought her back as Miss December 1955 and Miss October 1956, making her the only three-time Playmate of the Month other than the calendar model who established the record by stealth. Post-Pilgrim Playmates were customarily photographed in "natural" settings, often the photographer's home or a staffer's apartment, with the presence of a male signaled by props: a pipe, a necktie, an extra cup of coffee or glass of wine. In one of the funniest centerfold shots, Myrna Weber, Miss August 1958, was pictured roasting two weenies at the beach. Outdoor settings became common also, adding sunshine to the magazine's wee-hours feel. For Hefner, the wee hours were the "whee hours," the time when "romantic dreams were more likely to come true."

But, indoors or outdoors, each centerfold was like a still from a movie co-starring the viewer, who was invited to assume the role of the phantom male roasting weenies at the beach with Myrna Weber or relaxing after a foxhunt with Nancy Crawford, Miss April 1959, or rendezvousing with Miss March 1960, Sally Sarell, at her Greenwich Village art studio. The viewer was likewise invited to acquaint himself with the Playmate off-screen, as it were, through the candid photos that preceded the centerfold; but not until the seventies did the magazine permit mention of an exclusive offscreen boyfriend, though boyfriends and even husbands, identified as casual dates, sometimes made cameo appearances in Playmate stories. Gloria Waldron, a.k.a. Allison Parks, Playmate of the Year 1966, was seen giving swimming lessons to anonymous toddlers in her *Playboy* debut as Miss October 1965. The toddlers were hers. According to Art Paul, "In the early days of *Playboy*, the number of Playmates who were pregnant when they were shot was amazing." June Cochran, Miss December 1962, was seven and a half months along in her encore pictorial as Playmate of the Year 1963, but the photographer managed to disguise it without resorting to a trick as retroactively transparent as the one used with Joan Staley, Miss November 1958, whose centerfold had her idling in a dressing room on a television set, hiding her belly with a script. No trick would suffice when Lorrie Menconi, Miss February 1969, showed up heavily pregnant at a Playboy party on the day her issue was published. Hefner was furious, and Lorrie Menconi, as might be surmised, did not become Playmate of the Year 1970. That was Miss November, Claudia Jennings, the nom de centerfold of Mimi Chesterton, who almost didn't test for Playmate, thinking she wasn't buxom enough. A few Playmates of the seventies and before had their breasts augmented, but perceived deficiencies at the time were ordinarily corrected with lighting and airbrushing. Hefner maintained that centerfolds received "relatively little retouching," but even if that were true, he copied the old Hollywood star system in every other way, renaming his protégées and finessing their marriages, pregnancies, toddlers, and anything else that didn't fit the prescribed fantasy. For instance, recycling the legend of Lana Turner's discovery by Hollywood at the soda-fountain counter of Schwab's Pharmacy, *Playboy* claimed to have discovered Miss November 1955, Barbara Cameron, at a soda-fountain counter; in reality, Barbara Cameron was dating Victor Lownes III, the Playboy organization's recently appointed head of promotions.

At sixteen, Hefner, the reticent child of prim Methodists, had retooled his own image, becoming "Hef," the kind of "High School kid you'd see in a movie," a "Sinatra-like guy with a love for loud flannel shirts" and "his own style of jiving and slang expressions." He reinvented himself again after his wife filed for divorce and he resolved to personify the life he espoused in *Playboy*. His style mentor was Victor Lownes, a silver-spoon sophisticate and much better casting as the aristocratic rake than Hefner, whose penchant for Pepsi, fried chicken, and orange clothes betrayed his parochial roots. So did his lack of curiosity about subjects other than sex. "Visiting Paris just to see the sights would bore me," he once said, as if tourism and travel are identical, though he would readily visit Paris "if a girl I was romantically involved with were there and couldn't come to me." He was wise, then, to defer to his second in command, A. C. Spectorsky, in literary matters. It was Spectorsky, an author and former staffer at *The New Yorker*, who fostered *Playboy*'s reputation for first-rate writing, and Lownes who proposed that the company should start a nightclub. Lownes further proposed the bunny costume worn by club waitresses. Hefner had imagined the waitresses in abbreviated nightgowns.

The first Playboy Club opened in 1960, four months after the premiere broadcast of *Playboy's Penthouse*, a syndicated television variety show that introduced Hefner in his suave new persona as the host of a black-tie party in his high-rise bachelor pad. The show was taped on a set at Chicago's ABC affiliate, and once the taping was complete, Hefner and his guests—musicians, comics, and the requisite Playmates—would reconvene for a real party at Hefner's real bachelor pad, a vast Gilded Age mansion two blocks from Lake Michigan. The mansion had carved wood paneling, marble fireplaces, and a ballroom the size of a regulation basketball court. Numerous *Playboy* pictorials were shot there, including "Playmate Holiday House Party," which was published in 1961 and showed Hefner celebrating Christmas with a dozen centerfold models. He was "romantically involved" with all of them, he later euphemized, except Miss April 1960, Linda Gamble, though, in his generosity, he designated her Playmate of the Year "just the same." Presumably he had become "romantically involved" with Elizabeth Ann Roberts, another "House Party" Playmate, after she turned eighteen. She was sixteen when she appeared as Miss January 1958, arousing the ire of Chicago officials. The case never went to trial—Roberts had posed nude with her mother's written permission—but Hefner would remain controversial in Chicago, a city dominated, from the mid-fifties to the mid-seventies, by its autocratic mayor, "Boss" Richard J. Daley, and his Catholic constituency. Chicago Catholics had lobbied for film censorship during the Great Depression, resulting in the repressive Hays Code that all but spoiled movies for young Hefner.

But without repression, *Playboy* would have had no raison d'être, and if Chicago Catholics were Hefner's unwitting boosters, his Protestant work ethic likewise served him well. He labored exhaustively during *Playboy*'s ascendant years, popping Dexedrine, washed down with Pepsi, to stay awake in the master bedroom of the Playboy Mansion and micromanage his editors with fastidious memos about every aspect of the magazine and the growing empire it ballasted. He ventured outside as seldom as possible, attending business meetings in the robe and pajamas that eventually became as much a part of his persona as the pipe he adopted to keep his nervous hands busy on *Playboy's Penthouse*. Of course he played as hard as he worked. Bunnies from the nearby Playboy Club rented rooms at the mansion, and they brightened the Friday-night party and Sunday-night movie screening, weekly mansion events, as well as the parties on almost every other night, impromptu affairs that continued long after Hefner returned to his round, rotating bed to work again on the magazine or tryst with his "special lady" of the moment or a Playmate or Bunny or five. The special lady wasn't always a Playmate or Bunny, but she was always held to a double standard, so that Hefner didn't afford her the sexual license he granted himself, just as he didn't encourage her ambitions beyond pleasing him, or as he once put it, "If I start going out with movie stars then I wouldn't have someone who was more interested in me than in herself." Jealousy was similarly a one-way street, though infractions predictably occurred. "When Cynthia got mad she threw things," Hefner recalled of a special lady weary of being two-timed. Another special lady "lost it," "screaming and yelling," when she saw the hook coming from stage left, while a semi-special lady pushed a rival into the mansion's indoor swimming pool: "Her mascara was all running down and her dress was shrinking, but her slip stayed the same size. It was the best thing I ever did."

But these incidents, and others like them, weren't recounted in *Playboy*, which sustained the sunny view of sex dreamed by Hefner in his world of perpetual night, made that way by the blackout curtains that covered his windows and excluded any hint of noir.

MIKE DAVIS, IN HIS ESTEEMED BOOK about Los Angeles, *City of Quartz*, refers to noir as the "great anti-myth" of L.A., a city mythologized in its original boom period, the late nineteenth century, as the capital of sunshine and robust health. Davis traces noir to the 1934 publication of James M. Cain's *The Postman Always Rings Twice* and "a succession of through-the-glass-darkly novels—all produced under contract to the studio system—[that] repainted the image of Los Angeles as a deracinated urban hell." This was not Los Angeles as Hefner saw it. For him, it was the place "where most of my earliest dreams came from," and he had been making trips there since the late fifties to canvass centerfold candidates. In 1962, he commissioned the Playboy Building on the Sunset Strip, with the penthouse apartment reserved for his visits, but he used it infrequently until Screen Gems approached him in 1968 with an idea for a television show, *Playboy After Dark*, to be taped on a set in L.A. *Playboy After Dark* would follow the same format as *Playboy's Penthouse*, long since canceled, and Hefner signed on as host "because I knew that would force me out of the house and into new areas of activity." Film production was among these areas. Movie fans with money are almost always snared by the siren song of Hollywood, and Hefner was forty-two and having a midlife crisis, a novel concept at the time, so that he delegated more of his Playboy editorial duties to A. C. Spectorsky, who guided the magazine to new heights of prestige matched by its circulation, freeing Hefner to ponder his future and fly to L.A. every other weekend for *Playboy After Dark*.

Then, during the taping of the show's third episode, he was gobsmacked by a pert brunette dancing in a blue minidress to a live performance of Iron Butterfly's "In-A-Gadda-Da-Vida." Her name was Barbara Klein, and she was an eighteen-year-old premed student at UCLA and occasional model with designs on a singing career. A Hefner associate had hired her as an extra for the show, certain that Hefner would find her appealing, but no one could have guessed that Hefner would fall as hard as he fell for Barbara Klein, who soon adopted Barbi Benton as her stage name. Hefner coined the name. He forgot that he wasn't in the market for an ambitious girlfriend, starting a Playboy record label, which naturally released the music of Barbi Benton, who naturally posed for *Playboy*, though not as a Playmate. She was too special to be a Playmate. She was the most special of Hefner's special ladies to date. She loved travel, as he didn't, but he bought a DC-9 jet and whisked her away for holidays in Europe and Africa. He also bought a house that she discovered one day as she was searching for a place to play tennis. The house was off Sunset Boulevard on a street called Charing Cross Road after a street in the heart of London. But that Charing Cross Road is famous for its bookstores; there were no bookstores within a reasonable walking distance of Hefner's new house, which was in Holmby Hills, between Beverly Hills and Westwood, on five and a half acres of redwood trees that evoked an English forest, while the house pretended to be an English castle built by Henry VIII or one of his Tudor relatives. In fact, it was built by a department-store scion with an evident taste for fantasy and, perhaps, the sort of class anxiety that would prompt a Californian to construct and inhabit an English castle in the midst of a fabricated English forest on a street that affected an English name. He would not have been alone. The hills of Los Angeles are full of castles, English and otherwise, that stand on fabricated grounds.

Barbi Benton was athletic, unlike Hefner, who preferred board games to sports. He did enjoy bowling, but Playboy Mansion West, as his new house came to be called, couldn't accommodate a bowling alley like the one inside the Playboy Mansion in Chicago. He wanted Mansion West to be "interconnected to nature as the Chicago Mansion had never been," stocking the grounds with exotic animals, including two dozen squirrel monkeys who gave the lie to his sentimental notion of nature when they sprang from the redwoods to ransack a buffet table set up in a neighbor's yard for a wedding reception. Hefner added a swimming pool, a grotto, a koi pond, and the tennis court that Barbi Benton had failed to find on the day she discovered the house. His landscape architect rightly thought it "paradoxical" to witness Hefner "relate...to nature" at the California property, since "in more than ten years at the Playboy Mansion in Chicago [he] had probably seen the light of day five times."

Playboy After Dark stopped airing eight months before Hefner threw his first party at Mansion West in April 1971, but he continued to commute between Chicago and L.A., where his production company was based. Barbi Benton moved into the California mansion, and while she knew that Hefner dallied with other women in Chicago, she was unaware of his deepening involvement with Karen Christy, a baby-faced platinum blonde with a figure that once led her to leave a White Sox game for all the commotion it caused. Karen Christy reminded Hefner of "the pre-Production Code beauties in Busby Berkeley musicals" when he met her at the Chicago mansion a month after the inaugural party at Mansion West, and because she was loath to live on his largess, he made her Miss December 1971, which paid well enough that she could quit her Bunny job and devote her evenings to him. It was supposed to be a fling, but she satisfied him sexually like nobody else in his prodigious experience, and she shared his enthusiasm for board games, so that she soon became his special lady in Chicago, though she accepted, at least for a while, that Barbi Benton remained his priority. He was, after all, the founder of a media empire, and Barbi, the poised daughter of a prominent Sacramento physician, could hold her own in public as Karen, a diffident waif from small-town Texas, could not. She was his nighttime girlfriend, and Barbi was his daytime girlfriend, and since they lived in different cities, their paths didn't cross, even when Hefner tempted fate by flying Karen to L.A. on his private jet, arranging with the security staff at Mansion West to alert him if Barbi arrived home earlier than expected.

Then *Time* magazine reported Hefner's relationship with Karen, upsetting Barbi, who moved out of Mansion West. Hefner was in Chicago when he learned of her departure, and he flew to L.A. to coax her back, upsetting Karen, who had lately concluded that Hefner cared more for her than he did for Barbi. His mission to L.A. was successful, but things were never the same with either woman. Both slept with other men, the foremost sin in Hefner's book, and Karen tormented Barbi, another sin, by leaving clues of her presence at Mansion West. Karen was herself tormented by the triangle, so that she lost weight and woke friends with late-night calls to complain of feeling trapped at the Chicago mansion, where the atmosphere was already fraught due to the drug charges faced by Bobbie Arnstein, Hefner's longtime secretary and confidante. Chicago authorities orchestrated the charges, clearly hoping that Arnstein would implicate Hefner in a scheme to sell cocaine along with her boyfriend. Only the boyfriend was guilty of selling cocaine, but he finally received a lesser sentence than Arnstein, who withstood the pressure to reduce her sentence—fifteen years in federal prison—by incriminating Hefner. Instead, Bobbie Arnstein killed herself with sleeping pills.

This noir scenario played out against the parallel noir scenario of Hefner's obsession with Karen Christy. Once, when she stole out of the Chicago mansion to see a friend, Hefner, terrified that she had left him utterly, turned up with security guards to retrieve her. She was shaken by his briefcase-throwing meltdown on another occasion. Ultimately she hatched a prison-break plan for her exodus to Texas, packing her belongings and shipping them to needy relatives, or so she told spies at the mansion before she absconded while shopping one day, vanishing through the rear door of a boutique as her chauffeured limousine waited out front. Elsewhere, a couple of girlfriends were standing by with a car to drive her to Texas, and once Karen joined them, they all took turns at the wheel, staying alert with the help of Dexedrine, Hefner's pet pick-me-up in the days when the magazine was his chief obsession. But those days were over, and so were his nights in Chicago. His mansion there was tainted by abandonment and suicide and conspiratorial authorities, and he fled it so quickly that, visiting four years later, he could pinpoint his departure by the dated newspapers in his "virtually untouched" quarters. Now he was committed to the restorative world of sunshine and nature at his faux English castle, but he was unable to commit to Barbi Benton, and after they parted amicably, his sex life became orgiastic on an unprecedented scale. Meanwhile, as he had done since he purchased what would eventually be the sole Playboy Mansion, he courted Hollywood with parties, though one Playboy executive observed that Hefner was "regarded by Hollywood as an interloper. They'll come to his parties and play his games. But they won't give him respect." His production company had financed and overseen three films—Roman Polanski's *Macbeth*; a half-animated adaptation of *The Naked Ape*, Desmond Morris's bestselling sociobiology primer; and *The Crazy World of Julius Vrooder*, an antiwar dramedy about a Vietnam vet—and the latter two were yanked from theaters almost as soon as they opened. *Macbeth* likewise flopped commercially, but it was named the best film of 1971 by the National Board of Review, as Hefner would mention with justifiable pride. Critical acclaim means little in Hollywood, of course, unless it's corroborated by accountants, but even if Hefner had produced blockbusters, he would have received grudging respect in Hollywood, which has always deeply frowned upon fortunes founded on sex. Covert whores and pimps are uneasy with the overt kind. But Hefner wasn't subjected to inquisitions as he had been in Chicago, so he could manage an illusion of acceptance in L.A., and he was a genuine son of Hollywood in his appetite for illusion.

Playboy's circulation peaked at 7.2 million in 1972, when Hefner was still commuting between L.A. and Chicago. By the end of 1976, some two years after he deserted Chicago, *Playboy* had lost nearly two million readers to bawdy *Playboy* imitators like *Penthouse* and *Hustler*. Hefner was wary of estranging corporate advertisers, so he launched *Oui*, a racier magazine with the European accent suggested by its title. But *Oui* also stole *Playboy* readers, so Hefner began to imitate his imitators in *Playboy*, printing fewer everyday candid shots of Playmates and more nudes, bold nudes that stopped short of gynecological detail as Playmates were seen fondling themselves in splay-legged poses. A notorious cover featured a bare-breasted Playmate-to-be masturbating, hand on groin, as she watched a movie. *Playboy* never ran another cover as off-putting to advertisers as that one, but the changes in its pages remained, and they weren't limited to photography. A. C. Spectorksy died of a stroke in 1972, and while his staff perpetuated most of his policies, he had taken with him some ineffable ingredient that made *Playboy* feel essential. Now it felt anachronistic. Playboy Clubs were increasingly desolate. Playboy Records was in the red. Playboy Productions couldn't afford to greenlight films. The Playboy jet was too costly to fly. However, in England, there were lucrative casinos that momentarily kept Playboy Enterprises afloat. Victor Lownes had opened the casinos after moving to London in the sixties, and he continued to operate them, living out the role of the aristocratic rake, hunting foxes and mingling with the likes of Prince Charles. At Hefner's request, he returned to the States to play bad cop to Hefner's good cop as they restructured the company, and Hefner stepped down as the president of Playboy Enterprises, a post that would eventually pass to his daughter, Christie, who as an infant had slept while he pieced together the first issue of *Playboy* at his card table. Christie Hefner had the sober business sense her father lacked. When Playboy tried to open a casino in Atlantic City, Hefner was ill prepared for questions that required him to search his memory at a hearing to determine if the company should be granted a gambling license. "Ask me whom I was dating," he responded at one point. The license was denied. Hubris on the part of Victor Lownes would lead to the loss of Playboy's gambling operation in England.

According to "Death of a Playmate," Teresa Carpenter's Pulitzer Prize-winning article published in the *Village Voice* in 1980, Hefner was preoccupied in this period with the screen careers of Playmates as he sought Hollywood approbation as a star maker, a function that in theory should have come naturally to him since, starting with Janet Pilgrim, he manufactured a calendar's worth of starlets each year. "Yet," writes Carpenter, "with all those beautiful women at his disposal, he [had] not one Marion Davies to call his own," referring to the mistress of newspaper tycoon William Randolph Hearst, who promoted Marion Davies to movie stardom in the silent era. But Davies's stardom was always suspect in the eyes of Hollywood, just as Barbi Benton was always suspect as Hefner's would-be Davies. Barbi Benton did some acting, mostly on television, a utilitarian medium for Hefner where film was an exalted one. He saw Dorothy Stratten, Miss August 1979 and Playmate of the Year 1980, as a probable movie star, describing her to Carpenter as "a curious combination of sensual appeal and vulnerability." It's a familiar description often applied to Marilyn Monroe, and Dorothy Hoogstraten, as she was known before *Playboy* abridged her name, had a pearly luminosity and soft-spoken sweetness that amounted to a Monroe quality unmatched by any Playmate since the early sixties. She came to the attention of *Playboy* through test shots arranged by her manager-boyfriend, Paul Snider, a former pimp with nebulous dreams of Hollywood success, which he assigned to Dorothy after they met in British Columbia, where they both grew up poor. *Playboy* accepted Dorothy as a centerfold almost immediately, flying her to Los Angeles and introducing her to an agent with a number of Playmate clients, but Dorothy clicked with casting directors as they did not. She booked six acting jobs in a year, including the title role in *Galaxina*, a sci-fi spoof, and the lead in *Autumn Born*, a cut-rate *Story of O*. They were bad movies, to be sure, but useful training for an inexperienced nineteen-year-old; and shortly before she turned twenty, Dorothy was cast in *They All Laughed*, a romantic comedy starring a Hollywood grande dame, Audrey Hepburn, and directed by Peter Bogdanovich, a Hollywood bête noire following a string of box-office lemons, two of them showcasing his girlfriend, Cybill Shepherd, who, like Dorothy, was tall and blonde. Bogdanovich and Shepherd were equally haughty and equally unpopular in Hollywood, but their relationship was finished by the time Dorothy was picked to play John Ritter's love interest in *They All Laughed,* which Bogdanovich obviously hoped would reverse the trend confirmed by his latest empty-seater, *Saint Jack*, a portrait of a pimp, executive produced by Hugh Hefner. His own flops couldn't deter Hefner from another spin at the roulette table. Dorothy, meanwhile, had married Paul Snider, though the marriage was naturally hushed by *Playboy* and Snider's influence on Dorothy's life and career was already waning, so that the unfolding noir scenario seems inevitable in hindsight: Dorothy, an unspoiled Cybill Shepherd, became Bogdanovich's new girlfriend, and Snider, confronted with her bid to divorce him, reacted in magnified pimp form, blasting her face off with a shotgun and turning the gun on himself. Dorothy's remains were cremated and buried within sight of Marilyn Monroe's crypt in Westwood Village Memorial Park. Hefner was nearly as devastated as Bogdanovich. He had lost his most promising protégée in a manner that would horrify anyone but especially horrified him, a bloody refutation of his make-believe world of breezy coupling. He was further dismayed by Teresa Carpenter's article, which posited that Hefner, Bogdanovich, and Snider were variations on the same sexist male, but only "small-time" Snider had taken sexism to its logical extreme. Hefner had always been disconcerted by feminist critiques of *Playboy*. As far as he was concerned, he had done a great deal to liberate women from the scourge of puritanism, and those who disagreed under any flag were themselves puritans.

"Death of a Playmate" was the basis for *Star 80*, a movie directed by Bob Fosse, with Mariel Hemingway as Dorothy, Eric Roberts as Snider, and Cliff Robertson as Hefner. The Bogdanovich character was renamed and played by a Brit, Roger Rees, in a kind of Groucho-mask move to evade a possible lawsuit from Bogdanovich, who purported not to have read Teresa Carpenter's version of the case even as he disparaged it. Hefner revised her version in *Playboy*, while Bogdanovich wrote a book about Dorothy, *The Killing of the Unicorn*, in which he accused Hefner, a "hygienic superpimp," of forcing himself on her, contradicting Hefner's credible claim that he and Dorothy had never had sex. Even Carpenter accepted that "fucking Hefner is a strictly voluntary thing. It never hurts a career, but Hefner, with so much sex at his disposal, would consider it unseemly to apply pressure." Bogdanovich apologized after Hefner suffered a stroke that he attributed to the strain brought on by *The Killing of the Unicorn* and, to a lesser extent, his latest special lady, a young Canadian who flouted all his bylaws, sleeping around while demanding his fidelity and raging when her whims weren't indulged. Friends urged Hefner to break with the girl, afraid she would thwart his recovery, but he allowed her to stay until she elected to leave, as if to punish himself for any overlooked part he might have played in the death of Dorothy Stratten.

THERE HAD BEEN PROMISING PLAYMATES before Dorothy Stratten, beginning with Jayne Mansfield, who appeared anonymously as Miss February 1955 and soon became famous as "the poor man's Marilyn Monroe," signed and groomed by Monroe's studio, Twentieth Century-Fox, as a replacement for its most troubled and troubling star. But Monroe was irreplaceable, as Fox came to realize, and Mansfield was finally more famous for being famous than she was for her movies, though one of them, *The Girl Can't Help It*, a rock & roll musical, is still noted for its Technicolor performances by Little Richard, Eddie Cochran, and Gene Vincent. The director of that movie, Frank Tashlin, later worked with Stella Stevens, a cash-strapped single mother, recently dropped by Fox, when she posed as Miss January 1960, to her regret: "All of a sudden I got sidetracked into being a sexpot. Once I was a 'pot,' there was nothing...legitimate I could do." Her words are pertinent to other Playmate actresses and even to Hugh Hefner, consigned as he was to the same Hollywood ghetto as his discoveries. Marilyn Monroe never entirely escaped it. She mined publicity gold when she acknowledged her nude calendar photos, but it was a Faustian bargain that sealed her image as a sex symbol and compromised her credibility as an actress. Stella Stevens, an earthier Monroe type, was directed in the course of a long career by the likes of Sam Peckinpah and John Cassavetes, but she never quite broke through as a major star. Still, until the nineties, she was the sole Playmate, aside from Mansfield and Monroe, to headline a "respectable" movie.

Claudia Jennings, who had thought herself too modestly proportioned to test for *Playboy*, and Victoria Vetri, who was called Angela Dorian as Miss September 1967 and Playmate of the Year 1968, were the two most successful Playmate stars of less-than-respectable movies in the pre-VHS era. Vetri reverted to her real name on the advice of Roman Polanski while shooting a small part in *Rosemary's Baby*, his horror classic. Jennings had a small part in a sci-fi classic, Nicolas Roeg's *The Man Who Fell to Earth*, but she was better known for drive-in fare like *Truck Stop Women*, *Gator Bait*, and *The Unholy Rollers*, the last a knockoff of *Kansas City Bomber*, which starred Raquel Welch, the premier sex symbol of the day, as a roller-derby queen. Vetri, in *When Dinosaurs Ruled the Earth*, approximated Welch's role as a cavewoman in *One Million Years B.C.*, but after a final drive-in movie, *Invasion of the Bee Girls*, she all but disappeared from public view. Jennings persevered. Her audition as Kate Jackson's replacement on *Charlie's Angels* is said to have been a grand slam, but she was rejected by network executives because of her *Playboy* association.

Another drive-in-movie actress, Yvette Vickers, may similarly have been hindered by her *Playboy* association. A moon-faced blonde of conspicuous acting talent, Vickers had lead roles in *Attack of the 50 Ft. Woman* and *Attack of the Giant Leeches*—behemoths loved to attack her, it seemed—but after she appeared as Miss July 1959, she was reduced to bit parts, including one in *Hud* on the arm of Paul Newman. It's a pity she never made a film with Russ Meyer, who photographed her centerfold, just as he had photographed his wife, Eve, as Miss July four years earlier. Unlike many exploitation directors, Meyer apotheosized strong women in movies that became wildly popular with hipster kids of the eighties and nineties, especially *Faster, Pussycat! Kill! Kill!*, with Sue Bernard, Miss December 1966, and *Beyond the Valley of the Dolls*, starring Dolly Read, Miss May 1966, and Cynthia Myers, Miss December 1968. Roger Ebert, the screenwriter of *Beyond the Valley of the Dolls*, saw wasted potential in Cynthia Myers, a voluptuous pinup favorite of American troops in Vietnam. *Playboy After Dark* was the only television show that hired her, and despite her affection for horror movies, she never acted in one.

Horror, ostensibly the antithesis of *Playboy*, is nonetheless about mating, more often than not, so that it's the genre most receptive to Playmates, the one that makes them pay for the futile lust they inflict on men and the absurd standard they impose on women. Hence, Ruthy Ross, Miss June 1973, who had the quirky charisma of a Warhol Superstar and a Mensa-level IQ, was stalked by a homicidal maniac in *The Centerfold Girls*; Jean Manson, Miss August 1974, was chained and bullwhipped by a maniac played by the same actor in *Nightmare Circus*; and Ashlyn Martin, Miss April 1964, was scalped by a maniac played by a different actor in *Blood Feast*. Meanwhile, because beautiful women are inherently cruel, or so they're perceived by ignored admirers, there are horror movies with Playmates as monsters rather than victims. Anulka Dziubinska, Miss May 1973, a radiant Brit of Polish extraction, was one of the eponymous *Vampyres*, while the creature of *Frankenstein Created Woman* was Susan Denberg, Miss August 1966, an Austrian based in England, where both movies were filmed. Denberg and Hefner once double-dated with Sharon Tate and Roman Polanski, who was also acquainted with Misses October 1970, Mary and Madeleine Collinson, the stars of *Twins of Evil*, a period vampire movie with a sister-act gimmick. Polanski remembered the Collinsons as the "spectacular Maltese twins" sent by Victor Lownes, whose London residence they shared, to console him after Sharon Tate died at the hands of the Manson Family.

When they weren't killing people or being killed, Playmates typically served a decorative purpose in movies, per Jean Bell, Miss October 1969, dancing in pasties in Martin Scorsese's *Mean Streets*; Azizi Johari, Miss June 1975, stripping at the nightclub owned by Ben Gazzara in John Cassavetes' *The Killing of a Chinese Bookie*; and Donna Michelle, Playmate of the Year 1964, cavorting wordlessly with Warren Beatty in Arthur Penn's *Mickey One*. Donna Michelle was one of several Playmates to garnish the beach-party movies of the sixties. Another, Sue Williams, Miss April 1965, is the first officially confirmed to have had breast implants, though she got them after her centerfold was published, using the modeling fee to finance the surgery. Jo Collins, Playmate of the Year 1965, had forgettable parts in two beach-party movies, but when she traveled to Vietnam to personally deliver a lifetime *Playboy* subscription to a wounded soldier, she loosely inspired the indelible Playmate sequence in Francis Ford Coppola's *Apocalypse Now*, which had Linda Beatty, Miss August 1976, and Cyndi Wood, Playmate of the Year 1974, choppered to a burlesque stage in the jungle, where, vamping to a cover of "Susie Q," they caused sex-starved GIs to riot. Linda Beatty and Cyndi Wood were both brainy Playmates, like Ruthy Ross, and Wood later counseled emotionally disturbed children while pursuing a Ph.D. in psychology. Jean Bell, after starring in a blaxploitation movie, *T.N.T. Jackson*, attracted international press attention as Richard Burton's post-Elizabeth Taylor girlfriend. Jean Manson tweaked her first name to become Jeane Manson, a pop star in France. These are the kind of Hollywood endings that *Playboy* is pleased to recount, and there are surely many more entailing matrimony and motherhood and satisfying, if quotidian, jobs.

But Dorothy Stratten isn't the only Playmate who figures in the Hollywood anti-myth of noir. Five years after Marilyn Monroe fatally overdosed in a noir scenario with long legs, Jayne Mansfield was killed in a grisly car crash, along with her abusive boyfriend and their twenty-year-old driver, an employee at the Mississippi supper club where she had been reduced to performing. Claudia Jennings, who had acquired a taste for cocaine, an occupational hazard of her time, was also killed in a car crash, this one in Malibu. Ashlyn Martin led "a rather sad life," according to her *Blood Feast* co-star Connie Mason, Miss June 1963, and attempted suicide at least once before a mortal attempt in her forties. Susan Denberg likewise attempted suicide and spent much of her late twenties in and out of mental institutions while working as a topless dancer. Victoria Vetri, paying the bills as a waitress in her sixties, "would walk up and down Hollywood Boulevard and go, 'People recognize me,'" or so a witness was quoted after Vetri shot her husband, fifteen years her junior, as he walked away from an argument. He survived, and Vetri was sentenced to nine years in the California state penitentiary for a crime that reminded some of *Sunset Boulevard,* Billy Wilder's iconic noir that concludes with a man being shot as he walks away from his older lover, a faded movie star with delusions of enduring celebrity. Yvette Vickers made her screen debut in *Sunset Boulevard*, but it was her drive-in movies that led to long-distance friendships with late-arriving fans, though she barely interacted with her neighbors in Benedict Canyon. One of them, noticing that Vickers's mailbox was deluged and receiving no answer when she knocked at the door, broke into her cottage and found her dead amid countless empty liquor bottles and a trove of memorabilia later junked by Vickers's philistine half-brother. Her corpse had been mummified by a space heater still running approximately eight months after she collapsed beside it and died at age eighty-two. This case too has been compared to *Sunset Boulevard*. Yvette Vickers is visible in that film for less than thirty seconds. She has no lines.

HEFNER REGARDED THE EIGHTIES as a "dark decade" for Playboy, which continued to tank until it was gradually reconfigured by Christie Hefner as, in her words, a "global multimedia lifestyle brand" that drew "on the heritage of the magazine and the good life" for a "new generation of young women [who]...thought the rabbit head was cool." This cool factor was due largely to the rise of hip-hop and its veneration of the pimp, a close relative of the aristocratic rake in his dandyism and sweet tooth for quality merchandise, animate and otherwise. Hefner spent much of the early hip-hop era married to Kimberly Conrad, Playmate of the Year 1989, after he tellingly forgot to bring the ring to the ceremony and joked to ex-girlfriends at the reception that the marriage was a mistake. If he was seeking sanctuary, he didn't find it, and when he and his wife separated in 1998, he was startled by the excitement he stirred as he made the rounds of L.A. clubs with his "party posse" of three blondes, two of them twins who referred to each other, gangsta-style, as "nig." The original party posse was replaced and expanded to seven, a blonde for each day of the week, and if one of them dropped out on reaching her centerfold goal or was discharged for cuckolding Hefner or for neglecting such duties as watching classic movies with him—some of the girls had never seen a black-and-white movie until they had no choice—there was always another blonde waiting to assume her spot and receive a weekly stipend, with bonus money provided for breast implants and other cosmetic procedures, including the professional application of chemicals that kept her blonde, and more money still for the gowns she wore to the Hollywood galas frequented by her benefactor, who, flanked by his chorus line of blonde replicants, would pose for paparazzi like the star of a musical with two distinct scores: the Irving Berlin or Cole Porter score of his dreams, and the hip-hop score heard by young people, especially young males, as they cheered for him in the same way they cheered for Ron Jeremy, the middle-aged, overweight porn star as preposterous and therefore heroic as Hugh Hefner. Young females, on the other hand, tended to see Hefner as a kind of pimp Santa Claus who could give them everything they wanted except sex, which would have to come from less doddering sources. Sex occurred offscreen, mercifully, on *The Girls Next Door*, the "reality" television series that documented life at the Playboy Mansion, spotlighting the three blondes—Hefner was back to three: Holly Madison, Bridget Marquardt, and Kendra Wilkinson—who were tenured there. None of them were Playmates, but the show made them almost as recognizable as three other blondes—Pamela Anderson, Miss February 1991; Anna Nicole Smith, Playmate of the Year 1993; and Jenny McCarthy, Playmate of the Year 1994—who had finally fulfilled Hefner's bygone hope that mainstream stars would emerge from *Playboy*, even if they didn't achieve stardom in movies. Two more blondes—Shannon Tweed, Playmate of the Year 1982, and Erika Eleniak, Miss July 1989—had some success in movies, and Eleniak starred in a few major-studio releases. All of these women, save for Bridget Marquardt, had their breasts augmented, in three cases after their initial *Playboy* appearances. So did the three blondes who became *The Girls Next Door* after the first three vacated the mansion. In a striking exchange on the series, Hefner told Barbi Benton, who had surfaced as a reminder of his pre-blonde past, that plastic surgery had improved to the point where it was hard to distinguish real breasts from synthetic ones, a remark less incisive about plastic surgery than it is about Hefner's Californicated vision. As the novelist John Rechy wrote of Los Angeles in *City of Night*: "You can rot here without feeling it."

But Hefner never really lived in Los Angeles; he lived in an English castle in a redwood forest near Beverly Hills, insulated from the L.A. where bottle blondes and breast implants are scarce compared to his side of town and, certainly, the five and a half acres he owned of it. Yet after residing in that town since the early seventies, he was still unable to navigate it as well as he could navigate Chicago, as demonstrated on another episode of *The Girls Next Door*, one that saw him return to Chicago for the first time since the nineties and play backseat driver while being chauffeured with his blonde phalanx on a promotion tour that stopped at the erstwhile Playboy Mansion, a stately building with no pretensions of being anywhere other than Chicago's Gold Coast. Maybe it's happenstance that the Playboy empire began its decline when Hefner abandoned Chicago, but regardless, he should have left his trademark costumes behind. Pajamas aren't suited to the California sunlight, and a tuxedo is best seen indoors at night, as any classic-movie fan should know. Meanwhile, a koi pond is to nature what silicone breasts are to real ones, and the most convincing personal use Hefner ever made of his tennis court was during the roller-disco era, when the court was converted into a rink skated by Hefner in a feathered "Indian" headdress borrowed from one of the Village People.

Playboy Enterprises closed its headquarters in Chicago in 2012 and followed its founder to Beverly Hills, where it splits an office complex with a talent agency. The magazine, marginalized like most in the digital age, can only afford to publish six issues a year. Christie Hefner resigned from the company in 2009 and her much-younger half-brother, Cooper Hefner, is now its "chief creative officer" after standing in for their declining father at events such as the annual media luncheon, held on the lawn of the house on Charing Cross Road, to formally announce the Playmate of the Year. Hugh Hefner was bedridden with back pain during the 2014 luncheon, but later that day, accompanied by his third wife, the former Crystal Harris, Miss December 2009 and one of the replacement blondes on *The Girls Next Door*, he hobbled downstairs to pose for photos, appearing sadly shrunken next to Crystal, Cooper, and the newly named Playmate of the Year, Kennedy Summers, an aspiring plastic surgeon who might have been the cousin or niece of Nicole Kidman. A celebrity resemblance was always a boon for Hefner, the decisive ballot in Playmate selection almost to his death at ninety-one in 2017. Jessica Ashley, Miss June 2014, calls to mind Natalie Wood in *Bob & Carol & Ted & Alice*, a movie that simultaneously epitomized and satirized the bourgeois permissiveness wrought in part by *Playboy*. Jessica Ashley's aspirations were literary, and on her Playmate Data Sheet, a centerfold accessory added in 1977, she professed a single "turnoff": "I can't really get warmed up for a man who doesn't stimulate my mind. We'll read Henry Miller together or we won't be together, baby. Sorry!"

The apology was gratuitous. Jessica Ashley may not have known it, but by plugging Henry Miller in *Playboy*, she did what the magazine did best in its heyday. Men and boys would buy it or steal it for the nudes, but later, leafing through it, they found themselves at a paper cocktail party where writers like Miller and Nabokov and Vidal were mentioned, and foreign films and destinations, and posh drinks and dishes, and Latin terms—fellatio, cunnilingus, coitus interruptus—for common sexual practices that seemed uncommon until *Playboy* confirmed their universality. Only in Hollywood movies had most Americans glimpsed the world they encountered in *Playboy*, but those movies omitted references to subversive writers and "lewd" acts, partly to placate moral guardians but also because Hollywood considered its audience too moronic to apprehend them. Hefner, by contrast, welcomed his audience to the cosmopolitan party that he himself wanted to attend, supplying readers with some of the needed nomenclature, as well as paper dates who, in addition to playing the bait in a bait-and-switch operation that ended in edification, were fighting puritanism by being good girls who liked sex. Of course, if he had digested some of the very writers he published, he might have stressed other factors as being more pernicious to healthy sex, and health overall, than puritanism. How is puritanism at fault for the erratic mood swings of Miss February 1971, Willy Rey, who, like Marilyn Monroe and Anna Nicole Smith, was a prescription-drug casualty? Was it puritanism that caused an obsessed fan of Miss January 1991, Stacy Arthur, to drive from California to Ohio, where she lived, and gun down her husband in a murder-suicide? Is it the reason that Star Stowe, Miss February 1977, turned tricks on the street in a downward spiral that placed her in the path of a likely serial killer? Her strangulation murder remains unsolved.

But Hefner would sooner have traded night for day than probe that kind of darkness or, for that matter, the kind that clouded his personal life, as if his controlling nature and Frankensteinish need for duplicates had nothing to do with the fits and indiscretions of his speedily replaced favorites. There's no defeating the pathologies of noir as decisively as he believed he could defeat puritanism by challenging censorship laws—he challenged them with admirable success—and winning hearts and minds with his starlet factory. As of 2018, the factory has produced some 750 variations on its patented line, discounting the calendar reprints of *Playboy*'s first year, though they too acted as bait in its bait-and-switch operation, which never worked as well on the Internet, where the click-happy pace is an obstacle. The magazine in whatever form isn't as edifying as it used to be, and even if it were, America is a harder place emotionally and economically than it was when Hefner was planning *Stag Party*, so that fewer people identify profit in learning "interesting" things for the sake of learning them. Will it get them a job? Will it make them popular? It might with Jessica Ashley, but she's an exception. She's *Playboy*'s Playmate of the Month, model No.

715, and somehow her line perseveres now that Hefner is interred alongside Marilyn Monroe in Westwood Village Memorial Park. He purchased the vault twenty-five years before he occupied it, because, he said, "Spending eternity next to Marilyn is too sweet to pass up." Hence, to cap a life packed with realized fantasy, he has realized a final fantasy as the mate of a stranger, though they once spoke briefly on the phone about a cover photo that would feature Monroe clasping a white fur stole given to her for Christmas by "Playboy," the company or its rakish rabbit mascot. She died soon after that chat and Hefner proceeded with the cover, substituting Sheralee Conners, Miss July 1961, for the *Golden Dreams* girl whose Hollywood ending cut to black, while his own would slowly dissolve.

2014/2018

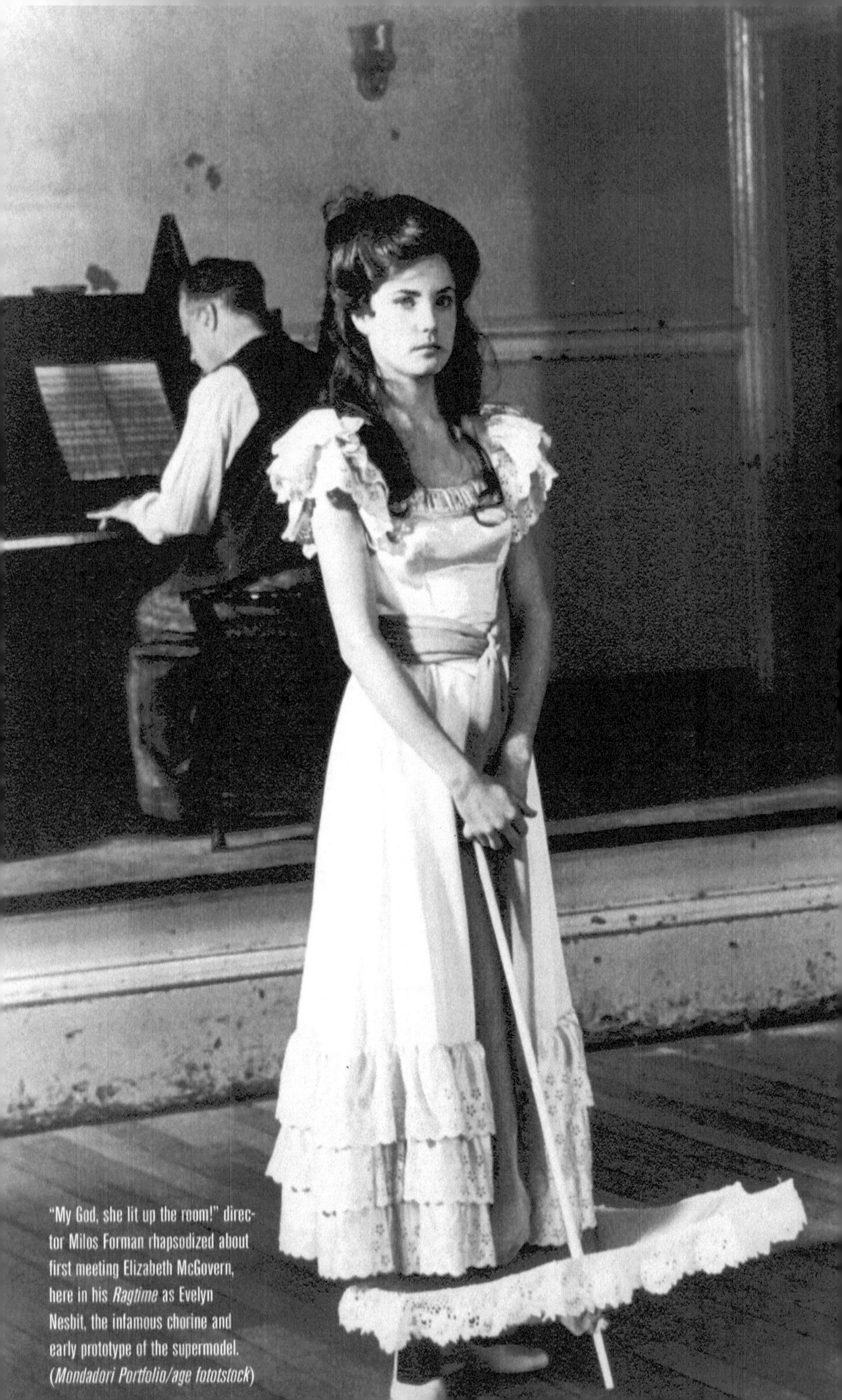

"My God, she lit up the room!" director Milos Forman rhapsodized about first meeting Elizabeth McGovern, here in his *Ragtime* as Evelyn Nesbit, the infamous chorine and early prototype of the supermodel. (*Mondadori Portfolio/age fototstock*)

THE PHANTOM OF THE PUBLIC THEATER

I BOUGHT MY PENGUIN PAPERBACK of *Moby-Dick* on February 23, 1988. I'm certain of the date because it's scrawled on the first page, just above a thumbnail biography of Herman Melville. I used to have a habit of noting a book's purchase date on its first page, and sometimes I would add the store where I bought it, though I only added the city in this case: "NYC." I remember the circumstances vividly. I bought *Moby-Dick* at St. Mark's Bookshop on St. Mark's Place while headed to see, for the third time, a Brazilian-themed production of *A Midsummer's Night Dream* at the Public Theater. Then, at a stationery store, I bought a blank greeting card with a Monet landscape on the front. The card was for Elizabeth McGovern, who was playing Helena in *A Midsummer's Night Dream*, and I inscribed the card at a coffee shop cater-cornered from the Public Theater on Lafayette Street. "I'm an actor and writer in town from L.A.," I wrote, "and I'm planning to see the play tonight and I'd like to say hello afterward," describing myself briefly—"I'm tall and wearing a black leather jacket"—so that Elizabeth McGovern—or "Liz," as she was known to friends—could recognize me after the performance. I listed a few mutual acquaintances without mentioning Orrin, as I'll call him, who was also in the cast of *Midsummer* and had advised me against trying to contact Elizabeth McGovern, and I certainly didn't mention that I had seen the play twice already. She might take me, rightly, for a stalker.

An hour or so before curtain time, I bought a ticket at the Public. I had wanted to work there ever since I moved to New York from Virginia, but I could never infiltrate the Public or Playwrights Horizons or Circle Rep or any of the other prestigious Off-Broadway theaters. My paid acting and writing jobs had all been in film and television, so it made sense for me to live in Los Angeles, where I had spent most of the previous year. I met Orrin in L.A. I hoped he wouldn't spot me, yet again, in the lobby of the Public. Staffers didn't wear uniforms, but I noticed a kid, slightly younger than me, who looked like a probable staffer, and I approached him with the card in hand and asked if he could deliver it backstage.

"Sure," he said. "Who's it for?"

"Elizabeth McGovern."

The kid's helpful expression dissolved. "Oh," his eyes seemed to say, "a stalker." Still, he took the card and hurried away, possibly to alert the cops or bouncers, and I busied myself elsewhere until curtain time. My memory of that hour is hazy, but if I returned to the coffee shop to begin *Moby-Dick*, I doubt I got much further than "Call me Ishmael." Orrin had told me that Elizabeth McGovern was reading *Moby-Dick*, and I would brandish my copy as an ice-breaker or, as I dared to imagine she might interpret it, a potential sign of destiny. Stalkers are often deluded romantics, if "deluded romantic" isn't the redundancy I believe it is.

MY OBSESSION WITH ELIZABETH MCGOVERN started with *Ordinary People*, the movie that launched her as an It girl of the early eighties. I was in the midst of my James Dean phase when I saw it, mumbling my way through acting classes in thrift-store clothes bought near my flat on the Lower East Side, and *Ordinary People* was about a kind of James Dean character, played by Timothy Hutton, though his family had money, unlike mine, and his teenage angst, unlike mine, had a tidy cause: his brother's death, which led him to attempt suicide, a subject avoided by everyone in the movie save for his therapist and Elizabeth McGovern, his love interest and classmate. She reminded me of former classmates of my own in Virginia, preppy girls who wore plaid skirts and knee socks and Fair Isle sweaters, and favored the "wedge" hairstyle popularized by the Olympic figure skater Dorothy Hamill, and greeted friends pretentiously with *Bonjour* or *Hola*. All of that was true of Elizabeth McGovern in *Ordinary People*, but she was the bighearted opposite of the preppy girls I had wooed in vain in Virginia. Misfits, especially poor misfits, weren't on their menu, and I aimed to punish them and other former classmates, those who rejected me socially, by becoming the James Dean of our generation, and an equally famous paramour would salt the wounds. A sample caption for a fantasy paparazzi photo: "Elizabeth McGovern, an Oscar nominee for *Ragtime*, with her boyfriend, Darel Haeny, soon to be seen in *Roaring*." I spelled my name "Darel Haeny" at the time because I considered it more eye-catching than "Daryl Haney," and *Roaring* was a screenplay I co-wrote with my manager (the title, which I hated, was his); but even if *Roaring* had been realized on film, it surely would have starred a celebrity and not Daryl Haney, as I reverted to spelling my name on hearing "Darel Haeny" mispronounced once too often. However, Elizabeth McGovern really was nominated for an Oscar for *Ragtime*. It was her second movie, and she was only twenty.

She lost the Oscar but won an Obie, the Off-Broadway counterpart of the Tony, the same month she appeared on the cover of *Newsweek*. *People* named her one of that year's twenty-five most intriguing personalities. *Harper's Bazaar* declared her one of the world's ten most beautiful women. Was she that beautiful? "She looks like Tweety Bird," a young actress remarked to me. "She walks like a duck," another young actress said. They were jealous, presumably, but I knew what they meant. She had a round face and puffy cheeks, and there was something a bit gawky about her, but her peachy skin and periwinkle eyes made her springtime personified, as far as I was concerned, while I identified her dark hair with winter, for whatever reason, and in *Ordinary People* she was shown walking to school on a path covered with dead leaves, and she never entirely lost that autumn association for me. It was hard to picture her in Los Angeles, mythically a city of perpetual summer, but she moved from Evanson, Illinois, to an L.A. suburb at age ten, when her father became a professor of law at UCLA. (He had previously taught law at Northwestern University in Evanston.) Academic parents were practically mandatory for the preppies I knew in Virginia, and if any of those preppies had been interested in acting, they probably would have studied at exclusive Juilliard, like Elizabeth McGovern, and lived near Juilliard in uptown Manhattan, also like Elizabeth McGovern, and upscale uptown and boho downtown were worlds apart in those pre-gentrified days. I had swapped the class divisions of Virginia for the class divisions of New York and show business.

I learned that Elizabeth McGovern lived uptown through "Captain" Arthur Haggerty, the best-known dog trainer in New York and a frequent guest on *Late Night with David Letterman*, though, since I didn't own a dog or a television, I had never heard of Captain Haggerty before we met in Frank Corsaro's acting class. He was a fiftyish man with a shaved head and a sumo-wrestler's build, a good type for a scene I wanted to perform in class, and he agreed to be my scene partner as long as we rehearsed at Captain Haggerty's School for Dogs, where some of his pupils were kenneled out of sight and silenced by Captain with a single command—"SHUT UP!"—when they barked during rehearsal. His assistant, meanwhile, manned the phone, and one day she interrupted rehearsal to announce that she'd just gotten a call from Elizabeth McGovern.

"Oh my God," I said. "I am in *love* with that girl. I want to *marry* her."

"She has beautiful breasts," Captain volunteered. He had seen *Ragtime*, obviously. Elizabeth McGovern had a nude scene in *Ragtime* and a Boston terrier in urgent need of Captain's housebreaking services. *Rolling Stone* had recently run a photo of Elizabeth McGovern and her Boston terrier in a short item about her latest movie, a romantic comedy with the apropos title of *Lovesick*. I had pestered my manager, John, to introduce me to her, but John had only met her once through an actor named Todd, and Todd wasn't about to introduce me to Elizabeth McGovern or assist me in any way after hearing John praise my acting talent. Now, maybe, I could meet her at Captain Haggerty's School for Dogs.

But she was never at the school when I was there. I asked about her, of course, and Captain affirmed his judgment of her breasts, while his assistant said she was very nice and lived on the Upper West Side. Somebody else supplied the intersection, and I walked past it the next time I went to the Thalia, a repertory cinema on West 96th Street, and decided Elizabeth McGovern lived in a particular building; and for weeks, whenever I saw a movie at the Thalia or otherwise found myself on the Upper West Side, I would return to that building and stare at the windows, wondering which were hers, and sometimes loiter for a few minutes at the corner or across the street, hoping she emerged from the building and so corroborated that I had it right. At least Jay Gatsby, one of the foremost stalkers of American literature, knew he had Daisy Buchanan's residence right, but her dock was rigged with a green light that directed his gaze and reinforced his yearning.

One summer day I dropped by Writers & Artists, a talent agency in the Fisk Building on West 57th Street. Writers & Artists represented Elizabeth McGovern, but my visit was unrelated to her. I was with John, who had some business there, and we had just left the building when John froze on the sidewalk and said, "That was Liz McGovern," motioning toward a tall girl in new jeans and a yellow polo shirt. Her back was to us—she was walking in the opposite direction—and I thought John was mistaken or putting me on, so I turned around and followed her. She entered the Fisk Building and crossed the lobby with me four feet behind her, and as we neared the bank of elevators, an elevator door opened and a girl stepped out, a girl who knew the girl I was following, and they stopped to chat, and finally I saw the face I had longed to see in life since *Ordinary People*, and no images—or words, for that matter—could do it justice. She *glowed*: her skin, her eyes, her smile. I fled before she noticed me gaping. Then, outside, I reproached John for failing to introduce me when he had the chance. Why didn't he say hello?

"Because," he said, "I ogled her before I realized it was Liz McGovern and she saw me do it, so I didn't want to remind her we'd met before. Did *you* speak to her?"

"I couldn't, goddamn it. I don't want to meet her like that." But I did regret running away so quickly. A glance could reveal instant attraction, I believed, and I hadn't waited for a glance that proved or disproved reciprocal attraction, even if nothing came of it.

MY PLAYWRIGHT FRIEND PETER, who had been produced at the Public Theater, knew Elizabeth McGovern, but not well enough to arrange an introduction. He had a celebrity crush of his own, Rob Lowe, and when he teased me about my celebrity crush, I would retaliate by saying, for example, "I hear Rob Lowe is cheating on you with Nastassia Kinski."

"Oh, that Rob. At least it's not with Dudley Moore."

Dudley Moore was Elizabeth McGovern's co-star in *Lovesick* and her rumored lover offscreen. I was mystified by the rumors, since he was half a foot shorter than her and old enough to be her father. Surely she would prefer a tall, young James Dean type who read classic literature and could turn her on to hip New York, or so I joked to friends. I always treated my crush on her as a joke, while part of me believed that I might genuinely have a shot at dating her if we met through someone with clout, like Peter. Once, after he had coffee with Elizabeth McGovern, Peter called to inform me, and I said, "Great, thanks. I don't suppose you could have called me *while* you were having coffee. I could've joined you, you know."

"It wouldn't have worked. It wasn't just the two of us."

"Did you talk about me?"

"I'm hanging up now."

Then calamity struck: Elizabeth McGovern became betrothed to Sean Penn, her co-star in *Racing with the Moon* and, according to *Rolling Stone,* "the next James Dean." I refused to accept Sean Penn as the next James Dean, though my James Dean phase had ended. I was growing up, a little. I had a girlfriend, and we lived together in Soho, across the street from Madonna, who married Sean Penn soon after he broke up with Elizabeth McGovern. By coincidence, not by design, I broke up with my girlfriend at the same approximate moment, and for a period I crashed on the Upper West Side, where I occasionally passed Elizabeth McGovern's building, assuming she still lived in that building, if she had ever lived in it in the first place; but I never saw her on the Upper West Side, just as I didn't see her outside the WPA Theater when I attended a play she did there. I met more and more people who knew her, and one of them told me that she was now involved with Rob Reiner, a beauty-and-beast combo as unpleasant to me as the Dudley Moore rumors and, possibly, the engagement to Sean Penn. "*Please* introduce me to her," I begged. "This is a goddamn emergency!"

Finally, at the Actors Studio, I had another brush with her. I was an observer at the Studio, not a participating member, and one day, after a session, I went downstairs to use the pay phone and found myself waiting behind Christopher Walken, who was waiting behind Harvey Keitel, who was waiting for a girl to finish her call. The girl was facing the phone on the wall, her back to the line, and suddenly she turned to survey the line and shock me inadvertently. She didn't glow as she had glowed in the lobby of the Fisk Building four years earlier. She looked at Harvey Keitel, then at Christopher Walken, then at me. Our eyes met for a second or less. Then, listening but not speaking, she turned back to the phone and replaced the receiver and hurried away. I didn't follow. I had gotten the glance I wished I had gotten at the Fisk Building, and it didn't reveal instant attraction or even modest curiosity. On the other hand, she was rushed and distracted, and she hadn't been perceptibly impressed by Harvey Keitel or Christopher Walken, so I was in famous company, at least.

A YEAR LATER I FLEW TO L.A. to star in a Roger Corman movie. I planned to stay only until the movie wrapped, but it immediately begat more work, which kept me in L.A. for another six months. Orrin auditioned for the Corman movie. He was bicoastal, an increasingly quaint term in an era of preposterously overpriced rents. I wanted to be bicoastal, but I held the lease on a place in Brooklyn with a fluid cast of roommates and I couldn't fill the frequent vacancies from afar. No, for the time being, I would have to commit to L.A., a city I didn't love but seemed to love me, offering me the kind of opportunities reserved by its rival for the privileged, with token exceptions that proved the rule. New York is one of the great unrequited crushes of my life, and when I returned in December to officially terminate my lease and ship my belongings to L.A., I lingered for a long goodbye. There were nightly games of poker and pool with friends, and we bar-hopped and club-hopped until last call at quarter to four in the morning. Interrupted flings were resumed and new flings initiated. Weeks passed, and at one point I bought a biography of Jack Kerouac and wrote, on the first page, the purchase date—"8 Feb. '88"—as well as the bookstore—"Shakespeare & Co."—and this unique note: "How many days to L.A.?" By then, I'm almost positive, I had seen *A Midsummer's Night Dream* twice. It opened in mid-January, Google reminds me, and I read the *New York Times* every day and the *Village Voice* every week, so I would have known about it while it was in previews. Well, well, well. Orrin was doing Shakespeare with Elizabeth McGovern. I would have to renew acquaintance with Orrin in the lobby of the Public, where actors mingled with well-wishers before and after performances, and if a certain someone happened to pass us in the lobby, maybe Orrin would flag her down as a favor to me and vouch for a few of my virtues. He owed me such a favor, by my reckoning. I had introduced him to a lusty Nordic type—I called her the Viking— in L.A. The Viking was too imposing for me, but she made a snack of Orrin and vice versa. Orrin was lusty in his own right.

He received me warmly in the lobby of the Public, but he hardly had a moment to speak, and the certain someone was nowhere in sight. He invited me to see the play again as his guest. I sat next to his latest girlfriend that time, and he left with her almost as soon as the performance ended. I tried to stall him. I asked for help in meeting one of his castmates, and he guessed without a hint or pause the castmate I had in mind.

"Liz," he said. "This isn't a good time to meet Liz." But that was as far as he went at the Public. He was more forthcoming later on the phone.

"She just broke up with Rob Reiner," he told me, "and she sits around reading *Moby-Dick* and eating a lot of popcorn and drinking a lot of coffee, and do you know what happens when you eat a lot of popcorn and drink a lot of coffee? *Do* you?" he repeated for dramatic effect. "You *fart*. We'll be onstage in the middle of a scene and she'll let one rip, a silent but deadly one, and I've got to just stand there in this cloud of blue smoke and gag through the rest of the scene. Trust me, you don't want to be around her right now. She's not in a good place."

But I was in a good place, now that my career was kicking in, and I rarely thought of the preppy girls who rejected me in high school and laid the foundation for my crush on Elizabeth McGovern. The very notion of a celebrity crush seemed puerile to me now, but something of this one had stuck after years of moonstruck speculation, and if nobody was willing or able to introduce us, I could introduce myself. She was single again, but, farts or no farts, she wouldn't stay single for long, and I knew where she spent part of every day, except when the house was dark, and I was far more confident than Darel Haeny, so that I wouldn't gape or fawn or otherwise embarrass myself as that green kid would have done. It was a good idea. It was a bad idea. Back and forth I swung, and I had to act before Roger Corman or some other producer offered me a job that would force me back to L.A. Should I bring or send her flowers? No, flowers were too solicitous. I should keep it simple with a backstage note that cited some of the people we knew in common, people like Peter, not Orrin, who might speak ill of me if she showed him the note to confirm that I wasn't a stalker—"He *is* a stalker, and he *farts*!"—and I could manufacture a coincidence by buying a copy of *Moby-Dick*, a book I intended to read anyway, and if *Moby-Dick* or something else sparked a conversation in the lobby of the Public, I could invite her to have coffee across the street, where I would feign surprise if she mentioned, for instance, her breakup with Rob Reiner or the Boston terrier that used to have a problem of the excremental kind.

Lord, what a fool this mortal be!

I WASN'T EAGER TO SEE *A Midsummer's Night Dream* a third time. It was an agreeable production with a competent cast, but as a broad rule, I preferred and prefer Shakespeare's histories to his tragedies, and his tragedies to his comedies, and the fairy characters and transformative spells of *Midsummer* work better on the page than they do onstage. Then again, I've never seen a British production of *Midsummer*, and the British could surely pull it off, with their overall feeling for Shakespeare that's as much a matter of blood, I'm convinced, as it is of training and tradition. Even mediocre British actors make music and sense of Shakespearean language, while American actors sound off-key and clueless by comparison. Marlon Brando is among the anomalies. He electrified as Mark Antony in the 1953 film adaptation of *Julius Caesar*, and if he had played Oberon, the king of the fairies, or Theseus, the duke of Athens or Bahia or wherever in Brazil this version of *Midsummer* was set, I would gladly have seen it a third time. As it was, I thought of skipping the play after dropping off my card with the Monet landscape on the front and returning to the Public when the play was nearly over; but if I did that and something freakish occurred, if a stage light exploded or a heckler got ejected or an actor collapsed mid-soliloquy, I would know nothing about it, and I would have to know to comment persuasively later.

No lights exploded that night. There were no hecklers. None of the actors collapsed, despite the alleged flatulence. Maybe Elizabeth McGovern had changed her diet. Her performance was the same. She played Helena as a kind of exasperated wallflower, coltish and a bit nasal, and she was effective: comedy was more her métier than drama, I had come to decide. Evelyn Nesbit, her character in *Ragtime*, was a real-life siren at the center of a sensational murder case in Gilded Age New York, but she was mined for laughs by Elizabeth McGovern, who implied an unwritten line: "Somebody killed for *me*?" The fictional siren and object of Robert De Niro's decades-long obsession in Sergio Leone's *Once Upon a Time in America* was played by Jennifer Connelly in the movie's puberty scenes, but the obsession became less credible when Jennifer Connelly matured into Elizabeth McGovern, who didn't seem to own or recognize her sexual power, not just in the movie but generally. There were hints of the wallflower in everything I had seen her do and the charm of it had started to fade for me, if it hadn't faded already, but that was voided by the image of her reading my card in her dressing room before the play that night. Finally, I thought, she had tangible proof of my existence, and she knew I was now watching her, unless that kid, the staffer, had ditched my card after I gave it to him in the lobby. But he wouldn't do that. Would he?

Orrin's girlfriend was in the lobby when the play ended. If she had been in the audience I would have noticed her—it was a weeknight and the house was half full—so she had evidently turned up after the play, and since avoiding Orrin meant avoiding her as well, I ducked behind a column before she saw me. There were several columns that made for convenient hiding places, but Orrin appeared quickly and disappeared with his girlfriend, freeing me to mill openly, and soon the lobby was almost empty except for me and a gay couple with the buzz cuts and trimmed facial hair and pristine lumberjack clothes that were then fashionable on Christopher Street. What had happened to Elizabeth McGovern? As far as I knew, there were no stage doors at the Public, so she must have exited through the lobby invisibly, on cat feet, a third time.

But she hadn't. Here she was, walking toward me in ankle-high basketball shoes and a plush coat almost as dark as her black tights, a boho style she wore well. She looked better than she had looked ten or fifteen minutes earlier, taking a bow onstage. Her hair was attractively disheveled. Her skin shone if it didn't glow. I was about to speak, to say hello, but she walked past me and over to the gay couple, greeting them instead. She was friendly or friends with one or both of them, clearly, and I was a stranger, so of course she would speak to them first. She would get to me in a minute, I thought, and I expected a glance that said as much—"Oh, hey, you must be the guy who sent me that note"—and I moved a little closer when there was no glance and stared in lieu of clearing my throat ("Ahem!") or otherwise intruding, but she went on talking to her friends, oblivious to me or pretending to be. I wasn't close enough to eavesdrop, but whatever she was saying, she said it theatrically, mugging a bit and gesticulating, and I began to wait theatrically; I paced and stopped to stare or thumb my copy of *Moby-Dick*, then I paced again and so on in a pantomime of waiting that pleaded for attention. Eventually one of her friends murmured a question about me, "Do you know this guy?" or "Do you have plans with him?" or something like that, and she shifted her gaze a hair in my direction and said, tersely, "No." Her flashing glance at the Actors Studio had been a study in duration compared to this one. Then she resumed chatting with her friends.

I gave up. She may or may not have gotten my card, but the situation was too awkward to continue in any case. I went to make a call on the pay phone in a corridor to the side of the lobby. I had wasted the evening by seeing the play again, but the night was still salvageable, and the purpose of the call was to get the night rolling. The phone was at the end of the corridor, and I headed back to the lobby after hanging up, and there at the other end of the corridor, alone and again walking toward me, was Elizabeth McGovern. She passed me again, eyes averted. Apparently she needed to use the phone, but here was my chance to speak to her, if I could summon a voice. My confidence had ebbed in the lobby.

"Did you get my Monet?" I managed to say; and she slowed and turned with a puzzled expression.

"Oh," she said, "yes. Thank you." She beamed as she said it, still moving toward the phone, and I reached for inspiration to stop her. I had a short reach. Essentially I repeated what I had written in the card—I was in town from L.A., and we shared friends and acquaintances, and I just wanted to say hello—and she half turned and said again, "Thank you," not beaming so much as smiling politely. Then, having gotten to the phone, she went to make her call. Her back was to me. I left the theater.

It was a mild night for New York in winter and a quiet night for New York in any season, or so it seemed, but I was numb to the point where sound and temperature barely registered. I walked a block from the Public to Astor Place, and as I was about to cross the street, the last few minutes caught up to me suddenly with the force and sensation of a blow to the head, and I steadied myself against the big black sculpture of a cube near the Astor Place subway station, rubbing my brow to relieve the pressure I felt there, or really—that is, unconsciously—I think I was trying to rub reality through my brow and into the part of my brain that was stunned to discover how deluded I'd been about this person, the part that didn't treat my crush on her as the joke I knew it was in the sensible part of me. I should have listened to Orrin when he warned that now wasn't a good time to meet her, but there would never have been a good time; I had seen nothing in her eyes when they met mine that day at the Actors Studio, and I had to embarrass—no, humiliate—myself to learn what instinct told me then, even though my attraction to her had since largely faded. Was I out of my mind? I must be, I thought while I walked in a daze around the cube sculpture, again and again, as if that would help to repattern my brain, and maybe it did help: I'm obsessive by nature, but I would never obsess again about her.

A FEW DAYS LATER I called Peter. He was often away overseeing a production of his work or serving as writer-in-residence at this or that regional theater, so we hadn't spoken in a couple of years, but he surprised me by answering his phone and I surprised him by announcing my move to L.A. I had called to leave a message about the move, but naturally, once we started talking, I recounted my encounter with Elizabeth McGovern, and he laughed gently here and there and said, when I had finished, "Well, you know how the Public is. It's sort of gothic-looking, and it's got those stairs by the phone, and she may have had *Phantom of the Opera* fantasies of you chasing her up and down the stairs."

"I never thought about that. I guess I thought my motives were transparent. I never thought she would find me threatening."

"Well, you are pretty cute. Not as cute as Rob Lowe, but cute."

In fact, since we lost touch, he had met Rob Lowe at a regional theater where Melissa Gilbert, Rob Lowe's on-off girlfriend, was doing a play. He spent the better part of a day with them, so he could technically claim to have had a date with Rob Lowe, though I gathered that personal contact had been almost as deadly to his celebrity crush as it had been to mine.

"He said he was trying to improve himself by reading more books," Peter told me. "I said, 'Oh, like what?' and I thought he was going to say, you know, *Leaves of Grass* or *The Brothers Karamazov*, but he said, 'Well, right now I'm reading a book about the Actors Studio.'"

That was the last time I spoke to Peter, who later had some success as a television writer. Orrin also had some success in television, co-starring on a crime show, and John, after we parted ways, became the manager of a multimedia phenomenon whose empire began in television. Elizabeth McGovern, meanwhile, moved to England, the genesis of the preppy look, where she married a producer-director, had two daughters, and worked predominately in television, enjoying a second wave of fame as Cora Crawley, Countess of Grantham, on *Downton Abbey*. Few remember the first wave, so that when I refer these days to Elizabeth McGovern, as I very seldom do, she's usually confused for Elizabeth Montgomery, the lead witch of *Bewitched*, and I'll say, "No, no, she's on *Downton Abbey*. She's the American, and Shirley MacLaine plays her mother." I can't say more because I never watched *Downton Abbey*, or *Game of Thrones* or *Breaking Bad* or any of the other television shows that obsessed most people I know. Nor, despite numerous attempts, have I read *Moby-Dick*, the story of a singular obsession that ends badly; but I was familiar with that story long before I bought the book, and I would give my farewell New York performance of it offstage, like always, at the Public Theater.

2015

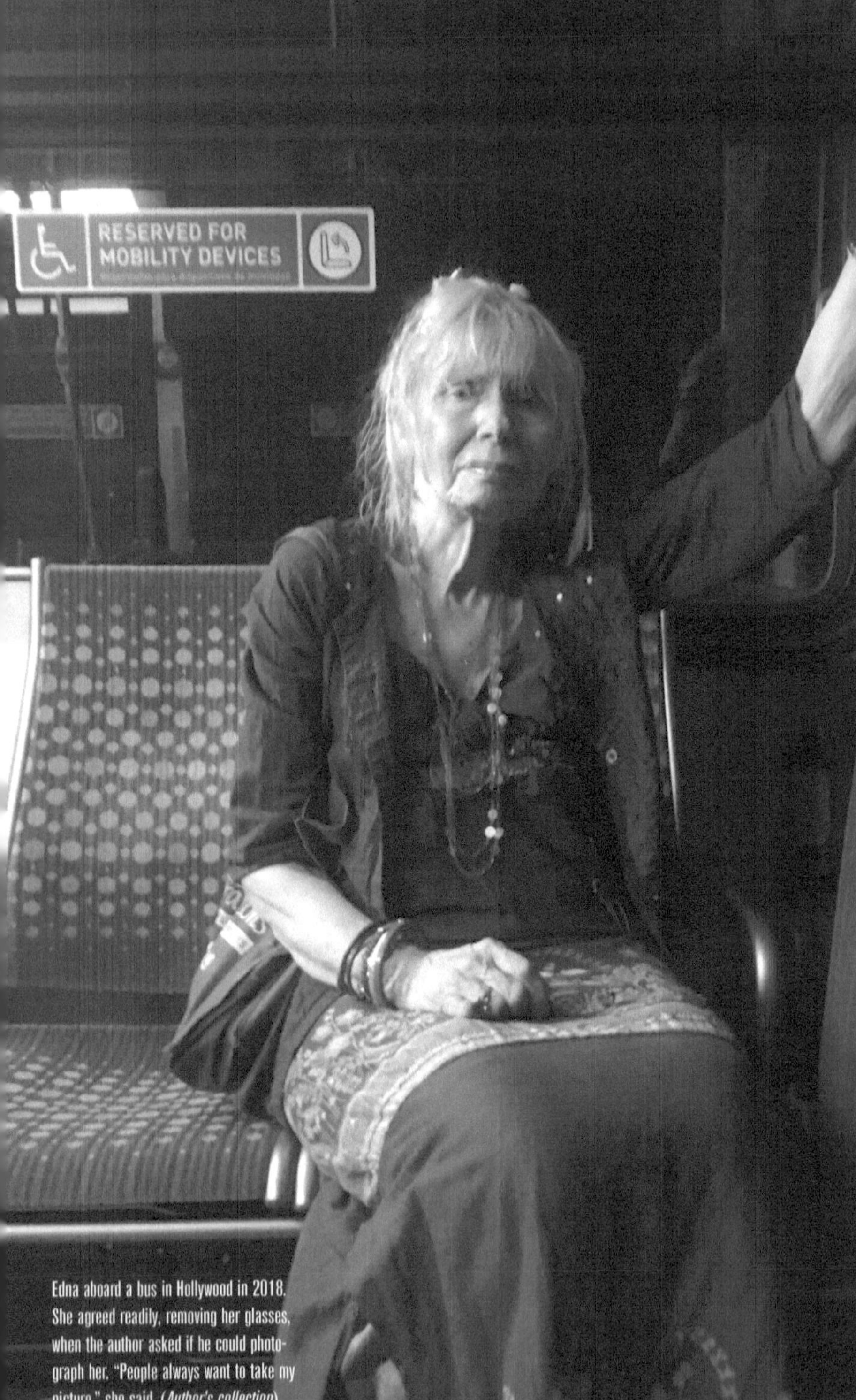

Edna aboard a bus in Hollywood in 2018. She agreed readily, removing her glasses, when the author asked if he could photograph her. "People always want to take my picture," she said. (*Author's collection*)

THE PURPLE LADY SENDS HER REGARDS

IT WAS TWO WEEKS before Halloween, and I was on a Metro bus headed toward Hollywood on Sunset Boulevard. Ahead I saw the ninety-year-old Vista Theater, which is just down the hill from the strip mall where Jerry's video store used to be, and this was the season when I particularly missed the store. Its owner, Jerry Neeley, claimed an inventory of 20,000 titles of every genre, but horror was his specialty, so that I would observe Halloween by renting movies that only he would insist on stocking: *The Astounding She-Monster*, *The Hideous Sun Demon*, *The Thing That Couldn't Die*. In his twenties Jerry had contributed articles to *Famous Monsters of Filmland* magazine, my preadolescent bible, and to rent a movie from him was to invite anecdotes like this one about *The Astounding She-Monster*: "You'll notice that the lead actress never turns her back to the camera. That's because she split the back of her costume open on the first day of shooting and they didn't have time to repair it." Jerry's knack for trivia was a magnet for regular customers, and it was shared by his wife, Mary, an animal lover who taped snapshots of customers' pets to the side of a filing cabinet behind the counter. She and Jerry could both be peevish, and the store was frankly homely, with its cinderblock walls and ramshackle racks, while its musty smell must have been off-putting to some; but there was no shortage of corporate alternatives that smelled vaguely of plastic and were staffed by cheerful teenagers who consulted computers when asked about offbeat titles and said, as expected, "Sorry, we don't carry that." Jerry's store wasn't computerized. Everything there was done by hand: the bookkeeping, the checkout slips, the signs that distinguished the Fellini section from the Fassbinder section, the Gable section from the Garbo section, and so on.

The bus passed the Vista and stopped at the corner of Sunset and Virgil, where it was boarded by "the purple lady," a seventyish platinum blonde, nearly six feet tall, famous locally for dressing exclusively in purple. I used to see her daily at Jerry's store, scrutinizing video boxes with a lorgnette—spectacles on a stick—or chatting with Jerry in a dizzy, fluty voice that turned the heads of customers who had somehow overlooked her remarkable appearance. She was like the missing link between human and bird of paradise, but my curiosity about her was trumped by a reflexive wariness of her eccentricity, so that I kept my distance at Jerry's and later, when I saw her occasionally in Hollywood, especially at Amoeba Music, the last of the great L.A. record stores. Jerry once told me her name, which I remembered as Edna, though I was sure I must be mistaken, since Edna suited her a little too well. I had forgotten everything else Jerry told me about her, save that she idolized a certain actor—was it Richard Burton? Stewart Granger? Kirk Douglas?—whose movies and memorabilia she collected, and I wondered if that had anything to do with my recent sightings of her at Amoeba, where DVDs are also sold.

She sat behind the bus driver, in a seat reserved for the handicapped, and stared straight ahead with a rapt yet vacant expression. As always, her hair was gathered in a high ponytail, like a white plume on a Victorian cavalry helmet, and of course she wore purple from neck to toe, with a purple Hello Kitty tote bag and pink-tinted, purple-framed glasses. A stop later, she relinquished her seat to a man in a wheelchair and alighted next to me. She didn't tacitly acknowledge me as people sometimes do when they find themselves brushing against strangers. She continued to stare vacantly ahead, while I oscillated between my usual wariness and curiosity.

"Excuse me," I said finally. "Didn't you used to go to Jerry's video store?"

She flinched. I had startled her. "Oh," she said in her dizzy voice, "yes, I used to go to Jerry's, but I couldn't walk up that hill no more. I have a heart condition."

"I'm sorry to hear that."

"Yes, and some kid ran into me on the street and hurt my wrist, but I can't afford a doctor." She seemed eager to relate her collision with the kid, but I couldn't make out if he had been walking or running or skating or biking, and that wasn't the point anyway. The point was her pain and penury.

"I don't know what I'd do if I lost my job," she trilled. "Or my apartment. My landlord tried to evict me."

"There's a lot of that going on. The same thing happened to me. Where do you live?"

"Behind the Vista."

"Right, you just said you used to walk up the hill to Jerry's. Well, that neighborhood has really gotten hot. All these Westside types are invading the east side now, and the rents are going through the roof. It's the same in Echo Park, where I live."

"My landlord said he needed his apartment for himself."

"It's called an owner occupancy, yeah. That's how landlords usually evict tenants in L.A. They claim they need your place for themselves, but you can beat them if you take them to court. You just have to establish that they're trying to get you out so they can jack up the rent."

But that was no longer a problem for the purple lady; her landlord had died and bequeathed the building to his sisters, who dropped the eviction and let Edna stay on at a reasonable rent. I had remembered her name correctly: it was Edna, she confirmed, though she appeared to welcome the exchange only when it concerned her financial and medical worries, responding to my questions as if trapped by a Jehovah's Witness on her doorstep. No, she wasn't a native of L.A., but she had lived here since the age of eight. Yes, she worked in Hollywood, as either a seamstress or designer—I couldn't quite tell—for a fashion company. Now I wondered if she made her own clothes, but I couldn't think of a way to ask without it coming off like "What's the deal with purple?" She worked constantly, she said, even at home, and didn't have time for a social life, even of the digital kind—she had no use for computers—but she did make time for watching movies, and Charlton Heston was one of her favorite actors. Others included Christopher Lee and Peter Cushing, who often played adversaries in British horror films of the fifties and sixties, but Heston was the favorite mentioned by Jerry.

"Well," I said, "no wonder you got along with Jerry. He could recite the complete résumés of Christopher Lee and Peter Cushing."

"What *happened* to Jerry? One day I walked up to the store and it wasn't there anymore."

"He closed it."

"Why?"

"Well, he'd been talking about it for a while. The neighborhood was changing, and he didn't like the new breed of customer he was getting, those self-important Westside types, and he wanted to retire and take it easy. That's what he *said*, you know, but I later heard the store was losing money. I mean, Netflix must have taken a bite out of business, but Jerry said he was going to keep it going for another year. Then the landlord raised the rent, and he decided not to wait."

"When was this?"

"The summer of 2007. It happened really quickly. The landlord raised the rent toward the end of August, and the store closed right after Labor Day. I was devastated. That store gave me a place to go, you know? I could be sitting around, feeling lonely, and I'd think, Oh, hey, I'll just go to Jerry's and hang around and talk to him or Mary or John Sullivan. Do you remember John? He used to work there, and he knew everything about westerns. I thought he and Jerry were related when I first started going there. You know, they were both in their forties, and John had a mustache and Jerry had a beard, and sometimes John wore a cowboy hat and Jerry *always* wore that Greek fisherman's cap. He was in the hospital the first time I ever saw him without it. He had all kinds of health problems with his diabetes, you know. Did you ever notice his fingernails? He had that fungus thing you get with diabetes, where the fingernails are yellow and kind of scaly, the poor guy."

Edna had avoided my eye before the subject turned to Jerry. Now she faced me and asked if I had stayed in touch with Jerry after the store closed. Yes, I told her. He and Mary lived just up the street from the store, and whenever I was in the neighborhood, I would drop by to watch movies or play Trivial Pursuit. They were both formidable players, naturally, and unbeatable when they broke out the Silver Screen edition of the game.

"But how did they support themselves?"

"Well, at first they sold memorabilia. Jerry had been collecting that stuff since he was a kid, posters and props and all that, and he used to sell it at the store—you used to buy from him, didn't you?—and then they started selling it online. But they ran into some kind of problem with eBay, so Mary started a dog-walking business, and Jerry would help out with that. I mean, he couldn't *walk* the dogs, because his diabetes had gotten so bad he could barely walk at all, but Mary would also sit for dogs when their owners were out of town, and she would be at one place and Jerry would be at another. It was the perfect job for Mary. You remember how she used to post photos of pets at the store. Yeah, she didn't miss the store at all. Neither one of them did. They ran it for twenty years."

"Is she still walking dogs?"

"I assume she is. I haven't talked to her in a year and a half. The last time I called, they didn't call back, and Mary used to keep in touch by e-mail and that stopped, so I thought she and Jerry were mad at me for some reason. Then Jerry died—"

"When?"

"Six weeks ago. It was the weirdest thing. I was having lunch with these friends of mine, a married couple, and we were talking about the Manson murders, and Mary knew everything about that case. And I mentioned that, and I was telling my friends about the store—they just moved to L.A. a couple of years ago, so they never went—and I said, 'Well, the murders happened in a house right up the street from the store, and the house is still there; want to see it?' So we got in the car and we drove by the store—it's now a Thai massage parlor—and I said, 'Oh, hey, that's where Jerry's used to be. Oh, and see that building there? That's where Jerry lives—if he's still alive.' Because, you know, his diabetes had gotten really bad, like I said. He had trouble walking, he was blind in one eye, and he was sixty-seven and he always said he didn't think he'd live to see seventy. Anyway, I pointed out the Manson house and my friends dropped me off at my place, and an hour later I got a text message saying Jerry was dead. I mean, I hadn't been up that street in *months*, and then to say what I did and an hour later—it was really spooky."

I had gotten the text message from a friend who had heard the news from Jerry's brother. "It was a heart attack, apparently," I told Edna. "Mary went out to walk a dog, or something, and when she came back, she found Jerry dead. I sent her a card and she wrote me a note to thank me, but she wasn't up to talking, which is understandable. They'd been together since 1978. But she did send me a picture of his urn. Well, technically, it's not an urn. She put his ashes in a King Kong bank—you know, like a piggy bank? *King Kong* was his favorite movie."

"Was there a service?"

"He didn't want one, but I think one of her clients held some kind of service for him. You know, when the store closed, I wanted to write something about it for the *LA Weekly*, but he said no, he wanted the store to close quietly. I don't think he realized how much it meant to people. I wasn't the only one. People still talk about that place, the ones who haven't been forced out of the neighborhood. It's kind of a local legend."

"Like you," I almost added. Edna's oddness had always, in my mind, symbolized the oddness of the store itself, even if I had nothing to do with her there, and talking to her now was therapeutic, though she seemed to have run out of questions, again staring straight ahead. I took her withdrawal for shock at learning of Jerry's death, and I left her in peace until the bus approached Sunset and Ivar, the site of Amoeba Music, and Edna pressed the stop button and moved her purple tote bag from her lap to her shoulder.

"Amoeba," I said. "I'm always going to Amoeba. Haven't I seen you there?"

"That's where I buy movies," she nodded absently. "Nobody rents anymore." Then she stood and, just before she stepped to the front of the bus, she turned in my direction and said, "Say hello to Jerry for me. I think about him a lot."

Say hello to Jerry? Did she foresee me joining him soon? But she had probably already forgotten what I told her about him, and now she stood by the driver as she waited for him to pull up to the curb, apprising him of her idée fixe: "This kid on the street ran into me and hurt my wrist." The driver ignored her, and so did nearby passengers, as if the world were overpopulated with platinum-blonde amazons dressed entirely in purple. Maybe she would find solace at Amoeba, which I imagined was struggling now that so many people applauded the death of physical media; and when Amoeba became another casualty of progress, Edna and all the other oddballs, including me, would effectively be rendered homeless.

2015

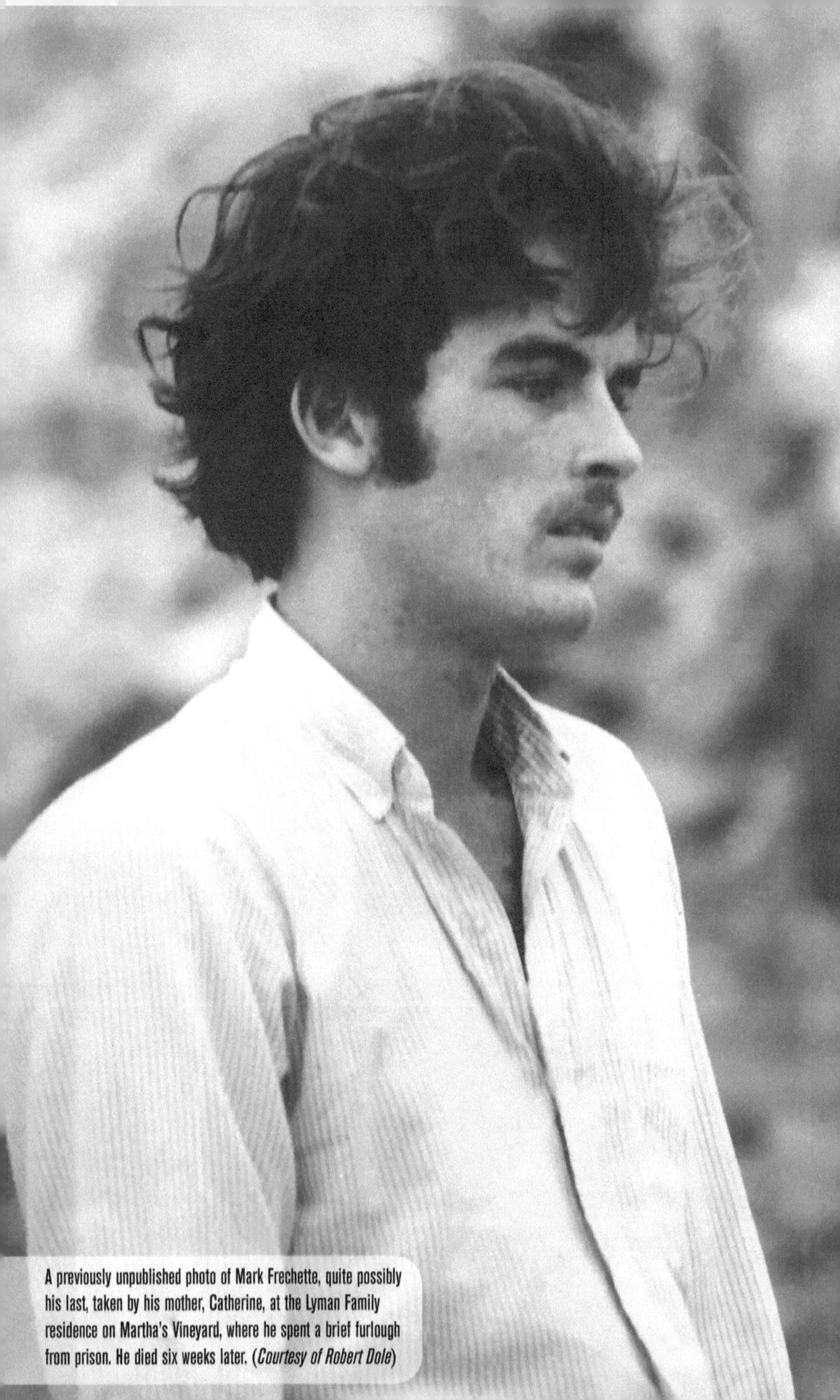

A previously unpublished photo of Mark Frechette, quite possibly his last, taken by his mother, Catherine, at the Lyman Family residence on Martha's Vineyard, where he spent a brief furlough from prison. He died six weeks later. (*Courtesy of Robert Dole*)

PLUTO IN THE TWELFTH HOUSE

MARK FRECHETTE, MOVIE ACTOR and bank robber, believed in astrology. His interest in it started before he joined an astrology-obsessed commune, based in the Fort Hill district of Boston, that called itself the Fort Hill Community and eventually answered to "the Lyman Family." Like all cults, it denied being a cult, despite being led by a despot who proclaimed himself the Second Coming and was tagged the "East Coast Charles Manson" by *Rolling Stone* magazine in a 60,000-word exposé that appalled his apostles. Here's how they characterized themselves in a pamphlet published in 1973, the same year Mark Frechette botched a bank heist and feathered a reputation already tarred by *Rolling Stone*: "We are a group of people between the ages of 16 and 30 who have been experimenting with communal living for seven years now and have come up with some amazing results which we would like to share with you." The pamphlet advertised the courses they offered to the heathen, including two in astrology: "By studying your own chart, you will learn to make astrology work for you in your relationships with other people by a greater understanding of them, an understanding to which there are no limits." Mark Frechette would certainly have studied his own chart, but whatever understanding he gained from it, he was captured and died cryptically in prison. His FBI file includes a photocopy of the Lyman Family pamphlet.

"People who dismiss astrology do so out of ignorance or rationalism," Camille Paglia wrote in a rare defense of astrology by a teacher with an Ivy League doctorate. "Rationalists have their place, but their limited assumptions and methods must be kept out of the arts. Interpretation of poem, dream, or person requires intuition and divination, not science." Recalling this passage from *Sexual Personae*, it occurred to me that an astrological interpretation of Mark Frechette might shed light on his view of himself, providing a kind of inside approach; otherwise any attempted portrait would draw only from the usual magazine and newspaper accounts and the smattering of more elusive material I had managed to collect: the FBI file; a DVD of a short documentary about Mark; his correspondence with his friend and early mentor, Robert Dole, who was interviewed in the documentary and happy to speak to me, unlike most other former intimates and associates. I never reached out to the Lyman Family, which, remarkably, was still intact. They, least of all, would welcome the subject of Mark Frechette, I imagined.

My knowledge of astrology was confined, almost, to the twelve signs of the zodiac, but I did know that specifics of time and place are essential to a comprehensive natal chart. The Internet disgorged the location of Mark's birth—St. Margaret's Hospital in Boston—but not the moment he was born on December 4, 1947. For that I would need a birth certificate, and for days I phoned the Massachusetts Bureau of Vital Statistics, unable to get through. Online efforts were also fruitless. Now I had an excuse to do something I had long wanted to do as a fan of film noir: hire a private investigator. I called one at random from an online list of PIs in the Boston area and asked about a rate. "I'll give you three hours for three hundred dollars," he said in the jaded tone of noir cliché. The casting was too perfect for me to shop for a cheaper rate, and a few days later he called to say, with a surprising hint of boyish excitement, that he was holding the birth certificate. Mark had been born at 10:25 p.m.

Now to find a professional astrologer. A friend suggested Antero Alli, originally from Finland and now living in Berkeley. Like the detective in Boston, he was perfect casting, an author and filmmaker who had directed his own plays when Sam Shepard was active in the same theater circles, and Shepard wrote the early drafts of *Zabriskie Point*, Mark's most notable film. I preferred a "blind" reading of his chart, unbiased by his fame or infamy, however faded; but Antero's code of ethics precluded readings of third parties. Nothing ventured, nothing gained: I messaged him the name of the third party in question. "Interesting person," he messaged back. "Like Morrison, Joplin, Hendrix, Cobain, & other anonymous great ones, Mark died at the age of 27—a year before his Saturn Return. There's an entire mythos around this passage. OK, Duke. If you can pay my regular fee, I will agree to interpret his chart for you and send it to you on a CD."

That was before I decided to attend a film-noir festival in San Francisco. I messaged Antero to ask if we could meet in person and, if so, how to get from San Francisco to his place. It was as simple as taking a BART train, he answered; and two weeks later I walked out of a BART station in downtown Berkeley and up Shattuck Avenue, per Antero's directions, passing a sign that announced Hearst Avenue and reminded me of the case that informed my earliest impressions of Berkeley: the 1974 kidnapping of newspaper heiress Patricia Hearst by the Symbionese Liberation Army, or SLA, a small cadre of Maoist urban guerrillas, and Patricia Hearst's subsequent reemergence as "Tania," a gun-brandishing, rhetoric-spouting, bank-robbing compañera of the SLA. No one ever seemed to connect the Hearst case and the Frechette case thematically, as I did. The SLA was a late-blooming product of the revolutionary sixties, and it fully cohered in Berkeley at the very moment that Mark determined to rob a bank in Boston as "a personal revolutionary act," with a secret beneficiary.

Antero's A-frame house was on Rose Street, and I followed him upstairs to his consultation room, where he handed me a printout of Mark's chart. I had brought along a cassette recorder, an analog backup should something go wrong, and during the ninety-minute session he paused just once, to turn the cassette over at the forty-five-minute mark, and a long time later I edited the transcript for brevity and clarity.

> ***Each chart to me*** *is a kind of fingerprint, quite distinct, quite unique, and one of the key distinctions of this chart is that he's got Mars conjunct ascendant tightly in Virgo, and Mars, of all the symbols in the chart, really represents the force of action, doing; it's the embodiment of a strong masculine force. However, what's really interesting is that because it's in Virgo—with the confluence of Mars in Virgo, and Saturn and Pluto both in the twelfth house—we have here a character that I will call a misanthropic critic of society. There's a mysticism here. A chart is divided into twelve areas, sort of like pieces of a pie, and each of these areas the language of astrology refers to as houses, which represent very specific areas of human experience and activity, and the twelfth house is the one most directly linking to solitude or withdrawal. It's traditionally associated with prisons, with hospitals, any kind of experience that places the individual apart from society. Pluto represents where and how a person comes into some sense of their own power, and Pluto in the twelfth house is really defined as power derived directly from personal experience, communion with the divine, some kind of merging with higher power; and often times when Saturn is in the twelfth house it represents an absent father or a disappearing father or a father that was there physically but not emotionally.*

MARK'S FATHER managed the cafeteria at the Electrolux factory in Greenwich, Connecticut, long one of the wealthiest towns per capita in the U.S. and, in my thankfully brief experience of it, also one of the snobbiest. Most employees at the factory, best known for producing vacuum cleaners, commuted to work, and so it was with Mark's father; the Frechettes lived in nearby Stamford before they moved a few miles north to Fairfield when Mark was fourteen. His mother was Irish Catholic, his father Franco-American. Both parents were born and raised in Massachusetts. Given all this, Mark would seem to have been drawn to Jack Kerouac, a literary sensation of the day, lionized by youth, and a working-class, Catholic, Franco-American originally from Massachusetts; but Robert Dole can't remember Mark ever mentioning Kerouac. "He enjoyed reading," Robert wrote me, "but he didn't really have much of a literary education." Still, he was a straight-A student until he started high school, approximately.

Around that same time, a pivotal figure entered his life. Despite their move to Fairfield, the Frechettes remained parishioners of the Church of St. Cecilia in Stamford, where Father Laurence Brett had become assistant pastor, and Larry, as Father Brett preferred to be called, was a polyglot and world traveler, then around twenty-five, who drove one of the original muscle cars, a 1962 Pontiac Tempest, and dazzled all who met him with his charm and erudition. As a "cool" priest unlike any they had met before, he was especially popular among boys in their early to mid-teens, and he organized an elite group among them to discuss liturgical reform within the Church. Mark was one of them. Their name, Brett's Mavericks, was derived from a television program, and Father Brett smoked and cursed in their company, and took them on road trips, allowing them to drive his red Tempest, whether they did or didn't have learners' permits. Manhattan was a frequent destination. Brett accompanied the boys to grindhouse theaters in Times Square and even helped them to hire hookers, some of them said decades later.

By now you've surely guessed where this is headed, but priests were trusted, even revered, figures in the early sixties, and the parents of the Mavericks couldn't conceive that their sons were being molested by Brett, whose seduction formula had a blasphemous twist: after the standard grooming and isolation, he would explain fellatio as another way of receiving Holy Communion. The Mavericks had not been singled out for their superior minds, as Brett had led them to believe, but for their desirability, and Mark was "likely to his own regret, an extraordinarily good-looking boy," or so the *Boston Phoenix* would remark postmortem with his acting career in mind, not the Father Brett business. Mark never spoke publicly of Brett, and there's some question as to what happened between them. Robert Dole was under the impression that Brett propositioned Mark, no more; but according to a *Hartford Courant* story published in 2002, "Frechette told a friend that Brett performed oral sex on him after hearing his confession." His "reaction was extreme," the *Courant* continued. "Within months of his...fateful encounter with the priest...[he] dropped out of school, started burglarizing homes and, eventually, landed in the state-run mental hospital." Here's a more detailed version of the story, from my correspondence with Robert Dole:

> Mark himself told me he had run away from home, went to Greenwich Village, came home for Christmas, got in a fight with his father, and then his parents had him taken off to the Hartford Institute for Life, a mental hospital from which he managed to escape after six months of incarceration by making love with an Afro-American attendant in an elevator and receiving her keys to the hospital as a recompense. He then came to Cambridge and that was when we met. I once spoke to his father on the phone and he told me that he had nothing good to say about his son. His mother, however, was a very sweet lady, who suffered greatly from Mark's misfortunes.

He got in a fight with his father. His father had nothing good to say about him. An absent father or a disappearing father or a father that was there physically but not emotionally. Was that the case before Father Brett? It would certainly help to explain Mark's investment in him, which must have been enormous, judging by the meltdown that followed. He seems to have lost not just a mentor—a surrogate father—but his faith in institutions: the Church, formal education, the nuclear family, the entire politico-economic system, which as he may have seen it—and I don't believe he would have been wrong—was rigged by and for the lords of Greenwich and beyond. He did not lose faith in faith itself, however, or in mentorship.

The other Mavericks, each in his way, suffered quietly for years before admitting, in some cases to themselves, what had happened to them; but Mark told his parents and denounced Brett in a meeting with the vice chancellor of the Diocese of Bridgeport. Brett was a priest of the diocese, and the vice chancellor made a curious note in a memo about Mark: "He really has his astrology down!!!" Why did the subject arise? The Church frowns upon astrology as fatalism, so Mark could have been implying his defection by talking of it. He had just turned seventeen, and after he was removed to a mental hospital a year later—three "thugs" ambushed Mark in his bedroom, according to Robert Dole, and forced him into a van—his parents petitioned the diocese to contribute to the cost of his care and were told there was no proof of any wrongdoing on Brett's part.

In fact, there was proof, as the diocese knew very well. A few months before Mark's meeting with the vice chancellor, Brett was reassigned to

Sacred Heart University in Fairfield, and a student there had complained of being of bitten on the penis by his chaplain—Brett—in what today would be classified as a sexual assault and handled by police. In 1964, however, it was handled by the diocese, and Brett was sent to a treatment center in New Mexico, where he claimed to have been cured and, assigned to local schools and parishes, he molested more boys. He did the same in the Sacramento area and again in Baltimore, all while remaining technically a priest of the Diocese of Bridgeport. Finally, in response to a lawsuit filed by one of the Mavericks in 1993, the diocese effectively defrocked Brett, who disappeared and was found nine years later by the *Hartford Courant*, "living a secretive but comfortable life on the tropical island of St. Maarten in the Caribbean." He refused to speak to the *Courant*, of course, but his neighbors said that "young men and teenagers were frequent visitors" and that Brett "identified himself to acquaintances on the island as a writer, a businessman or, at times, a CIA agent."

For protecting Brett, the Diocese of Bridgeport was ordered to pay a million dollars to the former Maverick whose lawsuit may have prompted other victims to come forward. Criminal charges were filed and, now being sought by the FBI, Brett fled St. Maarten for Martinique, where, still at large and evidently drunk, he fell down a flight of stairs and died of a head injury on Christmas Day 2010. The date of his death can be viewed as ironic happenstance or as meaningful in a cosmic scheme that astrology purports to delineate; or maybe it's simply poetic that, for instance, Mark's father died days before the first anniversary of Mark's death, as if to avoid it, and that Mark's mother died days after the twenty-first anniversary, as if to absorb it. They never saw any restitution from the Diocese of Bridgeport.

***I haven't talked** about his Sun sign. His Sun is in Sagittarius, but it's conjunct Jupiter, so there's kind of a double emphasis in what we'll call the character of the seeker. This is who he was deep down. People who really got to know him found out this guy's a real seeker, and that seeker energy would have been accompanied by what I would call a feral spirit of recklessness, okay, someone who would pretty much do anything just to get at the truth of something, who would put the truth first, and in doing that, there's a natural inclination to just open yourself up to whatever, to more opportunities and situations, and therein lies serendipity or coincidence or synchronicity. This is, in part, amplified by this other element with Pluto in the twelfth house. There's a channeling element here. This guy had kind of a medium-mystic quality about him, where there was some-*

thing in him that acted as a screen for the projection of the zeitgeist of the time.

AFTER HE ESCAPED from the mental hospital, Mark would have, in a two-year period almost exactly, three momentous encounters with strangers who, in each case, approached him on the street. The first was Robert Dole, an undergrad at Harvard with troubles of his own. They had started at prep school, when he confessed his homosexuality to his roommate. The roommate initiated sex. It was a gratifying experience for both of them, Robert thought, but the following day, apparently distraught, the roommate confided in the campus physician and requested a new roommate. Robert was summoned to the dean's office and told that he would have to keep a weekly appointment with a psychiatrist in order to remain at school. The psychiatrist practiced what's now called conversion therapy, and Robert realized the failure of it quickly. He grew more and more depressed, consoling himself by listening to Joan Baez records, and praying as he hadn't prayed since he realized at fourteen that he was gay and therefore persona non grata to God. His prayers now were answered in the form of beatific visions that led to a self-diagnosis of schizophrenia, and later, at Harvard, his behavior so alarmed others that he was escorted to McLean Hospital by three interventionists, much as Mark was escorted to the Hartford Institute of Life by a team of three. Robert spent fifteen months as a psychiatric inpatient, and because he decided early on that homosexuality wasn't the cause of his condition, it was actually the cure, he refused to discuss it with any psychiatrist. He also had a vision in which God promised him the ideal lover of fantasies that began before Robert grasped their implications. In fact, this person was the new Messiah, God told Robert, who would recognize him at once by his superlative good looks.

Need I say it? A week or so after he was discharged from the hospital, as he was leaving a class at Harvard in June or July of 1966, Robert set eyes on Mark and "knew immediately that he was the true Messiah," to quote one of Robert's two books that cover much of the same territory with minor variations—hence the hedging about the month. Mark had already run away to Greenwich Village so, figuring the police might search for him there, he had found his way to Cambridge and picked up a job as a sandwich-board man, advertising a bookstore in Harvard Square. That's where Robert saw him, and he was there again, the Messiah as walking billboard, when Robert returned to Harvard Square the following day. Now Robert shared his find with another former inpatient at McLean, the friend he calls Maria Maddalena in his second book, and she accompanied him on his pilgrimage to Harvard Square the next day. He hadn't described Mark to her. He wanted to see if she could spot him in the crowd. She did so without hesitation. Then, taking Robert by the hand, she crossed the street and began to talk to Mark. It was trivial talk, a ploy for Robert to meet Mark, and when Robert proved tongue-tied, Maria Maddalena said, "Young man, my friend here would like to tell you that he finds you an aesthetically pleasing ornament to Harvard Square." There is never any variation on that remark in Robert's writing or his conversation. Maria Maddalena went on to provide Mark with Robert's address, inviting him to stop by after he was done with work that night. Robert, embarrassed, was sure he would never turn up.

But he did turn up. They traded life stories and bonded as recent mental patients. They were similarly angry with just cause and then some, but Mark was a high-school dropout with sensibility and limited learning to support it, while Robert was an academic whiz kid who had started Harvard as an advanced-placement sophomore and had read, by age twenty on his own, a long list of authors from Sartre to Proust to Bertrand Russell to James Baldwin. He was especially interested in the German-born theologian Paul Tillich and, like Mark, in the subject of religion overall. Like Father Brett, he was a polyglot, but, unlike Brett, he was readily forthcoming about his homosexuality. Mark made good on God's promise, though as Robert clarifies in his first book:

> Mark was profoundly heterosexual and he was probably unable to make love with any other man than me... Whenever we made love, he made it known that it was for my pleasure. His only pleasure consisted in giving me pleasure. He loved me in a way that no homosexual could. But Mark also needed my love. After the humiliations and horrors that he had known in the mental hospital, my worshiping him came as a balm. He needed a real friend to whom he could say anything. He also needed a crash pad.

I believe there's an additional reason that Mark became Robert's lover: he was correcting his experience with Father Brett by sleeping with a man who was Brett's intellectual equal and his moral superior by leagues. Meanwhile, if Brett, with his talk of liturgical reform, was something of a rebel who started Mark on the same path, Robert was the next step in that way. "We detested bourgeois American society," he writes, "and its materialism, its war in Vietnam, its racism, its sheer stupidity." Mark was "the most idealistic person I have ever known," "a true prophet who knows that his country is not what God wants it to be," yet Robert was the prophet's tutor, contextualizing and supplementing his intuitions. In a sense, they were both students at Harvard, though only one of them was enrolled there.

It was never an exclusive relationship. Mark had a girlfriend, Betsy, in Fairfield, and at some point that autumn she told him she was pregnant. His FBI file mentions an arrest for breaking and entering and aggravated assault in Fairfield in September 1966, so possibly this had to do with a freakout on Mark's part. Nevertheless, two days after Christmas and three weeks after his nineteenth birthday, Mark married Betsy in a civil ceremony, and they set up house near Robert, who was always ready to accommodate Mark when he and Betsy quarreled. They quarreled often, but she didn't insist on monogamy. There are indications that, with her blessing, Mark slept with other women, and she accepted, Robert says, that he and Mark were lovers. I was unable to speak to Betsy, but I would guess that, like most teenage newlyweds, she and Mark fought about chores and money, particularly once their son was born. Mark worked a series of odd jobs, selling pot on the side, and his FBI file also mentions an arrest for possession of pot in February 1968, which may have precipitated his split with Betsy. They would reconcile long enough to conceive a second son, and in the meantime Mark learned of the Fort Hill commune through the *Avatar*, the underground newspaper it published and hawked on the streets, though Mark's first copy was a gift. Here's the story as recounted by a communard in a later edition of the *Avatar*, with punctuation and emphasis intact: "See, one of the lovely ladies on the hill was very attracted to him and picked him up on the street. She said 'WOW, did you see that guy that walked by?' And she said 'Hey kid, do you want an *Avatar*?' And he says 'Yeah.' Two days later he moved up to the hill, right, with his kid on his back... She thought he was *be-au-ti-ful*!"

In fact, Mark did not move "up to the hill" two days later. By his own account, he continued to read the *Avatar* for "several months" before the move, and what surely struck him right away was its preoccupation with astrology. There was a regular column on the subject, articles about it, and the Sun signs of editors and contributors appeared alongside their names on the masthead. The most important contributor was Melvin Lyman, a self-taught banjo and harmonica player who had drifted to the Boston area when it was winding down as the folk-music mecca that produced Joan Baez. He was self-taught in almost every way, save the degree in computer programming he had picked up at a night school in San Francisco. He made films. He exalted himself in writing, shelling the reader with capitalized word grenades: "I traveled a lot, I preached for years all over this country until I FOUND my people, the few who could UNDERSTAND me..." Kay Boyle, the Lost Generation novelist and mother of two children who were among "the few who could UNDERSTAND" Lyman, thought him "very insignificant looking and very weak looking," and she's borne out by photographs, though in one taken by Diane Arbus, we observe the weird gleam that must have electrified the thirty or so people who, around the time Mark met Robert, followed Lyman to Fort Hill, then a slum, and, pooling their resources, bought or rented seven dilapidated Victorian houses and began to restore them as self-taught carpenters. They wouldn't be known as the Lyman Family until the Manson Family became infamous on the very eve of the seventies, and Lyman's commune, like Manson's near Los Angeles, was a utopian alternative to establishment America with a musical motive besides: Lyman and Manson both had bands composed of Family members. Both grew more tyrannical as they tested their disciples for loyalty and realized the hold they had on them; both had hodgepodge philosophies slopped together from crackpot hunches and spotty schooling; and both sought to familiarize their followers with "reality," as if either man dwelled in reality, but that wasn't required of them, since they were both Christ incarnate. In the *Avatar*, Lyman wrote of his mission as the new Messiah: "No turnin water to wine and raisin the dead this trip, just gonna tell it like it is." If Mark never read Jack Kerouac, it's clear that Lyman had read him and adopted the worst of Kerouac's "first thought, best thought" prose style.

To Robert, of course, Mark was the Messiah. He "played such an essential role in bringing me to a life of sanity," Robert wrote to me. His theory is that "Mel Lyman simply replaced me as Mark's guru." A void had to be filled. Mark "wanted to have a guru in his life," and Robert decided to start a new life abroad. He would leave the U.S. permanently as soon as he graduated from Harvard, he announced to Mark, who raged at him "for the only time in our relationship... He said, 'America needs you. You will spend your life like a tourist, living out of a suitcase.'" But Robert feared a relapse if he stayed in America, and with Betsy gone already, ostensibly for good, Mark moved to Fort Hill, where he watched the communards from a distance. By now there were around fifty of them, and as Mark would say later in the *Avatar*, he was struck by their "vitality," and "even though I didn't know them, just even their physical presence on the top of this hill helped me through an awful lot of changes." He longed "to contribute something to what was going on up here," but he didn't know what that could be, since "they had enough people with hammers in their hands."

Serendipity would supply a solution. One evening in June 1968, a few weeks after Mark moved to Fort Hill and a week after Robert flew to London, never to live again in the U.S., as promised, Mark was waiting at a bus stop in Cambridge, while, next to him, a sailor argued loudly with a lady friend. A third-floor tenant of a nearby apartment building, angered by the noise, hurled a potted geranium at the sailor. "This was real slapstick," Mark would later tell a journalist, "and I started to laugh, but when the sailor looked over at me for laughing at him, I felt bad about it and started yelling at the guy in the window." He specifically yelled "Motherfucker!" The tenant replied in kind, and Mark "tried to open the front door and go up after him," and just then a man walked up and said, "Hey, kid, how old are you?" "Twenty," Mark snarled. "Follow me," the man said without identifying himself. He worked in public relations in Boston, Mark learned later, and for some reason—was it the "seeker" in Mark?—he followed the man a few blocks to a waiting limousine and stood while the man shouted to someone inside it, "I found one. He's twenty and he hates." Then "a groovy-looking blond chick" emerged from the limo to say that she was scouting talent for a movie. Her name was Sally Dennison, and she was an assistant to the Italian director Michelangelo Antonioni, who was prepping his first—and, as it turned out, only—American production. Mark had never heard of Antonioni. Even so, in an Aquarian-age twist on golden-age Hollywood legend, the hat-check girl or cabana boy in the right place at the right time, Mark had just been discovered.

***This is an extremely** private person. However, there are other indications in the chart where he's, let's say, destined for public exposure, and that would be the North Node conjunct, the very top of the chart, which has to do with the marketplace and profession. And North Node—that little loop up there, every chart has one—is going to give some indication of where an individual tends to be pulled forward. We're called to that area, and here it is, he's called to the public, he's called to make an impact, okay, but it's also the most challenging area of any chart. So if you want to find the area that comes easiest for a person, like their comfort zone, you look to the South Node, the bottom of the chart, and with him, he's totally safe in the realm of his mind. To come out and expose himself up there, okay, that's like the front lines of battle. It's really tough, and he can do it, but he needs to come back to regroup, and then he can go out a little bit. The combination of the forces in the twelfth house also represents a very strong inclination throughout life of retreat and* *withdrawal, over and over again. Wherever Pluto is in the chart, it represents a place where you power up, okay; and typically, people who are born with Saturn in the twelfth house have this overriding sensitivity, almost like a crab without its shell. So, throughout his life, he would be constantly searching for some kind of sanctuary, some place where he can find psychic protection. And often times when this happens, people will make a home either in a wilderness region or some kind of commune that is defined by principles and visions that are set apart from society.*

AROUND THE TIME Mark married Betsy, *Blow-Up*, Antonioni's film about Swinging London, was released in the U.S. Antonioni was already a hallowed name on the arthouse circuit, but *Blow-Up* was an international breakout hit with special appeal to college students, so possibly Mark had passed a theater in Cambridge with a long line of students waiting to see it or heard someone at Harvard reference it. He would later watch a number of Antonioni films and say in an interview with Roger Ebert, "Nothing happens, man; it's just a lot of people going nowhere." He didn't miss the point; he nailed it. Antonioni was the auteur of alienation, a master of composition whose frames were filled with victims of the automated modern world, characters who yearned to connect but couldn't and often dragged themselves through desultory affairs set against desolate landscapes. *Blow-Up* was a kaleidoscopic exception that captured the spirit of sixties youth culture, even though its director was in his fifties. It was notorious at the time for a scene with full-frontal nudity. In Hollywood, where the hoary Hays Code was still in effect, nudity was prohibited.

Blow-Up was distributed, not financed, by MGM, which, like all major Hollywood studios, was struggling with the decline in movie attendance due to television. Exploitation filmmakers might have the right idea, they decided: leave television to families and target youth with sex, blood, and salty language. *Blow-Up* opened with modest expectations and without code approval, the beginning of the end of the code, and MGM was thunderstruck that an art film directed by an inscrutable European could take in so much money. Who was this wizard, this youth whisperer? Let's get him over here to make an American *Blow-Up*. He could do whatever he wanted at MGM's expense, and Antonioni embarked on a tour of the country, chasing inspiration. He found it in Death Valley at Zabriskie Point, just outside the Nevada border in California. A sign at Zabriskie Point encapsulated its origins: "This is an area of ancient lake beds deposited five to ten million years ago. These beds have been tilted and pushed upward by earth forces, and eroded by wind and water." Five to ten million years! Nature had been working that long to sculpt the perfect location for Michelangelo Antonioni. He merged it with a recent newspaper story about a young man who stole a light aircraft in Arizona and, when he went to return it, was shot and killed by authorities. Antonioni added a girl to the story. She and the boy would somehow converge here, a kind of contemporary Adam and Eve in a fossilized Garden of Eden.

Antonioni spoke fluent English but not the American vernacular. For that he would need an American writer, and he preferred someone young, a Hollywood outsider like himself. He read novels and plays by young Americans during his travels, and while staying in New York, he tracked down Sam Shepard, the author of a one-act play, *Icarus's Mother*, produced in Greenwich Village at Caffe Cino, which was to theater in the sixties what CBGB would be to rock & roll in the seventies. There was an offstage airplane in *Icarus's Mother*, and Antonioni "figured that since he had an airplane in his movie we had something in common," Shepard remembered. Antonioni headed back to Rome, awaiting Shepard's arrival to collaborate on the screenplay. They weren't very compatible. Most Italian intellectuals of the day were Marxist to one degree or another, and so it was with Antonioni, who was enamored of youthful radicalism and titillated by the widespread sense of imminent revolution. For Shepard, then twenty-four, it was sufficient to be part of a revolutionary theater movement. Ideology wasn't his métier, and he found the sixties "terrifying": "It felt like everything was going to get blown up sky-high. It didn't feel like flower power. It felt like Armageddon."

Shepard gave the screenplay an anticapitalist subplot about real-estate development in the desert, but Antonioni, he said, wanted "a lot of Marxist jargon and Black Panther speeches. I couldn't do it." He was replaced by Fred Gardner, a Marxist journalist and antiwar activist, and the airplane thief became a student radical suspected of gunning down a cop. Three other writers were credited for the script, including Antonioni, but there was never really a final draft of it; the film would be semi-improvised as Antonioni shot footage of actual campus protests and staged an encounter session between Kathleen Cleaver, a prominent member of the Black Panther Party, and fledgling revolutionaries. He decided against casting professional actors as his two main characters. The people he chose would *be* the characters; if the boy was named Steve in life, that would be his name in the film. He didn't know what he wanted exactly; he would know it when he saw it, and he saw it relatively quickly in the case of the girl. A colleague showed him *Revolution*, a documentary about the Haight-Ashbury hippie scene, and there was a dance troupe in it, a naked dance troupe performing in a psychedelic light show, and Antonioni was impressed by one of the dancers. "She was so beautiful, she'd knock you right off your feet," Mark would say later in *Rolling Stone*. "I guess I was nailed to the floor when I first saw her, otherwise I would've been blown over." She was a freshman at the University of California at Berkeley, where she was making a pot in the ceramics department when she was called to the phone and told that Antonioni had her in mind for the lead in his new film. Unlike Mark, she had heard of Antonioni. Her name was Daria Halprin and, within days of the call, she was flown to Los Angeles for a screen test, and the girl of *Zabriskie Point* was "Daria."

But finding her male counterpart was a problem. Production was delayed for weeks while Sally Dennison, Antonioni's proxy, searched for "a boy who's been involved in the student revolt" and "what you see when you go to Berkeley." When he didn't turn up in Berkeley or Haight-Ashbury, the search extended to Hollywood, as if such a creature existed there, and then to the counterculture capitals of the East Coast, Harvard Square and Greenwich Village. In the latter alone, well over a thousand contestants responded to a cattle call and were asked to say "Fuck you." That was the audition. It had to be said with conviction, and Mark had aced the audition unwittingly by shouting "Motherfucker!" at a bus stop. He had a beard at the time, which might have evoked Che Guevara, one of the character's alleged prototypes. Daria was tall and Mark was taller, so he wouldn't have to stand on an apple box in a two-shot. Both he and Daria had brown hair and light eyes, hers green, his blue. Sally Dennison must have realized he was a likely finalist before he met with the film's executive producer the next day and with Antonioni ten days later in New York. He shaved his beard reluctantly for a screen test, and learned he had been given the part after the requisite flight to L.A. He wasn't sure he wanted the part. "Hollywood scared me," he would tell the *Boston Globe* in 1973. "I felt lucky if I could get out of it with my skin."

He was persuaded to go forward by Mel Lyman. He had already tried, more than once, to speak to Lyman, who couldn't be bothered. The purpose of the Fort Hill Community—*purpose* was one of its loaded words—was to assist its *moving spirit*, Lyman, in his various creative endeavors, and too many people were looking for *a free ride*; they were deficient in *feeling*; they ran from *pain*; they had yet to *wake up*, and were unable to be of *service*. A worthy recruit would have—check one or more—a trust fund, reputable parents like Kay Boyle, arty credentials, media connections, an exploitable skill or skill set. Possibly Mark was thinking of the last by becoming an apprentice carpenter, his job when Sally Dennison discovered him; and back in Boston, before he packed or didn't pack for a long stay in Hollywood, he called again on Mel Lyman. Antonioni, did he say? The lead in a movie? Have a seat! There were so many things the community needed, practical things, equipment, and if Mark accepted this part—and he really should accept it—maybe they could finally acquire those things, and he could certainly help Lyman as a filmmaker by forging valuable contacts in Hollywood. So it went for a couple of hours, at least. Mark had a guaranteed place in the Lyman Family now, and as far as he was concerned, that was the first of just two rewards that would come from *Zabriskie Point.* You may already have surmised the second.

It was a star-crossed shoot from the start. Antonioni's extemporaneous directing style was an aberration in assembly-line Hollywood, and MGM accused him of wastefulness, not without cause. For one shot he insisted that a new floor be added to a skyscraper in downtown Los Angeles to improve the view from its windows, and for outdoor shots with billboards in them, he ordered the billboards changed. It wasn't him but Hollywood that was wasteful, he said; he had sought and gotten a small, young crew, but the labor unions forced him to hire extraneous tradesmen, reactionary types who regarded Antonioni as a "pinko dago pornographer" and repeatedly halted production with de-facto strikes and complaints to the unions about minor infractions of industry regulations. They may also have informed the FBI that hundreds of hippie extras were being bused from Nevada to the desert location in California to have sex in the film's "love-in" scene, a fantasy orgy intercut with Mark and Daria making love in the sand. Antonioni was already being surveilled by the FBI because of his association with Kathleen Cleaver and other perceived enemies of the state, and the love-in scene supplied the FBI with an excuse to openly investigate him for violating the Mann Act, an antiquated federal statute that forbade the transportation of "any woman or girl" across state borders "for the purpose of prostitution or debauchery." In fact, what was transported to the set by the truckload was a powdery grade of sand that wouldn't chafe the skin of the seventy or so extras, not hundreds of them, as they mimed sex in the scene. One extra recalled Antonioni "dashingly commanding" Mark off the set for "laughing uproariously...at our feeble attempts to create 'love noises'" for a wild-track recording.

Mark was another hindrance to Antonioni. Like countless young men opposed to the war, he was a draft resister, and the draft board ordered him to report for a physical exam, which must have alarmed everyone with a stake in the film: how would it ever be completed if its star were shipped to boot camp? The physical was a rite of passage for Mark's generation, and the freakout at the induction center was a common tactic of draft dodgers, but it succeeded in Mark's case, backed as it was by his madhouse stint and a police record with a recent arrest: during a break in filming, he attended a concert in Connecticut and spat in the face of a plainclothes cop and probable narc, though Mark was charged with breach of peace and resisting arrest, not again with possession. In the same period, he spent a weekend with Lyman at Fort Hill and, as he reminisced in *Rolling Stone*, they "stayed up and smoked some of [Lyman's] fantastic weed, and listened to his music. All the music he ever recorded he played for me that weekend." Drug use, prevalent in the commune's early phase, impeded reality, Lyman later decided, and he frowned upon drugs, except when they suited his agenda; and what was his agenda in scrambling this kid with "fantastic weed," sleep deprivation, and aural bombardment for two days? He wanted to compose the score of *Zabriskie Point*, and he inculcated a zealous agent in Mark, who, back in California, began to pester Antonioni to listen to the recordings he had brought with him from Boston.

But Antonioni had his own ideas about the score. He envisioned bands like Pink Floyd, the Grateful Dead, and the Doors writing songs for it, and while he would reject "L'America" by the Doors, Jerry Garcia of the Grateful Dead contributed a guitar instrumental for the love-in scene and eerie Pink Floyd sound collages would play over the film's title sequence and its unforgettable finale: a series of dreamlike explosions, the revolution as imagined by Daria. Eventually, to placate Mark, Antonioni listened to Lyman's recordings. "It's hard to say what he thought of them," Mark related in *Rolling Stone*:

> I noticed that during one of the more spirited pieces he was twitching in his chair quite a bit. I mean, he had a terrible slant on what was happening here in America; he had a real European outlook. I tried to make him aware of what was happening here. I told him about Fort Hill, about *Avatar*. I told him about Mel and what he meant to this country. But he never understood. It was really frustrating.

It's frustrating to read of Mark's frustration. Why was "a real European outlook" necessarily negative? Did every view of America have to conform to America's view of itself, and was Antonioni obliged to make *the* film about revolutionary youth of the sixties? Couldn't he present a few personal impressions expressed poetically and not, as Americans tend to prefer, literally? And what exactly did Lyman mean to the country? He was a minor celebrity to folkies and *Avatar* readers, idolized only by his Family, but he would be idolized by all if Mark could manage it; and for the rest of the shoot, Mark proselytized on behalf of his "good" father, Lyman, in defiance of his "bad" father, Antonioni. I believe that's how, unconsciously, he graded male authority figures, even when they weren't much older than him, and while he may have recognized his actual father, a factory worker, in the Teamsters on the set, he approached them anyway with the *Avatar* in hand, trying to save their souls. Lyman had equipped him with multiple issues of the *Avatar*, some with Lyman on the cover, and Mark used them in a failed product-placement campaign: he would dress the set with an *Avatar*, arranging it so that Lyman's face was legible to the camera, and the raptor-eyed Antonioni would snatch it out of the frame. Antonioni was often aloof with his leading men and magnanimous with his leading ladies, and that applied to *Zabriskie Point*, so Mark's cold war with the director wasn't entirely one-sided, but he handled it poorly. An assistant director described him as "incorrigible." Delivering him to the set was a routine struggle, since "he always seemed to have something better to be doing," and he created "a bad environment for Daria," his sole convert to the Lyman sect.

The climactic battle of the cold war was fought in March 1969, when Mark flew to Boston, possibly to see his new son for the first time, and showed up unexpectedly in Fort Hill to announce that he wasn't going back. It was all "a big Hollywood lie," he told Lyman, and he had decided to toss "a monkey wrench in the works" by quitting the movie as it was finally winding down. Lyman hid his horror. Mark was his ticket to Hollywood expansion, and the ticket was trying to cancel itself. Out came the stash of pot again. Antonioni would yield if Mark played hooky instead of quitting, Lyman suggested; and sure enough, when Antonioni phoned Fort Hill to negotiate, he agreed to reshoot scenes with dialogue that addressed Mark's concerns—a spiritual revolution was just as important as a political revolution, Mark lectured him—and to meet with Lyman in Boston as soon as the film wrapped. Instead, fleeing MGM, the FBI, the subversive crew, and Mark and his furtive guru, Antonioni returned to Rome, taking with him the 50,000 feet, or roughly nine hours, of footage that he had shot for the last eight months, which he began to edit without interference. "Most everything we worked out was left on the cutting-room floor," Mark would complain. It's impossible to identify what remains of it in the final cut, but there's an intriguing line delivered by "Mark" about pot: "This group I was in had rules about smoking. They were on a reality trip." The response of "Daria" is likewise intriguing in light of forthcoming events: "What a drag."

__Going back__ to the concentration of Virgo—he's got Moon in Virgo too, with Virgo rising, and Mars in Virgo—that can naturally lend itself to a kind of introspective nature, and also things around him are not falling in line with his expectations of them. One thing with people with Virgo rising—they're born with this fine-tuned, discriminating intelligence that enables them to pretty much see what's wrong with any picture that's given to them, so that they are persistently not only perceiving what's wrong or incorrect, they're adamant about correcting it. And the downside of that is that the world at large, as you know, is going to be constantly producing one imperfection and flaw after another, and sometimes Virgo-rising people have to figure out, "How do I live in a totally flawed and imperfect world when I just want to keep correcting it? It's like the job is never done." And so he may have had to struggle with that kind of perfectionist outlook and this compulsion to correct stuff that, in essence, would never be corrected, even though he's compelled to continue trying.

I DIDN'T EXPECT to hear from Daria Halprin when I e-mailed her about an interview, so I wasn't disappointed by her silence. She has seldom given interviews about *Zabriskie Point*, and the little that's known of her involvement with Mark comes predominantly from him and David Felton's exposé in *Rolling Stone*. It began, in fact, with silence. "Mostly we just stared at each other," Mark told David Felton. "For months I was just completely overwhelmed by her." That was likely because of her manner as much as her appearance. Her father, Lawrence Halprin, was a distinguished landscape architect, and her mother, Anna Halprin, was a modern-dance pioneer with a company that included Daria. It was Anna Halprin's company that performed naked in *Revolution*, which of course led Antonioni to contact Daria, a pedigreed, cultured native of San Francisco. She might have reminded Mark of the blue-blooded girls of Greenwich, Connecticut, and he might have struck her as a blue-collar bad boy, and "Look but don't touch" seems to have been the initial rule for both.

But how could they resist one another? They were accidental actors and lottery winners, unique among those they knew, and neighbors at the Chateau Marmont, at least in late 1968, when their romance on film became a romance in fact. What a place Chateau Marmont must have been in 1968! Sharon Tate and Roman Polanski were residents that year, and Jim Morrison and Pamela Courson, who was juggling Morrison and the actor Christopher Jones, another resident, and we can picture one or more of these people saying to the concierge or valet, "Who's that beautiful girl with the long hair, the one who's always with that good-looking guy? Are they those kids in the Antonioni movie? Do you know what I heard about that? Hundreds of hippies are really going to ball in a big orgy scene." We can also picture Mark telling Lyman about this stellar girl who would hopefully move to Fort Hill when the movie was over, and Lyman all but drooling. Daria's background made her a better recruit than Mark, and with both stars of *Zabriskie Point* in his thrall, Lyman would have Hollywood at his feet. Then too, in the Family way, Mark had been forwarding his earnings to the commune, minus what he presumably sent to Betsy, and if Daria joined, that would be gravy. As newcomers with equal screen time, each probably received the same amount for *Zabriskie Point*—in Mark's case it was $40,000: nearly $270,000 when adjusted for inflation—and Daria, unlike Mark, had no kids to support.

For weeks he tried to sell her on their future in Boston, but Daria, to her credit, balked. Finally, while they were shooting in Berkeley, she had a vision of Lyman and a change of heart. "Mel just paid me a little visit one night in California," she would say of her vision in the *Avatar*; and after production wrapped in April 1969, she and Mark took the scenic route to Fort Hill, driving across the country. "It was," David Felton writes, "a very happy time in their lives. They were the center of attention on the Hill, and they were in love." Now, largely because of their revenue, the Family would colonize New York, New Orleans, San Francisco, and (of course) Hollywood, and buy a farm in Kansas; and the moving spirit would move from branch to branch and reduce his leadership role. Every hardcore communard *was* Mel Lyman, effectively, so the original could leave the minutiae to them and occupy more time with creating and procreating. He fathered twelve children by seven Family members, and one of his daughters was named Daria in tribute to his star apostle, or maybe to appease her. He must have sensed immediately, with his nose for potential dissent, that she would never thrive as Mark did on the spartan life and confrontational "honesty" of Fort Hill. *What do you mean by that? Show me your feelings! Get real! Wake up!* That, I think, was the appeal of the place to those who stuck it out there: the jolt of the ongoing group therapy made the outside world seem dull by contrast. Lyman's Jesus charade was superfluous. The Family's mysticism had mostly to do with astrology—visitors were asked their Sun signs in the manner of traffic cops demanding proof of insurance—and politically they were anti-establishment in some ways and reactionary in others. There was a feminine quality about Lyman, who mandated gender conformity in his followers, as if to bolster his own. Fort Hill men wore their hair relatively short and the women wore modest dresses, never pants; and everyone got together every Sunday in autumn to watch football on television. Lyman loved football.

Mark missed most of the regular season in 1969. Having worked with Italy's best-known filmmaker after Fellini, he was offered a starring role in *Uomini contro*, a film about World War I to be directed in Yugoslavia by another well-known Italian, Francesco Rosi, starting in September. He told a newspaper columnist that he "wanted a few months to reflect on what all had happened to me" and he "might do other pictures, but not right away." He *might* do other pictures? *Must* is the obligatory verb for a cash cow; and while Mark was in Yugoslavia, Daria's honeymoon with the Family ended. The specifics are limited to a single anecdote. According to David Felton, Daria called a publicist at MGM to say that she was broke and staying at the Family outpost in New York and hoping to book a few television commercials. "Without any trouble," Felton quotes the publicist, "I lined up some jobs for her. But when I called her back in New York, she wasn't around. They said Daria had to be sent back to Fort Hill for retraining, that she was too much of an individual." What did "retraining" entail? Felton, citing "fairly reliable, anonymous" sources, writes that Daria was physically assaulted by Family women, and he documents other instances of members beating heretics or confining them in a kind of dungeon, which is consistent with Lyman's view that "FORCE" would change those who "won't learn gracefully." Kay Boyle, who once observed a shrine to Charles Manson in the children's playroom at Fort Hill, believed that "the notoriety of Manson had an effect" on Lyman, that "he saw even greater dimensions that he might rise to in some way," and she may have been right. He exchanged letters with Manson and expressed interest in meeting him, and though Lyman never incited his followers to kill, rumor has implicated him in the bank robbery that left one of them dead—or two, if we count Mark's later death in prison.

Anyone who has ever been in love can appreciate Daria's probable reason for remaining in the fold after finding herself at odds with it. Surely at some point she spoke to Mark in Yugoslavia, but how private was the setting? He would have urged her to stay in any case, and once he returned, they were both busy with promotional duties for the soon-to-be-released *Zabriskie Point*. Mark was photographed by Richard Avedon for *Vogue* with run-of-the-mill results, certainly compared to Bruce Davidson's timeless images of Mark and Daria on location in the desert, looking like the older siblings of Leonard Whiting and Olivia Hussey, the teenage stars of Franco Zeffirelli's *Romeo and Juliet*, a pop-culture phenomenon of the previous year. MGM seems to have noted the resemblance and angled for

Mark and Daria to decorate the dorm rooms of college students, just as Whiting and Hussey were tacked to the walls of high-school girls. Davidson's photos were used in most of the promotional material for *Zabriskie Point*. One of them ended up on the cover of *Rolling Stone*, though not in connection with David Felton's article, and a more striking image made the cover of *Look* magazine, a lesser *Life*, inviting a rare public comment from Mark's mother. Surprised by a reporter, she said that "we don't really want the publicity," perhaps anxious that the Father Brett matter and Mark's subsequent breakdown would come to light. "Let us wait until the movie is out before calling him a star," she added with a touch of admonishment. We can only imagine the reaction of this pious, beleaguered woman if she ever saw her son fornicate in the midst of a hippie orgy, but we know the reactions of Mark and Daria. He disparaged the film on record—at the premiere, yet—as "a revolutionary Disneyland. Antonioni has given us a lot of pretty pictures, but otherwise it's a void—there's no context, no feeling." Daria, handed the cudgel, judged that Antonioni "doesn't understand people—he didn't give his characters enough room to be human." Mark's opinion of the movie worsened over time, but Daria, fifteen years later, said that while she used to be "quite embarrassed" by it, "at my age it becomes enjoyable." Still, she regretted that "it wasn't a silent film. I would have been better off." She and Mark were both pilloried for their flat performances.

Yet, for all of Antonioni's disagreements with Sam Shepard about dialogue, *Zabriskie Point* essentially *is* a silent film, with the score by Pink Floyd, Jerry Garcia, and so on, functioning as the live piano or movie-house orchestra of the 1920s and earlier. Even in the encounter session with Kathleen Cleaver, the film's only garrulous scene, what's said is far less important than the faces of the people saying it, and so it is with Mark and Daria. To gaze upon them is to know as much as Antonioni cares for you to know. Their sparse youthspeak is filler, and already sounded dated to the cognoscenti in 1970. Pop culture was evolving at hyperspeed, and *Zabriskie Point* arrived a minute late with insurmountable expectations. It was the Edsel of movies, scorned by critics and snubbed by audiences, and its stars were in the awkward position of having to promote a film that they disliked as much as, or more than, anyone. When they went on *The Dick Cavett Show* and the host mentioned that he was planning to see *Zabriskie Point* the following week, Mark told him to save his money. "It was clear from their grim-visaged entrance that they were soiling themselves by appearing on a commercial television program," Cavett said in an interview about his torpid guests—"I wondered if they were zombies of some sort"—but I interpret the episode differently. It was taped in April 1970, and by then their relationship was shaky, per Mark to David Felton, and their demeanor on the show implied squabbles and a brittle truce. Then too one of their fellow guests was the critic Rex Reed, whose bellicose review of *Zabriskie Point* had fired a shot at them—"two of the worst performances of the decade"—and Daria, wearing a long dress in the Family style and undoubtedly conscious that the show would be watched attentively at Fort Hill, may have been wary of repercussions. In fact, when another guest, Mel Brooks, asked if their commune was like the one in *Easy Rider*, Daria finally perked up, eager to exhibit her training or retraining, while Mark corrected Cavett's misapprehension, deploying the Lyman lingo to define the *purpose* of the *community*, not "commune." *The Dick Cavett Show* was an oasis of intelligence on mainstream American television in 1970, but showbiz banter was its bread and butter, and because he had to wrench it from Mark and Daria, Cavett mocked them on camera and decades later in interviews, though I would say they gave him something better. He had scores of cooperative guests who aren't memorable precisely because they were cooperative.

On a legendary episode of *The Merv Griffin Show*, Mark and Daria were joined by combative guests: Abbie Hoffman, the anarchist cofounder of the Youth International Party, or "Yippies," and Tony Dolan, a conservative journalist and folk singer. Yes, you read that accurately. Either in earnest or to parody progressive folkies like Joan Baez, Dolan would accompany himself on guitar while deploring the liberal bias of the *New York Times* or opponents of McCarthyism. Young conservatives are absent from the popular narrative of the sixties, but Dolan, who later became a speechwriter for Ronald Reagan and an adviser to George W. Bush, was twenty-one at the time he appeared on *Merv Griffin*. Abbie Hoffman, meanwhile, wore a shirt fashioned from an American flag, and lest the shirt offend viewers, the network erased Hoffman electronically. Everyone on the panel was visible but him, a blurry pattern heard arguing with Dolan. Mark got a piece of the action, siding with Hoffman. The argument continued backstage when the taping was over, and Mark punched Dolan in the face; but a gossip column reported that they met accidentally a few nights later at a diner in Connecticut and discussed their differences amiably.

Despite the failure of *Zabriskie Point*, and for roughly a year following its release, gossip columns covered its stars in a forgotten format, the items about them separated by ellipsis from items about others: "...Mark Frechette and his wife got the divorce..." "...Daria Halprin and Mark Frechette say they're moving from their Boston commune to Manhattan's East Village..." The Family's New York branch was in the East Village, and

Mark and Daria moved to it to pursue their film careers. Los Angeles was "such a vacuum," Mark said, that he couldn't imagine himself living there, but when the commune began its Hollywood expansion in July 1970, he and Daria were among the first residents at the Family's rented house in L.A.; and that September, Daria moved out of it and into the apartment of a girlfriend who lived in the area. She never returned to retrieve her car: that's how finished with the Family she was. Lyman had recently landed in L.A., which "sort of brought it all to a head," Mark told David Felton, so Daria seems to have had a problem with Lyman in particular. Was it sexual? The Family practiced serial monogamy, save for its polygamous leader; but if he desired Daria, surely he wouldn't have acted on it and risked losing Mark, who earned $20,000 while working abroad and made his usual endowment. Mark furnished no details of Daria's decision to leave, only that she "just didn't want to give what was asked of her."

But she still wanted Mark, as she let him know, and he was forced to choose between her and the Family. It was "a terrible situation," he would say. "I was really a basket case—boy, was I torn." Wisely and shockingly, he chose her—for the moment. If a romantic relationship is inevitably a cult of two, it undermines a cult at large, so Lyman discouraged couples from spending time alone. Now this couple had some time alone. They had no real chance of longevity—they were too young, and he was lost and irascible—but, picturing them free of hovering meddlers, it's impossible not to root for them. They lasted less than a week: three Family members knocked on their door and handed Mark a plane ticket to Boston. The moving spirit had spoken, and Mark obeyed, flying back to Fort Hill, where he would "let time wash away the pain." It may never have washed away entirely. When he returned to L.A. a few months later, he called on Daria, but she was gone and he left her a book by Lyman. He had learned nothing.

Daria, terrified of the Family, had moved twice in the interim. "They came after her and threatened to beat her up," a friend informed Felton. "She kept calling home, saying she was afraid she was gonna get killed." She had very nearly stolen the commune's chief breadwinner, though he was about to be eclipsed by the Fort Hill Construction Company, the Family putting its carpentry skills to profitable use. At a film festival in Yugoslavia in early 1971, Daria met the director of *Easy Rider*, Dennis Hopper, and she married him, pregnant with his daughter, a year and a half later. Out of the fire and into the frying pan! Hopper, addicted to drugs and alcohol, was given to shooting guns indoors, and Daria fled home to San Francisco, where she became interested in movement therapy and cofounded, with her mother, a dancer's workshop. Her interest in therapy, she said, "came out of my commitment to save myself"—she was "very close to burnout"—and one wonders if she ever, in hindsight, considered Mark in clinical terms and concluded that he was salvageable or too far gone, a casualty of his past and temperament, if not the times or constellations.

> ***I forgot to mention this.*** *I should go ahead and say it now. This is the chart of an extreme individual. This is not a casual person. This is a person of extremes. And part of that—with Pluto in the twelfth house, this is kind of the signature of a fanatical nature—if they're going to participate and go into something, it's going to be all the way or nothing. This is not someone that is going to be at peace with mediocrity, for example. Mediocrity is death to this kind of individual. So this person is going to have extreme reactions because his soul depends on it.*

"WHEN MARK IS JUST STANDING THERE," a Lyman Family member once remarked, "he's handsome but rather bland; but when Mark is excited or angry, something extraordinary takes over." Movie rebels are usually excited or angry or both, and Mark always played rebels, but he was languid, in the Antonioni way, in *Zabriskie Point* and stoical as an army officer in *Uomini contro*, which was released as *Many Wars Ago* in English-speaking countries. Only in his third and final film, *La grande scrofa nera*, or *The Big Black Sow*, is he as combustible as he was in life. It was made in Italy at some point in 1970, and its plot paralleled his dilemma with Daria, as he must have recognized. His character in the film, the forward-thinking son of a domineering peasant farmer, marries a city girl who fails to mesh with his insular family, and when they brutalize her, he retaliates with patricide, fratricide, and sororicide, as if to articulate Mark's unacknowledged rage at Lyman and the rest for driving Daria away. Italian films of the period often featured foreigners who performed in their native languages and were dubbed in postproduction, and that may have led Mark to feel like a puppet and limit himself to American projects; but with his lacerating reviews for his flop debut, how many projects came his way, and what kind? Most actors in his shoes would have accepted small roles in mainstream movies, lead roles in exploitation movies, and guest-starring roles on television shows like *Gunsmoke*—Mel Lyman was a huge fan of *Gunsmoke*—but such jobs wouldn't have paid much or elevated Mark's stock in Hollywood. The latter was of no concern to him, but it mattered to Lyman, who must have decided that it was better for Mark to wait for a vehicle that proved his value than it was to work and depreciate irredeemably.

Mark was lucky to have a simpatico agent: Joe Funicello, the brother of Annette Funicello, famous in the fifties as a Mouseketeer on *The Mickey Mouse Club* and in the sixties as the star of beach-party movies, *Beach Blanket Bingo* and so on. Joe Funicello knew the sort of material that would appeal to Mark, and somewhere around the beginning of 1973, he received the very thing: an adaptation of *Crime and Punishment* set not in nineteenth-century Russia but a contemporary American suburb. It was written by its attached director, Dezso Magyar, a young Hungarian émigré, and inspired, Dezso told me, by the climate of violence in the U.S. at the time: "I personally saw a couple of frightening episodes in Santa Monica, where I lived." Only the strange tragedy of Mark Frechette could mix Annette Funicello, Dostoevsky, and political oppression in Hungary: Dezso was under surveillance there after directing three films that were considered subversive and banned, though praised abroad. He had been in California for less than a year when his reputation attracted a pair of novice producers with the funds for a movie if there was one he wanted to make. *Crime and Punishment*? Okay, fine. Now they needed a cast, and the script was sent to Joe Funicello, who recommended Mark, of course, and Dostoevsky would doubtless have agreed that Mark was the perfect Raskolnikov, described in the novel as "remarkably handsome," "taller than usual, slim and well-built," with "dark, chestnut-colored hair." Mark had something of the mind-set of Dostoevsky's soulful killer as well. Funicello was eager to introduce him to Dezso. "I believe that you guys will hit it off because you are not like a typical Hollywood guy who wants to make a movie," Dezso remembers him saying.

He was dead on. It's refreshing to hear Dezso's take on Mark: "a totally natural human being" and "a very sweet man, certainly to me," who was "low-key and very real" as well as "innately intelligent" and "sensitive; but I don't think that he was terribly cultured, you know; I don't think that he had the literary curiosity to go read Russian novels." However, Mark did read *Crime and Punishment* to compare it to Dezso's version, and he liked that Dezso injected politics into the moral inquest at the core of the novel: is a crime—in this case murder, with incidental theft—truly a crime if society is improved by it? Having worked with nonprofessional actors in Hungary, Dezso was unfazed by Mark's lack of formal training, and he believes that his "naïve and honest and enthusiastic" approach endeared him to Mark, as did his confidence that Mark could pull off the Raskolnikov part, easily the most layered and challenging of his scant career. This film would correct *Zabriskie Point*, not in the sense of commercial triumph or making an idol of Mark; rather, he was treated as a full partner, often meeting with

Dezso to analyze the script, sometimes at Mark's house, meaning the Family's house, though—and this too is refreshing—Dezso never once mentioned the Family to me. They had purchased two houses in Hollywood, but Dezso couldn't recall the street of the one where he got together with Mark, only that it was in Laurel Canyon or someplace like it "where the people lived in a typical hippie lifestyle," and Mark would strum a guitar, everything "nice" and "laid-back," while they planned their film. They even scouted locations.

Then the inevitable happened: their producers were revealed as frauds. They had never had the money to make the film; they were hoping to secure a bank loan, which had been denied. Mark and Dezso were devastated. Joe Funicello, who "loved" Mark and was "very attached" to him, Dezso said, tried to find new funding, and Mark and Dezso did the same on their own, but they were unsuccessful and Mark's master was calling him out of town. He left in July 1973, and Dezso never saw him again, not in person, though he would see him soon on television.

Mark headed to Martha's Vineyard, where Lyman was holed up at the summer retreat owned by one of his most devout disciples. He and the Family had circled the wagons following the publication of the *Rolling Stone* article at the end of 1971.They mirrored each other so intently, their reflections seemed distorted in David Felton's mirror. It was all lies, they claimed, with a single exception: Felton had written fairly about the moving spirit after finally gaining access to him. But Lyman was cannier than his flock, of course, who spoke too freely with the journalist embedded among them, one differentiating his commune from another thus: "The Manson Family preached peace and love and went around killing people. We don't preach peace and love. And we haven't killed anyone—yet."

In fact, thousands of communes were established across America in the late sixties and evacuated in the early seventies by hundreds of thousands of young people weary of being bullied by their "brothers" and "sisters." Daria Halprin wasn't an anomaly. The collapse of the commune movement contributed to the end of the sixties at least as much as the popular catalysts, the shootings at Kent State and the Manson murders. Idealism turned to cynicism. The pace of pop culture slackened. Activism continued in hotspots like Berkeley, but Russ Little, a founding member of the Symbionese Liberation Army, was disgruntled by the mood there: "We were pulling out of Vietnam [and] a lot of people were going, 'Well, everything is over, we'll go back to college,' and it wasn't over at all. The same stuff was going on, you know; the same criminals, murderers and stuff, were still running the government." Russ Little "couldn't believe that Nixon got reelected in '72"—and it wasn't a narrow victory as it had been for Richard Nixon in 1968, when the nation was polarized. In 1972 college-aged voters and older voters both supported Nixon overwhelmingly, tuning out news reports that linked him to the growing Watergate scandal, which by the summer of 1973 couldn't be disregarded: the game shows and soap operas of daytime television were preempted by live coverage of the Senate Watergate Committee's hearings about the case, a miniseries with a stern audience on Martha's Vineyard, where Mark and other Family members were remodeling Lyman's retreat.

Meanwhile, in Santa Monica, Dezso was still trying to raise the funds to make his film, and every so often Mark would call for an update and offer encouragement. Then one day he called and said, "Good news: I found the money, man. It's all done, and I'm arriving tomorrow in L.A. with the financing." Dezso is almost certain that he received the call on Wednesday, August 29, and that night, watching the eleven o'clock news, Dezso was "profoundly shocked and devastated" by the headline story: Mark Frechette, the star of *Zabriskie Point*, had been arrested with an accomplice at the scene of a violent bank holdup in Boston. "It was a rather traumatic introduction to America" for Dezso.

Mark had two accomplices: Sheldon "Terry" Bernhard, the thirty-one-year-old pianist in the Lyman Family band, and Christopher Thein, a husky twenty-two-year-old known in the Family as "Herc," short for Hercules. Thein was a drifter who wandered into the Family orbit in New Orleans, its sole recruit there, and while he's identified in some accounts as Mark's "best friend," they met for the first time on Martha's Vineyard that summer. They traveled to Fort Hill a week prior to the robbery, a "spur-of-the moment idea" Mark told the FBI, and enlisted Bernhard, who, interviewed decades later in *Death Valley Superstar*, Michael Yaroshevsky's half-hour documentary about Mark, said "they were going to do it without me if they weren't going to do it with me" and he went along only because "I always tried to look out for them." There were no cameras inside the branch of the New England Merchants National Bank they robbed that day, but more than half of Mark's eighty-page FBI file consists of witness statements, and Mark and Bernhard were semi-cooperative with investigators, anxious to quell any question of the Family's complicity before it was broached.

They had walked to the bank, a mile from Fort Hill, and "planned to escape on foot," Bernhard stated, and leave town immediately afterward, "possibly going to the West Coast." Thein wore a security-guard shirt, and Mark and Bernhard both wore fake mustaches, Mark well dressed in a dark suit and tie. All three men carried fully loaded .38 caliber Smith & Wesson revolvers, the FBI file confirms, contradicting folklore that their guns were unloaded. Family members were armed of necessity in their early days in Fort Hill—the neighborhood was lethal and they were under near-constant siege—but Mark and Bernhard naturally said that the revolvers used in the robbery were obtained elsewhere. They entered the bank around five p.m., and Thein pretended to fill out a deposit slip while Mark sat with a bank officer and talked about a loan before quietly announcing the robbery to her, directing her to beckon to the security guard, whose post by the front door was assumed by Thein. Mark disarmed the guard and prodded him to unlock the door that led to the tellers' area. Bernhard joined them now, slipping past the door with the guard and Mark, who, sotto voce, instructed the tellers to stand and line up next to the vault. Few customers at this point had any inkling that a stickup was underway. Some noticed that the arm patch on Thein's shirt said MEDICAL CENTER, but there was a hospital across the street, so the patch didn't appear odd, and his .38 was hidden in a paper bag with his hand inside it. Mark covered his own hands with gloves before touching anything, and Bernhard guarded the guard in an adjacent anteroom, waiting for Mark to fill their briefcases with cash.

If this all sounds like a professional bank heist, it wasn't. Mark had one of the tellers collect the cash, but he "did not check to see that [the teller] got all the money," another teller stated, "and further did not know which drawers contained the cash" and "was not very attentive" to the packing of his briefcase, since he was simultaneously watching the tellers beside the vault, none of whom could open it. Only the head teller, gone for the day, knew the combination to the vault, Mark was told, and again the guard opened the door to the tellers' area so that Bernhard could hear what Mark had just heard about the vault and, together, they decided it must be true. Because they hadn't seen or heard anyone set off an alarm, they assumed it hadn't happened; but two tellers had triggered the alarm surreptitiously, and though Bernhard, unlike Mark, expressed concern about the time factor within earshot of the tellers, he "then stated that they had enough time" to seize more loot—$10,150 was stolen altogether—and this is where they made their critical mistake. The robbery lasted as long as eight minutes, and "when we got to prison," Bernhard recalled in *Death Valley Superstar*, "the bank robbers all came up to Mark [and] said... 'We could've told you you've got to be out of there in two minutes, you dumb fucks.'" Even fleeing was silent-film comedy. They struggled with the door that led to the lobby while the tellers advised "that the handle had to be turned to the left." Finally the guard opened the door for them, and as they approached Thein in the lobby, the comedy ended. Two policemen had just entered the bank, and the person they took for the security guard ordered them to drop their weapons. He had, one of them saw, "a brown paper bag in one hand and his right hand inside the bag," and the second cop lunged for him and lost his balance, falling to the floor. Then Thein's "hand came out of the bag holding a gun," and he was shot twice in the chest by the fallen cop's partner. Mark and Bernhard surrendered without further incident. Thein was pronounced dead on arrival at the hospital across the street.

When the Symbionese Liberation Army held up a bank eight months later in San Francisco, the robbery lasted just over a minute and netted $10,700 with no fatalities. Its real success, however, was the spotlight role it afforded Patricia Hearst, now Tania, the SLA's manufactured star. They wanted to make an agitprop movie using the bank's security cameras, while Mark's ruse of enquiring about a loan was, consciously or unconsciously, a restaging of the loan application for the arthouse movie he wanted to make, with a decidedly different outcome: the loan is approved, motherfuckers! Were his accomplices aware of the movie? The *Boston Globe*, quoting unnamed friends, reported that Mark was "worried about whether the film would be made" and "edgy for most of the summer," which, of course, he spent alongside Thein on Martha's Vineyard; but this does not mean that Thein knew he was robbing a bank on behalf of a screen adaptation of *Crime and Punishment*, or that Mark would have delivered the money to the production company once he realized that he hadn't stolen nearly enough—and he couldn't have stolen enough, not with two briefcases, even if the vault had been opened. It's hard to believe he thought otherwise, though his phone call that day to Dezso, now an eminent film teacher, would seem to be the smoking gun. Neither Mark nor Bernhard ever spoke of *Crime and Punishment* to the FBI or the media. They didn't discuss motive at all with the former, and questioned by the latter, Mark defined the robbery as "an act of political protest" against the ultimate bad father: "We had been watching the Watergate hearings on television and... saw the American people sinking deeper into deeper into apathy and we felt an intense rage... Because banks are federally insured, robbing that bank was a way of robbing Richard Nixon without hurting anybody." He was echoed less effusively by Bernhard and with gusto by other Family members. "To me," one of them declared, "robbing a bank is like robbing the government. Everybody's money is insured." Did she get that line from Mark, did he get it from her, or did they both get it from Mel Lyman?

The Family started the folklore about the unloaded weapons, telling the *Globe* that "the first chamber of Thein's six-chamber pistol was empty" and "this is evidence that he did not plan to use it," which is rather like saying that no noise was intended because one of six firecrackers wasn't lit. The FBI file notes that they harassed the bank staff for a few days, demanding to know which teller had set off the alarm, but apparently it dawned on them that they might get more bad publicity that way and they backed off. Lyman craved fame, not infamy, and for that reason, if no other, I assign authorship of the robbery to Mark, who had effectively confirmed that, yes, the Family was the dangerous cult portrayed in *Rolling Stone*. Of course that wasn't his conscious intention, but Mark was fractious by nature while servile to Lyman, a conflict that possibly festered beneath his awareness until it exploded in passive-aggressive form, with Nixon as the patsy.

Dezso believes that Mark had pondered *Crime and Punishment* ever since he read the book—what exactly *is* crime?—but Mark may finally have aspired to play Robin Hood, not Raskolnikov, in designating the film his charity du jour. Then too the cash wouldn't be as easily traced to the production company in California as it would be to the Family in Boston, though Mark would probably have shared some of it with them—or all of it, once he saw how little he had stolen—to affirm his value as a breadwinner. His reduced stature in the Family has been floated as another motive, and still another is that Mark aimed to authenticate his revolutionary character in *Zabriskie Point*; but the character was him—that's why he was chosen—and as Bernhard pointed out in *Death Valley Superstar*, "we never expect anyone who's played a bad guy"—an outlaw—"to live out the role." The outlaw was a heroic role to Mark, obviously, as it was to the SLA and, we can guess, Hercules Thein. We can also guess that Hercules was powerless to resist the "something extraordinary" that overtook Mark in states of excitement or anger, and that Mark was haunted by Thein's death, even if he never addressed it in the interviews he gave at the Charles Street Jail in downtown Boston, where he and Bernhard would languish for eight months. But ghosts are often unaddressed, as if the silence will hold them at bay, and Mark himself would be a ghost a little over two years after his "personal revolutionary act."

> ***So we're looking*** *at the death chart, and there's a particular transit happening that month, and that is what astrology calls the transit of Neptune. This is a once-in-a-lifetime transit, and when Neptune crosses an area, often this will bring about experiences of either apathy or depression. The other transit that happened right around his death, Saturn was starting to enter his twelfth house, approaching his natal Saturn, what we call his Saturn Return. See, Saturn Return represents an era, kind of a rite of passage that happens to every-*

body between the ages of twenty-eight and thirty. A lot of people who become famous young never make it to the Saturn Return.

ROBERT DOLE HAD MOVED from England to Ireland and eventually became an English professor in Quebec, but he made an annual trip to the U.S. to see his parents, and in 1973 the trip coincided with the bank robbery. Robert learned that Mark was in the Charles Street Jail and visited him there, sidestepping talk of the robbery "because I did not want him to think that I was judging him." Afterward they corresponded by mail, Robert writing at length on a typewriter, Mark responding tersely by hand. In one note he sounds like the biblical prophet of their Cambridge days, asking if Robert has "any notion of the blood that will soon flow" in America: "She is going to bleed & burn & crumble." Mark had enjoyed listening to Robert read poetry when they lived together, and Robert approximated the experience in letters by transcribing poems like W. B. Yeats's "The Second Coming," a vision of the apocalypse that Mark must have devoured. He updated Robert about his case: "we pleaded guilty" with "no deal involved" and "the judge followed the DA's recommendation of 6-15." He and Bernhard ended up at Massachusetts Correctional Institution in Norfolk, an hour's drive from Boston, and this struck Robert as "lucky": "The man who started it, as an experimental progressive place, is a friend of my parents', and I've had the pleasure of hearing him praise the ideas that are behind its liberality." He went on to advise Mark to "let your prison be your university": "I assure you that there is much more to human knowledge and wisdom than what Mel Lyman and astrology can offer you."

To some extent, Mark heeded the advice. In the lengthiest article written about him during his time at Norfolk—it ran in *Oui*, the sister publication of *Playboy*—it's mentioned that he "has set himself a regular program of reading" and "read Solzhenitsyn straight through and clearly sees himself as the prototypical Solzhenitsyn hero, the political prisoner." He met with the journalist—Julia Cameron, the future wife (and ex-wife) of Martin Scorsese—in the prison library, in fact. But the slant of the article is the Lyman Family, and Mark speaks of Lyman with the ardor of an alcoholic who attends twelve-step meetings three times a day. He was visited by Family members three times a week, the article says. It doesn't say if Julia Cameron attempted to interview them, but regardless, the Family shunned the media until it tentatively lifted the veil fifteen years after the robbery, by then "less a commune" and more "a conglomerate," *People* revealed in 1986, with "income from the family-owned construction business expected to reach $3.5 million this year." The business renovated celebrity homes—

Steven Spielberg and Dustin Hoffman were clients—while in their own homes, still shuttling from one to the next in areas they helped to gentrify, the Family savored "good food and wine," "happy we no longer have to eat radish soup." Mel Lyman had died in 1978, but they were cagey about specifics because he "pleaded for privacy" and it was "still too painful to talk about." The living can't be sainted, however, so he may have been more valuable to them as the holy spirit invoked every time they watched *Gunsmoke*, as they did faithfully, or one of the films he had catalogued in "The Lord's List of All Time Movie Greats." Every Family household had a copy of the list. *Zabriskie Point* wasn't on it.

In her profile of Mark, Julia Cameron describes him as having bulked up since his *Zabriskie Point* days—"Frechette attributes this change to the prison diet, mainly starch, and a weight-lifting regime"—but he doesn't look any heavier in his final media appearance in March 1975, when he directed a theater production, *The White House Transcripts*, which recreated Nixon's tape-recorded conversations in the Oval Office with aides played by thieves and murderers at Norfolk, an amusing concept that made national headlines. The project was proposed to Mark by its creator, a public-relations man in Boston, possibly the one assisting Sally Dennison that fateful evening in another life. Here was Mark's chance to correct the bank robbery, characterized by some as political theater, with unmistakable political theater and to do with others as Antonioni had done with him, coaxing performances from amateur actors. It was "amazing how Mark got us into our parts," one of them told *People*. Terry Bernhard, interviewed for *CBS Evening News* in the putty nose he wore as Nixon, spoke of the irony of impersonating a figure whose actions had ostensibly motivated robbery. Mark was interviewed in the same broadcast, his convict number appearing beneath his name on the screen, too beautiful to be a convict and a blatant class act who might finally have found his calling, though he downplayed the production in typical fashion, saying it was simply a way to pass the time and "we all have a lot of time on our hands."

Norfolk may have been "an experimental progressive place," but it was still a prison, the most daunting of all institutions, and Mark had repudiated institutions in the wake of the Father Brett business, so it isn't surprising that a court-appointed psychiatrist warned at his sentencing that he would become "increasingly depressed" in prison, or as Bernhard would say: "Confinement's not easy for anybody, but being in that kind of a place for somebody like Mark was absolutely hell, just intolerable." He applied for early parole at the beginning of 1975, and the parole board favored it, but it was vetoed in June by the Norfolk superintendent, who declared

Mark of "questionable stability." Robert saw him once at Norfolk, and Betsy would visit with their kids and think, "Gosh, I hope he makes it through," or so she recalled in *Death Valley Superstar*; but that summer, as the second anniversary of the robbery approached, he hit rock bottom. He didn't eat. He couldn't sleep. He stopped working out. All that stood between him and parole was a good mental-health report and, after the anniversary passed, he scheduled an appointment to begin psychotherapy. He seems to have wanted to prepare for it by resuming his workout regime, and though he had lost weight and muscle, he may have assumed that he was capable of lifting what he had lifted weeks earlier. Whatever happened, another inmate discovered him dead on September 27, lying on a bench in a rec room with a 150-pound barbell squashing his throat. There were no signs of a struggle, and he was "well-liked by the other inmates," the *Boston Phoenix* said, with "only relatively minor hassles with the Norfolk guards," so "for now" nobody was "seriously doubting the official explanation" of accidental asphyxiation.

I'm satisfied by the official explanation. I was almost asphyxiated once when my arms suddenly buckled while I was bench pressing alone, and Mark's deterioration was confirmed by the person who knew him best in the last two years of his life, Terry Bernhard, without innuendo of foul play. If his death was deliberate, I tend to think that Mark surrendered to despair when his arms gave; but of course there have always been fingers pointed at shadowy assassins. Joe Funicello, in a phone conversation with Dezso, speculated that Mark had been murdered by guards because he "organized some protest plays and whatnot." Robert Dole, in his correspondence with me, theorized "that some fellow inmate put the make on Mark and Mark rejected the advances and the man then killed him," citing "a friend who was in prison in Concord, Massachusetts, at the time" and told Robert "that all the rumours going around the Massachusetts prisons claimed that Mark had been killed." It's possible, though I'm as skeptical of jailhouse rumor as I am of jailhouse religion, and more intrigued by Robert's reading of the death as symbolic crucifixion, with the bench and the barbell forming the shape of a cross. I see Mark as the Family Messiah and Lyman as the Moses, the lawgiver who led the elect to Mount Sinai—that is, Fort Hill—and from there spied the Promised Land, which they settled later, after Mark arrived. As much as they refused categorization with the other communes of the period—they were, again, a *community*—they might have gone the way of the rest if bad publicity hadn't united them in indignation at the decisive moment. Mark doubled down on the bad publicity and ultimately died for their sins, freeing them to become the yuppies they may always have been at heart, with their real-estate prescience and foodie affectations. They earned their perks, to be sure, and maybe it's true that they were never like other communes—and that's what they were: semantics don't determine reality, contrary to fallacy more popular today than ever—but they personify the distrust that younger generations have of theirs. If a conservative is a liberal who got mugged, as the old joke goes, a bourgeois baby boomer is a revolutionary who got scolded.

It was cinephiles born in the sixties and seventies, for the most part, who rescued *Zabriskie Point* from ignominy. It didn't matter to them—it didn't matter to me—if it was or wasn't a bona-fide record of boomer radicalism; they granted the film the poetic license it wasn't afforded in 1970, certainly not by Mark, whose notorious act in life is a footnote to the film, just as his death was only newsworthy in 1975 because of it. Cinephiles are a moribund breed, and long after the last copy of *Zabriskie Point* has vanished, its titular location will remain; but for as long as film archives exist, Mark will exist as Antonioni's idea of the young male American revolutionary circa 1968, and that accords him an artistic legacy that surpasses anything achieved artistically by Mel Lyman and, for that matter, skilled actors who worked in countless movies that were considered good, even excellent, and are now forgotten except to a handful of aging cinephiles. Mark never sought an artistic legacy, of course, and when cinephiles and pop-culture fans write about him, they usually do so sneeringly. That stupid, untalented pretty boy! That crumb, that zero, who got lucky! But Mark was impetuous, not stupid, and he demonstrated real talent as the director of *The White House Transcripts*, from every account I've read of it; and to me the saddest thing of all about his sad but exasperating life isn't just that he didn't live to realize his talent but that he probably wouldn't have tried to realize it had he survived. Terry Bernhard returned to the Family after being paroled, and Mark would unquestionably have done the same, but I prefer to believe that he would have felt uncomfortable watching *Gunsmoke* while sipping chardonnay and snacking on foie gras. The same month he died, there was an attempted assassination of Nixon's successor, Gerald Ford, by a die-hard member of the Manson Family, Lynette "Squeaky" Fromme, and Tania and two other members of the SLA were arrested after a year and a half on the lam. Six more SLA members had been killed in a ferocious shootout with police in Los Angeles, and two others, including Russ Little, were already in prison. "I just felt like, you know, we got to keep something going," Little would say years later of the SLA's inception, referring, of course, to the radical spirit of the sixties, and in that way alone Mark was similar to the SLA and Squeaky Fromme, though Tania instantly reverted to Patricia Hearst behind bars—a victim of mind control, she claimed, and it must be admitted that few heiresses would commit armed robbery voluntarily. I've been robbed at knifepoint and twice had guns trained on me, so I don't defend violent crime or the threat of it, but I will submit that Mark, unlike 99 percent of his generation, took its antiestablishment rhetoric to its logical extreme, or as he said when he and Bernhard were interviewed in September 1973 at the Charles Street Jail, now a luxury hotel: "In 1966, '67 and '68 there was something happening. There was incredible interchange. We haven't changed. Everybody else is gone. Where did they go?"

> ***Now, the transits that are happening** today are really quite fascinating. His spirit or his character, even though he's passed away, is returning. There's a ripeness for that part of his character I would call a misanthropic critic of society. One of the effects of this oversaturation of the media culture can be like a numbing down of people, their sensibilities. There can be also a kind of isolating, isolationist tendency where people actually go to their computers for their social life because it's easier, more comfortable online. Back then, people hung out, they talked, they went out to the pub or to the bar; and people still do that today, but not nearly as much. So there's something about him that I'm thinking may relate to a certain mind-set today of a misanthropic critiquing of society not necessarily to make society better, but it's almost like a more anarchistic death wish for society so that we can rebuild something after the annihilation of all that has gone wrong.*

THE "PREDICTIVE PART OF ASTROLOGY," Camille Paglia wrote in *Sexual Personae*, "is less important than its psychology, which three thousand years of continuous practice have given a phenomenal subtlety." It was the unexpected subtlety of Antero's reading—the complexity of it—that most impressed me. If I was less impressed by the accuracy—and that impressed me also—it was because, again, it wasn't a blind reading and I knew that I wasn't immune to confirmation bias. But I could understand now what Mark saw in astrology, and when I told Antero that he might have made a believer of me, he was ready with a standard joke: "I always say I don't believe in astrology—except it works."

That was in 2014, and for that year and the next, I postponed writing about Mark while I worked on other projects. I still hoped to interview a few people other than Robert Dole who knew him, especially Dezso, and the more I researched Mark, the more I decided that to somewhat do his story justice, I would have to expand on the sketch I had in mind at the outset. The fragments of his life were scattered like the dismembered body parts of the Egyptian god Osiris—here in this nook was Father Brett, and over there was Daria Halprin, and so on—and nobody aside from Michael Yaroshevsky, in a different medium, had tried to locate them all and reassemble them, as far as I could tell, since Mark didn't warrant the effort. That wasn't my position, obviously, and whenever I studied the pieces I had collected so far, I was struck by new insights and questions. I wondered, for instance, how Mark might have reacted to two lines in "The Second Coming": *The best lack all conviction, while the worst / Are full of passionate intensity.* Was he as perplexed by them as I was when I first read the poem at age twenty or so? Passion and intensity were the traits I prized most in myself and others. Surely Yeats had it backwards and the worst, not the best, lacked all conviction.

I wrote very little in 2016, paralyzed by the spectacle of an election as ghastly as the one I witnessed in Yugoslavia when I lived there in the waning days of the Slobodan Milošević regime. My memory of the late sixties is hazy, since I was a child at the time, but the polarization of America was plain to me, with longhaired young people, whom I identified as "students," not "hippies," inexplicably clashing with older people like my Southern Baptist grandfather. I never thought I would see anything like that again, not in America, not on that scale, but I was corrected by the election of 2016 and its aftermath. A young woman protesting a rally of white supremacists in my hometown, Charlottesville, Virginia, was mowed down literally by one of them, while in Alexandria, Virginia, where I lived briefly at eighteen, a fanatical progressive shot and wounded conservative lawmakers. I removed myself repeatedly from social media because I couldn't take the rancor it permitted and, as far as I was concerned, instigated by isolating people rather than "connecting" them. Everyone was so fucking certain they were right, including me. I lost friends because of the election and may never speak again with certain relatives by mutual agreement.

Mark Frechette's spirit was returning, Antero augured in 2014; the transits favored the reappearance of the "misanthropic critic of society." Maybe now his relevance can be appreciated as it wouldn't have been three years ago, and maybe I was guided by intuition when I postponed writing about him. Mark himself had prophesied that America would "bleed & burn & crumble," though he saw it happening sooner rather than later, unlike the architect of his celebrity. "Perhaps in fifty years things will arrive at a crucial point and these forces that are now underneath will explode," Antonioni said when asked if there would be a violent revolution in America. He said that almost forty-eight years ago, as I write these words, and by now I agree that, yes, the best lack all conviction while the worst are full of passionate intensity.

2017

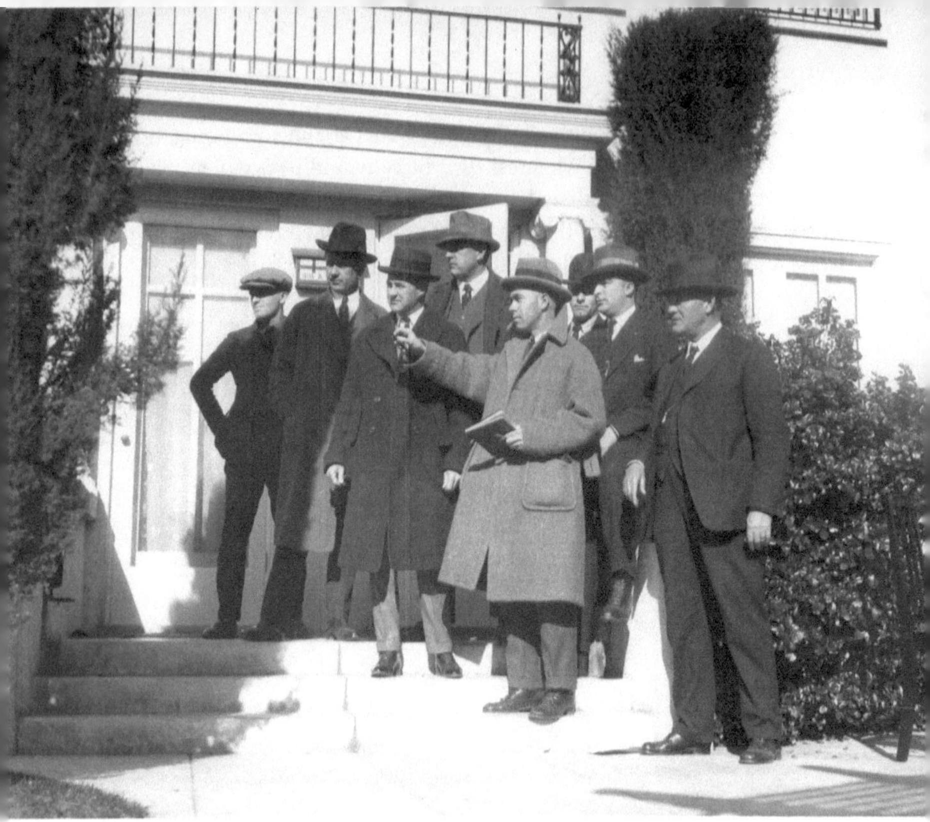

William Desmond Taylor's killer left in the opposite direction faced by investigators on Taylor's porch two days after the murder, and apparently struck after lurking in the alley where this puzzling sign now looms. (*Top: Bison Archives; Bottom: Author's collection*)

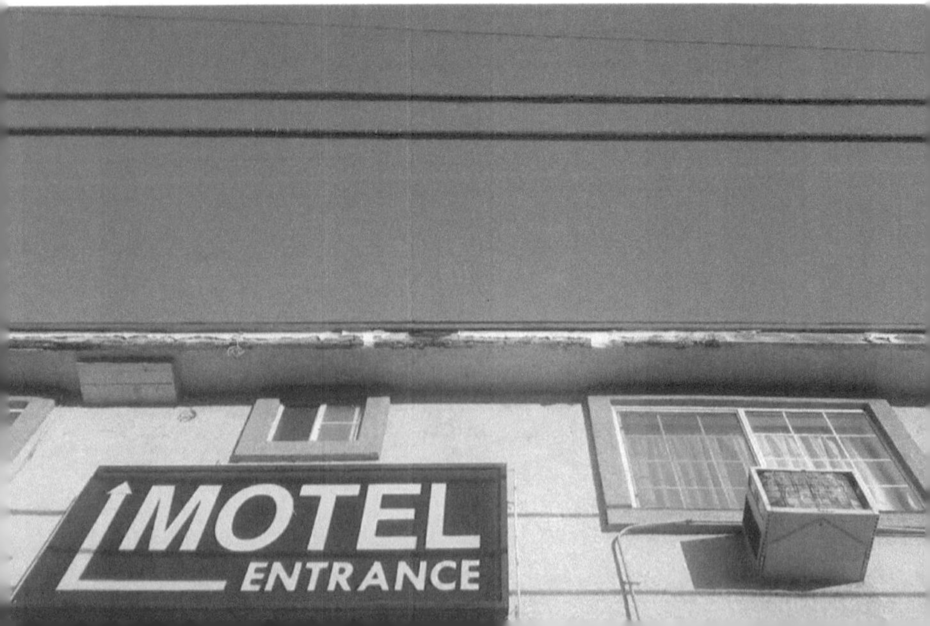

WILLIAM DESMOND TAYLOR DIED FOR YOUR SINS

WALKING UPHILL IN WESTLAKE, a neighborhood just north of downtown Los Angeles, I paused at the site of the most intriguing whodunit in local lore, save the Black Dahlia case. Here, on February 1, 1922, in the living room of his duplex bungalow, one of sixteen units at the Alvarado Court Apartments, William Desmond Taylor, a film director and former actor, was shot and killed by an unknown intruder, though a number of plausible suspects have been identified by professional and armchair detectives, based partly on the eyewitness account of Faith MacLean, who, with her screen-star husband, the since-forgotten Douglas MacLean, lived next door to Taylor. Shortly before eight that night, Mrs. MacLean stated, she heard what she thought might be a "muffler explosion," and when she opened her door to investigate, she observed, standing in Taylor's doorway, a "funny looking man" dressed "like my idea of a motion picture burglar"—a disguise, perhaps. He—or possibly she, since Mrs. MacLean later allowed that this person could have been a woman in a man's suit and cap—seemed ready to leave through the garden courtyard that led to Alvarado Street, but he hesitated, as if "Mr. Taylor [had] spoken to him from inside the house." Then, in what I regard as the eeriest detail of the case, he met Mrs. MacLean's gaze in the darkness. He didn't seem bothered by a witness. "No," she said, "he was the coolest thing I have ever seen"; and in that unruffled spirit he closed Taylor's door, "then turned around and, looking at me all the time, walked down a couple of steps that go up to Mr. Taylor's house," vanishing in name but not deed through an alley that led to Maryland Street.

That alley is gone, but another still exists, the alley where the MacLeans' maid heard someone pacing in "flat shoes" thirty minutes before the murder. It ran behind the Alvarado Court Apartments, which were bulldozed in 1965 to make way for what's now a Ross Dress for Less store, or rather, the store's parking lot. This is where I paused while walking uphill on Alvarado. The alley is flanked on one side by the parking lot and on the other side by a plaque-colored fleabag with a sign that says MOTEL ENTRANCE and an arrow that points to the roof, as if guests were expected to arrive by parachute. There are several fleabags in the neighborhood, some in worse shape. There are pawnshops, one with a mural of Jesus walking on water, and "check-cashing" companies, legal loan sharks for illegal immigrants and other indigents, and photo-menu restaurants with names that emphasize speed—China Express, Atitlan Express—and storefront churches next to liquor stores next to bargain stores that stock the same items—toys and toiletries, "gold" jewelry and "leather" belts—sold by sidewalk vendors across the street from MacArthur Park. The park is the heart of Westlake Park, as the neighborhood was called when it was settled by the smart set, including the "picture people" who later forsook it for higher ground, literally, north and west. Douglas MacLean, for instance, died of natural causes in 1967 in Beverly Hills, where murder is as anomalous as it used to be in Westlake in the silent-film era. It isn't anomalous now, and while most students of the William Desmond Taylor case believe the victim was acquainted—probably well acquainted—with his killer, murder in contemporary Westlake is often random and tied to street crime. Every sort of crime is practiced in and around MacArthur Park, with none of the seedy glamour it receives in popular entertainment.

But Westlake is entering a new phase. On 6th Street, before I turned onto Alvarado and paused at the parking lot where sixteen duplex bungalows once stood, a twentysomething white man rode past me on a bicycle. Winos were the only white people I saw intermittently in Westlake when I discovered it in the 1990s. Latins were and are the majority there, and over the years I noticed a surge in black residents and, eventually, a few of the young white "creatives" prized by corporate America as first-wave colonists of dicey urban areas. They wore tight pants, plaid shirts, and smug expressions, all tribal signifiers, just as bicycles are a totem of their kind, and this one passed me at an apropos spot: the former location of the Hotel Californian, another relic of the silent era, where a $28-million apartment complex, the so-called Paseo at Californian, is under construction. Quaint old buildings are being demolished all over L.A. to accommodate charmless yet costly replacements, a trend justified by politicians and real-estate developers as a solution to the city's housing crunch, as if they aren't contributing to the crunch by displacing tenants now compelled to seek every homeless Angeleno's chimera: affordable rent. Possibly the cyclist moved to Westlake because he was priced out of downtown, itself a dicey area before a dramatic facelift a few years ago, and he may well be priced out of Westlake a few years hence. First-wave colonists are personae non gratae once they've braved and bettered conditions for the affluent second wave, and I write from experience as a first-wave colonist in Manhattan and again in Brooklyn when New Yorkers carried a little cash in their wallets to appease muggers—twenty dollars was considered a reasonable minimum—and hid the rest in their shoes.

A block from Maryland, I passed St. Vincent's Hospital, where I was treated once for a foot injury. It was an older and more serious leg injury that concerned me now, and I was headed to a clinic five or so blocks away to schedule an appointment with an orthopedist. Then I retraced my route, headed now for the Metro Rail station across from MacArthur Park, and found myself dodging traffic on 3rd Street at Alvarado. Lunchtime was over and rush hour hadn't begun, so traffic was relatively light, and when I say that I found myself dodging it, I mean I was daydreaming as usual and didn't fully realize that cars were buzzing around me until a woman somewhere, possibly a driver, yelled something about jaywalking. I had injured my leg this way, a habit picked up in New York, where I had obviously failed to learn that daydreaming is apt to result in disaster on busy, cutthroat streets. I deserved to be admonished for jaywalking.

But the voice didn't have an admonishing tone. It was a friendly voice, and when I looked around to place it, I saw an astonishing woman who was dodging traffic a lane behind me and smiling as if to imply complicity. She was in her late thirties or early forties, tall and powerfully built and definitely female, though I wondered momentarily if she was transgender and if her straight black hair, waist-length and cut in bangs, was a wig. The Ikettes, backup singers for the Ike & Tina Turner Revue, had hair like that, and Claudia Lennear, the ex-Ikette who purportedly inspired the Rolling Stones' "Brown Sugar," had a similar espresso complexion; but this woman's skin was streaked with ashy gray, as if she had been mixing mortar or cleaning a chimney, and she wore a powder-blue hospital gown and matching slippers, while lugging a tote bag that may have contained the clothes on her back when she checked into St. Vincent's, where I supposed she had been a patient. The gown didn't fit her. It exposed her muscular legs from groin to ankle, yet she hadn't bothered to change out of it on being discharged, such was her haste to leave. It couldn't have been pleasant in the psych ward, if that's where she was held, and while I preferred her smile to the haughtiness of the cyclist, I quickened my pace to put some distance between us, just as she seemed to be putting some between distance between herself and St. Vincent's, jaywalking to catch a bus or train, if she didn't live in the neighborhood.

It's a photogenic neighborhood, from my perspective. The fleabags, the pawnshops, the vendors and their wares: I've photographed them all. The camera likes squalor. It likes grit. It likes the sort of mystery posed by a woman wearing a hospital gown in public, or it likes it if the framing is right, and I jogged ahead of her, downhill on Alvarado, to scout for a frame that she would complete when she stepped into it unwittingly; but I hadn't found an acceptable frame by the time she appeared at the top of the hill, so I abandoned the idea and continued on my way. The Taylor murder site was half a block in front of me, and I wondered if the two old apartment buildings across the street, the Roxy and the Ozmun, existed at the time of the murder. The Roxy went up seven years later, I would learn online, but the Ozmun dates to 1917, and I imagine its tenants were questioned by police about any suspicious-looking people they might have seen in the neighborhood, maybe especially anyone matching Faith MacLean's description of a "motion picture burglar," on that winter night in 1922.

Suddenly, from behind me, I heard a scream. I was sure it came from the woman in the hospital gown, and I was afraid she had somehow divined my discarded plan to photograph her and the scream announced a confrontation that I aimed to quell by walking on as if I had heard nothing. Then there were sounds of a scuffle and I turned to see the woman charging downhill in my direction while glancing backward and screaming, repeatedly, "Leave me alone!" to invisible assailants, ghosts or demons, hot on her trail.

Then they became visible to me: three or four uniformed cops and paramedics, some wearing latex gloves and all of them bunched together, so that they fairly collided when they stopped short on the curb, abruptly giving up the chase. The woman had leapt off the curb and was now racing across Alvarado with a stride that made me think of scissors opening as far as they'll reach on the hinge, her gown inching upward, her thighs streaked with spilled black ink as well as the ashy gray. In fact the black was an illusion and the ink was urine, I realized a second later. She may have been an escaped mental patient with a history of violence—that's what the chase suggested—yet she was frightened to the point of pissing herself, still screaming, again and again, "Leave me alone!" like a battered child trying to fend off worse; and I urged her silently on. Yes, leave her alone. Real-estate developers and the politicians who enable them are a greater menace by far in the long run. Persecute them instead.

The northbound lanes of Alvarado were strangely empty, and the southbound lanes were filled with traffic at a standstill. The traffic slowed the woman, who wove through it, and by the time she reached the sidewalk, two cops were waiting outside the Ozmun as if for a blind date arranged by a poor judge of character. Their appearance startled me; I hadn't seen them arrive. They moved slowly toward the woman, who backed away from them, then turned and started running toward the Roxy; but two more cops were advancing on her from that direction after appearing, like the first two, seemingly from nowhere. They converged on her by the gate of the Hollywood Delux Inn, which is sandwiched between the Ozmun and the Roxy and advertises rooms that rent for $59.95 ("+ tax") per day. She didn't try to fight her way out of the trap. It was over and she knew it, and I watched until I was satisfied that she wouldn't be manhandled, then continued downhill, where two more cops were standing on either side of a patrol car that obstructed traffic on Maryland. There were patrol cars further downhill, I now saw, rerouting northbound traffic on Alvarado, and still more patrol cars stalling southbound traffic at the top of the hill. The entire block had been quarantined to ensure the capture of this apparently unarmed and demonstrably terrified woman, naked except for a hospital gown and slippers; and I said to the cops on Maryland as I passed them, "What did she do?" Surely nothing short of murder could warrant such overkill.

But one of the cops, young and Mexican, shrugged and grinned as if to say that my guess was as good as his, and I walked on, past the parking lot and the alley where someone was heard pacing a half-hour before a verified murder. Presumably this was the man, or the woman dressed like a man, who emerged from William Desmond Taylor's bungalow a minute after the pistol report that prompted Faith MacLean to open her door, though she dismissed the incident until Taylor was discovered dead the following morning by his black valet. The murderer was white. That's certain, even if his gender has been questioned. No wonder he walked away so casually while meeting Mrs. MacLean's gaze and disappeared into an alley that itself disappeared more than forty years later. No wonder he didn't seem dangerous to those who crossed his path on Maryland or Alvarado, or not so dangerous that the police were alerted. His race permitted him to come and go without trouble in Westlake as it was then and will be again, once the grit and squalor have been expunged and the streets have been cleared of all suspected criminals but the licensed kind.

2016

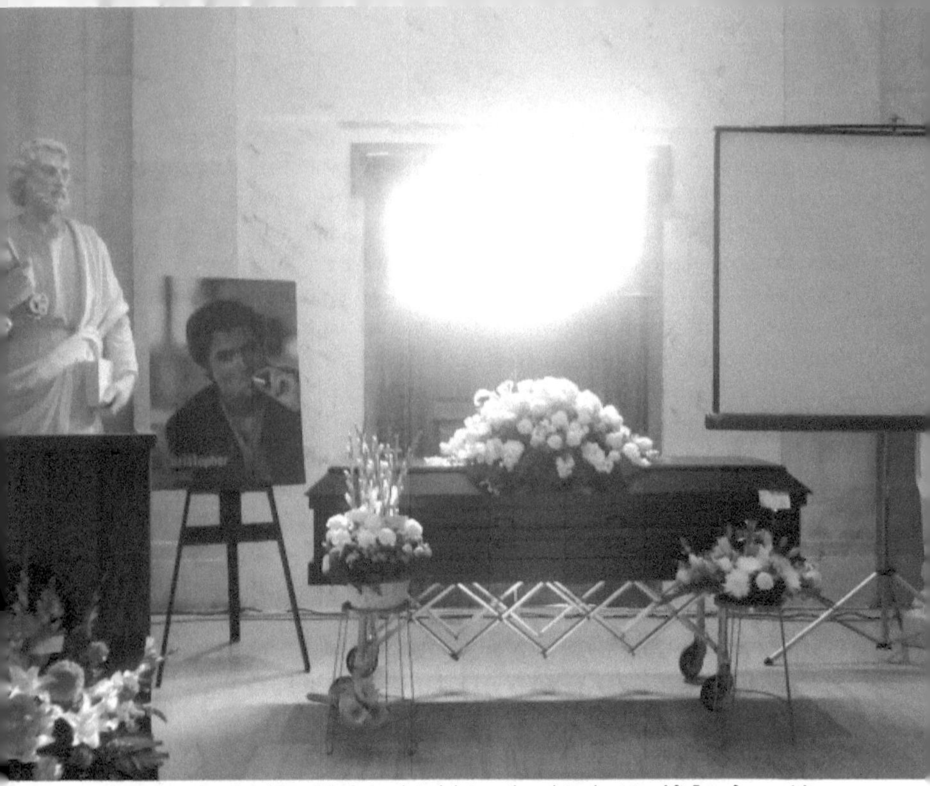

Scenes from a funeral. A picture of the deceased stands between the casket and a statue of St. Peter. Someone left roses and a handwritten note on the casket lifter by the mausoleum wall. "I love you Christopher Jones ♥," the note read. (*Author's collection*)

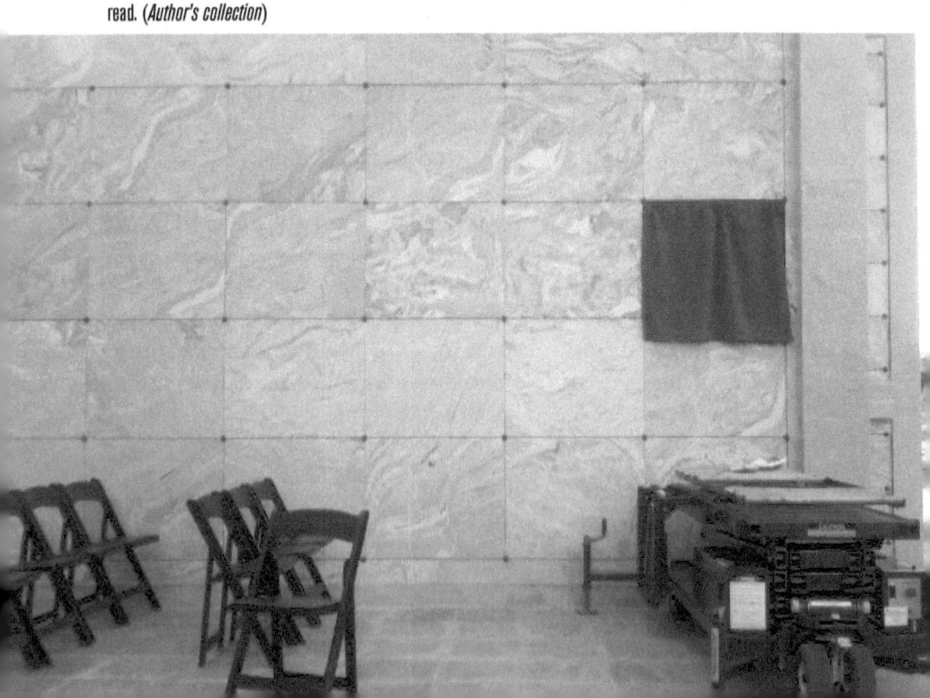

CATCH ME

THIS IS A LOVE STORY, and it begins, for me anyway, with the death of Christopher Jones, "an heir apparent to James Dean who starred in such films as *The Looking Glass War* and *Ryan's Daughter* before quitting show business at the height of his brief but dazzling career," as he was summarized in the lede of his *Hollywood Reporter* obituary. He had been likened to James Dean since the late fifties, when he was a teenager living in a home for orphaned and abandoned boys in Memphis, Tennessee. He had Dean's blondish bedhead and a similar build and stature, but with his snakelike eyes and exotic cheekbones, there was also a resemblance to Rudolph Valentino, as noted by a cameraman on the set of *Chubasco*, the first of six movies Jones made back to back in the late sixties. He played a rock star in the prophetically titled *Wild in the Streets* and a captive stud in *Three in the Attic*, and he was ideally suited to both parts as a real-life romantic rival of Jim Morrison and an exhibitionist with just cause, or as he would say to an interviewer long after his heyday, "I wasn't John Holmes, exactly, but nearly." He was dangerous to know and a danger to himself. He brandished guns and knives, and narrowly escaped death in two car crackups, the first in Italy, where he made another prophetically titled movie, *Brief Season*, and the second in Ireland, where he shot most of *Ryan's Daughter*, a kind of Irish *Madame Bovary* directed by David Lean. He claimed to have had an affair with Sharon Tate while making *Brief Season*—she was working on a different film, her last, in Rome—and when he learned of her murder by the Manson Family a few months later, he snapped and disappeared from the spotlight, even as *Ryan's Daughter*, released at the end of 1970, established him as a top-tier star. Offers poured in, and he was already committed to making more movies, but he ignored the commitments as rumors of schizophrenia, of drug addiction and turning tricks on the street, swirled around him. Pamela Des Barres, the celebrated former groupie and author, had an encounter with Jones outside the Psychedelic Conspiracy, a Sunset Strip head shop, in 1973, and as she wrote later in *Movieline* magazine, now defunct, "his long hair was disheveled, his clothes in tatters, his feet dirty and bare. Since he was obviously having a private conversation with himself, I didn't intrude." I read that story shortly after it was published in 1996, and it haunted me to the point where I eventually retooled it for *Banned for Life*, my novel about a punk-rock pioneer said to be panhandling on the streets of Hollywood following his perplexing withdrawal from the underground music scene.

Jones fathered six children by three women, not including the son he insisted was his by Susan Cabot, a B-movie actress best remembered as the star of *The Wasp Woman*; but he was legally married just once, to another actress named Susan. Her father was Lee Strasberg, the artistic director of the Actors Studio, and she played the title role in the original Broadway production of *The Diary of Anne Frank*, so Susan Strasberg was New York theater royalty when she met Christopher Jones, then studying acting with Frank Corsaro, my acting teacher more than twenty years later. In Hollywood, Susan Strasberg appeared in a couple of drug movies, *The Trip* and *Psych-Out*, and in life she was introduced to drugs by Jones, or so she wrote in her 1980 memoir, *Bittersweet*. He was violent emotionally and physically during their time together, so that she finally took out a restraining order against him, and even then she had to phone for help when he showed up at her door and threatened to kick it in, adopting "his wistful hangdog look when [the police] arrived. I thought I detected a flash of antagonism in their eyes: What's she doing to this nice young man?" This occurred before his crucible while making *Ryan's Daughter*. Though he and Strasberg were divorced by then, she visited him on the set in Ireland and thought he was "acting strangely."

Jones admitted to abusing his ex-wife in a talk with Pamela Des Barres for *Movieline*: "I hit her a few times. But I wouldn't hit a woman now." It was his first interview in more than twenty-five years and a chance to set the record straight, Des Barres told him in print, to which he replied, not unfairly: "Yeah, right, set the record straight. For who? For *who*?" Even so, prompted by Des Barres, he did attempt to set the record straight, in his semi-coherent fashion. He denied ever having abused drugs, contrary to what Susan Strasberg had written in *Bittersweet*: "She's lyin' like a dog. She just wanted to be in with the scene. She's so square." He also denied, initially at least, that Pamela Des Barres had seen him ostensibly homeless on the Sunset Strip in 1973, but he relented when Des Barres held her ground: "I admit I was living like Tarzan, a bit." That had nothing to do with drugs, however: "I wasn't high. I was flipped out on the agony and the ecstasy. Let me tell you, if you have two managers trying to rob you, an ex-wife driving you crazy, and everybody's after your fucking money—I went through a Howard Hughes kind of thing." The murder of

Sharon Tate was another factor, and for the first time, though not for the last, he spoke publicly of their alleged affair: "I didn't fuck her. *She* fucked *me*." Yet another factor: "I had done three pictures in a row in Europe, and had so many love affairs I was exhausted." And another: "The death of Jim Morrison fucked me up more than anything." And then there was the matter of one of his managers conspiring successfully to squelch his betrothal to Olivia Hussey, the Raphaelian star of Franco Zeffirelli's *Romeo and Juliet*, and the same manager, Jones said, later kidnapped him in the guise of arranging psychotherapy at a place in Virginia where members of a Mansonesque cult tried to turn him into a "sex slave" before he escaped and "stayed very much in the background" when the cult was busted. He could easily have topped that far-out tale by recounting the facts in the 1986 murder of Susan Cabot by her son Timothy, who clubbed his mother to death with a barbell, hid the barbell in a box of laundry detergent, and attributed the killing to ninjas. The facts of the case were known to Jones, but when Des Barres asked about it, he claimed paternity of Timothy with little elaboration and added, with no elaboration at all, that the murder was self-defense. So a judge ruled. Timothy was born with a growth-inhibiting condition that Susan Cabot tried to reverse with injections of a hormone derived from the pituitary glands of human cadavers, but the treatments ultimately resulted in folie à deux and may have contributed to Timothy's early death of heart failure in 2003.

The *Movieline* interview coincided with the surprising return of Christopher Jones to the film business. Quentin Tarantino had sought him out for the part of Zed in *Pulp Fiction*—Tarantino is a fan, as am I, of *The Looking Glass War*, an oft-derided adaptation of the John le Carré novel, with Jones as a Polish spy—but Jones said no to Tarantino and yes to Larry Bishop, who had played one of his bandmates in *Wild in the Streets* and asked him to play a hit man in *Mad Dog Time*, Bishop's directorial debut. But *Mad Dog Time* would be Jones's swan song as an actor: in 1997 he had another close brush with death, this time from an abdominal hemorrhage. The cause remains characteristically mysterious: at times Jones said it was perforated ulcers, at other times that he drank "something caustic." His old friend Bill Dakota would tell me firmly it was drug-related, and in fact Jones looked as gaunt and glassy-eyed as a jailhouse junkie in the recent photos that accompanied the *Movieline* piece. Bill Dakota published a notoriously salacious tabloid, *The Hollywood Star*, in the late seventies, but I nevertheless found him credible. During the *Hollywood Star* period, he managed an apartment building where Jones was a tenant and the object of Dakota's blatant infatuation: almost every edition of the *Star* carried an item about him. Still, Dakota was forced to evict Jones, who, in addition to falling behind in his rent, had captured snakes and wild birds and set them free in his apartment. There were bird droppings all over the walls and floor, Dakota said, and a snake crawled down the bath drain and emerged in the tub of another tenant.

The hemorrhage left Jones with a permanent feeding tube. Dakota visited him at the start of a long convalescence, most of it spent at a Hollywood rehabilitation facility, Brier Oak on Sunset, where a furtive camera grabbed a grainy shot of him, pajama-clad in a wheelchair, outside the entrance at night. The shot was for a 1999 episode of E! Channel's *E! True Hollywood Story* series, but Jones declined to participate. He knew he had come off badly in *Movieline*, and he blamed alcohol and Pamela Des Barres, who further vexed him by lending her tapes of their talk to E! Channel and reenacting for the camera her encounter with Jones outside the Psychedelic Conspiracy. Others shared memories and impressions: Larry Bishop, Quentin Tarantino, and Jones's manager, Sherry Dodd, who predicted that we hadn't heard the last of him. She was accurate in the sense that, following his release from Brier Oak, he surfaced on rare occasions to speak with print journalists. I know of a single possible on-camera interview: Skip E. Lowe, the epicene host of a public-access talk show, *Skip E. Lowe Looks at Hollywood*, swore to me that Jones once appeared on it, but I hadn't seen the tape and Skip was prone to confusion. A sample from his show: "Marilyn Monroe went back with Joe DiMaggio after she committed suicide, didn't she?"

I became friendly with Skip while researching a piece about another actor, someone he didn't know as well as he knew Jones, who lived with him for a while after being evicted by Bill Dakota. Skip spoke of having me on his show. A career in show business, successful or not, was his sole criteria for booking guests, and we met one morning—it was June 25, 2013—to discuss the possibility. I'm certain of the date because he inscribed it in a copy of his memoir, *The Boy with the Betty Grable Legs*, which he brought to the meeting and sold to me for twenty dollars. ("Enjoy my journey," the inscription continued.) I was then about to begin a piece about Jim Morrison, and in the course of reading about Morrison, I was reminded of Christopher Jones, who was as enigmatic as ever, going by the few updates I found online, like this one written in digitalese on the message board of the Internet Movie Database: "Chris Jones is a recluse in west hollywood. I met him a few times thru Sherry Dodd. he never left his room till night and never went out. he did paint really beautifully though." Jones was "a man with demons chasing him," this person added, "very thin, alot of health woes," and I gathered that he had been taken in by Sherry Dodd, who posted her e-mail address on the IMDb message board for those who sought to contact him, though there were complaints on the board that she failed to respond to e-mails, even from potential buyers of his artwork. He had been drawing and painting since childhood, and he studied art briefly in New York before he turned to acting, but the study wasn't evident in the portraits I discovered elsewhere online of Marilyn Monroe, James Dean, and Rudolph Valentino, all derived from photos. It was fan art, the work of a hobbyist. I had seen worse, but I had also seen better.

Sherry Dodd was an enigma in her own right, a manager with an exclusive client whose interests she didn't seem to protect. Who was she? What was her game? I thought I detected a clue in a 2009 update of Jones provided by Dodd. "Chris is constantly getting requests for interviews and now he will only do them for money," she responded to a movie blogger who had obviously hoped to interview him. "He spends a lot of time with his children at his beach house. When he's in Hollywood, he stays with me in our place near the Sunset Strip and we are the closest of friends." Skip told me that Jones had been living for years with Paule McKenna, his de-facto wife, and their four children in Seal Beach, but Sherry Dodd had erased Paule McKenna, Soviet style, while emphasizing her own close relationship with Jones. Later I learned that he and McKenna (whose first name is pronounced as it's sometimes spelled: "Paula") had split at some point in the nineties and that McKenna owned the place in Seal Beach where he was a kind of platonic house guest, which made her the latest in a long line of lovers and former lovers and wishful lovers who had given him shelter. Skip fell into the final category, but which category was Dodd's? Regardless, she seemed covetous of him, so that when I decided to follow my piece about Jim Morrison with one about Christopher Jones, I was sure she would snub my interview request. He expected to be paid for interviews in any case. No matter; I would collect the necessary research materials—books, magazines, DVDs—and interview Skip and Bill Dakota and my friend Nadine Bass, who had known Susan Strasberg and Jones's colleague and loyal supporter Shelley Winters, both now dead. Nadine also knew Jones's daughter Jennifer, by Strasberg, as well as Pamela Des Barres, while I had mutual friends with Quentin Tarantino and Larry Bishop, and a few mutual acquaintances with Jones—I had never met him—and after I had spoken to as many of these people as possible, I would petition Sherry Dodd to interview Jones, and however she answered, that would conclude my piece. I didn't anticipate an answer, of course, and almost didn't want one, since I aimed to work the mystery angle, and the less we know of a mystery, the more it finally intrigues. The punk pioneer of *Banned for Life* was a disappointment to the fan who managed to track him down.

But I would never prove so lucky—or unlucky—with Christopher Jones. One morning, in my Facebook feed, I saw a link to the *Hollywood Reporter* obituary that announced his death of gallbladder cancer. I was stunned. He was seventy-two, so I suppose I shouldn't have been stunned, but I somehow believed that, like Keith Richards, an equally implausible survivor of the sixties, Jones would beat the odds indefinitely.

THE *REPORTER* OBITUARY was published online hours after Jones died on January 31, 2014. It mentioned nothing about a memorial service, and an account of one, if I were able to attend, would function as well as a response or non-response from Sherry Dodd as an ending for my piece; but even Sherry Dodd said nothing of a memorial service on Facebook, where I found her profile and "followed" her without "friending" her. She acknowledged Jones's death by uploading a recent and rather elegant photo of him—she had taken it—and a few days later she posted that she was quoted in Jones's *Los Angeles Times* obituary, in which she was identified as his *former* manager. Was that by choice? And wasn't someone going to hold a public service for this once public man? If so, it was omitted by the *Times*.

I called Skip. Yes, he knew Jones had died. No, he didn't know about a service, but he was stuck in a nursing home anyway, recuperating from a nasty fall. I thought Nadine might have heard something from Jennifer Strasberg Jones or even Pamela Des Barres, but she hadn't, she told me when I called her also. Finally, on the verge of giving up, I discovered a communiqué from Paule McKenna on Twitter about a memorial service to be held at Hollywood Forever Cemetery on February 7. Rudolph Valentino is interred at Hollywood Forever, and Jones's portrait of him had been displayed there, according to the *Reporter* obituary, presumably at one of the annual memorials for Valentino, the cemetery's star resident. His supporting cast includes Mel Blanc, the voice of Bugs Bunny; Fay Wray, the unrequited love of King Kong; punk-rock legends Johnny Ramone and Tomata du Plenty; Maila Nurmi, a.k.a. television horror host Vampira; and William Desmond Taylor, the silent-film director and victim of a sensational murder. Toto, the terrier from *The Wizard of Oz*, is buried elsewhere, but a statue of Toto stands beside the cemetery's Cathedral Mausoleum, where the vases on either side of Valentino's crypt are always filled with fresh flowers. Christopher Jones hadn't left show business after all. In death he was back in the thick of it.

After Paule McKenna tweeted about the service, a few more announcements popped up on Facebook. It was scheduled for two p.m. at the Cathedral Mausoleum and open to "the interested public," so I invited Nadine to meet me there and asked her to alert Jennifer and Pamela. I didn't like the idea of attending alone. I pictured Sherry Dodd playing the gatekeeper that she seemed to have enjoyed playing when Jones was alive, limiting access to him one last time. Nadine told me that Sherry Dodd couldn't have been kinder in their only exchange, but I was wary even so as I neared the mausoleum on the day of the service, passing the statue of Toto and a marble wall of honeycomb crypts without inscriptions. The lid had been removed from one of the crypts and a black curtain covered the square hole in the wall, and beneath it, a casket lifter was parked and awaiting cargo. I hadn't realized the service would include interment, but the weather was perfect for it, the overcast winter sky agreeing with the gray of the wall. I was thirty minutes early, and Nadine had beaten me there; I saw her chatting with Jennifer and a few other people beside the wall, and, not wanting to interrupt, I walked on, about to enter the mausoleum when a woman effectively blocked me, stepping into my path. "Who are you here for?" she asked.

"Christopher?" I said in a harmless tone usually reserved for cops. I left it at that initially, since a first name implies familiarity, and when the woman didn't step aside, I said, "Christopher Jones?" I had solved the riddle of the Grail: the woman smiled and handed me a program card with black-and-white head shots of Jones at his movie-star peak on the front and back, and a color still from *Ryan's Daughter* in the middle.

Inside the mausoleum, I recognized Pamela Des Barres by her burgundy hair. She was sitting in one of the folding chairs that faced the casket at the far end of the room, her head turned to me. I felt an instant sense of humility on seeing the casket. It was the near-black of fertile earth, and a lush bouquet of white roses seemed to be growing out of its belly. Two more bouquets of white flowers bookended the casket, and there was a projection screen on one side of it and a poster-size color photo of Jones on the other. He was young in this photo also, and his name was printed at the bottom, as if the guests could use a reminder of the name of the person they had gathered to mourn. In fact, after taking a seat at the back of the room, I overheard a ponytailed guest in his seventies explain to a companion that Christopher Jones was an actor who had been in this and that movie. Heroic statues of the twelve Apostles stood like pillars, six beside the left wall and six beside the right, and those statues must appoint this the "cathedral" room of the mausoleum, I decided. Valentino's crypt was in a separate room adjoining this one.

I was trying to be unobtrusive by sitting in the back, but then Nadine walked past and waved for me to join her and Pamela Des Barres in a row closer to the casket. I had met Pamela once before, I reminded her, though I hadn't asked then, as I had wanted to ask, how she had come by that interview with Christopher Jones. Well, she said, she had been trying to learn what happened to him for a long time, and then her friend Gabriel Byrne mentioned that he was making a movie with him, *Mad Dog Time*, so she approached him about doing an interview and he canceled again and again before he finally went through with it. Of course he was unhappy with the result, but she tried to make him look as good as possible while editing the transcript. It wasn't easy—he said worse than appeared in print—and persuading him to pose for new photos was another trial. "He looked *haggard*," she said. Aging is especially brutal for those blessed by Aphrodite in youth.

Now the family entered the room, sitting ahead of us. I recognized Paule McKenna from her Twitter profile photo, and with a single exception, her children resembled her more than Jones. The exception was their teenage son, who was darker than his father, but otherwise remarkably similar. I hoped that Quentin Tarantino would show, but he didn't, which made Pamela or the actress Peggy Lipton, best known for TV's *The Mod Squad*, the most famous guest, followed by Larry Bishop. Bill Dakota had long since moved to Ohio, and Skip, of course, was in a nursing home, where I planned to visit him after the service. Sherry Dodd was sitting in the row opposite mine, though I didn't realize it until she stood and walked over to Pamela. In the *True Hollywood Story* episode, broadcast more than fifteen years earlier, she had shoulder-length dark red hair and a creamy complexion, but there was a hint of unhealthy gray in her complexion now and her hair was longer and dyed a lighter color. Her Italianate eyes hadn't changed. She leaned down to whisper to Pamela—I heard this much: "He would have wanted you to be here"—then returned to her seat, and I rose to take a few photos of the casket. Others had taken photos, so it must be permissible, though I felt uncomfortable doing it. A lot of these people—most of them—had known this man and loved him. I was a voyeur, a vulture.

The service commenced with a brief statement from a representative of Hollywood Forever, not the woman who had stopped me at the door but a different woman who said, in essence, that she was pleased to add Christopher Jones to the cemetery's well-known collection of the well-known. Then she welcomed to the podium a Methodist reverend whose voice, like hers, reverberated in what was effectively an echo chamber. Jones wasn't perfect, the reverend began, and he probably would have done some things differently if he could have lived his life a second time, but "this is the day we remember the best and bury the rest." He divided Jones's life into two parts, the first starting with his birth as William Franklin Jones, a name he changed after he moved to Hollywood and learned of another actor named William Jones. The reverend was right about the reason for the change, but it happened earlier, before Jones's professional debut in the original Broadway production of Tennessee Williams's *The Night of the Iguana*. Shelley Winters was in that production, and per the reverend, Winters introduced Jones to Susan Strasberg. Again, this was only half right: Jones was with Winters when he first set eyes on Strasberg, but he met her later, during a visit with Frank Corsaro on Fire Island, where Strasberg kept a summer house. These errors were unimportant save that they led me to wonder if the reverend had been personally acquainted with Jones or if he was a kind of hired gun. So far the eulogy seemed have been quilted together with "facts" culled from the Internet.

But the tone became more intimate when the reverend turned to the second part of Jones's life, the part that began when he quit movies, freeing him to pursue his love of art, which he may have inherited from his mother, whose permanent removal to a mental institution, when Jones was four, was reduced tactfully to an "emotional downturn" by the reverend. Jones was fascinated by "historical mysteries and the unknown," the reverend said, and with his "classical bent," he collected ancient coins and statues of ancient deities. He read philosophy and poetry, particularly the works of Byron and Keats, and wrote poetry in "a beautiful hand." He enjoyed watching the History Channel, and hiking the trails of Griffith Park, and cooking for friends and family, and most of all, he loved his children. He wanted to be a family man, a good role model, the reverend said, and as he spoke, sobs echoed around me, while ahead of me, I saw someone consoling Jennifer Strasberg Jones, gently stroking her neck and shoulders. The reverend concluded with a quote from Jones: "I want my epitaph to read that some things are better left unsaid." That struck home, since any effective piece about Jones would ineluctably violate his wish for privacy. Again, I felt like a vulture.

Then the lights were dimmed and "The Crystal Ship," the most elegiac of songs by the Doors, began to play on the mausoleum's loudspeakers, and the projection screen came alive with a slide-show video of photos of Jones. The majority were from *The Looking Glass War*: lobby cards with, in some cases, Japanese titles on them. None were recent or snapped by friends or relatives. Then, when the song and video ended and the lights were switched back on, the pallbearers, which included Jones's sons, gathered around the casket and began to move it outside for the interment. The guests followed. The clouds had dispersed; the sun was now shining. The casket was placed on the casket lifter, and the family sat in folding chairs while everyone else stood. My phone had vibrated inside the mausoleum, alerting me to a text message, and I removed the phone to glance at the text, and when I looked up, the reverend was glowering at me. Point taken: I pocketed the phone. Then the reverend plucked a rose from the bouquet atop the casket and held it for all to see. Life, he said, is short and sweet, and he lifted the flower to his nose and savored its fragrance, and a moment later the casket vanished behind the curtain that covered the unsealed crypt.

AFTER THE SERVICE, as Nadine and I were catching up inside the mausoleum, we were approached by another guest, a youngish guy I had observed sitting alone in the row ahead of us with the slouch of a Method actor of the fifties. "Where's that portrait Chris did of Valentino?" he asked. "I thought it was supposed to be hanging here." I proposed my theory that the portrait had been displayed at a Valentino memorial service, and we all walked back for a look at Valentino's crypt and others, chatting while doing a bit of morbid sightseeing. I had guessed correctly that the youngish guy was an actor. His name was Jason, and he had some success as a "juvenile" type in the nineties, around the time he met Christopher Jones through his acting teacher, Shelley Winters, who saw them as kindred spirits. He also met Skip E. Lowe through Shelley Winters, and when I mentioned that I was about to visit Skip, he offered to drive us both to the nursing home in West Hollywood.

We arrived at suppertime and found Skip in his room, picking at his food and watching *From Here to Eternity* on a tiny retro television. The movie sparked a typical Skip reminiscence: in long-ago Manhattan he came upon Montgomery Clift, who was drunkenly wandering the nighttime streets, and Skip guided him to his brownstone apartment and crashed there. A different version of that story appeared in *The Boy with the Betty Grable Legs,* and now Skip was readying a follow-up book for publication and planning to resume his talk show once he mended and the nursing home released him. Jason asked about the episode of the show with Chris Jones—like me, he hadn't seen it—and Skip recalled a second guest, John Barrymore Jr., and during the taping, Jones either broke a camera or threatened to break one. These details, new to me, were persuasive, but I weighed them against Skip's fanciful account of the Manson murders, based on a confession Jones purportedly made to him. In *The Boy with the Betty Grable Legs* and again in conversation with me, Skip stated that Jones was romancing Sharon Tate at her rented house on Cielo Drive on the night she died there and he missed the killers by minutes when he left to buy cigarettes. In fact, Jones was on location in Ireland with his managers, Rudi Altobelli and Stuart Cohen, at the time of the murders, but there was a Weimaraner dog named Christopher on the Cielo Drive property that night. The Weimaraner was owned by Rudi Altobelli, who also owned the property, and one of the killers testified to seeing a dog peer through a window of the house before the carnage began. This dog was probably Christopher, Jones's namesake, and possibly Jones related the killer's testimony to Skip, who confused Christopher the dog with Christopher the actor and added a separate anecdote about running out for cigarettes to garnish his mangled account. It's also possible that Jones misled Skip for sport or sympathy. He could be manipulative, as demonstrated by the "hangdog look" he adopted for the police when he violated Susan Strasberg's restraining order.

Skip was a die-hard lottery player. Even bedridden in a nursing home, he somehow managed to acquire lottery tickets, which in California can't be bought online. He was sure he had divined the winning numbers for the next day's drawing, and he repeated them to me and Jason more than once in the course of our visit, urging us, as we said goodbye, to buy tickets. They cost only a dollar after all, so Jason stopped at a convenience store near the Sunset Strip, and we lingered for a while in the parking lot, talking mostly about the Manson case and Jones's affair with Sharon Tate. In his most detailed interview about Tate, which he gave to the *Daily Mail* in 2007, Jones remembered that Rudi Altobelli dined with them in Rome on the night the affair started, and I gathered from the *Daily Mail* that Altobelli introduced them. Not so, Jason said; they knew each other from the Chateau Marmont, a block from where Jason and I were now standing. The Chateau Marmont was Jones's usual residence when he wasn't working abroad in the late sixties, and his occasional neighbors there included Jim Morrison and Pamela Courson, Morrison's longtime girlfriend, who propositioned Jones in the hotel's parking garage by way of avenging Morrison's infidelities and guaranteeing his jealousy. Sharon Tate and Roman Polanski, her husband, lived at the Chateau before they moved to Cielo Drive, and Jason said that Jones sensed Tate's interest in him even then, though, per the *Daily Mail*, nothing happened until she invited him to her room in Rome, asked if he wanted to smoke opium, and pulled him into bed with her. This is all in the spirit of the swinging sixties, but it isn't in the spirit of Sharon Tate, an expectant mother who ceased her casual drug use the instant she learned she was pregnant, her friends concurred post-mortem. She wouldn't even touch a glass of wine, Polanski told homicide detectives, and there wasn't "a chance of any other man getting close to Sharon." Again, her friends concurred, save the one quoted anonymously in *The Roman Polanski Story*, an unauthorized biography published in 1980, about Tate's affair with an unnamed man in Italy while Polanski was in London, collaborating on the screenplay for what would have been his next movie. Supposedly Tate confided in the anonymous friend after she returned to Los Angeles without Polanski, who had their house sitters remain with Sharon as her due date neared and he finalized the screenplay in London. He was the spouse who ordinarily strayed, and according to the friend, Sharon wanted to pay him back by taking a lover of her own, à la Pamela Courson, though Sharon's revenge was private, or as the friend said of Polanski: "I'm sure to this day he doesn't know that she was unfaithful to him in Italy."

The Roman Polanski Story is a flagrant hatchet job written by Thomas Kiernan to capitalize on Polanski's infamous statutory-rape case, but it's worth noting as the sole account of an Italian affair that doesn't cite Jones as the source. Possibly Jones read the book, or anyway read the crucial passage, and decided he was the nameless lover and, perhaps unconsciously, converted his friendship with Tate into a full-blown affair, and so settled on a romantic narrative for his breakdown while making *Ryan's Daughter*, a dreary experience for everyone involved. The fickle Irish weather caused constant delays, as did David Lean's perfectionism. Jones was a charismatic but unruly actor, a common combination, and the more Lean tried to control him, the more fractious he became. The remote location was a gulag to him, and seems to have aggravated a second legacy of his institutionalized mother, if his flair for art was the first. Susan Strasberg, in *Bittersweet*, observed early inklings of mental illness unrelated to drugs. Jones spoke of a generic *them* who were out to get him. He gave Strasberg a black eye after he imagined a conversation between her and another man. He had a "love affair" with a female ghost, informing Strasberg that the ghost was jealous and "told me to get rid of you." That ghost may have been a harbinger of Sharon Tate. I never doubted that Pamela Courson threw herself at Jones precisely as he said she did—it's perfectly in tune with her bold character—but I was more skeptical of his affair with Tate than I was of his paternity of Susan Cabot's son. Cabot was living in New York when she became pregnant in 1963, weeks before Jones met Strasberg on Fire Island, and both women were petite, brunette, and Jewish, so it isn't inconceivable that Jones could have abandoned Cabot for a younger and more prestigious actress of the same type.

But Jason accepted the Tate affair as fact, having discussed it with Jones personally; plus, it was confirmed by Rudi Altobelli when Jason met him and Jones for drinks one night. I was surprised that Altobelli would even associate with Jones after being maligned by him as a career wrecker and embezzler, draining his savings while obstructing deals. Stuart Cohen, Altobelli's partner who preceded him in death, was similarly maligned, but Altobelli alone was accused of interfering in Jones's romance with Olivia Hussey (Altobelli was her godfather) and of luring him to the sex-cult compound in Virginia. Plus, Jones alleged, Altobelli made light of Sharon Tate's death by displaying her bloodstains to visitors to the house on Cielo Drive. As a witness in the trial of Charles Manson and three of his minions, Altobelli testified that Manson strolled onto his lawn one day in search of the previous tenant and came face to face with Sharon Tate—their only known encounter. No words were exchanged between them, and she and her house guests were later slaughtered solely because they occupied a residence familiar to Manson and the proxies he dispatched there for reasons still debated by armchair detectives. Jason was open to revisionist theories of the case, which I rejected; but despite ourselves, I think we both believed that we each possessed a winning lottery ticket, thanks to Skip, whose foresight was as reliable as his hindsight.

SHERRY DODD was a fleeting topic in the parking lot that night. Jason knew her and dismissed her as less a manager and more an oddball groupie. Once, he said, he went to visit Chris at Brier Oak and Sherry loaded Jones into her car while babbling inexplicably about cults and sped off with him. Jones told Jason about another outing with Sherry, who spotted Quentin Tarantino sitting outside a café and said, "Oh, look, Chris, it's Quentin! Let's go talk to Quentin, Chris! Don't you want to talk to Quentin?" Chris had no pressing need to talk to Quentin, Jason said, but Sherry turned the car around and forced a sidewalk summit. This all fit my notion of her, and I decided she was best avoided if I ever moved forward with my piece about Jones. I was ambivalent about the piece after the memorial service.

Then Sherry Dodd sent me a friend invitation on Facebook. I had forgotten that I had "followed" her there, and she clearly must have noticed. It couldn't hurt to accept her invitation, I thought, and over the next month or so, she "liked" a few of my innocuous posts. Her posts were also innocuous. She recycled holiday memes with cute animals, and linked to classic rock songs on YouTube, and uploaded blurry photos from her past. Vintage Los Angeles was a recurring theme: postcard shots of the city in the sixties and earlier. Christopher Jones wasn't the recurring theme I expected him to be. Most of her posts about him predated his death, and none of them were in egregious taste.

Finally I sent her a private message. We hadn't met at the memorial service, I said, but I had been there to gather material for a forthcoming piece, and I wondered if we could get together for an interview. Sure, she answered quickly. I had her figured as a lady of leisure who had managed Jones as a hobby, but she alluded to jobs and medical snags, so she was only free on Thursdays, she wrote. Fine, I wrote back, and we met the following Thursday at Barney's Beanery, a place I suggested partly because I knew she lived nearby. She recognized me right away, though I almost never posted recent photos of myself on Facebook, and sat across from me in a booth with an unobstructed view of Santa Monica Boulevard. She ordered scrambled eggs. We made small talk. She was a native of L.A., she said, and used to work as an extra in movies and TV shows. She took it as a compliment when I told her she looked Italian. There was a calm about her, a lack of hurry. She seemed to smile even when she wasn't smiling. Her long brown hair helped to obfuscate her age, but I guessed her to be in her mid-sixties.

Barney's Beanery was one of Jim Morrison's hangouts. That was the other reason I had suggested it: mention of Morrison might jumpstart the interview. I was right. Sherry was at the Doors' Hollywood Bowl show in 1968, she said, and Chris was there also. She saw him. She had a crush on him from *The Legend of Jesse James*, the TV show that launched him, and she used to see him all over town, but she never approached him because he was always with other people. Then he stopped making movies, and she heard that he was flipped out and living on the streets, and it was true that he was flipped out, she said, but it wasn't really true that he lived on the streets. Shelley Winters had rented a motel room for him on Sunset Boulevard, and James Dean's friend Jack Simmons owned a trailer home that he donated to Chris, who himself owned a house in the Hollywood Hills, though he never spent any time there. Sherry believed the house was on one of the streets named for birds, like Blue Jay Way. George Harrison lived on Blue Jay Way, which he immortalized in the Beatles' song about it—possibly my favorite song about L.A.

In any case, Sherry said, she didn't meet Chris until 1973. She was specific about the date. It was the Fourth of July, and she had gone out for lunch at Ben Frank's, a diner on the Sunset Strip, and Chris was standing in the parking lot, looking much as Pamela Des Barres described him in *Movieline*, with long hair and disheveled clothes, though he wasn't barefooted; he was wearing worn-out shoes. Sherry was with her ex-husband

Greg and a friend of theirs, and they all entered the restaurant, and later she went alone to her car to retrieve something and Chris walked up and asked if he could borrow a hairbrush. He told her his name was James. She humored him, lending "James" her hairbrush. "Come with me," he said, and she knew she was crazy to do it, but she followed him into an alley, where he suddenly grabbed her. She pulled away. She had to get back to her friends, she said. He asked where she lived. In the Hollywood Hills, she said, on Paseo Del Serra, off Hillcrest Road. "Maybe I'll see you," he said, and she returned to Ben Frank's with this strange story of being grabbed in an alley by Christopher Jones after letting him use her hairbrush. She wasn't scared so much as intrigued, despite his aggression and obvious madness.

Then, at three in the morning a month later, somebody threw a toy metal car through an open window in her kitchen. She was woken by the sound of it hitting the floor, and when she looked out the window, there, staring up at her, was Chris, who said, "It's me, James." She invited him up, and he stayed for months. She went on calling him James at first. Even people who knew James Dean, like Jack Simmons, were always telling Chris how akin they were, so that had become part of his madness. To Sherry he seemed "possessed" by James Dean, but one day he spoke of Ireland and she said, "I love *Ryan's Daughter*," and so broke the spell. "You know who I am," he said. He had lived with her for two weeks at that point, and some days he was lucid and other days he would wake her by grabbing her face and threaten to tie her up. Sometimes, in the middle of the night, he would slip outside and swim naked in the koi pool of Yamashiro, a Japanese restaurant atop a neighboring hill, and return, still naked, to the apartment. She mentioned the moonlight swims on the *True Hollywood Story* episode, but she kept the rest to herself. She knew his kids would see the show, and one of them, Christopher Jr., was on it, along with his mother, Carrie, who was Chris's girlfriend after Sherry and before Paule McKenna. Carrie and Chris Jr. now lived somewhere in the South, Sherry said, and they didn't make it back for the memorial service for whatever reason.

One day Sherry came home to the place on Paseo Del Serra to find her television smashed and Chris gone. Periodically he would disappear to the room that Shelley Winters had rented for him or Jack Simmons's trailer. The trailer was parked just down the hill, and Sherry drove there, furious, and told Chris she was done with him; the TV was the last straw. He apologized in his fashion. There had been a broadcast of *The Looking Glass War*, and he was so upset by the way it was cut, he threw a rock through the screen. He promised to buy a new TV, so she relented, and soon became so frightened by his escalating violence and threats of further violence that she sublet her apartment for two months. She hoped the two months would cool things with Chris, but he turned up again when the sublet was over, and late one night, as she arrived home, he came up behind her and covered her mouth and dragged her inside the apartment and pushed her onto the bed. Somehow she managed to free herself and scramble outside and run screaming down the hill. He chased her and caught up to her, and she yanked his long hair while screaming for help, and one of her neighbors, an actor named John, walked out to investigate with a knife in his hand. The knife was serendipity—John had been peeling an apple when he heard Sherry scream—but Chris saw it and stopped short. He was only kidding, he said, he wasn't going to hurt her, but John escorted Sherry into his house, and she gave up her apartment shortly afterward.

"So that," she told me, "was the end of my relationship with Chris for years." She read in *The Hollywood Star* that he was living at the building managed by Bill Dakota on Argyle Street, and she dropped by one day to see if Chris was any better, and he did seem better, and he seemed better still when she saw him one night a few years later, but the big change occurred after the hemorrhage that almost killed him. He was declared clinically dead in the ambulance en route to Cedars-Sinai Hospital, where emergency surgery saved his life, and she didn't know if it was the near-death experience or what, but he was a different person when she saw him again by chance at Brier Oak. The darkness was all gone. There were no bad vibes anymore. She visited him at Brier Oak as often as possible, and E! Channel contacted him about this show they were planning to do, and he didn't want to be interviewed for it—he looked terrible and felt as bad as he looked—so he asked Sherry if she could handle the *True Hollywood Story* thing and any other business while he recovered. That's when she became his manager. His esophagus was blocked, so he couldn't swallow solid food, and she arranged for corrective surgery at UCLA—she knew a good doctor there—but he ultimately decided to forgo the surgery because he was afraid something might go wrong and he wouldn't see his kids grow up. He didn't mind living with a feeding tube, but he was frail and still bleeding from the hemorrhage, so she started bringing him protein shakes with vitamins, and gradually his condition improved to the point where he could leave Brier Oak for daily excursions. Once, she said, as she was driving him around, he spotted Quentin Tarantino and asked her to turn back so he could say hello. Jason told me that story, I said, though I didn't share his reversed version of it. Sherry's expression soured when I mentioned Jason. He was obsessed with the Manson case, she said. She didn't think it was good for Chris's recovery to have somebody like that around him, so she would try to truncate Jason's visits at Brier Oak.

But it was Sherry's visits that irked the staff. They were strict about curfews, and sometimes she kept Chris out too late, or they talked too long in the parking lot. Eventually he was ordered to leave, and she moved him into the two-bedroom apartment that she shared with her ex-husband Greg and their son on La Cienega Boulevard. Space, not jealousy, could be a problem. She and Greg were just friends. She and Chris were now just friends. He had a girlfriend, Jyl, and he also spent time at her place, and when he stayed with Sherry, she would give him tube feedings and clean the tube and otherwise play nurse, and he painted and considered movie offers—yes, he still got them—and they collaborated on a screenplay, since he spoke of wanting to direct. He and Paule had made their peace, and she would drop their kids off, sometimes without notice, and it was a cramped arrangement already, and looking after Chris was one thing and looking after his kids was another. Finally, when it happened once too often, Chris moved to Paule's house in Seal Beach. Sherry saw less and less of him after that, but they always kept in touch by phone. They had last spoken a few months before, on Thanksgiving. Chris said he wasn't feeling well. He was diagnosed with cancer a few days later. She was never able to visit him at the hospital. The cancer claimed him so quickly, and she called friends to let them know, people like Skip E. Lowe, who said, "Christopher *who*?" We both laughed. She and Skip went back years, and she went much further back with Jones than I had realized, relating from start to finish a complicated relationship of decades, meanwhile eating her scrambled eggs. She had brought something to show me as well: a fist-sized plaster bust of Rudolph Valentino in *The Sheik,* his signature role. The bust had been sculpted by Jones, of course, and I was touched by her tacit pride in it and also by the bust itself. He was gone but this remained. *Ars longa, vita brevis.*

She showed me something else: a photo of Jones outside Falcon Lair, Valentino's estate in Benedict Canyon, half a mile or less from where Rudi Altobelli's house once stood on Cielo Drive. I was flabbergasted. Jones looked to be in his late thirties, yet he was sixty-four when Sherry took the photo in 2005. "I guess I brought him back to health," she said. She always thought he turned down movies because he didn't look as good as he did in his twenties. He hated being photographed. I hate it too. Vanity, thy name is former actor.

TWO WEEKS TO THE DAY after our first meeting, Sherry drove me to her old place on Paseo del Serra. Contractors were doing work on the garage, and she explained to them that she used to live upstairs and wanted to have a quick look. She led me up a wooden staircase and onto a deck with a view of Yamashiro. That was Chris's path, she said, when he would go skinny dipping. Then she turned and, peering through the uncovered windows of the apartment, pointed to the approximate spot on the floor where the toy car landed. It was a small place but prohibitively expensive now as it wasn't in 1973, and she reminisced a little about the area as it was then, and lingered as if to listen for phantom music that only she could hear.

It was now two and a half months since the memorial service, and Sherry wanted to see if Chris's crypt had been engraved, so we drove to Hollywood Forever and past the gates to the mausoleum. The crypt had been sealed, of course, but there was no engraving on it. Sherry seemed disappointed, if not quietly peeved. Peacocks roamed the grassy parts of the cemetery. I had been there many times and never seen peacocks, and I chased this one and that one, trying to take a picture. Sherry joined the chase, and finally a peacock froze in front of a tombstone and fanned out for the camera, like a cornered celebrity appeasing a paparazzo. The photo was a bore compared to the chase. Sherry was fun and free-spirited, a throwback to the kind of L.A. woman who inspired songs of the seventies like "Tiny Dancer." Chris, she said, used to tell her that he argued inevitably with every woman but her. I could believe it. There was something soothing about her. The sense of calm I had felt in our first meeting was infectious.

I devised a new angle for my piece about Jones—or "Chris," as I started to think of him—and shared it with Sherry the next time we got together. It was based on the mondo movies of the sixties: episodic documentaries like *Mondo Mod* and *Mondo Hollywood* that titillated provincial audiences with gonzo footage of trippy parties and wiggy people. This passage from *Bittersweet* has a mondo feel: "We'd go to a discotheque almost every night until the sun came up, and then we'd sleep away a good part of the day. Between the marijuana and the pills we were taking, we were exhausted the next day." The Manson case, the Susan Cabot case, *The Hollywood Star*, Chris's "homeless" period, his apartment with free-range birds and snakes: that was all the stuff of a mondo movie, and I would title my piece "Mondo Christopher Jones," I told Sherry, who seemed amused by it, though I wondered if she, like me, had reservations. It was a sneering slant on someone who had been mentally ill, and I questioned Sherry hoping to discover a better approach in a telling detail, some hidden "Rosebud." How did Chris and Jim Morrison get along? Not well; Chris liked the Doors' music but Morrison was "menacing" toward him. Did he know the reverend who eulogized him? Probably not; he believed in God but he was never a regular churchgoer. What caused his near-fatal hemorrhage? Not even Chris knew the answer to that; he blacked out and woke a week later in Cedars-Sinai with no memory of how he got there, but the doctors thought he had tried to kill himself with a caustic liquid. Chris always denied it, though he was depressed at the time because he had just broken up with Paule—"again"—and he couldn't see their kids. Sherry didn't believe drugs were involved. She never saw Chris do drugs.

We were sitting in the courtyard of Cat & Fiddle, a Mission-style pub in Hollywood that served as a location for *Casablanca* and later became a hangout for rockers. It was a Thursday afternoon, as usual, and we basked in the glorious May weather, snacking on fries and talking occasionally about subjects other than Chris. She was impressed by my knowledge of vintage L.A. and said I should work as a tour guide. She had two jobs, she said, one of them running errands for a geriatric woman, buying groceries and that sort of thing. She glossed over the second job, and told me nothing about the weekly medical appointment that she mentioned every time I tried to schedule a meeting with her. She canceled our next meeting because she had to see a specialist, or so she wrote, again without elaboration, and I started a new piece while I argued with myself about "Mondo Christopher Jones." All communication stopped, of necessity on my part. I'm irascible when I'm writing. I couldn't account for Sherry's silence.

Then she interrupted it with a couple of brief e-mails about tour-guide jobs. She was quite the job bloodhound, sending me links to Craigslist ads, none of which called for knowledge of vintage L.A. These messages were followed by a longer one concerning a matter that had puzzled Sherry for years: the Sharon Tate affair. We had discussed it at our first meeting at Barney's Beanery. Sherry was inclined to believe Chris, but there was never any proof, and she was dubious that Rudi Altobelli had confirmed the affair to Jason. However, Olivia Hussey might be able to confirm it to me. She had been staying with Chris in Ireland at the time of the Manson murders, and Sherry and Olivia had a mutual friend, and now Sherry wanted me to contact this person to request an audience with Olivia. It was a wild-goose chase in the making, I wrote back to say with ill-disguised impatience. Sherry didn't respond. Good, I thought. That's one less distraction while I work.

Weeks passed. The silence continued and guilt set in. I knew Sherry meant well, and she was right in any case: this might be the Rosebud I needed, the very Rosetta Stone. I wrote to Olivia Hussey's friend, her husband, and finally, on Facebook, to Olivia Hussey herself, all, as expected, to no avail; but I spoke to Debra Tate, Sharon's sister, at an event for her coffee-table book, *Sharon Tate: Recollection*. She was familiar with the story about her sister and Christopher Jones, though she didn't hear it from Sharon and Sharon told her "everything." Debra Tate is often denounced as a liar and worse in the strange world of Manson-case devotees, but her denial to me was credibly inconclusive. As for Rudi Altobelli, I spoke to his decades-long assistant Woody McBreairty, who said that Rudi never alluded to a romance between Chris Jones and Sharon Tate, and for that matter, Chris never talked about it either, not when he lived in the guesthouse on Cielo Drive after *Ryan's Daughter*, or later, when he would visit to read scripts in a room above the garage. In fact, Woody learned, he wasn't reading scripts at all; he was drawing pictures—Woody still had one of them. Then he withdrew utterly from his career and vanished, and Woody recalled being alone in the house on a spooky night when someone kept phoning and hanging up without a word, so that he finally called the LAPD and Rudi's partner Stuart, who instructed him to say immediately, "Chris, Stuart wants you to come inside and wait for him," the next time he answered the phone. Stuart seemed certain that Chris was lurking somewhere outside by the gate, but if so, the LAPD didn't find him.

I also spoke to Quentin Tarantino, not about Sharon Tate but Sherry. Yes, he remembered someone approaching him one day to say that Christopher Jones would like to have a word with him. No, he didn't feel coerced. He walked to a car where Chris was sitting in the passenger seat and they chatted for maybe ten minutes. Chris had a feeding tube. He did not seem "deranged"—in fact, Quentin cringed when I used that word. Their encounter was as pleasant as their first meeting to discuss *Pulp Fiction*, though shorter by several hours, and his implicit admiration of Chris would probably have pleased Sherry more than his exoneration of her.

I SENT SHERRY UPDATES of my research, apologizing more than once for my curtness in our last exchange. Finally she replied. She didn't feel well enough to get together, she wrote, but I was welcome to call. It was the first time we had spoken on the phone, and I asked about her living situation, a minor mystery, and was told she still lived with her son, though, cagey as ever about subjects other than Chris, she never disclosed her son's name. The larger mystery of her health had deepened. She sounded weak and wheezy, as if deprived of oxygen after surviving a fire, and I said, "Sherry, this is hard for me, but for weeks you've been talking about doctors' appointments, and then you disappear and I call and, you know, it's obvious something isn't right. Do you want to tell me what it is?"

It was cancer. She had had it for a long time, she said. It started in her breast and now it had spread, and while she wasn't explicit about the metastasis, she did say that she had fluid in her lungs, and when I heard that, I thought, Oh my God, she's a goner. I had been through this with a former girlfriend, a cancer patient who died days after calling me to say that she had fluid in her lungs. Her name was Kerry. Sherry and Kerry: the rhyme was itself a portent; but of course I was mum about it. Sherry now had to have her lungs drained once a week at a hospital, and there was talk of equipping her with a kind of pump so that she could drain the fluid herself, at home. She was apprehensive about the pump. A lung would have to be pierced, and she was used to the daily discomfort of living with cancer, but this was pain of a different order. I asked if she wanted me to accompany her the next time she went to the hospital. No, she said, and she didn't want me to visit her at home either. She wasn't up to visitors.

We spoke again a week or so later. She had gotten the pump. She had no choice, she was told, and the procedure was as painful as feared. It was still painful. All she did was lie in bed and move as little as possible. It hurt even to talk. She had tried so hard to stay positive, she said, and her only recourse now was chemotherapy, which, if she were lucky, could extend her life for as long as a year, and between the pain and the indignity of losing her hair, she might be better off dead. Kerry had faced a similar dilemma, and I couldn't advise her any more than I could now advise Sherry; it was a private matter for Sherry to decide, and since she was still adamant that she didn't want visitors, all I could do was call, and if she felt strong enough to answer and talk, I would listen, though for the most part she listened while I talked about the one topic that seemed to assuage her. Yes, she agreed, Chris should have received more attention when he died, at least as much as Philip Seymour Hoffman, who fatally overdosed three days later. Facebook lost its hive mind when Philip Seymour Hoffman died, and sure, okay, he was a better actor than Chris, but no contemporary actors—no celebrities—were charismatic on a par with Chris because they weren't authentically wild like he was; they were milquetoasts by comparison, and yes, the people close to Chris paid a price for that, but it was worth it in the end: no friction, no fire. She never referred to him as the love of her life, but that's what I took him to be. "I remember," she said, "he told me once, 'I'm going to die before you, but don't worry; when you die, I'm going to be there to catch you on the other side.'" I wondered if he told her that before or after her diagnosis. I didn't ask. It was her prerogative, not mine, to raise the topic of cancer. She rarely raised it.

Then, toward the end of September, Skip E. Lowe died. I had passed him on the street in Hollywood during the summer, but he was oblivious and I wasn't in the mood to tax his memory by greeting him. Now I regretted not greeting him. He was eighty-five and died of emphysema, according to obituaries, which, shades of Chris, said nothing about a memorial service, and Sherry spoke of attending if there was one. That gave me hope. She sounded sturdier when I called her about Skip. I was walking near Hollywood Forever, and Sherry thought someone there might know about a service, so I ducked into the cemetery and, finding the office locked, kept walking to the Cathedral Mausoleum, hoping to spot an administrator. Sherry had been to the cemetery since our visit together in April, she told me, and Chris's crypt still wasn't engraved then, but it was now, I was happy to report. I described it to her. ALWAYS IN OUR HEARTS, the inscription read, and bronze flower holders had been added to the lower corners, while in the center there was a small picture of Chris, a still from *Chubasco* with his co-star Susan Strasberg cropped out of it. I snapped some photos and posted them on Facebook for Sherry to see, and as I was about to leave, I was stopped by a mother and daughter with Southern accents, tourists seeking the statue of Toto. The mother especially seemed smitten by the still of Chris, forever young in Hollywood Forever, and I encapsulated his life and career and pointed the way to Toto, assuming the role of tour guide that struck Sherry as an ideal match.

A MEMORIAL SERVICE was held for Skip in late October at an Italian restaurant in Beverly Hills where he used to host an open-mic night. Sherry seldom answered the phone by then, but she sent me a note to say that she couldn't make it and afterward wrote to ask how it went. It felt, I replied, like a cast party for a variety show at a lesser casino—Siegfried & Roy without the lions—but, as an alien to that side of show business, I was glad to have gotten a peek at it. She didn't respond. Cat & Fiddle was closing, a victim of the gentrification that would eventually claim Yamashiro, and I posted something on Facebook about it, but she didn't respond to that either. Calls weren't returned. Possibly, I thought, the cause was chemo. She had never shared her decision about it, not with me, and my encouragement might be a nuisance to her now. I would try again after the holidays.

Then I received horrifying news, not about Sherry but my friend Corey Brandenstein, a talented filmmaker who hung himself on Christmas Day, leaving behind a wife and five-year-old son. Why? No one could fully explain it. Corey was thirty-nine and a mainstay in a circle of friends that had started to disperse but reunited for a wake, and two days after the wake—it was New Year's Day, in fact—I read an open letter to Sherry posted on Facebook by William Richert, the director of such films as *Winter Kills* and *A Night in the Life of Jimmy Reardon*. Bill Richert and I were Facebook friends because of Sherry, who saw us as simpatico, and he phoned her, I knew, as often as I did. "I'm glad you kept your hair," he wrote publicly to her. "You wouldn't let the chemo take that away and you wouldn't let doctors break your spirit." So she hadn't gone forward with chemo. I could guess what followed, though not the specifics. She had died in her sleep at a hospice two weeks earlier. Her son had left a message for Bill after speaking with a hospice worker who "sounded positively happy to give him this otherwise terrible news, it seemed she was almost laughing with joy" because, as Bill reasoned it, she "got a whiff what happiness was in store" for Sherry: "If what goes around comes around, you're in paradise."

But that was no comfort to me. I never expected to like Sherry as much as I did, and now, too quickly, she was gone, the climactic death of a year filled with it and a catalyst for the grief I hadn't expressed for Corey, whose suicide had numbed me while I pondered the motive. I knew Corey for thirteen years, yet he was finally as mysterious to me as Chris, a stranger who had come to feel like an intimate, and Chris in turn was finally mysterious to Sherry, his fan, then lover, then manager, then nurse, yet after all that, she couldn't swear that he had an affair with poor Sharon Tate or that he once tried to kill himself with a caustic liquid. *Some things are better left unsaid*, he wanted his epitaph to read, and so it would have to be in my piece about him—about him and her both. Yes, I had my angle. What else could it be? She had given me her time when her time was running out, playing the tour guide that she projected onto me, driving us to the place on Paseo del Serra and then to Hollywood Forever, where there would never be a service or a vault for Sherry. I couldn't even find an obituary. Her Facebook page was her only memorial, and just when I felt sound enough to begin writing, I discovered something there that crushed me all over again. It was a relatively recent photo of Chris that Sherry had uploaded during the summer, when her illness entered its terminal stage, and as if to compensate for his crypt, which was then unmarked, she had noted his birth and death dates above the photo, and followed that with a plea that would have been mysterious if I had seen it months before: "Catch me!"

2017

STEVEN BAUER

JENNIFER RUBIN

WILLIAM KATT

IN THE DARK...

CAN YOU TELL

A KILLER

FROM A COP?

STRANGER BY NIGHT

The sell sheet, a double-sided brochure distributed to film buyers, for *Stranger by Night*. The restraint here was corrected on the VHS sleeve, which emphasized Jennifer Rubin's cleavage and Steven Bauer's gleaming Beretta 92F. (*Author's collection*)

HELLO STRANGER

BY MY COUNT, I wrote seven "erotic thrillers," a largely and justly forgotten genre that combined noir and softcore porn. It was a favorite of tight-fisted producers of the VHS era, since it required no special effects, aside from squibs and silicone breasts, and the action was confined to a few affordable locations. Much of *Stranger by Night*, for instance, was set in the apartment of a distraught cop and the office of the female psychologist who was trying to help him determine if he had murdered any hookers during his alcoholic blackouts. She helped him as psychologists usually helped their clients in erotic thrillers: she had sex with him. Her husband was murdering hookers to frame the cop. Most spouses in erotic thrillers were predators or prey.

Stranger by Night was directed by Gregory H. Brown, as he was credited on that movie. He was called Gregory Dark in his dual career in hardcore porn. We were introduced by his cameraman, a friend who knew I was in need of a job, and my first for Greg Dark was the screenplay for *Mirror Images II*, an erotic thriller about a hooker scheming to kill and assume the identity of her demure twin sister. Greg or one of his business partners wrote a paint-by-numbers outline for *Mirror Images II*, which none of them appeared eager to make, but the success of the original *Mirror Images* demanded a sequel and Greg cranked one out. Everybody in Hollywood seemed to crank things out, including me, so that lately I fantasized of moving to Montana, where the cost of living was low and I could focus on the novel I had started that winter. The novel was meant to conclude, in fact, with a disillusioned actor moving from Hollywood to Montana. I was so disillusioned with acting that I was no longer pursuing it.

Mirror Images II was a paycheck, a way to finance my novel, but I cared about *Stranger by Night*, at least initially. I knew it was unlikely to turn out well, with its budget constraints and compulsory clichés, to say nothing of a director best known for *New Wave Hookers*, Greg's hardcore apogee; but I was a writer best known for *Friday the 13th Part VII*, and if I wanted people to believe that I was capable of better, it behooved me to believe it of Greg. He provided the premise for *Stranger by Night* and left the mechanics to me, though he approved and vetoed suggestions in our story conferences. He envisioned the movie as a moody map of the soul of a kind of Raskolnikov character, and I invested that character and others with my own neuroses as I wrote the script from dusk to dawn for the better part of a month, chain-smoking and knocking back shots of whiskey while Bernard Herrmann's ominous score for *Taxi Driver* played on repeat in the background. Maybe I won't move to Montana to work on my novel, I thought. Maybe I'll stay here and get back into acting, starting with *Stranger by Night*. Greg would surely cast yesterday's news as Bobby, the Dostoevskian lead, but maybe I could play Troy, Bobby's fellow cop and barfly. I was moved to tears when I wrote Troy's death scene. Poor Troy. He was going to go over big.

Troy went over big as expected, but Greg and his partners were iffy on the script overall. "I don't understand Bobby," one of them said. "He doesn't understand himself," I said. "That's why he's seeing a psychologist. That's what the movie's about." But that wasn't what the movie was about. The movie was about hookers, I decided in subsequent meetings with Greg, who seemed concerned that there weren't enough hookers in the script, if not in life. His partners requested less angst and more action, and I revised accordingly, but my next two drafts were also received coolly. Even so, the movie was rushed into production, and soon afterward I learned from the cameraman that the script had been rewritten by a former military officer from the U.K. with no experience as a writer or as a producer, though Greg had appointed him co-producer and given him credit for the script. I would share credit, in other words, with a stranger to me and a relative stranger to Greg, who had met the Brit on the set, I was told, and succumbed to his tales of international adventure. Tales of international hookers is more like it, I thought.

But the sting healed quickly. I was used to shabby treatment in Hollywood, and I had returned to my novel, so that even if Greg had listened when I hinted that I wanted to play Troy, the shoot would have been a distraction from the work that mattered. I heard that William Katt was playing Troy and the crew was really wowed by him, which didn't surprise me: I had rigged that role for scene stealing. But that was unfair to William Katt, whom I remembered fondly as one of the surfers in John Milius's *Big Wednesday*. I remembered Steven Bauer, who was playing Bobby, from *¿Qué Pasa, U.S.A.?*, a sitcom that I watched as a teenager, mostly because I thought it made me worldly to appreciate a show about Cubans who spoke half their lines in Spanish; and when I passed Steven Bauer in New York a few years later, I had an impulse to say, "Weren't you on *¿Qué Pasa,*

U.S.A.?" I thought he might like that, since most people knew him only as Al Pacino's sidekick in *Scarface*, but I had a sore throat, so I said nothing. It was Halloween 1984, and I had just bought medicine at a pharmacy a block from the southeast corner of Sixth Avenue and 8th Street, where Steven Bauer, dressed completely in black, had paused to light a cigarette. Halloween helped to crystallize the surrounding details in memory.

One day Greg called with a question about the script. "Where's your limey rewrite guy?" I felt like saying. "I'm sure he can answer your question if he isn't too busy co-producing. Besides, I'm packing for a trip to Montana." It was true, I was going to Montana, but I wouldn't stay long and I would shelve the novel that I more or less completed there after judging it a hopeless mess.

But it would have been foolish to feud with Greg. Despite his misgivings about my script for *Stranger by Night*, there was a tentative plan for me to write *Animal Instincts II*, and a shared credit was one thing and money was another, and so far I hadn't lost a penny to the Brit. Not that the subject of the Brit was ever broached by me or Greg. I asked how the movie was going, anticipating raves for William Katt; but the actor who seemed to please Greg most was Jennifer Rubin, who was playing Bobby's shrink. He was calling from the set of Bobby's apartment, which was in or near Westlake, not far from my place, and he invited me to stop by. It wasn't my first invitation to the set, but it was my first from Greg, and now I decided to risk the awkwardness of running into the Brit. Naturally I was curious about him, and I wanted to say hello to the cameraman, and it might be fun to meet William Katt. That's right, I wrote Troy for myself. No, it's cool. I'm really a novelist anyway.

Unfortunately I missed William Katt and, fortunately or unfortunately, I also missed the Brit; but Steven Bauer and Jennifer Rubin were hanging out by the craft-services table behind the apartment building. I had met Jennifer Rubin at a party four years earlier. She didn't remember me or the party; but remarkably, when I mentioned to Steven Bauer that I had seen him in New York on Halloween 1984, he remembered standing that day at the corner of Sixth Avenue and 8th Street. I believed him. I saw the lights come on when the memory came to him. We talked about *¿Qué Pasa, U.S.A.?* and a movie I had wanted badly to do, *The Beast of War*, which starred Steven Bauer.

"You know," I said, "my agents in New York were always sending me out on bullshit, some commercial for the Army or a soap opera or some shit, and I was like, 'God*damn*, man, get me an audition for a *movie*.' Then they *got* me an audition for a movie, and I get the script and, goddamn, it's actually *good*."

"It was a good script," he agreed. I didn't ask what he thought of *Stranger by Night*, which hadn't been my script since the first draft, and even that draft wasn't altogether mine.

I had never seen Greg as upbeat as he was that day, and I would never see him so upbeat again. He banished me after *Animal Instincts II*. We didn't quarrel, exactly. He wanted the protagonist to be a hooker, an untenable idea to everyone but Greg, so that he was never satisfied with the script, and at a certain point, I refused to rewrite it. Nor did the Brit rewrite it. He took his credits for *Stranger by Night* and ran, but if he thought they would do more for him than tales of international adventure, they were the Hollywood equivalent of Monopoly money, as I would guess he soon discovered.

Montana beckoned, but I lingered to watch Greg shoot a scene. It was a short scene of Bobby opening his door to the lovely Dr. Richmond, who knew he was in particularly bad shape, otherwise he wouldn't have crashed her cocktail party a scene earlier. Lovemaking would follow in the bedroom, but this scene was in the foyer, while the camera was in the living room, where I was sitting next to Greg on a black leather sofa, Bobby's sofa, though it didn't look like the sofa of a cop. For the matter, the apartment didn't look like the place of a cop, but realism was hardly the point. The room was filled with grips and production assistants and makeup artists and so on, and Greg was flirty with some of the girls and they were flirty back; jokes were made and laughter was heard, so that the set had something of a party atmosphere, which is so often the case on sets. I wasn't immune. I was joking and laughing too, and I may even have gone on talking after an assistant director announced a rehearsal and called for silence, and I watched the foyer as Steven Bauer, now dressed completely in black as he had been that Halloween, walked to the door and opened it and said to Jennifer Rubin, "It is me," meaning that he was murdering hookers. Then he walked past the camera and up to the sofa, where Greg and I had resumed joking and laughing, if we had ever stopped, and he leaned down and spoke in a low voice to Greg. He was very serious, and Greg also became serious, leaning forward to listen to Steven Bauer as he tried to explain something, stumbling and stopping and starting again, so that it came out like: *You know, it's...it's like that thing where you're... you're half like this, but you're half like...you sort of want to, you know, but you're also sort of...* He was looking at Greg while looking through Greg—he had a thousand-yard stare—and I thought, What in the world he is *doing*? What is he trying to *say*? Yet it also seemed weirdly familiar. *I've* done this, I thought. I used to do this all the time before I moved to L.A., and occasionally I did it now, but I had never *seen* myself do it. Is this, I wondered, how I looked and sounded when I was rehearsing scenes for acting class and sorting out my feelings, or the character's feelings, which will finally be the same? And is this the way I look now when I'm writing something that asks me to dig as deep as I can dig, and would I sound like him if I spoke my mind aloud while writing? Yes, I knew now what he was doing, but it had caught me off-guard because I hadn't expected to see it here, today, on this set, or any set. I couldn't even remember the last time I had seen it, it had been so long, so that I couldn't locate the word for it. *Was* there a word for it? And I sat there searching my memory while I watched him search his soul, and finally it came to me.

He was being *creative*.

2014

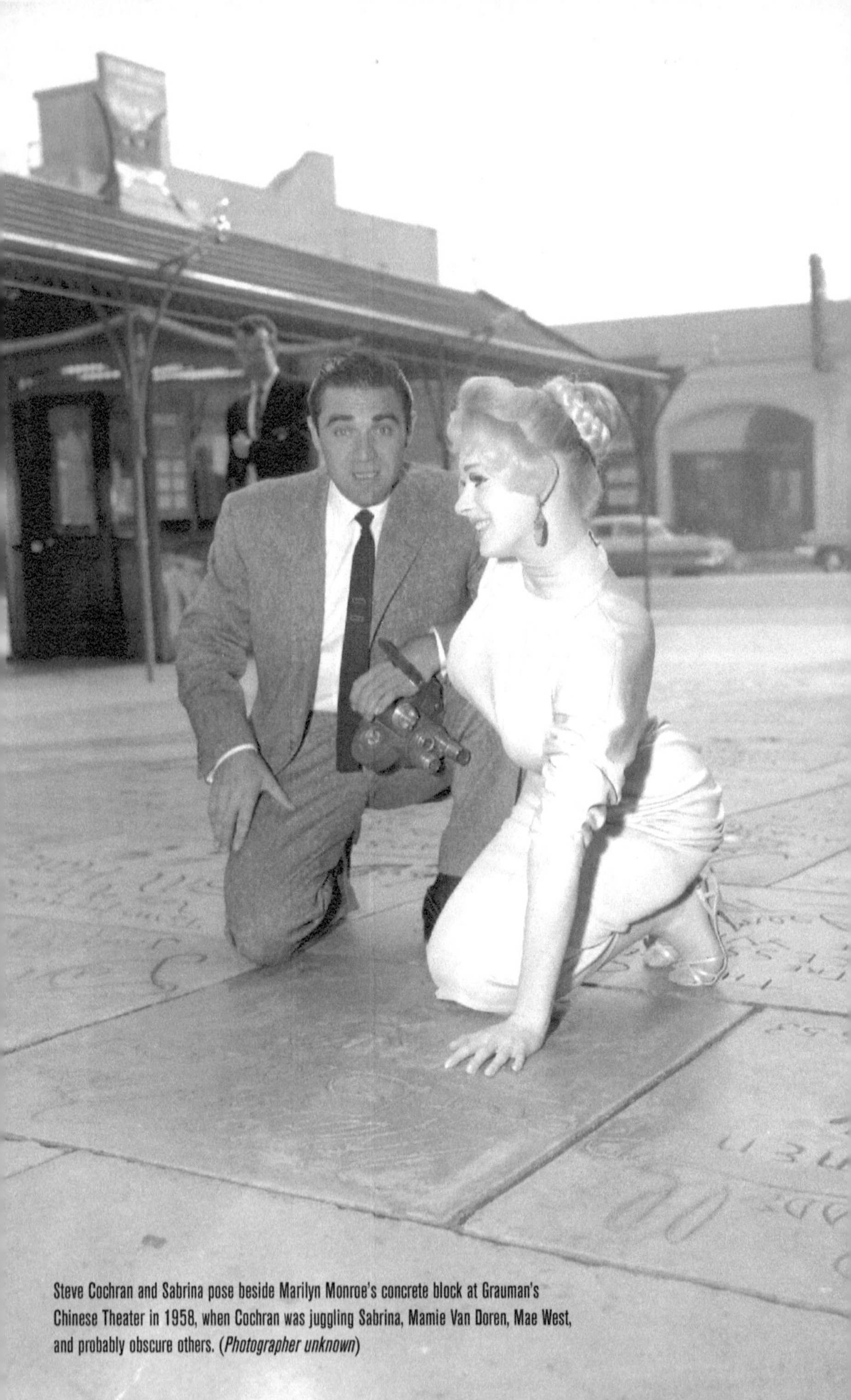

Steve Cochran and Sabrina pose beside Marilyn Monroe's concrete block at Grauman's Chinese Theater in 1958, when Cochran was juggling Sabrina, Mamie Van Doren, Mae West, and probably obscure others. (*Photographer unknown*)

THE END OF COCK RUN

THE BOOK, IF I EVER WROTE IT, would be titled *Steve Cochran: Badass Motherfucker*, I joked to friends. It was not a joke I shared with Ralph Hodges, who was eighty-three years old when I called him out of the blue in 2012 to ask if I could interview him about Steve Cochran and, specifically, how he came to be a passenger in Cochran's Porsche during a high-speed chase with a Culver City policeman on a Sunday morning in November 1953. A second passenger was identified in press accounts as a twenty-five-year-old model, and Cochran, then thirty-six, was reported to be wearing "a yachting cap, T-shirt, and jeans," so he might have been passing through Culver City on his way to San Pedro, where his boat was berthed, for a day of sailing with his latest fling; but this speculative scenario was complicated by the presence of "Air Force Sgt. Ralph S. Hodges, 24." I knew from research that Hodges had worked as an actor, though never alongside Steve Cochran, the most glamorous of film-noir heavies and God's gift to postwar gossip columnists, a hard-drinking, bed-hopping cop magnet "whose life," one hack wrote, "reads like the adventures of a grown-up Dennis the Menace." Ralph, by contrast, looked as wholesome as an Eagle Scout in stills from movies like *A Date with Your Family*, and he sounded, in our phone conversation, as wholesome as he used to look, emphasizing again and again his lifelong devotion to the motto engraved on his Hollywood High School ring: "Achieve the honorable."

At first he was wary of discussing Cochran with me, but he relented once I assured him that I wasn't preparing a hatchet job. At the time they met, Ralph said, he was amicably estranged from his first wife, Richye, and producing short films for the Air Force at the Federal Building in downtown L.A. Cochran, meanwhile, was under contract to Warner Bros. and promoting *The Tanks Are Coming*, his only war movie. As part of the promotion, he was sent to the Federal Building to glad-hand military personnel, and when he was introduced to Ralph, he recognized the name and said, "Are you married to Richye?" He *was* married to her, Ralph corrected. "Well, for heaven's sake," Cochran said, "could you please call her and get her off my back?" It seemed she was stalking him, more or less, and she was hardly unique; he attracted a lot of "headhunters," Ralph's term for starlets who wanted to date Cochran for status points, though Jayne Mansfield, one of his many celebrity lovers, diagnosed a different appeal: "He has the he-man charm that women fall for." Mamie Van Doren, another lover in the Mansfield mold, rated him "an exciting man in bed, partly because of the sense of impending danger he exuded," while Virginia Mayo, his recurring co-star but never, she insisted, more than a friend, rendered this wallet-size portrait: "He was tall, and in spite of the fact that he photographed as if he was a really big man, he wasn't. Steve was a man with a slight frame, had unusually dark, deeply smoldering eyes, thick black eyebrows, black hair, and was often cast as a gangster or a rough, hard man. Steve was none of those things in real life. He was polite and sensitive, and very kind. But indeed, he was extremely sexy and women just couldn't get enough of him."

Cochran's sailboat, the *Blackie Daw*, "leaked like crazy," Ralph said, and Ralph was a veteran sailor who "really knew the guts of a boat," so he was someone to be cultivated for reasons other than his influence on Richye. I was right about their destination in the Porsche that day. Cochran had bought the Porsche as a tax write-off while making a movie in Germany a few months earlier, and it had finally been delivered to him in California. Ralph had never seen it before Cochran arrived to pick him up, just as most Americans had never seen a Porsche in 1953, and Cochran was demonstrating its precision steering by zooming around corners in Culver City, oblivious to the police cruiser that started to chase him. Ralph was in the backseat of the Porsche, and he heard a loud bang and turned to see a cop leaning out of the window of the cruiser with revolver in hand. The cop had fired a warning shot, and Ralph said, "Steve, it's your car and I don't want to tell you what to do, but it might be a good idea to stop." Finally Cochran pulled over, and the cop walked up and said while admiring the Porsche, "I don't know how I stopped you, because I'm driving this old Chevy and you're driving this expensive sports car."

"If you hadn't pulled that gun on me," Cochran replied, "you *wouldn't* have stopped me." It was a good-humored remark and received as such, Ralph said, but in typeface it would read as insolence of the Baby Face Nelson sort. Cochran was arrested for reckless driving and evading arrest, and he handed Ralph the car keys and instructed him to phone a publicity man, presumably a "fixer," at Warner Bros. Ralph drove away in the Porsche with Cochran's date, who was, yes, a model from New York. They went to a movie, and the next day, at the Federal Building, Ralph's commanding officer presented him with a newspaper and said, "You want to explain this?" The paper was open to a picture of Cochran in his cell at the Culver City jailhouse. Rather than bury the incident, the publicity man had dispatched a photographer to capture Steve Cochran as the public perceived him, and his printed crack to the arresting officer was the olive in the cocktail. But Steve Cochran was "honestly a nice guy," Ralph said, "an honorable guy," and "the proof of the pudding" was his respectful treatment of Richye. He didn't take advantage of her as he might have done, and when headhunters called to ask if he would escort them to this or that event, he would beg off and attend with "a good, honest lady," "someone with character," not "some career-hungry lady" mired in "the Hollywood rat race." Only the second of his three wives, Fay McKenzie, had anything to do with Hollywood, and her screen image, chaste and cheerful, clashed with his. She starred in "singing cowboy" movies like *Sierra Sue* and *Home in Wyomin'*.

Every portrait ultimately says more about the painter than the painted, but Ralph's kindly Steve Cochran was corroborated by sources other than Virginia Mayo. He was profiled as an animal lover by the Associated Press in 1958 and pictured with a dog and an injured deer that he nursed back to health, two of his twenty-five pets. Jeanne Markham Keating, a longtime friend, noted his "abiding and genuine interest in people" in a eulogy published in the [San Fernando] *Valley News* the day after his lurid death came to light in 1965. He was "like an older brother" to James Westmoreland, an actor who debuted in a movie produced by Cochran. "He guided and supported me," Westmoreland posted online, "and always made sure to thank me and to tell me that I was doing a good job." I contacted Westmoreland through his Web site and he answered within hours, keen to be interviewed about "a great guy who left this world way too early."

Most of Cochran's friends were dead. Most of his girlfriends were dead. His first wife and only child were both dead. But his widow was evidently alive, as was Fay McKenzie, and she was foremost on my list of people to locate and interview. I didn't have a moment to spare, I thought. She was ninety-four years old.

I FIRST SAW HIM in *The Chase*, his first film noir, released when he and Fay McKenzie were an item in 1946. There were two villains in *The Chase*, Steve Cochran and Peter Lorre, and since nobody could steal a movie from Peter Lorre, I had forgotten about Steve Cochran by the time I saw him in another noir, *Private Hell 36*, this one about a good cop, a bad cop, and the lounge singer, played by Ida Lupino, who falls for the bad cop played, of course, by Cochran. I was put off by him initially. He seemed too slick and handsome for the part, a Hollywood notion of a tough guy. Then, halfway through the movie, he unfastened the straps on Lupino's dress to massage her shoulders—"Oh, Sergeant, dear, that feels great," she purred in her sultry voice—before he kissed her while caressing her throat. It was an uncommonly sensual scene for the period, but the clincher for me was a later scene in which he confessed that he was "stuck" on Lupino and slapped her when she refused to reciprocate, then pulled her close and, speaking through clenched teeth, forced her to admit her desire for him. The writing was pulp cliché but elevated by Cochran's unfiltered performance. I felt as if I'd made a major discovery: the unsung Brando of noir.

He wasn't quite as unsung as I imagined. Film-literate types knew him from *White Heat* and *The Best Years of Our Lives*, his undisputed classics, and a few recalled that he died aboard a boat with an all-female crew; but he was obscure to most, and as such, he struck me as an ideal subject for a short book along the lines of Henry Miller's *The Time of the Assassins: A Study of Rimbaud*. It's less a study than a rant that proved a chore to finish, but while I was still excited by it, I thought, "There ought to be more books like this: artists writing about artists in a personal way. Somebody ought to do something like this with an actor. Maybe *I* should do something like this with an actor." I had been struggling to start a novel for two years to no effect, and it might rejuvenate me to work instead on a quirky tour of a neglected career and colorful life—an appreciation with elements of biography. Cochran made forty movies and nearly thirty-five guest appearances on television shows, and I had seen maybe ten of the former and only one of the latter—"What You Need," a 1959 episode of *The Twilight Zone*—so I embarked by watching those titles that were streaming online and hunting down copies of the rest.

He fizzled in sympathetic roles, I found, unless the character had a dark or shameful past, like the reformed drunk in *Come Next Spring* and the naïve ex-con in *Tomorrow Is Another Day*, a wonderfully atmospheric noir with an absurdly upbeat ending. He was obvious as a Ku Klux Klansman in *Storm Warning*, overdoing the white-trash accent and widening his eyes to indicate stupidity; and he was unpersuasive as a wunderkind director of stage musicals in *She's Back on Broadway*, yet he managed a couple of sterling moments, a hangover scene in particular, and he didn't strike a woman as he did with alarming frequency onscreen, though he did torture a woman emotionally. He shot two women in *Highway 301*, one of his best films and performances, but he merely maligned a woman in *The Damned Don't Cry*, in which he played a debonair hood based on Bugsy Siegel—no relation to Don Siegel, who directed *Private Hell 36* and regarded Cochran as "a good actor, but not when he was loaded, and I had a hard time catching him even slightly sober." In fact, it was probably booze, I decided, that accounted for his uncharacteristic rawness in *Private Hell 36* and the all-too-credible hangover scene in *She's Back on Broadway*. He was typically smooth and calculated, closer in technique to a conventional leading man of his day, Cornel Wilde, say, or Rock Hudson, than he was to Marlon Brando. I had overrated him.

But while there were undoubtedly actors more deserving of reappraisal, they hadn't figured in newspaper stories of this kind: "Ex-fighter Lenwood Wright testified Friday that movie tough guy Steve Cochran was naked when the actor hit him with a softball bat during a New Year's Eve party." He personified film noir for me as they didn't, and he seemed to have died accommodatingly when the Hollywood of television, rock & roll, and the Whisky a Go Go had displaced his Hollywood of movies, big bands, and Mogambo. This cultural shift had been a background theme in my original plan for the book, but I moved it to the foreground as the plan evolved. Now the book was more biography than appreciation, and I wrote to the FBI to request its file on Cochran, if one existed, meantime trekking to the L.A. courthouse to search through its records on microfiche. I considered trips to Eureka, California, where Cochran was born and spent part of his childhood, and to Laramie, Wyoming, where, as a high-school student, he started acting, possibly in the production seen in a photograph that I excavated online. The photo was captioned "Junior Play, Laramie High School, 1934," and the play, like Cochran, wasn't identified, but it appeared to be a drawing-room comedy with Cochran unquestionably the kid at center stage, the standout in a crowded cast. So he must have thought: he later dropped out of the University of Wyoming to pursue acting professionally.

He apprenticed in summer stock and regional theater, most significantly in Carmel-by-the-Sea on the Monterey Peninsula. Carmel had been an arty town since its colonization decades earlier by Jack London and his literary entourage, who were seeking an alternative to overpriced San Francisco: *plus ça change*. The poet Robinson Jeffers was the resident lion when Cochran arrived in Carmel, and he would take pride in knowing Jeffers and marry a local actress, Florence Lockwood, often confused with her mother, a portrait painter likewise named Florence Lockwood. Cochran was the namesake of his lumberjack father, Robert Alexander Cochran, and in his salad days as an actor, he sometimes went by Robert and sometimes by Alexander before adopting Steve as his stage name. Jeanne Markham Keating mentioned in the *Valley News* that Cochran was "a very talented realistic painter [who] did many fine portraits of friends," and he may have been influenced by his mother-in-law, just as Carmel may have influenced his informal style: he once greeted a journalist "in blue jeans, dirty shirt and bare feet—he's no beatnik, just likes comfort." He would be buried in Monterey, such was his love for the area. His parents are buried in the same cemetery.

Twice, in the late thirties, he tried Hollywood without success. Broadway was equally inhospitable. He was, at various points, "a Wyoming cowpuncher, a railroad section hand, a fireman, private policeman in a New York department store, a shipyard worker, a carpenter and a hobo," according to an early profile. He was declared ineligible for the draft because of "athlete's heart" and passed World War II as every enlisted man's nightmare: the wolf guarding the lambs on the home front. Broadway finally warmed to him and, during the L.A. stop of a touring play, he was signed by Samuel Goldwyn, who saw him as "a younger Clark Gable." That was how he saw himself, but there was something unmistakably libidinous about him, a muskiness that Hollywood associated with criminals, so those were the parts he was given generally at Goldwyn and at Columbia, which purchased half his contract.

He divorced Florence Lockwood three months after his first film, *Wonder Man*, premiered in 1945, and two months after the divorce, this tidbit ran in a gossip column: "Fay McKenzie's fiance [*sic*], Steve Cochran, talked her into taking her first speed boat ride the other afternoon. The boat capsized, and the Coast Guard had to go to their rescue." There were nautical disasters to come, none involving Fay McKenzie, the woman in the wings while the curtain closed on Florence Lockwood, though surely the marriage was over long before lawyers interceded, with Cochran performing on the road and Lockwood elsewhere caring for their infant daughter, Xandria. He hadn't seen Xandria for five years at the time of his death. Lockwood never remarried. She was a dainty brunette, like Cochran's third wife and Fay McKenzie, but the affinity ends there. McKenzie was born and raised in Hollywood, the daughter of actors, and worked in silent films as a child and in Poverty Row westerns as a teenager, eventually graduating to her popular singing-cowboy movies and a concert tour with Frank Sinatra. She entertained the troops during the war, onstage and at the Hollywood Canteen, a nightclub where battle-bound servicemen were feted by stars and starlets. It's said that Cochran also entertained the troops, organizing shows at army camps, but this is likely false, I would learn.

He reportedly married McKenzie twice: the first time secretly in Mexico in 1946 and again in Las Vegas on her twenty-ninth birthday in February 1947. Six weeks later, Hedda Hopper, the meaner of the two most formidable gossip columnists in Hollywood, announced that Cochran and McKenzie would file for "a friendly divorce." In May, Hopper's acrimonious rival, Louella Parsons, wrote that the newlyweds had "kissed and made up," only to write in June that Cochran "is out every night with a different girl" while McKenzie was doing a play in New York. In July, there was this from Parsons: "The reunion of Steve Cochran and Fay McKenzie in New York didn't work out, I am sorry to say." And in September 1948: "It's getting slightly monotonous, but Fay McKenzie has again reconciled with Actor Steve Cochran." Louella Parsons was wrong: McKenzie was quietly divorcing Cochran, who would forsake matrimony for the next twelve years. "I don't mind being alone," he was quoted by Hedda Hopper in 1954. "Friends often come by and find me cooking dinner for one and say, 'Poor Steve.' What they don't know is that I enjoy the solitude."

McKenzie remarried quickly. Her new husband, Tom Waldman, was a screenwriter, and she effectively retired from show business to raise their son and daughter, occasionally accepting small roles, three in movies directed by Blake Edwards, one of which, *The Party*, was co-authored by Edwards and Tom Waldman. She played the hostess of *The Party* and a memorable guest at the party thrown by Audrey Hepburn in *Breakfast at Tiffany's*, the woman seen laughing madly one minute and sobbing uncontrollably the next. She was married to Waldman for the rest of his life—he died in 1985—and from what I could determine, she was presently living with her son, an actor also named Tom Waldman, in Malibu. As of 2012, she had never spoken publicly about Steve Cochran since divorcing him at the peak of the noir period.

HE WAS DROPPED rather mysteriously by Columbia after making three movies there, but he continued at Goldwyn until his contract expired. The Goldwyn lot was on Santa Monica Boulevard at the corner of Formosa Avenue and across the street from the Formosa Café, a trolley car that was converted into a restaurant-bar in the twenties and favored by celebrities whose pictures lined the walls, black-and-white flashbulb shots of them cavorting at the Formosa. I was unaware of Cochran when I patronized the Formosa in the nineties, so of course it didn't occur to me to check the walls for a photo of him, though he must have been a regular in the forties, with his hardy thirst and Goldwyn so close. The Formosa still stands, amazingly, but the photos are gone.

Between his stints at Goldwyn and Warner Bros., he returned to Broadway, playing opposite Mae West in a revival of *Diamond Lil*, one of her early vehicles. Her name was synonymous with sex—literally so: another early vehicle was titled *Sex*—and she was rumored to be dallying offstage with Cochran, but he denied it at the time to reporters and ten years later to Mamie Van Doren, his co-star in two low-budget noirs. "No sooner would we finish a scene than we would disappear into my dressing room for a quick fuck while they set up the next shot," Van Doren remembered on her Web site. "There was no question of romantic love with Steve. Our attraction was purely physical." She didn't much mind, then, when she started to suspect that she was sharing him with Mae West. "At first he told me that they were working on a script together, but as time went on, it became clear to me that there was a good bit of other work going on too. Steve finally admitted that he and Mae had been lovers for some time... Mae always liked a man who was dark and dangerous-looking, and equipped with a large cock. Steve fit the bill perfectly."

The Cochran cock is legendary, known to people who know little or nothing else about him, but before I read Van Doren's confirmation, I dismissed the legend as the slash-fiction fantasy of panting fans. I believed what I had heard since childhood about the monstrous appendage of Milton Berle because the story was so persistent and incompatible with a rubber-faced comedian—if it's strange, it must be true, I reasoned as a rule—but I didn't hear the lowdown about Cochran until my research was underway, and it suited him too well. It was the most grating aspect of my book project: to speak of Cochran was to provoke a reflexive dick joke. He joked about it himself on a residence sign outside his one-bedroom house on Yokum Avenue in Benedict Canyon, spelling his name *Cock Run*. Ardent starlets volunteered their services as housekeepers and he didn't decline, at one point paying his best friend, Montgomery Pittman, to look after the place. He had to install iron bars around his liquor cabinet to prevent Monte Pittman, an aspiring actor and fellow lush, from devouring all the whiskey, and even then Pittman found a way to wrangle it. If he had fabricated a screenplay with Mae West, Cochran genuinely partnered with Pittman on several, and he would produce one of them, launching Pittman's notable career as a writer and director of television shows from *77 Sunset Strip* to *The Twilight Zone*.

Yokum is the surname of the hillbilly characters of Al Capp's *Li'l Abner* comic strip, and for as long as Cochran lived on Yokum Avenue, he hosted an annual costume party with a hillbilly theme. His neighbor Jayne Mansfield, dressed as Daisy Mae Yokum, Li'l Abner's voluptuous wife, crashed a party to meet Cochran. She was then unknown, and they dated during her breakneck rise to fame. Her predecessors included some of his co-stars—Ginger Rogers, Barbara Payton, Ruth Roman, Nina Foch—but he never worked with his steadiest girlfriend of this period, Denise

Darcel, a French-born actress and singer who, around the time Cochran died, became a stripper at age forty-one. Darcel died just as I was about to seek her out. Ralph Hodges attended parties at Yokum and later at Cochran's house on Coldwater Canyon Lane in Beverly Hills, and he was underwhelmed. "I think maybe they were things that were put on by his agent and people who were trying to increase his status in the Hollywood jungle," he told me. James Westmoreland, on the other hand, wrote online that "Steve's house was always jumping with music, booze, and plenty of *gorgeous* girls" and that his "parties were as legendary as Errol Flynn's. They usually went on all night and well into the next day. And, man, let me tell you, they were *wild.*"

But neither Ralph nor Jim Westmoreland knew Cochran at the time of his most notorious party, the one at Yokum on New Year's Eve 1951. Shortly before the stroke of twelve that night, a couple of strangers arrived, saying they were friends of an invited guest who was en route. Another guest was acquainted with the larger of the two, Marshall Wright, the younger brother of Lenwood "Buddy" Wright, a twenty-nine-year old bit player in movies and retired professional boxer. The two men were welcomed and they sat at the bar, munching snacks and drinking. Cochran had anywhere from ten to twenty drinks that night, he stated later. His guests started to leave at two a.m., and he suggested to the men at the bar that, since their friend had never joined them, they might want to go also. They stayed. By seven most of the guests had departed, but not the men at the bar, and Marshall Wright was talking on the phone. Cochran told him to hang up and get out. He continued to talk. Cochran reached for the phone and Wright gave him a shove and raised the phone as if to strike him with it, but Cochran struck first, punching Wright in the face and bloodying his nose. Wright seized a bottle as a makeshift weapon, but other guests intervened and he and his companion were ejected. Cochran went to bed, and thirty minutes later Wright returned, barging inside and yelling, "Where is the bastard? Where is the yellow cur?" He had brought his brother with him, and Cochran could hear Monte Pittman trying to mollify them, though Buddy Wright would testify in court that he came to the house not for vengeance but to retrieve Marshall's coat.

At someone else's party five years earlier, Cochran brawled with another guest and a showgirl caught in the crossfire had her eye blackened. He had "a violent temper," Mamie Van Doren wrote, and he could be rough in bed: "one night he very nearly beat me up." Probably he wasn't alone in bed when he leapt out of it naked and grabbed a softball bat to attend to Buddy Wright, who resembled the sort of swarthy thug that Cochran impersonated in movies. A fair fight is an oxymoron after puberty. I learned that the hard way in a fight as an adult: I used my fists, and my opponent used a chair to beat me almost unconscious. I was stunned by his cowardice, and in scrutinizing the Wright case, it was difficult for me to side fully with Cochran. Buddy Wright asked for trouble simply by turning up, and he had the advantage as a trained fighter, so the bat was an equalizer, but he was clubbed on the head before he inflicted a single blow, suffering, he claimed, permanent brain damage. He had dizzy spells. His personality changed "completely." He sued Cochran for $450,000, and Cochran's lawyers stacked the jury with women whose names, listed in court documents, encapsulate the era better than the evidence: Mrs. Gertrude H. Leavens, Mrs. Gladys Doane, Miss Lyn Andre, and so on. The lawyers must have supposed that proximity to Steve Cochran would weaken knees and sway sympathy in the jury box, but Wright won, even if he was only awarded $16,000, which was later reduced to $7,500. Later still, when the case was long forgotten, he developed dementia pugilistica—"boxer's dementia" or "punch-drunk syndrome"—as a result of repeated concussions, the one delivered by a softball bat maybe most of all. Marshall Wright would found a charity for ex-fighters with the same condition. Buddy Wright, sturdy in body and broken in mind, would die at seventy-eight in 2000.

JIM WESTMORELAND was seventy-six when I interviewed him on the phone, and eighteen when he met Cochran in 1954. They were introduced by Jim's agent, Henry Willson, at Republic Studios, where Fay McKenzie had made her singing-cowboy movies and Cochran was in preproduction for *Come Next Spring*, which he co-wrote with Monte Pittman, though he attributed the script to Pittman alone. His tenure at Warner Bros. was over, and like many stars of varying magnitude, he had formed his own company: Robert Alexander Productions. Jim was known then as Rad Fulton, the name assigned him by Henry Willson, who specialized in discovering and renaming neophyte actors with poster-boy looks: Rock Hudson, Rory Calhoun, Tab Hunter, and so on. Jim, a construction worker and underwear model, was Willson's latest client and a Cochran fan since high school—"I liked his look, I liked his attitude, I liked the way he moved"—so he was thrilled to be cast in a supporting role in *Come Next Spring* and signed to a long-term contract with Robert Alexander Productions. He had posted on his Web site that Cochran "saw a little of himself in me, a little vicariousness, if you will," and he said the same on the phone, but I wanted detail, and detail is typically jettisoned once people settle on the gist of a story. Then too Jim didn't believe in oversharing, so that he tiptoed around the italicized *wild* in his characterization of Cochran's parties. "Wild how?" I pressed him. Prolific womanizers, bored by easy conquest or intoxicated by it, often opt for group sex, and Jim had written that Cochran "used to call me all the time and invite me to his house telling me, 'Hey, kid, I've got a bevy of girls here with me. Come on over, and join in the fun.'" As to what happened after Jim arrived, he allowed this in conversation: "I was always in bed with one or two girls when I'd wake up, and he'd have a couple with him. I don't know how it'd end up that way, but it did." He recalled nothing about their partners. "Duke," he said, "it's a kaleidoscope."

Rebirth is implicit in the title of *Come Next Spring* and also in its premise—a ne'er-do-well farmer earns the trust of the family that he deserted—and rebirth was a primary goal of Robert Alexander Productions: Cochran wanted to rehabilitate his image, and for the next ten years he would play villains regularly on television but only twice in his movies, his preferred medium. *Come Next Spring*, mishandled by Republic, was a box-office flop, and *Embarcadero*, Cochran's first feature as a director, was never released; but he enjoyed a *succes d'estime* with *Il grido*, his improbable collaboration with Michelangelo Antonioni, filmed in Italy just ahead of the influx there of downgraded American stars, a former Willson client, Guy Madison, among them. Antonioni was shopping for such a star to secure the financing for *Il grido*, and Cochran accepted with the stipulation that he would co-produce. He had a gift for languages—he spoke several, according to Jim Westmoreland—and, on location, he absorbed enough Italian so that he could mouth the lines, later looped, and pass convincingly for a native; but there was a clash of cultures nonetheless. "If I gave him specific directions," Antonioni griped, "and told him to follow those directions to the letter, he would abruptly tell me, 'No.' 'Why not?' I would ask him. And he would reply, 'Because I'm not a puppet.' Now that was too much to tolerate... As a result, I had to direct him by using tricks, without ever telling him what it was I wanted." Cochran "never became aware of the tricks," Antonioni added; "he just went ahead and did everything he wanted."

He directed a couple of scenes for the American version of *Il grido*, or *The Cry* as it was called in English, and returned to the U.S. with an outspoken appreciation of Italian wives—they "stay home making themselves attractive for their husbands," he enthused to a columnist—and a sullen view of their American counterparts: "We spoil our women too much. Look at that bunch, wasting an afternoon and their husbands' money!" This was hardly a renunciation of American women; he dallied with many before and during his final marriage to an enigmatic Dane, but his most enduring and publicized romance in the late fifties was with Sabrina, Britain's answer to Jayne Mansfield. He was curiously more popular in the U.K. than he was at home—in a photo taken at Albert Hall in 1955, fans mob him with a frenzy that foreshadows Beatlemania—and Sabrina was an outrageously proportioned blonde ("41-19-36") with a talent for self-promotion and, by her own unflinching assessment, no other: "I can't dance. I can't sing. And I can't act. But I'm making a lot of money on the stage, in TV, and in films." The tabloids depicted them as volatile in articles headlined "Sabrina and Steve Make It Up" and "When Sabrina Crowned Steve Cochran with a Vase," and the paparazzi caught him suggestively feeding her a bratwurst in Germany and her blithely smashing a champagne glass in London: "Her hand bled and panic ensued." They were apart as much as they were together, and Sabrina, accustomed to fanfare, was frustrated by her lukewarm reception in Hollywood. Cochran might have empathized: most of his pet projects, those he initiated, failed to gain traction, and the budgets of his movies, those initiated by others, were dwindling. He and Sabrina split in 1960, and a year later a columnist reported that she and "Hollywood's Rad Fulton went home in a Central Park hansom after whooping it up" at a Manhattan nightclub. I neglected to ask Jim about Sabrina, who in 2012 was living in the San Fernando Valley, so I hoped to speak to her personally. Her fame was a fad, as even she must have predicted, and she subsequently married a Hollywood gynecologist, which I submit without comment.

Jim's contract with Robert Alexander Productions came to nothing. He performed also-ran roles in big-studio productions and the lead in a juvenile-delinquent movie before, like Guy Madison, he did time in Italy. When he returned to the States, Henry Willson, "in one of his moods," dropped him as a client and demanded that he relinquish "Rad Fulton," so he began anew as "James Westmoreland," working almost exclusively in television while moonlighting as a golf pro. Eventually he moved to a desert town near Palm Springs, where he concentrated on golf, his true calling. He and I hit it off on the phone and spoke of getting together in person, just as I had done with Ralph Hodges, who was living in a mountain resort northeast of L.A., following a long career as a television producer in Las Vegas and San Diego. Ralph last heard from Cochran shortly before his catastrophic final voyage in 1965. By then Jim had lost touch with Cochran, to his regret: "He was the sweetest guy in the whole world… I never saw a bad side. I never saw him angry." He did not regret leaving show business, however: "It's a total business now. The charm is gone."

COCHRAN WAS A LIGHT-PLANE PILOT who once pleaded guilty to "reckless flying"—that is, less than a hundred feet from the ground—and had "the dubious distinction," the *Los Angeles Times* sneered, "of getting the first flying ticket issued by the police helicopter." Police once blocked him from boarding a flight in Miami, where he had been appearing in a play, because he owed $300 to the Venetian Isle Motel for liquor, long-distance calls, and "miscellaneous items." While shooting *Mozambique* in Durban, South Africa, he was accused of adultery by the husband of an extra and arrested at his hotel so that he would remain in South Africa to face the husband in civil court. The producer of another movie, *Shark River*, accused him of malingering when, claiming sickness, he declined to report to the set, and sued him for shutting down production. Cochran sued the insurers of the *Blackie Daw*'s successor, the *Rogue*, for the full cost of it after it rammed a breakwater and sank in San Pedro Bay. Cochran was aboard with two girls in their late teens and three of his pets, a monkey and two dogs. All survived, the monkey clinging to one of the girls as she swam to the breakwater and climbed it, and the *Rogue*, a forty-foot schooner, was ultimately salvaged.

It must be said that Cochran was sometimes exonerated in his legal dramas—or comedies, as they were for the most part. The South African case, for instance, was thrown out of court quickly, and Cochran crowed to the press that he barely knew the wife in question, even if he had made a kind of flag from the undergarments of his several local lovers and flown it outside his hotel room. That was his sense of humor. He was always one for a sexual joke, and there *was* something funny about a middle-aged man flaunting his trophies like a high-school cad, though the joke was on him. It needn't be said, but I'll say it anyway, that the press would never have covered these scrapes if they hadn't concerned a celebrity; yet the press never covered the most serious charge, in every sense of *serious*, ever brought against Cochran. The story may have been killed to protect the victims, or the press may never have learned of it. I learned of it when I received Cochran's FBI file and saw immediately that it contained two newspaper clippings about Cochran's quickie wedding to Jonna "Heddy" Jensen, an "office worker" from Copenhagen, in Las Vegas in March 1961. She was nineteen and he was forty-four, though, employing Hollywood arithmetic, he gave his age as thirty-eight to the newsman or newsmen called to the chapel. "My friends will never believe this," he said; but he also said that friends had introduced him to Heddy while she was visiting L.A. "several months ago." Why would the marriage matter to the FBI? The answer began with a bombshell memorandum—"SUBJECT: ROBERT ALEXANDER COCHRAN, Aka Steve Cochran"—that had been sent to J. Edgar Hoover by "Legat, London" three days after the date in its opening sentence:

> While Legat was in Copenhagen, Denmark, on November 10, 1959, Mr. HUGH TELLER, Consul General, American Embassy, Copenhagen, advised that subject, an American citizen, was arrested in August of 1959 by the Danish Police for photographing Danish girls in the nude. The girls involved were quite young, some of them 13 and 14 years old. After the arrest, however, the parents of the girls involved refused to prosecute because of the publicity. COCHRAN was released and subsequently returned to the United States.
>
> Mr. TELLER stated that one of the girls involved with COCHRAN, [name redacted], is a local Danish girl born [date redacted]. She has applied at the American Embassy for a visa to go to California to see COCHRAN. COCHRAN has advised her that he has an apartment in California where she can stay or she can stay with COCHRAN's former housekeeper. Mr. TELLER informed that this appears to him to be an attempt on COCHRAN's part to get [name redacted] to come to the States for immoral purposes...
>
> It is requested that local police and other sources in New York and Beverly Hills be checked to determine if COCHRAN is involved in prostitution or other activities of interest to the Bureau.

Heddy Jensen was the girl seeking a visa, of course, and the FBI launched an undercover investigation of Cochran, its L.A. office contacting four informants who had "furnished reliable information in the past." The first informant, "Los Angeles T-1," had "a wide acquaintance among the pornography dealers of Hollywood" and the second, Los Angeles T-2, had "a wide acquaintance with prostitutes," and neither "had heard of Cochran's name or corporation being involved in such fields." Los Angeles T-3, a postal inspector, "determined that a very attractive and well-developed young lady resides" at Cochran's house and "that this young lady is influenced a great deal by Cochran and she attempts to emulate him in her style of dress and conversation." This was likely Sabrina, and T-3 seemed to hint at mind control in describing her thus, but in examining Cochran's mail, T-3 saw nothing that implicated him in the sex trade. The final informant, T-4, was a Warner Bros. executive who "pointed out that Steve Cochran is considered a 'playboy' in the motion picture industry and is apparently attempting to follow in the footsteps, as far as his sex life and personal adventures are concerned, of Errol Flynn." Cochran knew Flynn, infamous for seducing teenage girls, from Warner Bros.; and Patrice Wymore, Flynn's widow and Cochran's costar in *She's Back on Broadway*, was living on the coast of Jamaica in 2012, and another name on my interview wish list. T-4 went on to suggest that Cochran might have been contemplating Denmark as a film location—but even if he met his models through a casting call, what mainstream film in 1959 would have required them to be nude? And did he limit himself to photographing them? We can assume that, if he was charged with statutory rape, the aptly named Mr. Teller would have mentioned it, though possibly there were no such charges because the youngest girls were too scared or embarrassed to admit to more than modeling. Fifteen is the legal age of consent in Denmark now, and if it was the same then, Heddy Jensen would have been past it, whatever transpired in her case.

The FBI poked around in Cochran's police and financial records and, persuaded that he wasn't a pimp or pornographer, closed its investigation at the end of 1959 and reopened it fifteen months later, per a second memorandum to J. Edgar Hoover from Legat, London:

> There is enclosed a newspaper article appearing in the "London Daily Express" for March 24, 1961, and another which appeared in the "Star and Stripes" for March 25, 1961. These articles state that subject was married to [name redacted] in Las Vegas, Nevada.
>
> I spoke with Mr. TELLER by telephone on March 24 and he stated that he had also seen newspaper accounts of the marriage. He advised that for some time the Department of the State had alerted all posts that no visa was to be granted to [redacted] to go to the United States. TELLER was under the impression that [redacted] may have gone to Mexico and from there to California...
>
> This is furnished to the Bureau in view of the possibility that [redacted] may be illegally in the United States.

Teller's impression was correct: unable to obtain a visa, Heddy had been instructed by Cochran to fly to Mexico City, or so he confided in a columnist four months after the wedding. "I took her to Ensenada and told her to wait there until I could get things settled with the Immigration Department," he said. "But she got lonesome. She crossed the border with a Mexican woman and hitch-hiked to my house in Hollywood." A more plausible scenario is that he sailed to Ensenada, a hundred and fifty nautical miles from L.A., and smuggled her into the U.S. as a *fuck you* to the naysaying authorities, then married her in the belief that she couldn't be deported as the wife of a U.S. citizen. If so, he was mistaken: alerted by the FBI, immigration officials began to harass Heddy, who "got so nervous," Cochran told the columnist, "she was on the verge of a breakdown. We thought it was best to send her back to Europe." Heddy would remember a different reason for her retreat to Copenhagen, as documented in a court ruling reproduced in part here with syntax *sic*:

> Cochran placed her under constraints. He made these rules because, he said, "I'm going to keep you, to treat you this way...I don't want you to become Americanized." She could go to the Valley, but in Hollywood "only on one side of Hollywood Boulevard." She had no funds or property of her own. "It was very seldom she could go out." She could go to the movies with a girl friend, but only on condition she "clean the house" and she had to return to the house by 8:00 p.m. Her only money was what he gave her for groceries. If she wanted a candy bar, she bought it as "groceries." On occasion, she was able to buy material and make herself some clothes. Five months after marriage, when she complained because "something was going on in the house she didn't like," he ejected her and sent her back to Denmark, saying "She was getting to be too Americanized."

He had married her, he said in Las Vegas at the time, because she was "so European and devoted." He might have been speaking of an imported maid, but despite her slave wages and stern boss, she wasn't pleased to have been fired; she returned the following year, and he hired an attorney to help her with her immigration morass. He was preoccupied with film projects, as he would be to the end. He had co-written a dramatic screenplay, *Tell Me in the Sunlight*, about a sailor in love with "a lady of uneasy virtue," and he had an idea for a comedy, eventually titled *Captain O'Flynn*, about a long voyage aboard a yacht with a crew of "six beautiful girls." He wanted Alec Guinness to play the captain. The *Rogue* could play the yacht. He enlisted an advertising executive, who really wanted to be a writer, to flesh out the idea, and between his brief television roles and his increasingly rare roles in movies, he sought investors for his own productions. To be a film director is to be a fundraiser most of the time. This is why I never had any ambitions as a director: I knew I didn't have the personality needed to separate millionaires from their money.

At one point Cochran planned to make *Tell Me in the Sunlight* in Central America. He met in Panama with the widow of a recent president—Panama had several recent presidents: this one had been assassinated at a racetrack—and, still a woman of influence, the widow pledged her support, but the deal collapsed after it was reported by Louella Parsons.

She and Hedda Hopper, her sister in bile, were no longer women of influence: post-fifties Hollywood was as unmindful of them as it was of Steve Cochran. He struck a new deal with a cabinet official in Costa Rica, but this deal collapsed after he arrived in Costa Rica to start production. The bad luck continued in the States: Monte Pittman died a month later of cancer. As a heavy smoker, Cochran was himself a candidate for cancer, and the cigarettes and alcohol were taking a toll on his face: in one of his last photos, he looks like Dracula with a tan. To fund and distribute his films, he needed a star. He had a standby star in Steve Cochran, and when his face went utterly, he would lose his best advantage as a filmmaker. Women wouldn't melt as they had always done. Already they weren't melting. In a *Los Angeles Times* postmortem, a young actress complained that, when she auditioned for *Captain O'Flynn*, Cochran "put me in a very compromising situation. I told him I didn't need a job that bad." Brava.

All of this has to have compounded the tension in the house in Coldwater Canyon. By sequestering Heddy there, he ensured that she didn't become so independent as to file for divorce and depart with more than his first wife had gotten: he was still paying $100 a month to Florence Lockwood. He didn't own much when he divorced Lockwood, and his best years were ahead of him. Now the downslide was accelerating, even if he was finally, in the Bahamas, going to make *Tell Me in the Sunlight*. Heddy couldn't or wouldn't accompany him, and to keep her from pulling "any funny business" while he was gone, he drafted an "ante-nuptial agreement" and ordered her attorney to have her sign it. The funny business he feared was divorce, of course, and when the attorney explained to Heddy that, according to the terms of the agreement, "if the next day [Cochran] turned her out, she couldn't get anything, she would just be on the street," she looked "as if a bucket of ice water had been thrown on her," the attorney testified later. He advised her not to execute the agreement. Cochran's own attorney advised the same, imploring Cochran, in her presence, "to make some provision for [Heddy] in case something happened": she wouldn't get a dime even if he died. Cochran refused to modify the agreement. She refused to sign it. "Then you can go and pack and get out," he told her. She packed and reconsidered. "I didn't know that much English to go out and get a job," she would testify, so finally she signed; and after he returned from the Bahamas in the summer of 1963, he again shipped Heddy to Denmark and, now shielded from alimony and worse, announced their divorce to the press. She appears to have been corrupted—that is, "Americanized"—in his absence, precisely as he expected.

Yet he didn't file for divorce, and she returned from exile in 1964, either because she was committed to the marriage—but why would she be?—or her objective had always been U.S. citizenship. He was then shopping a rough cut of *Tell Me in the Sunlight* to distributors, to no effect, and trying to raise the money to complete it, also to no effect. Meanwhile, to court investment in *Captain O'Flynn*, he filled the *Rogue* with bikinied girls and invited news photographers to join them for an excursion in San Pedro Bay, where the *Rogue* had sunk four years earlier. The girls, a columnist shilled obligingly, "are a dozen seemingly ship-shapely aspirants for six top roles in Steve's next picture... Steve says the girls are ALL sexy and talented but this trip is necessary in order to see if they're seaworthy too." Newspapers showed little interest in the ensuing photos until Cochran died aboard the *Rogue* seven months later. Many accounts of his death, a front-page story around the world, were illustrated by shots of the publicity stunt in San Pedro Bay, and Heddy is in one of them, a diminutive figure all but obscured by the other women, who, gathered around the mast, do their va-va-voom bit for the camera. Heddy, at the stern, is having none of it. Unlike everyone else, she wears sunglasses. It isn't clear if she's wearing a bikini, but her expression is that of an indignant pet, a dog or a cat, that's been dressed in a silly costume for the amusement of its owner.

Ten days after that picture was taken, Heddy filed for legal separation. She filed for divorce a little over a month later. But the divorce had still to be prosecuted when, in May 1965, five weeks before Cochran died, Walter Winchell, the last of the bigtime gossip columnists, printed this: "The Steve Cochrans hope to resolve their difference-of-opinion without the assistance of buttinskies."

FOUR DAYS AFTER Heddy filed for separation, Cochran was accused of assault and "false imprisonment" by a young woman, Ronnie Rae, who had met him as strangers sometimes met in the era of analog telecommunication: their phone lines crossed. She alleged that he complimented her voice and, when she told him that she was a singer-songwriter, invited her to his house because he might be able to use one of her songs in *Captain O'Flynn*. He, on the other hand, claimed that she was "trying to plug a song" and that he "agreed to hear some of her work" after a mutual acquaintance vouched for it. "She seemed sane and normal when she arrived," he said. "I wasn't even in the room when the transformation took place." He was the one who transformed, she said; he became enraged when she spilled a drink, and he bound her with neckties, hand and foot, and gagged her with a dish towel while beating her. He *didn't* beat her, he said, and *she* became enraged because he didn't like her singing, and he *had* to restrain her when she "ran her head against a stone fireplace" and "threatened to jump off a 1,000-foot cliff near his home." Ultimately she was permitted to make a call, and her grandmother, a Mrs. Reba Lewkowitz, drove to the house to fetch her. "I wanted to scratch his eyes out," Mrs. Lewkowitz remarked to a reporter about Cochran. The police, however, sided with him. Ronnie Rae had been institutionalized at Camarillo State Mental Hospital and charged recently with disturbing the peace and possession of "hypnotic drugs."

But it's the accusation, not the outcome, that sticks, of course, and Ronnie Rae's accusation was backed by a published photo of her with a black eye and swollen nose and mouth. Then came Heddy's divorce suit, and that was followed by Cochran's arrest for "harboring an unlicensed dog," undoubtedly a rescued stray. This occurred in San Pedro two days after Cochran bought what would now be more than $500 in merchandise from Radin's Liquor Store in North Hollywood—the invoice is in his probate records—so possibly he was in San Pedro to stock the *Rogue* with whiskey in preparation for a long trip that would end in Costa Rica. The ostensible purpose of the trip was to scout locations and talent for *Captain O'Flynn*, but with his streak of woes, Cochran had cause to skip town, and the movie, which didn't have a start date, seems to have provided the rationale. Had he struck another deal with a shady *funcionario*, or was he hoping to strike one on docking in Costa Rica? The pace of the voyage points to the latter.

He sailed in mid-January with two companions: an anonymous Spanish teacher and a twenty-one-year-old actress named Julie Gambol, who was cast in one of the movie's six supporting roles. He was planning to cast the other five in or near Costa Rica, having determined that Americans would be too costly, and Julie Gambol was taught sailing by Cochran and Spanish by the teacher "so I could train the other girls for their roles in the picture," she said later. She didn't say why she had to be taught in Ensenada, where the *Rogue* dropped anchor for two and a half months, or at what point or why she returned to L.A., but if Cochran made unwanted advances, she did say that she meant to meet him in Costa Rica when the picture was ready to roll, so they must have parted on good terms. We don't know if the Spanish teacher went with her or stayed in Ensenada, but later that year, Julie Gambol filmed a bit part in John Cassavetes's *Faces* and disappeared: *Faces* is her sole credit.

Cochran now sailed almost 1,300 miles to Acapulco, arriving in mid-April. He was fond of the place. His alleged first wedding to Fay McKenzie, the secret one, was in Acapulco, and during his first estrangement from Heddy in 1962, he acted in a movie there, *Of Love and Desire*, opposite Merle Oberon, often classified as of the great screen beauties of the thirties and forties. *Of Love and Desire* was her failed comeback vehicle, but while she may have been obsolete in Hollywood, she was a star in Acapulco, where she lived in splendor with her industrialist husband and held court at Tequila a Go Go, the town's premier nightspot. She and Cochran are said to have been lovers offscreen as well as on, and some have speculated that, when he was again in Acapulco, he or she or both prodded her husband to finance *Captain O'Flynn*, just as the husband had financed *Of Love and Desire*. Whatever happened with Merle Oberon, it's likely that Cochran lingered in Acapulco with fundraising in mind, and the longer he postponed the last leg of the trip, the more precarious it became: hurricane season, on the Pacific coast of Mexico and Central America, begins May 15. This must have been known to Cochran—every sailor is a meteorologist of necessity—but it doesn't appear to have fazed him, and he wasn't fazed by illness either: the medicine chest on the *Rogue* was empty, as we'll see.

For over a year he had been talking about undertaking a lengthy voyage with a female crew, at one point calling Ralph Hodges, then living in San Diego, to invite him to come along as the only man save for Cochran. Surely this voyage was meant to be research for *Captain O'Flynn*, but, reviving the idea now, Cochran was probably thinking more in terms of the publicity stunt in San Pedro Bay: if he sailed into Costa Rica with an all-girl crew, the press attention—and he would make certain there was press attention—would better his odds of securing a deal there. His dawdling in Mexico indicates a growing apprehension of the odds; and if nothing came of the trip, if the movie was as doomed as he feared, he would have lived out the movie, at least.

He placed newspaper ads that promised a daily wage of 70 pesos, then roughly $5.75, to young women who would work as "maids" and "helpers" on a cruise that would last up to nine days, with compensation provided for their travel back to Acapulco. There's some confusion as to whether, through the ads, he was also casting extras and bit players for *Captain O'Flynn*, but if he expected media coverage on his arrival in Costa Rica, he would have wanted to be photographed with the prettiest women that 70 daily pesos could buy, and if he had discovered one with the looks of a youthful Merle Oberon, he would doubtless have signed her to play one of the captain's shipmates. Out of nearly two hundred applicants, he chose three: Eva Montero Castellanos, a twenty-five-year-old seamstress; Eugenia Bautista Zacarias, a nineteen-year-old laundress; and a fourteen-year-old girl, Lorenza Infante de la Rosa. In photos they all appear slight and guileless, if not pious, with faces old in the sense that they evoke the Americas before Columbus. *Fellaheen*, Spengler called such people in *The*

Decline of the West, a bible of the Beats. Jack Kerouac, in his travels abroad, was always searching for the fellaheen.

The *Rogue* left Acapulco on June 3. None of the women—I'll refer to them as women, though one of them was a child—knew the first thing about boats, so Cochran taught them how to steer and "took charge only when it was necessary to change course or for some other special reason," they told United Press International later. He would rise early, at eight, and exercise before eating breakfast with the women, then fish; and at night he would "drink two or three whiskies and sleep on the deck" before, in the wee hours, heading to his cabin. The cabin must have held many pungent memories for him, but if sex was a duty for the Mexican women or he initiated sex, they never said so publicly, which, as the nun-educated Catholics that we can assume they were, would have been out of character for them in any case. I would like to have interviewed them, of course, but I saw no affordable means of tracking them down.

They told UPI they were hit by a storm early in the trip; and weather records show that Tropical Storm Victoria formed some 600 miles southwest of Acapulco on June 4 and, moving north, peaked the next day. The *Rogue*'s foremast was damaged by Victoria, and Cochran repaired it, but the damage slowed their progress, and near Oaxaca on June 12-13, the women estimated, they were struck by a second storm. This has to have been the "unnumbered tropical depression" that formed off the coast of Guatemala, south of Oaxaca, on June 11. A tropical depression isn't as severe as a tropical storm and therefore isn't named, but the *Rogue* was on the fringes of Victoria and directly in the path of the depression, which terrified the women, with its 30-knot winds and roller-coaster waves. "We thought we were going to drown any minute," Lorenza, the youngest, said. Only Cochran could steer and keep the schooner afloat. He did so and "was completely exhausted and very sick when the storm ended," Eva, the oldest, said. He complained of a headache and pain in his legs. He was sweaty with fever and took to his cabin, feeling faint. The women massaged his back. They went to look for medicine. There was no medicine. "Please don't leave me alone," he cried. The pain in his legs spread to his chest and arms, and his temperature climbed, but he tried to assure the women, saying, "Do not be afraid, nothing will happen, just keep the course to the east, watch the needle on the compass and keep it always at 90." He became paralyzed, able to move his head only. "What will you do if I die?" he said now. "What will you do? Raise the red flag right away, so that some passing vessel will come to your help." His fever worsened and, delirious, he "died almost," Eva said, "in the arms of Lorenza, who had been bathing his fevered face with a wet towel." Lorenza remembered that he "let out a deep sigh, he opened his eyes, and then he no longer complained." He was forty-eight. He had suffered for two days. They had all suffered. "The death of Steve Cochran was very frightening," Eva said, not least because it left them on their own.

They flew a red flag from the tallest mast, as he had instructed them to do, and tried to follow his directions about steering, but they never spotted land and they were ignored by the several vessels that passed them at a distance too great to hear their screams for help. They were adrift with little food and eventually left only with potatoes, though Jim Westmoreland told me that they were rumored to have eaten a dog that Cochran had brought with him. They were also rumored to have poisoned Cochran or murdered him in some other fashion, yet they didn't toss the corpse overboard, as logically they would have done had there been foul play. Several times they were driven from the deck by battering rain and forced to take shelter alongside the corpse in the cabin. The stench of it, rotting in the equatorial heat, must have been unbearable. The women were afraid of it regardless.

Finally, on June 27, twelve days after Cochran died, an American tuna boat, the *Belle Portugal*, chanced upon the "hysterical" women and towed the *Rogue* to Puerto de Champerico in Guatemala. The women were held for questioning, and the U.S. consulate was notified. "The body was horribly swollen and completely unrecognizable," the vice counsel said, but "from the papers on the body we are satisfied that it is of Cochran." An autopsy was performed by a Guatemalan coroner who had known him, and while the coroner was unable to pinpoint the cause of death, the paralysis reported by the women was the result of "acute pulmonary edema," meaning a buildup of fluid in lung tissue. Two underlying causes of edema, unmentioned by the coroner, are liver damage and congestive heart failure. Cochran had a longstanding heart condition that smoking couldn't have helped, and the condition might have become deadly without him being aware of it: he avoided doctors. He had worked hard at liver damage for years. The case was soon closed, and Cochran's putrefied remains were flown in a pine box to San Francisco and evidently claimed there by his seventy-nine-year-old mother, Rose, who immediately petitioned a court to appoint her administrator of his estate, as did Heddy. The traumatized Mexican women were released, and back in Acapulco, they filed claims with the estate for their unpaid wages as "chambermaids." Radin's Liquor Store presented handwritten bills for whiskey bought in bulk on two occasions. Florence Lockwood wanted $2,000 in back alimony. The cinematographer of *Tell Me in the Sunlight* submitted a claim for his full salary. Probably he had agreed to defer the salary until Cochran had a distribution deal. There was some interest in the movie now. A corpse with a little meat on it will always bring out the steak knives in Hollywood.

The week before he eloped with Heddy in 1961, and possibly for reasons related to their marriage, Cochran filed a financial statement in which he estimated his worth at $323,550—over $2,700,000 in 2018 money—most of it in investments and property value. Heddy insisted to a probate judge that never "before or during their marriage did [Cochran] discuss monies or properties," and argued that she was under duress when she signed the ante-nuptial agreement. The judge nullified it and appointed her the administrator of the estate. She had been wise, if not wily, to stall her divorce suit; but the judge's ruling was but the first shot fired in an epic legal war between the widow and the mother, Rose Cochran, who wasn't about to let that Danish tart, as we can be sure she saw Heddy, load the wheelbarrow and roll it into the sunset. We might call theirs the Seven-Year War. Yes, it concluded in 1972, and the legalese in the paper trail was beyond my powers to translate it. Nor did I have the inclination. What interested me were the glimpses of life in this or that document. Inventories of Cochran's assets, for instance, included a sextant, $15,000 worth of paintings, an account with Banco de Comercio Del Sur in Acapulco, "A collection of Movie Scripts," and "Proceeds of settlement with Allied Artists Corporation re Quadrille's Raiders." Someone had misspelled the title of *Quantrill's Raiders,* a low-budget western in which he starred and an intermittent subject in his probate records. The receipts of *Tell Me in the Sunlight,* finally released in 1967, were raised more than once, and the estate denied the claim of its cinematographer: superfluous proof that it's all but impossible to collect a deferred salary. Far more shocking proof: the claims of Cochran's three graces—Lorenza, Eugenia, and Eva—were denied. It would seem that Heddy made that call as the administrator of the estate, but she approved Florence Lockwood's claim and wrote a check for the back alimony, perhaps in empathy, having likewise suffered as a wife of Steve Cochran. With her immigration troubles at last behind her, she remarried during the Seven-Year War, and her new surname appeared in subsequent documents, but she always signed them *Jonna Jensen Cochran* in her official capacity and tidy hand. Whether she remained married to her second husband or she divorced or outlived him, she kept his name and was apparently living in Ventura County in 2012. She would have been my mother's age, seventy-one, and if I were to continue with *Steve Cochran: Badass Motherfucker,* a joke I no longer made, I didn't feel the urgency about reaching out to her that I did with Fay McKenzie—but how to go about it? How could I convince a ninety-four-year-old woman to talk about a time that, if she hadn't forgotten most or all of it, she probably wished to forget?

Then I learned that I had a friend in common with her son, Tom Waldman.

THE MUTUAL FRIEND, Gill Gayle, is an actor. Tom, unlike me, was still working as an actor, but if you've ever worked as an actor in New York or L.A., the fabled six degrees of separation are never six and usually one or none. I called Gill and explained my book project, and he called me after interceding with Tom, who groaned, he said, when he mentioned Steve Cochran. Still, as a favor to Gill, Tom was willing to hear me out.

I was a little nervous about calling Tom. If I blew it, that was it; I wouldn't get a second chance. Our conversation began with an off-topic question: which candidate, he wanted to know, did I support in the 2008 presidential race? He commended my answer. My preferred candidate, who left the race early, had been his preferred candidate. Politics were important to him: one of his heroes was Phil Ochs, the protest singer of the sixties. He didn't care for Steve Cochran as an actor or, based on his mother's stories, as a human being. "He threw Nina Foch out of a window because she wouldn't make gravy," Tom said. I was baffled. Was "making gravy" an archaic euphemism for sex? He went on to say that his mother didn't like to talk about Steve, just as I had anticipated, but possibly she would make an exception for me, and if so, maybe I could drive out to their place in Malibu. That would more than work, I said, and a few days later I got the good news.

They lived in a condominium complex off the Pacific Coast Highway near Paradise Cove. The condominiums were on a hill that overlooked the ocean: paradise indeed. There was a swimming pool in the center of the complex and a pool house next to it, and when I phoned Tom to announce my arrival at the gate, he said that he and his mother would meet me by the pool house. I hadn't seen any images of Tom, and those I had seen of Fay dated to the sixties and earlier, so my impressions of them both were indistinct at best, and here they were, Tom so much larger than Fay that it was hard to believe she had given birth to him. She couldn't have weighed more than ninety pounds or stood any taller than five feet, but she didn't stoop even slightly, and there was strength in her voice and presence in her bright blue eyes, her white hair appearing phosphorescent in the sunlight. It was clear at once that her mind was as sharp as all the tools in the usual similes and that she was still a performer at heart—she had, after all, been born in a trunk, as people used to say when everyday language had flourish—but, as I would learn, she was a lifelong Christian Scientist who never drank and never smoked, and this was the sound result. How extraordinary that such a woman had been married to Steve Cochran!

But I would have to wade into that subject. I could see that Tom was concerned that it might upset her, so as a warmup, I said that I had recently watched one of her Republic movies and *Assassin of Youth*, a lesser *Reefer Madness*, in which, at age eighteen, she was cast against type as a pot-dealing bad girl. *Assassin of Youth* was directed by a former actor, Elmer Clifton, one of the stars of *The Birth of a Nation* and, what I regard as D. W. Griffith's masterpiece, *Intolerance*, and I had with me an out-of-print book, *A Pictorial History of the Silent Screen*, with a photo of Elmer Clifton looking like a rockabilly if rock & roll had existed in 1916. We were seated now at a table in the pool house and, thinking she might find the photo amusing, I opened the book to it and slid the book across the table to her, but she glanced at it and said, unimpressed, "Yes, it's Mr. Clifton when he was young." I couldn't remember when I had last heard *mister* uttered with authentic respect. Usually I sense undertones of condescension when I'm called Mr. Haney or, worse, sir; and it was condescending of me to believe that Fay had to be primed to discuss her husband of more than six decades earlier. She spoke readily of him, in fact, giving him his due whenever possible, while often referring to herself with gray, if not black, humor that was probably another key to her lucidity and longevity.

"When we met," she said, "we had the same agent, Helen Ainsworth, and anytime she wanted me to do anything and be anywhere, I was early, I did everything, I was so easy to get along with. And she had this character who just drove her nuts; he wouldn't do anything, he was always late, didn't show up; he was just horrible. So she had this idea that I would reform him so he would show up for interviews and all of that, and that's how I started going out with him."

Helen Ainsworth is most noted now for her role in arranging Marilyn Monroe's first studio contract in 1946. She played matchmaker to Fay and Steve Cochran at the start of 1945 or so, when he had just wrapped *Wonder Man*. He admired Monroe, who was briefly signed to Columbia three years after his own brief term there, but if they ever met, she wouldn't have been interested: she was attracted to protective men who could advance her intellectually or professionally, preferably both, as Cochran could not. Fay didn't consider him "all that smart," with an asterisk: "I think he was smart about his career." On the other hand, she recalled why he was dropped at Columbia, clarifying what for me had been a question mark: Harry Cohn, head of production, "saw him one day and said to him, he said, 'Look, you stay away from my girls.' And Steve said, 'Well, Mr. Cohn, just tell me which ones are yours and I will.' Gone! He was out of there. That wasn't smart."

She thought him "a good actor, playing the right thing"—she lauded his performance in *The Best Years of Our Lives*—and "a very handsome geek, he really was. He did have a way. Anybody could be charming if they want to be, and as I say, he was most attractive, and I certainly was smitten. I don't know that I was ever in love with him, but I did think that he was, oh, good casting, you know." At the same time she understood that she was "insane" to be involved with him, or as she phrased it to me poignantly at one point: "We met to part." Her dream date was not "scraping the barnacles" off his boat or occupying a booth at the Formosa Café. She imitated his voice huskily—*"I'll meet you there"*—when I asked if he used to take her to the Formosa. It sounded, as spoofed by her, like the threat of a night without end.

"He drank so heavily," she said. "Terribly. Oh my God. He started drinking so *early* in the day." He was moody: "He scared me to death. I didn't know what he was going to do." He was egotistical: "He didn't care about anybody else. It was all about him." He cheated on her, of course: "All over the place. With everybody. Ridiculous." They were political opposites: "I'm a liberal, and he was very conservative." This surprised me since I knew that he flew to Washington for the 1963 civil-rights march during which Martin Luther King delivered the "I have a dream" speech, but Fay promised me that, while he may have crossed the aisle later, he was "very, very right-wing" when she was with him. With the Buddy Wright case in mind, I asked if she thought Steve was a coward, and she said yes, because "the one time I can remember him hitting a man, it was some poor homeless guy"—a panhandler—"and Steve just hauled off and just whacked this guy and knocked him down. I mean, to me, to hit someone defenseless, you've got to be a coward." She was positive he never performed for the troops on behalf of the war effort: "If he said that, he's just using my history, because he knew that I did."

She supposed that he loved her—and he did love her, she believed still, "in his way"—because "I was the dumber of the ones he dated," though "he always had some poor benighted woman who was there to wash up." More seriously, she speculated that, of all the unmarried actresses then in Hollywood, "he really saw me as [having] the best name of anybody that would be printed" and "I would know people that I could get to come to the parties that he'd have." By "people" she meant studio executives and celebrities, of course, and she knew plenty of both as a professional actress since infancy: she was ten months old when she made her screen debut as Gloria Swanson's daughter in *Station Content*. She had dated Orson Welles and Oleg Cassini, among others, and Betty Grable and Lana Turner, among others, had been her classmates at the Little Red Schoolhouse on the MGM lot. "I'm like Zelig," she told me, laughing.

In *The Best Years of Our Lives* Cochran is the cocky repatriated soldier who has plainly been bedding Virginia Mayo, the wife of the sympathetic Dana Andrews, while Andrews was stationed overseas. "He's playing himself," Fay said. "That's Steve, it totally is." She attended the wrap party with him, and when he introduced her to William Wyler, the director, "I could tell Wyler didn't like him at all." He was then filming or about to film *Copacabana* with Groucho Marx, who knew Fay well and took her aside to say, "What are you *doing*? I *hate* this guy. Are you *nuts*?" In fact, with his selfishness and unprofessionalism, Fay "never met anyone who worked with him that didn't say 'That lousy S.O.B.,'" and apart from Monte Pittman, "a cute guy" and "a dear," she could name only one person who truly liked him: her fellow Christian Scientist Jack Lord, whose catchphrase on *Hawaii Five-O*—"Book 'em, Danno"—was a household expression for decades. I could name two people, I said: Ralph Hodges and Jim Westmoreland, and Jim had spoken gushingly of working with Steve. "He probably was nicer to guys than he was to women," Fay reflected, "so I'm thinking that there was obviously a rapport that he had with guys," or a few of them, discounting her father. Nobody in her family approved of him, and her parents intervened in late 1946, flying her with them to New York, where she got a call from Steve, whose own father had died. "I am suffering," she recalled him saying, and "You must come, I am going through this terrible thing," and she fell for the bait, as she later saw it—"I never want to hurt anyone's feelings"—and boarded a plane to L.A. and from there to Carmel for the funeral. She arrived too late for the funeral, and Steve showed off by taking her to the house of Robinson Jeffers—the favorite poet of her second husband, coincidentally. Jeffers was elsewhere, so she and Steve visited with Mrs. Jeffers—"I remember she had on a green eyeshade"—and later, for the first and last time, Fay met Florence Lockwood: "That was sort of a strange, cruel thing he would do. He would take someone that had loved him and then bring another woman over. I'm sure it was hard for her." It appeared to Fay that Florence, "a nice-looking lady," had been taking "a little comfort from the bottle," a habit she may have acquired from and because of her ex. As a teetotaler, Fay did not see her future in Florence in that way or any other: "I knew I had to get out of this." Yet, because "I do these dumb things," she ended up marrying Cochran, not twice, as reported, but once.

When they were on holiday in Acapulco in early 1946, he asked her to marry him there, but she squirmed out of it by saying she wanted a domestic wedding with a minister to officiate, and "he remembered everything I said" and "had everything all set up" a year later for her birthday, hinting that "he's going to give me this big surprise." She had an unhappy hunch about the surprise, but placing the feelings of others ahead of her own, as always, she flew with him to Las Vegas, where she feigned happiness when the hunch was confirmed. "You call Louella," he said, "and I'll call Hedda," or maybe it was the other way around, but probably not, since Hedda "really liked the fellas." A singer named Eileen Barton was one of two witnesses who met them at the chapel. Tom, who commented continually that day in the pool house, told me that Eileen Barton was a one-hit wonder, and Fay sang the chorus of the hit, "If I Knew You Were Comin' I'd've Baked a Cake."

"And she knew Steve?" I asked.

"She *knew* Steve," Fay said. "Oh, everybody did. There was no question about that."

Insofar as she had hope for the marriage, she looked to the example of her parents, actors who had been together for forty years. But they adored one another, and Fay "was with a guy who was always off in the bushes with another woman, and he was like, 'That's how guys are; don't you understand? I married *you*, I love *you*. This is *nothing*.' And he almost got me convinced." I asked about Nina Foch, still pondering what Tom had told me, and Fay repeated what she heard from Steve: "He said that he wanted her to make gravy, and she didn't know how and couldn't do it, so he threw her out the window."

"Did he think that was funny?"

"I guess it was to tell me that you'd better learn to make gravy—and I know I did learn to make gravy."

She laughed. Tom laughed. "She makes great gravy," he said. Because she was so relaxed, he was relaxed. I was becoming less relaxed.

During their courtship, such was it was, Steve had lived in a little house on Willoughby Avenue in Hollywood, Fay remembered, and after they were married they bought the house on Yokum. "He had me sign that he was the owner of it," she said, "and with his usual, delightful sense of humor, he had a sign that said THE COCK RUN." I knew about that, I told her. She described the house as a one-bedroom with "a nice big living room where you could play charades, and that's where we entertained, a nice big open fireplace." They had a party every Saturday night and one with a *L'il Abner* theme—"that was a real original," she cracked, so clearly the idea was his—and they always played charades at the Saturday parties. She remembered Virginia Mayo, who was "darling," at a couple of parties, and one "where Eve Arden and Lucille Ball were doing charades—you can imagine the two of them!"

"Wow," I said. "Did you have a hard time talking to Steve? Did you find yourself having to search for things to talk about?"

She was stumped. "We never really talked," she said. He did like to share his past "triumphs"— Eileen Barton, and so on—and they would discuss the invitation list for their next party, but usually "we were, you know, doing the mess-around or else we were fighting."

"Did you fight back?"

"Oh my God, *yes*. I mean, I was in there"—until she wasn't. He was never abusive physically before they married, but he assaulted her three times afterward, and Fay kept leaving "because I think that a lot of times women stay and then they wind up dead. I would say, 'Goodbye, dear,' and he would leave, and I would pack and call a cab and get out of there, and he would say, 'Oh, but I love you' and everything, and stupidly I would go back."

On one occasion she scheduled, without telling him, an interview about playing Ado Annie in the London production of *Oklahoma!* "Well, he heard I was going on the interview, and he just knocked me down."

On the second occasion "we had taken someone—it wasn't Monte, it was some friend—and let him off, and as soon as the guy got out of the car, he smacked me in the face because he said that I was flirting with this guy. Well, I wouldn't have *dared*."

The third occasion was "mind-blowing" to Tom, despite his having heard about it before, and the most perplexing and disturbing to me. Fay, while serving breakfast to Steve, remarked about the eggs—"I don't know if they're cooked enough," she believed she said—and "he probably was hung over and maybe the idea of eggs was making him sick," but "he got up and just socked me" so hard as to deck her, or possibly she fell because she "wasn't expecting it." Whatever happened, "I was on the floor, and he stormed out, he didn't help me up, he went out and got in his car and went away, and so then I threw some things in a bag and left."

She was uncertain of the sequence of the assaults but certain of this: after the third one, she went to New York and replaced Jean Parker in *Burlesque*, a Broadway show starring Bert Lahr. Steve followed her and tried, as usual, to reconcile, but Fay was done. Her sister Ida Mae was married to a rancher in Wyoming, and to get a divorce there, Fay had only to establish residence with a six-week stay. Elsewhere in those days, except for

Nevada, divorce was tricky. Adultery was the only grounds for it, "which of course I had," and even then photographic proof was needed, so it was much simpler to have Steve sign the paperwork for a no-contest divorce, if he could be enticed to sign it. He did when "finally his ego got to him," and Fay made for Wyoming, where he came of age and she had "a lovely divorce. My lawyer was married to the circuit judge, so we just went over to their house, and Ida Mae was my corroborating witness, and I got this divorce for a hundred and twenty-five bucks." She asked for nothing. All she wanted was her freedom, and when she met her second husband, "I wasn't too sure I even wanted to marry him. I met his mother and she said, 'Oh, it's so wonderful you're going to be my daughter-in-law,' and I was like, 'What? What did he say?' But that was a good move." She considered her second husband her only husband. They were best friends.

She heard from Steve once maybe three years after she divorced him. He was then seeing Ginger Rogers, another Christian Scientist, and the call, Fay remembered, had something to do with his injured leg. I had seen photos of him with an injured leg when he was promoting *Storm Warning*, the movie he did with Ginger Rogers and Ronald Reagan—in fact, he and Reagan promoted the movie together on a nationwide press tour. "That's just hilarious," Fay hooted. "I'd loved to have been there." She had the same agent as Reagan, and told me a funny story about him. She was full of funny stories. We had spoken for over two hours, and she didn't seem tired, but I didn't want to wear out my welcome, since I hoped to meet with her again once I had digested what she had told me already. I didn't treat Cochran's arrest in Denmark lightly, but if the case had gone to trial, he might have been vindicated. Likewise, if Heddy had faced him in divorce court, we might have heard his side of the story. There was one. There's always more than one. But while Heddy's story was grim, there was nothing in it about physical violence, and now I knew that, just as he slapped women in movies, he had done the same in life, at least with Fay, and Fay's story gave credence to Ronnie Rae's story, because any man who could belt a woman for undercooking eggs, if that was indeed the catalyst, could belt a woman for spilling a drink. Yet when I asked Fay if she thought Steve was a coward, she said yes not because of what he did to her but what she saw him do to a panhandler. What does that tell you? It told me quite a bit.

But not everything. I drove again to Malibu a couple of weeks later, and this time I sat at Fay's kitchen table for a longer session, with Tom sitting in again, and there was a little more detail in her stories about Steve, which were otherwise the same; but at some point I lost interest in Steve;

I was more interested in hearing about her. She remembered the first song she ever learned and sang a little of it: *Oh, Harold, you must come over...* It was taught to her by a neighbor who would babysit her when her parents were working at movie studios, and one day, when she was four, a studio called to ask if she was available to shoot a scene, and she waited with her little makeup kit on the porch for the studio car to arrive and drive her to the set. She remembered her father taking her around to the Poverty Row studios when she was a teenager, and how she came to be signed by Republic, as pure a Hollywood story as I ever heard: at the instigation of her sister Ella, she bought a new bathing suit and lounged by a pool where the head of the studio, Herbert Yates—"Mr. Yates"—was sure to see her. She remembered the Hollywood Canteen, where, as "the captain of the junior hostesses on Friday night," her job was "to find a lot of little actresses, little stars, that the guys had seen, and then they would dance with them." During wartime "there was such a unity," she said, and "people were so supportive of one another; it was such a good feeling," and she had this to say about the acting profession as a spectator and practitioner from birth: "I think that what happens with women especially is you're so sought after and you think you're the Queen of the May, but you really don't have any power at all—*nothing*." She quoted her father's advice, her compass throughout her career: "Book everything; you can cancel later." That was great advice, I said; I never understood actors who turned down auditions. Neither did she. Neither did Tom. I hate the sound of my voice, so that I could barely bring myself to play the recording I made in Fay's kitchen that day, but when I finally listened to it a long while later, what I heard were three actors—because once an actor, always an actor—jabbering about the craft and the business and the coworkers—"Did you know him?" and "Oh, I worked with her"—and it was all so much fun that I lost my vanity about my voice. And there in the middle of it was Fay, ninety-four years old and just as ebullient as me or Tom.

Every portrait ultimately says more about the painter than the painted. "Darling," Fay said of Virginia Mayo. Monte Pittman was "a dear." The painter can be seen in those microscopic portraits.

Oh, Steve, you fucker. You really blew it.

THERE WAS A GENRE of magazines that coincided with film noir, appearing and expiring at the same approximate moment. They had titles like *Man's Action*, *All Man*, *World of Men*, *Rugged Men*, and they contained "true stories" of military heroics and maritime or jungle expeditions gone awry after planes crashed or boats sank and the survivors, soldiers of fortune or prospectors, were attacked by cannibals or fanged animals. These stories were depicted on the magazine covers in vivid paintings that often included sexy women, since of course the islands and jungles were filled with curvaceous natives if the men weren't already accompanied by busty associates; yet the men were likewise meant to be sexy, with their square jaws and bare chests. They look like Steve Cochran, many of them.

The sensibility of men's adventure magazines, as this genre was called, dated to an earlier time when boys believed that two-fisted adventure awaited them if they went to sea or rode west. They read books like *The Call of the Wild* and *Two Years Before the Mast*, and heard tales of buried treasure and sin dens in exotic ports. Steve Cochran would have heard such tales as a boy, and his last voyage might have inspired a cover story for a men's adventure magazine if all but maybe two hadn't ceased publication. There was no need for them. The wild ride of the sixties was underway.

As much as I may have sometimes romanticized the postwar era, it was, I knew, stultifying in reality. America was being suburbanized, and worth was measured in dull respectability. The most common plot in film noir, the respectable man imperiled by erotic adventure, was an admonition not to stray, and men's adventure magazines were a compensation for the dearth of thrills and a reminder that thrills were available to the footloose, even if their notion of adventure was quaint. If you resembled the guy on the cover of *Men's Action*, you shouldn't be fending off pirates in Micronesia; you should be a movie star, which was not only lucrative but a far more credible adventure. Bohemia was also a credible adventure, though too odd and effete for the average man; yet Steven Cochran sought a life of adventure in that way and as a traditional man of action, a bizarre combination in the twenty-first century, when machismo and creativity intersect in hip-hop and nowhere else in the arts that I can see. In fact, machismo is largely reviled by the intelligentsia, or what passes for an intelligentsia now, and it should be where the result is brutality; but if, say, the maternal instinct shouldn't be a given in women, brutality shouldn't be a given in virile men; and while Steve Cochran turned out to be the pig and covert coward that many presume every virile man to be, he was a more nuanced pig than most. Even Fay acknowledged his talent and charm—yes, I know, all sociopaths are charming, but I don't believe he was a sociopath, and I direct you to Henry Lee Lucas if you buy that they're all charming—and had I contacted Heddy, she might have referred to his good qualities, few as they were, when asked why she didn't prosecute her divorce suit.

Jack Kerouac updated the adventure story for the late twentieth century, but I don't know what would constitute adventure in 2018. Taking selfies? Hooking up on dating apps? There's certainly nothing adventurous about the life of a writer—thanks for the bum steer, Jack—yet, having said that, I did feel oddly excited about my visits to the L.A. courthouse when I was researching Steve Cochran, and I was very excited when I was able to locate people who knew him, even if some of them—yes, you, Mamie Van Doren—ignored my messages; so I didn't regard it as a total loss when I shelved my book about him. He was always a dicey subject, being so forgotten, and once I learned the awful truth, I couldn't imagine using him even as the figure in the foreground of a larger portrait of postwar L.A. I could be accused of condoning him by simply writing about him, unless I waved the progressive flag while stressing my disapproval of him, and I've never written to preach or condemn. Then too I couldn't devote months or years to documenting the life of a person I had come to dislike, which doesn't mean that I could never again watch *White Heat* or *Private Hell 36* or *Highway 301* or *Tomorrow Is Another Day*: that was the best of him, and I can separate the artist from the person, as some, to their impoverishment, cannot. Also I had promised Ralph Hodges that I wouldn't write a hatchet job, and that was how he might view the book had I finished and published it. Jim Westmoreland might likewise regret talking to me. I couldn't face either of them after I received Steve's FBI file and interviewed Fay. They were old men and entitled to their warm memories of him, and I was afraid of spoiling those memories with a slip of the tongue.

So I put that book away and started this book without intending to start it. Brad Listi, the publisher of my last book, a nonfiction collection, had suggested that I do a second collection, this one about movies and L.A., but I declined because I didn't regard myself as a Kenneth Anger kind of writer and didn't want anyone else to mistake me for one. Yet I had published at The Nervous Breakdown, Brad's online magazine, a couple of movie-related essays, and when he asked me again to do a whole book of them, I said yes because I still couldn't get a novel going. I had planned, before there was a book, to write about certain personal experiences pertaining to the movie business, but it took me a long time to realize the pattern in my other subjects. Again and again, I chose to write about rebels, often violent rebels, and since I had gathered so much material about Steve Cochran, I thought momentarily of adding him to the list, then decided against it for the reasons I've cited already.

Then they started dying, those I had interviewed or hoped to interview. Patrice Wymore, Errol Flynn's widow, died in Jamaica in 2014. Ralph died two and a half months later, and Jim in 2016. Jim's death was a bit of a shocker. He was eighty, but as a lifelong athlete, he must have been in superb shape, and almost as soon as I heard of his death, I was leafing through an old magazine—research for a piece about the late sixties—and there, in a fashion layout, was Jim: he hadn't told me that, after Henry Willson dropped him, he went back to modeling. What else didn't he tell me? What didn't I ask him? I didn't ask him about Sabrina, and she died two months after he did. Did Steve ever hit her? If so, she had taken it with her. People die, and they take facts known only to them, the details that amount to a life, unless they write it down or tell it to someone who will write it down for them; and why did I waste Ralph's time, and Jim's time, and Fay's time if I did nothing with the details they imparted to me? The headhunters, Jim waking at Steve's house after an orgy there, Lucille Ball playing charades by his fireplace: to me that was worth preserving because it *was*, and they *were*, and it helped me to imagine a little better that time before I was born and longed to enter because, while it may have seemed colorless to the readers of *Man's Action* and the rest, it had to be more adventurous than now.

So, yes, I would do something with it. I had to do something with it. I would put Steve Cochran at the close of my book, the last of my collection of rebels, not the worst of them—Lee Harvey Oswald surely had him beat—but the one whose story had the most satisfying coda. He would be the protagonist of the story, but the hero was the woman who left an injurious man and outlived him by many years, for the most part very happily, and lives still, as I write these words, "as strong as an ox" at last report from her son.

She is a hundred years old.

2018

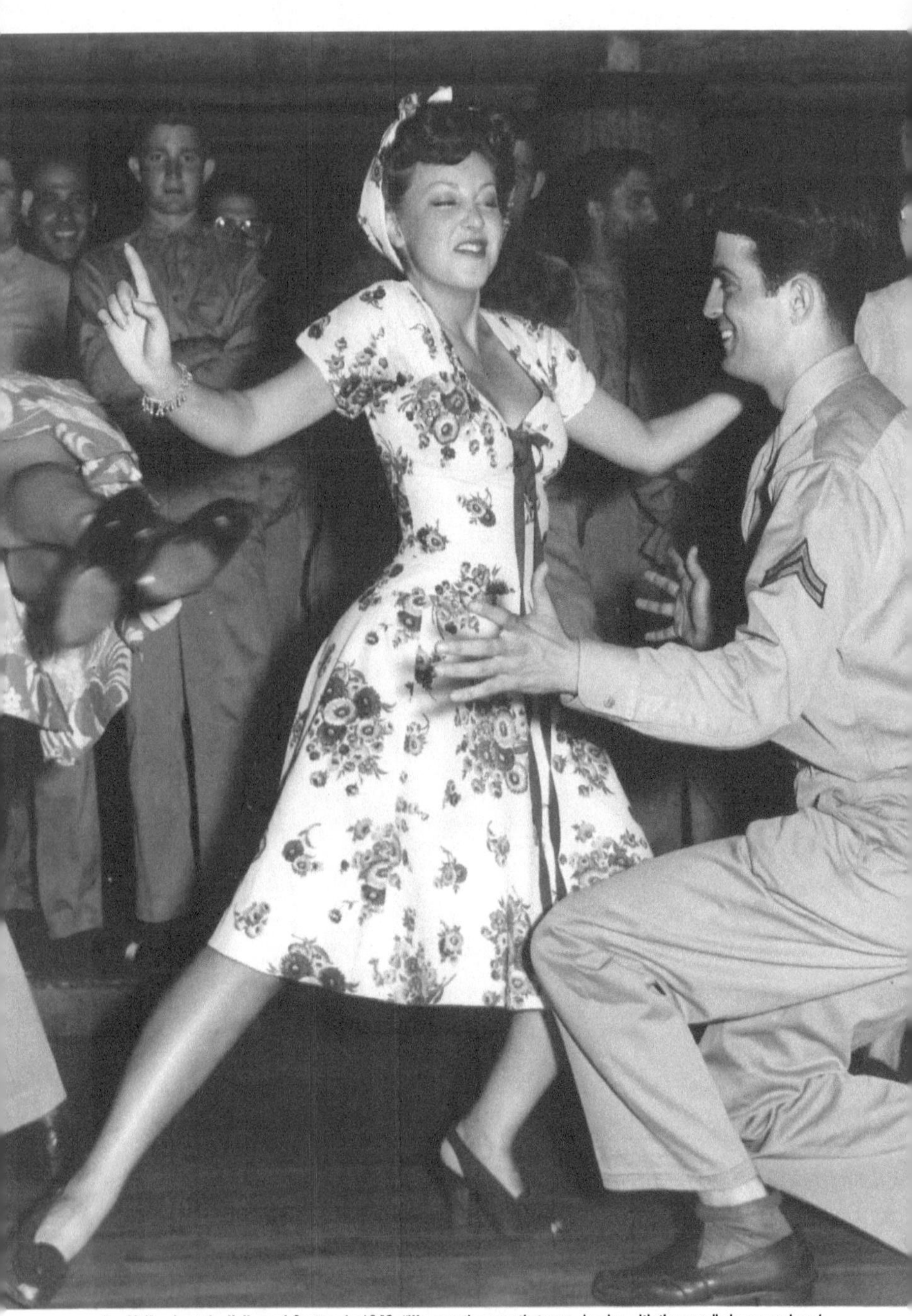

Fay McKenzie at the Hollywood Canteen in 1943. "We were the ones that were dancing with the guys," she remembered of the junior hostesses, "because they wanted to jitterbug and all that. The senior hostesses, Marlene Dietrich, Bette Davis, were serving food and sweeping up." (*hollywoodphotographs.com*)

AFTERWORD & ACKNOWEDGMENTS

HOW THIS COLLECTION came to be is recounted briefly a few pages ahead of this one in "The End of Cock Run," and its initiator, Brad Listi, is the first person I'll thank. I was a hare when I worked as a screenwriter, dashing off scripts in days, but I'm a tortoise as a writer of prose, as Brad was well aware, yet neither of us anticipated *Fifty Cents for Your Soul*, the collection's working title, taking so long to finish, and at a certain point it became obvious that Brad's imprint, TNB Books, would not be publishing it as planned. (The working title was from a quote attributed to Marilyn Monroe: "Hollywood is a place where they'll pay you a thousand dollars for a kiss and fifty cents for your soul.") This brings me to the next people I'll thank, Wai Wan Mok and George Porcari of Delancey Street Press. I've known George since I was nineteen, and I say in the book's opening essay, "When Dinosaurs Ruled the Earth," that I began to read seriously because I thought it would help me as an actor, and while that's true, I also aspired to be as smart and learned as George. Because he helped to shape the way I think, George's influence is everywhere in what eventually was called *Death Valley Superstars*. In fact, when I was about to change the title still again because so little of the book had to do with the geographical Death Valley, George persuaded me otherwise. For that matter I picked "When Dinosaurs Ruled the Earth" as a title with George's input in mind.

If, as I presume, you're reading this after, not before, "Pluto in the Twelfth House," you may remember that *Death Valley Superstar* is the title of Michael Yaroshevsky's documentary about Mark Frechette. I always admired the title, and since *Fifty Cents for Your Soul* was faring poorly in my informal polls, I asked Michael if he would object to a pluralized version of *Death Valley Superstar*, per the song by Murderdolls, as the title of my book. The song is written by Joseph Poole and Nathan Jordison, so naturally I'm grateful to them, Murderdolls, and Michael Yaroshevsky, who further demonstrated his generosity by mailing me, gratis, a DVD of *Death Valley Superstar* from his home in Quebec. I was the recipient of kindred generosity from Robert Dole, who mailed me, from his own home in Quebec, his correspondence with Mark Frechette and an English translation of his memoir *Comment réussir sa schizophrénie*; and from Francesco Borseti, who managed to locate in Italy a copy of *La grande scrofa nera*, Mark Frechette's last film, which was impossible then to find in the U.S. It was also impossible for me to find a copy of the Christopher Jones episode of *E! True Hollywood Story*, except by phoning E! Channel and explaining my predicament to an anonymous staffer who made a DVD of that episode and another (for an essay that I abandoned) and had them delivered before I could raise the matter of compensation. I wish I could thank her by name as I'll now thank my wondrous designer Michael Kronenberg; my astute copyeditor Ken Gee; and my friend Zara Potts, who, despite a harried schedule as the editor of *Dear Reader* magazine, made time to write an introduction.

Not everyone who was interviewed for the book, informally in some cases, was quoted in it, but I'm indebted to them all: Antero Alli, Ernie Andrews, Ruth Borusk, Bill Dakota, Pamela Des Barres, Sherry Dodd (RIP), Robert Dole, Ralph Hodges (RIP), Skip E. Lowe (RIP), Dezso Magyar, Jason Majik, Woody McBreairty, Nick Pearson, Howard Sobel, Quentin Tarantino, Debra Tate, Fay McKenzie Waldman, Tom Waldman, James Westmoreland (RIP), Duane Whitaker, Sean Flynn's mystery friend at the L.A. courthouse, and Edna, "the purple lady," surname unknown. Since many authors dread being asked to write blurbs as much as they dread being asked to read the manuscripts of strangers, I'm appreciative of those who answered the call: Brin-Jonathan Butler, Ronlyn Domingue, Art Edwards, Jonathan Evison, Mary Guterson, Donna Lethal, Greg Olear, Jim Ruland, and Paul Sammon. Every writer should be fortunate to know people like John Santana and Max Oravin, who wired me money when the wolf was at the door; Gill Gayle and Pamela Hodges, who helped to arrange interviews; and Elaine Jackson and Holly C. Slavic, who, well versed in some of my subjects, pointed me to reliable information about them. I had a lot of practical help and many boosters besides, and a list of those who supported me in either way, sometimes both, would include Tammy Allen, Margaret Arana, Mike Armstrong, Sanja Banic, Nadine Bass, Daniel Bernardi, Giavanna Bertelli, Jakob Bokulich, Corey Brandenstein (RIP), Harry Bromley-Davenport, Sean Brosnan, Guillaume Campanacci, Daniel Capuzzi, Steve Cattani, Heather D'Augustine, Joe D'Augustine, Jonathan Dunkle, Kerry McCombs Dunn, Vedrana Egon, Hillard Elkins, Carmen Gentile, Jeff Gittel, Sab Grey, J. T. Gurzi, David Gutowski, Slade Ham, Lori Hettler, Babette Hodis, Charlotte Howard, Sydney Hunt, Rachel James, Victor Janusz, Ramón Jurado, Terry Keefe, Jeremy Lowe, Billy Maddox, Dena Massenburg, Ted McCagg, Nathaniel Missildine, Jen Noble, TJ Nordaker,

Brett Ortler, Damon Packard, Joe Pasquale, Brandon Perras, Jude Potts, Thomas J. Quigley, Michael Rababy, James Reid, William Richert, Ben Roberts, Burke Roberts, Marcus Rummery, Ranjit Sandhu, David Secchiaroli, Todd Coleman Smee, Gary Socquet (RIP), Janet Steen, Stephanie St. John, Ryan Stockstad, Jason Tegtman, Gregg Tillery, Rahul Vithlani, Phil Wagner, Meghan Warner, Eileen Weiner, David S. Wills, Peter Winkler, Scott Witebsky, John T. Woods, Victor Marini of Computer Doctors, Marc Wanamaker of Bison Archives, Steve Trumbull of C'ville Images, and the staff of the New Beverly Theater, which was simultaneously a resource and a refuge. This is a long list, obviously, when it should really be longer, and my apologies to every friend who was omitted in the interest of (relative) economy. I should also apologize to Elizabeth McGovern in the improbable event that she should read or hear of "The Phantom of the Public Theater": I intended only to embarrass myself.

My models for *Death Valley Superstars*, not in terms of subject but of style and shape, were *The Air-Conditioned Nightmare* by Henry Miller and *A Long Desire* and *The White Lantern* (eventually merged into a single volume: *The Aztec Treasure House*) by Evan S. Connell, one of the most undervalued of American writers. Two collections about Los Angeles, *Black Swans* and *Eve's Hollywood*, by another undervalued writer, Eve Babitz, were also inspirational, as was, unoriginally and unavoidably, *The White Album* by Joan Didion. Prominent among beneficial Web sites, even if they don't appear in the selected bibliography at the end of this book, were Bruce Long's Taylorology, ground zero for anyone interested in the William Desmond Taylor case; Bill Hedley's Venus Observations, a history of erotica that covers in detail the taboo-smashing rivalries among men's magazines of the 1970s; and Steve Trussel's "Chronological Collection of Works by and about Mel Lyman and the Lyman Family." Research required me to watch or re-watch numerous films, one of which, *The Misfits*, had bored and confused me when I first saw it in my late teens, but now, despite its narrative flaws and halfhearted direction by John Huston, it became a favorite. *JFK: 3 Shots That Changed America*, produced for The History Channel in 2009, was easily the most haunting and illuminating of the several documentaries that I watched for "Oswald Has Been Shot"; while of the many playlists I compiled during the writing of the book overall, I will probably always associate certain songs with it: "Slip Inside This House" by the 13th Floor Elevators, "Pictures of You" by the Cure, "1983... (A Merman I Should Turn to Be)" by the Jimi Hendrix Experience, and "In the Long Run" from the *Beyond the Valley of the Dolls* soundtrack, to name only a few.

You may, after reading "Catch Me," understand why Sherry Dodd is one of two people to whom *Death Valley Superstars* is dedicated. The other dedicatee, Cynthia Bechhold Hawkins, was a professor of English at the University of Texas at San Antonio and, like me and Zara Potts, a contributor to The Nervous Breakdown, Brad Listi's online magazine, where many of these essays first appeared. Cynthia once profiled me for her local alt-weekly, the *San Antonio Current*, when I whined on social media that I had hit a wall in promoting *Subversia*, my book published by Brad Listi's imprint. We had never spoken before she called from Texas to interview me, sounding like the sweet Southern girl she seemed to be online, though here and there I detected a mordant sense of humor that might have chafed or lanced if not for her exemplary tact. She was exemplary in every way that I could see. She was blissfully married to her high-school sweetheart, Joe Hawkins, and the adoring mother of their young daughters, Hannah and Chloe (or "Firecracker," as Cynthia often referred to her); she was democratic in taste as a cinephile and music fan, despite her Ph.D.; and she was a statuesque beauty who, one year for Halloween, dressed as Mia Wallace, Uma Thurman's character in *Pulp Fiction*, and in the documentation I saw, rocked the character's "helmet" hairstyle, inspired by the silent-screen siren Louise Brooks, better than did Uma Thurman.

In 2011, months after I began this book unwittingly with "Life in Elizabethan Virginia," Cynthia asked me to contribute to *Writing Off Script: Writers on the Influence of Cinema*, the e-book she was assembling as a charity project: all proceeds were to benefit victims of the tornado that had devastated Joplin, Missouri, earlier that year. I was busy and said no, but determination was another of Cynthia's virtues: when she approached me again, I said yes, largely to return the favor of the *Current* story. The result was "When Dinosaurs Ruled the Earth," the longest essay I had attempted to date and, I believed, the best. To promote *Writing Off Script*, the essay ran at The Nervous Breakdown, though I was sure that few would read it, since almost nobody then, at TNB and elsewhere online, posted articles longer than 2,500 words, which was already considered prolix by Internet standards. In fact, "When Dinosaurs Ruled the Earth" was a minor sensation, and I decided afterward that I would never again confine myself to 2,500 words, that I would write at the length that a subject demanded. But for that liberating decision, I probably would never have proceeded with *Death Valley Superstars*, and in that sense I owe the book to Cynthia. She was the most effusive of everyone who cheered me on. At one point she urged me to please hurry and finish the book because she wanted to assign it to her students. In another exchange I explained that I had only written about Hugh Hefner after delving into *Playboy* history for a scrapped profile of an imprisoned Playmate, Victoria Vetri, who was unresponsive to the interview request that I forwarded in a Christmas card. "It's very difficult to choose the right Christmas card for a stranger in prison," I commented to Cynthia. I'm still tickled by her reply: "Well, now you have to write an essay titled 'It's Very Difficult to Choose a Christmas Card for a Stranger in Prison.'"

She loved Halloween, observing it at TNB with pieces about horror movies, and in early October 2013, I proposed that we collaborate on such a piece. She suggested Frankenstein as a topic—the novel, the films, the phenomenon—and during the next few weeks, as we exchanged e-mails and spoke on the phone, she never so much as hinted that she was undergoing a cancer scare. It was more than a scare: in November, some two months after her forty-second birthday, she announced that she had been diagnosed with breast cancer. This was distressing news, of course, but she handled it with her usual grace, starting a blog, Box of Monsters, about her treatment gauntlet, and posing for a photo in which, wearing a headscarf and flexing her biceps, she updated the Rosie-the-Riveter poster of World War II: *We Can Do It!* I believed very much that she could do it.

In October 2014, when her prognosis was optimistic, we spoke of another Halloween collaboration. It didn't happen, but our conversation produced the spark of "Hello Stranger." A year and a half later, as she was about to begin a new round of chemo, she wrote at TNB that, since her diagnosis, she had endured "a lumpectomy, the port removed, radiation, recurrence, a double mastectomy with reconstruction, a hysterectomy, another recurrence, and another surgery." She was "actually anxious to get started" again with chemo, she wrote, because "chemo isn't the worst thing. A particularly stubborn kind of cancer that keeps popping up again is." I'm sorry to report that the chemo was unsuccessful and the cancer spread, yet she always maintained a cheerful attitude, joking, in her final Box of Monsters entry, about how brittle she had become, or, as she titled the entry, "Here Lie the Broken Bones of Cynthia Hawkins." I can say, without exaggeration or sentimentality, that I was better for my every interaction with her, and it's a small consolation that I was able to convey that to her soon before the end. She took the high road all the way. She was the high road. I'm privileged to have known her.

"What makes you so sad?" Clark Gable asks Marilyn Monroe in *The Misfits*, a movie in which every character is sad for reasons both blatant and vague. Monroe deflects Gable's question, but I can tell you what makes me simultaneously sad and angry as I write this, and it takes the form of another question: Why Cynthia? I've known too many people who died too young, and these words from *A Farewell to Arms* are the nearest I've found to an acceptable explanation: "If people bring so much courage to this world the world has to kill them to break them, so of course it kills them. The world breaks every one and afterward many are strong at the broken places. But those that will not break it kills. It kills the very good and the very gentle and the very brave impartially. If you are none of these you can be sure it will kill you too but there will be no special hurry."

So, if I'm not very good or very gentle or very brave, at least I can pay tribute to the likes of Cynthia, who was all three; and as part of that tribute, I've included, as an appendix to the book she championed, our collaboration of 2013, with her introduction and my gratitude to Joe Hawkins for permission to reproduce it. Joe is the penultimate person I'll thank here. The last is you, the reader. *Je souhaite la vie éternelle au lecteur!*

Los Angeles
August 2018

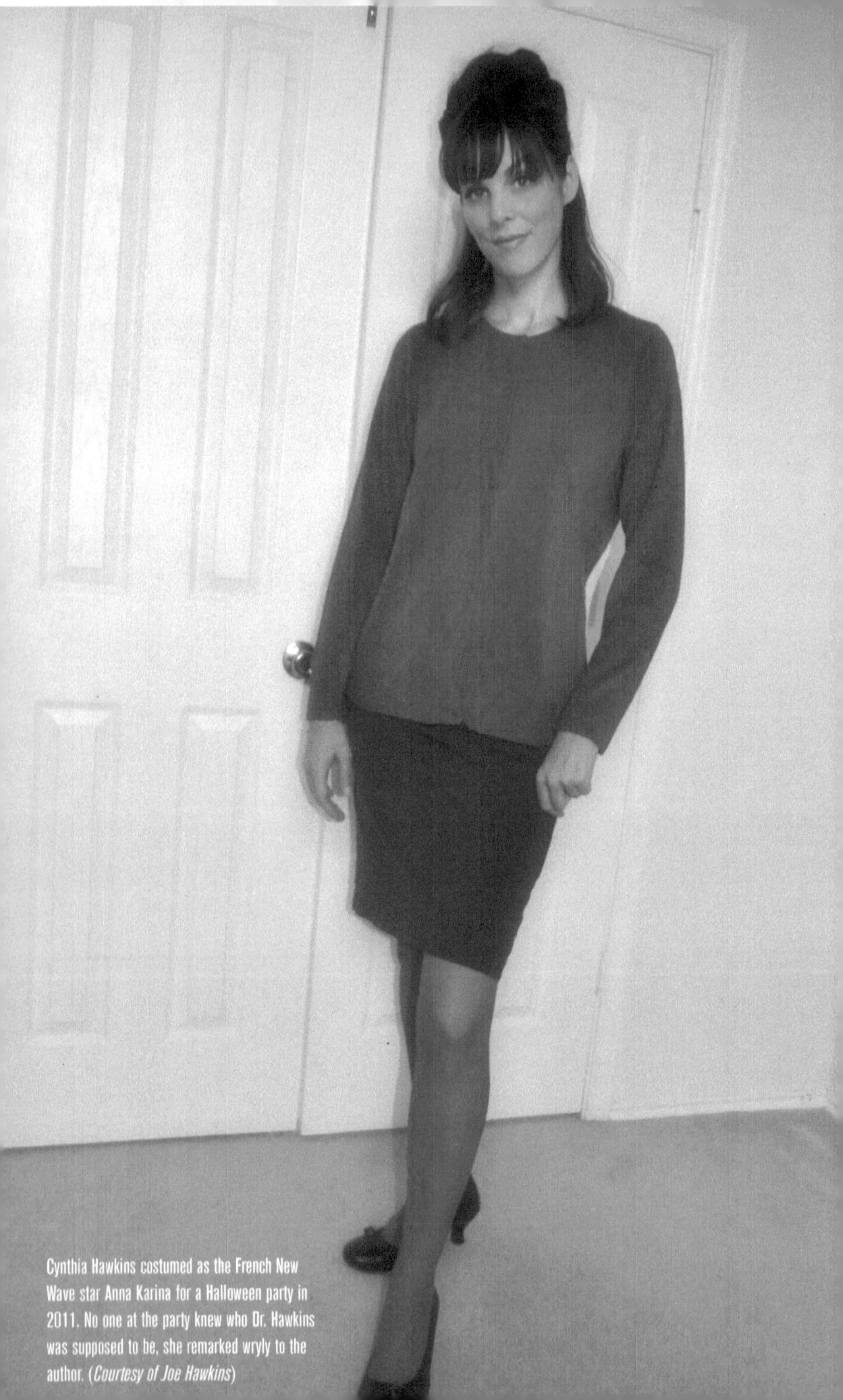

Cynthia Hawkins costumed as the French New Wave star Anna Karina for a Halloween party in 2011. No one at the party knew who Dr. Hawkins was supposed to be, she remarked wryly to the author. (*Courtesy of Joe Hawkins*)

MONSTER BISQUE: HAWKINS AND HANEY TALK FRANKENSTEIN

LAST HALLOWEEN, I'd asked a few Nervous Breakdown contributors to share their favorite terrifying movie scenes, and D. R. Haney was among them with his contribution from Rouben Mamoulian's 1931 *Dr. Jekyll and Mr. Hyde*. I, on the other hand, had picked the tunnel scene from *Willy Wonka*, which I explain so you understand why I like collaborating with Duke. My brain grows three sizes bigger by association. He's like a cinematic moral compass for which true north is James Dean. And this year for Halloween, Duke and I decided to discuss the classic tale that produced another old-school Hollywood icon.

HANEY: Do you remember your introduction to *Frankenstein*? Was it a story that had particular impact on you as a child?

HAWKINS: They must have shown the James Whale *Frankenstein* on network television every October, in the same way they'd show Edwin Marin's *A Christmas Carol* every December. I remember it being this big event because there were only four channels in my household at the time (two without a static scroll), and what else were we going to watch? *Chico and the Man*? So I'd seen glimpses of it in previous years before I'd actually sat down to watch the entire thing when I was maybe seven or eight. Informed by those early glimpses, I'd imagined, with much delight, that it'd be horrifying. But as it turned out the only horrifying thing about it was the way the monster was maligned. He just wanted to hold the sunshine! He didn't know Maria wouldn't float! He was just misunderstood! And Fritz was asking for it. What an asshole. And your introduction?

HANEY: Well, I first watched the James Whale movie when I was around nine. There was a television show called *Sir Graves Presents*, limited to two markets, Detroit and Washington, D.C., and we just managed to receive the D.C. channel where I grew up in central Virginia. The show would start with a panning shot of a no-budget cemetery where its vampire host, Sir

Graves Ghastly, emerged from his coffin to crack jokes while introducing the day's horror movie, and during intermissions he would return to perform skits, sometimes as other characters, including the Cool Ghoul, who was the ghost of a beatnik, or something like that. I think the show aired on Saturday afternoons, originally, but then it moved to Saturday nights at eleven or eleven-thirty, and it was a big deal for me to stay up to watch it, since I had to go to church in the morning. Well, one Saturday night Sir Graves showed *Frankenstein*, and I remember being especially struck by the scene with Maria—that and the one where her father, in a state of shock, carries her muddy body through the streets. I recently saw the movie again, and those scenes still stand out.

But, aside from the James Whale movie, the Frankenstein monster was always just *there*, you know what I mean? I had nightmares about him when I was three or four, and I would wake and go to my parents' room and say, "Can I sleep with you? Frankenstein is going to get me!" There was something about his walk, with his arms outstretched and those oversized boots, that really scared me. Also, the jagged scar on his forehead—that bothered me more than his flat skull or the bolts in his neck.

HAWKINS: He *was* just *there*, wasn't he. He was everywhere. And of course it's the Whale interpretation of him that became so prevalent in pop culture: the bolts, the blockhead, the scar, the walk. Henry Frankenstein (as Victor is renamed in Whale's film) calls the creature "Frankenstein," which also stuck. That's something Mary Shelley doesn't do in the novel, but the creature is in a way an extension of Victor—both transforming into monstrous beings, both hell-bent on revenge. In the silent film adaptation you introduced me to, the creature literally transforms into Victor's mirror image in the penultimate scene, which is such a striking moment. And when I was considering my introduction to *Frankenstein*, I'd first thought of his appearances on *Merrie Melodies* and *Scooby-Doo* and *The Monkees*. I'd thought of the goofily galumphing Herman Munster. So it's surely more honest to say that even before my proper introduction, Whale's Frankenstein iconography had already reached me in slapstick forms devoid of terror. I would have *loved* to have been terrified by that scar and that Karloff half-snarl. Then again, odd things terrified me back then, like the way caterpillar feet plucked free from the window screen when my sister captured them, and things that were meant to be terrifying never were. Which is also to say I was a weird kid, perhaps the true root of my affinity for Whale's monster.

HANEY: I was also a weird kid—hell, I'm a weird adult—and, as I've written before, weird kids often identify with movie monsters, or they do if they know they're weird. I did and I didn't. I knew that other kids, and even some adults, thought of me as weird, but I regarded myself as *unusual* in the tradition of great artists and scientists. That certainly helped to justify my routine tantrums: I'm a genius, and geniuses throw tantrums! At the same time, I thought I was deeply normal, and it was weird to me that people thought of me as weird.

Bear in mind that I was a preschooler when the Frankenstein monster scared me. He no longer scared me by the time I saw the Whale movie. I wasn't scared by horror movies generally. I was just fascinated by monsters, and particularly by the classic monsters of Universal: Frankenstein, Dracula, the Wolfman, the Mummy, and so on. I didn't care much for Godzilla or King Kong. I preferred my monsters on a human scale. Also, my favorite monsters tended to be products of the Romantic imagination—atavistic reminders that, no matter our scientific and technological advancement, we can never escape the irrational. That's something I couldn't have articulated as a child, needless to say, but I do think it was a factor. I was drawn to the ancient world, the primitive world, which seemed much more interesting than the mechanized modern world.

Of course, *Frankenstein* is literally the product of the Romantic imagination. The story of how of Mary Shelley's novel came to be written is better than the novel itself. What work of fiction can outdo Lord Byron and Percy Shelley trading wits at a party where they decide to write ghost stories, and Shelley's girlfriend and later wife, all of eighteen, conceiving of a ghost story that's still being read two hundred years later?

HAWKINS: Right! And you've mentioned to me elsewhere that Frankenstein's monster is unique in that he isn't a creature readily found in legend or folklore, like vampires or werewolves. Sure, Shelley cites the inspiration of Prometheus and one could draw parallels to the golem, but the articulate, intelligent creature formed from dead bodies and urged into being through science is all hers. And she does something extraordinary, I think, in stripping her story of any fantastical or supernatural elements in favor of science. In an era when there were still people debating spontaneous generation, it wouldn't have taken much for the monster-creation scenario to seem plausible. To that end, most of Volume I is spent building Victor up as a bookworm, a devotee of the "natural sciences" from a young age, a feverish researcher. His scientific advancements allow for the creature, which, in 1818, allowed for realism.

The film adaptations seem to struggle with how to make the creation scene seem just as believable for contemporary audiences, thus the variations (usually on the theme of electricity). Notable, for its kitsch value, is Kenneth Branagh's *Mary Shelley's Frankenstein*, in which Branagh's ripped, golden-coiffed Victor facilitates a giant shaft, attached to a giant sack, ejaculating giant sperm/eels to zap the creature into being. Actually, this visual didn't strike me as so overtly sexual until I showed the clip to a group of students at an all-girls Catholic school and it was suddenly *so obvious* my face flushed every shade of red in the visible spectrum by the time I'd reached the DVD player to shut it off. My closest friends have nicknamed me Demura for a reason. You have no idea the courage I had to summon just now to type "ejaculating giant sperm/eels."

HANEY: I assume you didn't summon it from a bottle. That's where I've found courage many a time, and I would require a lot of it to endure Branagh's *Frankenstein* adaptation. While we were discussing our collaboration here, you sent me a clip of the sperm/eels scene, and I was like, "Hey, why is Thor running around a nineteenth-century laboratory?" Then I remembered that Branagh went on to direct *Thor*. Clearly, his *Frankenstein* was foreplay for his *Thor*. I hope, Demura, that doesn't cause you to blush.

HAWKINS: I'd require liquid courage to endure the entirety of Branagh's *Frankenstein* again. I love that guy. He really is a fine actor (and competent director) when he's at his best, but his *Frankenstein* is a mess. Its high-brow attempts to be truer to the source material (De Niro's monster speaks, Victor works in isolation) are quickly undone by nonsensical aberrations from the source (Victor creates the "bride" from Elizabeth's dead body for himself, monster Elizabeth commits suicide by fire).

HANEY: In terms of the monster's creation, the most faithful screen version of the novel may be the first, the silent film you mentioned earlier, which was shot in 1910 at the Thomas Edison Studio in the Bronx. Victor is seen, alone, mixing a concoction in a bowl—a pinch of this and a dash of that—then emptying the bowl into a steaming vat, and—*voilà!*—a monster rises from the steam. It's like making instant bisque, and none of the ingredients are identified, just as the novel is necessarily obscure about Victor's "recipe"; Mary Shelley has him sidestep it in decorous language of this sort: "With an anxiety that almost amounted to agony, I collected the instruments of life around me, that I might infuse a spark of being into the lifeless thing that lay at my feet." There's some talk earlier in the novel about harnessing the power of lightning, but lightning isn't cited as one of the "instruments of life" that can "infuse a spark of being" as it does in, probably, every Frankenstein movie after James Whale. It makes poetic sense: the essence of life is electric in movies, a medium known in its infancy as "electric theater."

Another Whale addition is Fritz, the lab assistant whom you rightly call an asshole, and his inclusion underscores an unspoken concern of the novel: "...scientific man's desire to abandon womankind and find a new method of procreation that does not involve the female principle." So writes David J. Skal in his book *The Monster Show: A Cultural History of Horror*, and Skal continues: "The [Frankenstein procreative] impulse is thus autoerotic ('With my own hands!' as Dr. Frankensteins are usually fond of saying, all the time wringing them in glee—or is it guilt?) and/or homoerotic—life created with the help of male assistants (often cowering dwarves who are seen sticking their heads through portals and trapdoors, who spill precious concoctions, 'fuck things up,' etc.)."

That's Fritz: a "cowering dwarf" who "fuck[s] things up." He drops the "normal" brain marked for the monster and replaces it with a "criminal" brain, which accounts for the monster's violence—as if his utter alienation weren't motivation enough! Plus, he's tortured by Fritz. Why? The movie doesn't say, though we surmise that, finally, there's someone lower in the pecking order. As for "scientific man's desire to abandon womankind," the novel illustrates its implications by concluding in the North Pole, where Victor has pursued his creation far beyond the warm touch of woman. I didn't fully understand why the novel concluded in the North Pole until I read the Skal book, which I frequently recommend. As a matter of fact, I recommended the book to you, and you actually bought a copy. I'm not used to having my recommendations followed!

HAWKINS: Neither am I, and you watched *The Monkees* "Monstrous Monkee Mash" when I recommended it. Bless your heart! As we say in Texas. So, what a strange thing that the film company of Thomas Edison didn't consider electrical origins. I love the monster bisque approach, though. Primordial soup gone awry. And I think by "criminal brain" you meant "Abby Normal" brain. Maybe we can get around to *Young Frankenstein*, one of my favorite movies from childhood starring Gene Wilder, aka the man I thought I'd marry (didn't I say I was a weird kid?), but for now I'll comment on another aspect of that arctic setting.

Branagh's *Frankenstein* ends up with Walton on the ice-locked ship as per the novel, and it's in this chilly desolation that we have the brief convergence of three painfully isolated characters: Walton who longs for a like-minded friend on his expedition to the far reaches, Victor who has lost everyone he loves at the hands of his own creation, and the monster who is such an abomination of nature he has no place in it. De Niro, by the way, plays the creature unsympathetically, like a mangled Max Cady. But that moment in the novel in which the (more sympathetic) creature is sobbing over the body of Victor, all hope for acceptance obliterated, that moment, for my inner weird kid, is sheer horror.

The one chance the monster ever had was in the creation of another of his own kind, his Eve, and Victor destroys the would-be bride before she even takes a breath. Right at the monster's feet. And he does so because he suddenly fears that the two creatures will spawn a demon race. If we go with Skal's reading here, we might say Victor refuses to cede procreative power to the monstrous female. If we're talking Branagh's Victor, well, procreation is something only his giant monster-making phallus should do. And of course we get to see this Eve take a few steps in Whale's *Bride of Frankenstein* (played by Elsa Lanchester, who also plays Mary Shelley in the opening scene, oh the layers of meaning!).

HANEY: Yes, when I saw *Bride of Frankenstein* as a kid, I was perplexed by Elsa Lanchester's dual roles. I knew the author of the book was Mary Shelley, but I had never heard of her husband or Byron, who likewise appear in the *Bride* prologue to help remind the audience of where the first movie left off, as legendary poets are apt to do. "Would you like to hear what happened after that?" asks Lanchester as Mary. "I'm all ears," says the actor playing Byron. Meanwhile, the real Byron, spinning in his grave, triggers an earthquake.

But, seriously, I think *Bride* had a greater impact on me at nine than the original *Frankenstein*. I cried when the monster was taken in by the blind man, his first and only friend; and the movie's climax, when the monster's Eve, as you call her, comes to life and rejects him, is a highlight of horror history, with that haunting score by Max Waxman and Lanchester's staccato movements, which she modeled after birds, and Jack Pierce's visionary makeup, including the streaks suggestive of lightning bolts in the bride's electrified hair. Pierce, with input from Whale, also created the monster's look in the 1931 *Frankenstein*, producing one of very few twentieth-century screen characters still identifiable in the twenty-first century. Bela Lugosi's Dracula is another, though I doubt that many contemporary kids could name Lugosi or Boris Karloff, who brought a pathos to the monster that's never been equaled, even when other actors, among them Lugosi, played him in Jack Pierce's makeup. Of course, they played him in inferior films, none of them directed by Whale, but I still think Karloff's success in the part was due largely to Karloff.

Shelley's monster is an orphan with the history of deprivation that's become a cliché of criminal profiles, and as you say, he's intelligent and articulate, so that he can plead his case and draw sympathy. He almost never has that capacity in movies, where, apart from those with Karloff, sympathy seems beside the point. For instance, from the late fifties to the early seventies, Hammer Film Productions made a series of Frankenstein movies, each with a different monster closer in spirit to Leatherface or Jack the Ripper than Karloff's monster. These impulse killers are inevitably destroyed, causing Victor, usually played by Peter Cushing, to start anew in the sequel. Whale's Victor (who was probably renamed Henry because Victor, of course, means victorious) is redeemed by love and marriage after realizing that God's work should be left to God, but Cushing's Victor has no qualms about playing God; he's cold and ruthless—a psychopath cranking out psychopaths. But the lurid violence of the Hammer movies is what I like about them—that and their lush color and the retro factor. I imagine them as double features at the drive-in. Friday and Saturday only: *The Evil of Frankenstein* and *The Brides of Dracula*!

HAWKINS: And that particular pathos you mentioned was apparently Karloff's idea. According to James Heffernan in "Looking at the Monster: *Frankenstein* and Film," Whale had wanted Karloff's monster to violently throw Maria into the river and Karloff suggested it be a tender encounter resulting in an accidental drowning. I have to say, though, the monster's certainly more fun as a drive-in double feature psychopath. No gray areas to feel conflicted about. No wretched creature on whom to project your worst fears of rejection and alienation. But never is the monster more fun than when he's hoofing it in a tux onstage beside Gene Wilder's Frederick Frankenstein, chiming in on "Puttin' On the Ritz."

HANEY: *Young Frankenstein* was ruined for me by people acting out the best bits before I'd seen it. You can guess the result: when I finally saw it, I didn't find it as funny as I expected. Fun, yes, but laugh-out-loud funny, no, alas.

Every classic horror movie has been spoofed ad nauseam, but *Frankenstein* has been especially attractive to satirists, with the monster's cloddishness and the doctor's feverish megalomania. Versions of both characters appear in numerous animated shorts from the thirties, forties, and fifties—you already mentioned Bugs Bunny—and the Frankenstein skit was a constant of television variety shows, that extinct genre. Even Universal, the home of the franchise, played the monster for laughs in *Abbott and Costello Meet Frankenstein.* By then he had been milked dry of horror appeal, executives must have figured, and that went for their other star monsters, who were also featured alongside Abbott and Costello, Universal's star comedians.

My favorite *Frankenstein* parody is *The Rocky Horror Picture Show.* Tim Curry's Frank N. Furter may look like a transvestite vampire, but in fact he's a transvestite scientist who's building a bride—a male bride for himself. *Rocky Horror* could only have been made in the glitter-rock early seventies, though its cheeky pansexual decadence derives from Weimar cabaret, and to see it now is to realize how staid and rigid we are in the twenty-first century. Also, Tim Curry is flat-out brilliant in the kind of performance that usually goes unrecognized by awards committees. But that's true of Boris Karloff's performance in *Frankenstein.* Fredric March's Oscar for *Dr. Jekyll and Mr. Hyde* is an anomaly.

HAWKINS: *Young Frankenstein* is one of those things that might be hard for me to truly judge because I saw it as a kid and I'm still aping its best bits ("Walk this way!"). But I can tell you whenever I teach Shelley's *Frankenstein* I show *Young Frankenstein* clips to students and find I'm the only one laughing. The soundless, tears-welling-up laugh. Just me.

And of course the ultimate jokey, milked-dry-of-horror Frankenstein creature has to be his incarnation as a sixties sitcom patriarch on *The Munsters.* If it's funny to see him in a soft-shoe routine, it's even funnier to see him as Joe Suburbia muddling through TV-family shenanigans in his platform boots and bolt-screwed neck. In a weird way, Fred Gwynne as Herman Munster makes an indelible impression for some of the same reasons Boris Karloff had in Whale's films, though to far different effect. Like Karloff's, Gwynne's makeup was tailored to his unique features, allowing for that human connection, for that pathos in Karloff's case and that personality in Gwynne's. And, as you've told me, acting through makeup takes a particular talent. They keep trying to reboot *The Munsters*, and they keep failing at it. Probably because it was too schlocky to begin with, but most definitely because Gwynne is irreplaceable.

As for the equally irreplaceable Tim Curry….I have no idea how *The Rocky Horror Picture Show* didn't blip onto my radar until my early twenties. The first time I saw it, my friend had rented it because it was Halloween and we thought *Rocky Horror* was going to be something like *Creepshow.* I really wish I could be *that* surprised by a movie again.

HANEY: I wasn't that surprised, since I had heard a lot about it by the time I saw it. But I'm not *that* huge a fan. *Rocky Horror* is a relic of my midnight-movies youth, though I never dressed in costume or did the Time Warp, and I like it now mainly because of Tim Curry.

One underappreciated aspect of *The Munsters* is the way it reflects the America of Ellis Island, which still lived in memory when the show was current. Many young Americans of the sixties had heard their grandparents or even their parents speak of "the old country"—for the Munsters, the old country is Transylvania—and just as few Ellis Island immigrants could afford higher education, so that they worked at trades or in factories, the Munsters are maintained by Herman's low-level job at a funeral parlor. Herman's vampire father-in-law, meanwhile, is a retired vaudeville magician and garage inventor, though in his case the garage is a dungeon clearly based on the Frankenstein lab, and he's as much a mad scientist as he's an inventor. Grandpa Munster is Count Dracula and Dr. Frankenstein combined!

I was going to say that the mad scientist—a stock character of old movies, starting with *Frankenstein*—has disappeared, but on second thought, I'm not sure that's true.

HAWKINS: Well, there's Dr. Heiter, the mad surgeon, from the *Human Centipede* films, which I guess you could say is an evolution of the Frankenstein story itself.

HANEY: I haven't seen *The Human Centipede*, but to cast a wide net, any character who misuses science or technology is in the mad-scientist tradition, and there are bound to be many such characters in movies now. On the other hand, most Hollywood movies are now made for audiences in their teens or younger, and those audiences don't have much, if any, ambivalence about technology, so maybe there's no such thing as going "too far" in the mad-scientist way. Robot slaves? Hybrid animals? Computers that "feel"? Where can I, like, get one?

Frankenstein is a book you teach, right? Does it raise any questions of the "What does it mean to be human?" type for your students? Without your prompting, I mean.

HAWKINS: Not necessarily in those terms, though they often express surprise that the monster is more human than they'd anticipated. This is something, out of curiosity, I like to keep track of every semester I teach *Frankenstein*—what they focus on, where their sympathies tend to fall, what pre-formed knowledge of *Frankenstein* they bring to their reading of the novel. Usually, when I ask, only a few say they've read the novel before, and even fewer have seen any of the *Frankenstein* film adaptations (most have seen *The Human Centipede*). One thing they all know before digging into the novel is the image of Whale's Frankenstein monster. The fact that Whale's is the ubiquitous Frankenstein is fascinating to me (though we've already touched on Karloff's role in that). But it's also fascinating that filmmakers keep returning to this tale. *I, Frankenstein* releases this January [2014], and there's some talk about revisiting *Frankenstein* in a broader effort to bring back Universal's classic movie monsters, for example. Why do you think *Frankenstein*, in one form or another, endures?

HANEY: Well, Hollywood fears risk, so it seeks proven commodities: remakes and sequels of blockbuster movies, and adaptations of hit novels, plays, and television shows. Of course, there aren't many hit novels compared to the past, and the theater is kind of hobbling along as well. In fact, Broadway, with its endless revivals, has become more like Hollywood in recent years. Anyway, on the simplest level, I think *Frankenstein* keeps getting recycled because everyone has heard of it, and that suits producers and audiences alike. I'm consistently struck by the timidity of today's audiences. They stick to what they know.

On another level, the Frankenstein story is an early vision of technological man that's still relevant after two hundred years. It's *very* possible to go too far, though we don't always agree as to where the line has been crossed and we may not know until it's too late. But we push ahead blindly because that's what we do, trusting that science and technology will protect and save us, and works like Shelley's *Frankenstein* are there to warn of the potential consequences. What is it about that particular story? I would guess it's the characters. I haven't read much science fiction, but it may be that no characters have ever dramatized the stakes of "progress" as clearly and purely as Victor and his creature.

What do *you* think?

HAWKINS: Yeah, I think that's right, and I would add that not only is it a failure of science unchecked but a failure of human goodness as well. Science might have formed the creature, but it's rejection that makes him monstrous. I wish one of these movie reboots would finally get Shelley's *Frankenstein* just right. And I wish it could star James Dean.

HANEY: You know, I never thought about it until now, but James Dean, the chronically alienated epitome of teen angst, would have been ideally cast as the monster in a *Frankenstein* remake. As a matter of fact, he once played the monster in a school play called *Goon with the Wind*, and I understand he did his own makeup.

HAWKINS: Not bad! In the words of Mary Shelley: "His countenance bespoke bitter anguish, combined with disdain and malignity." I imagine Dean's was the most convincing monster to ever drag his platform boots across a high school stage.

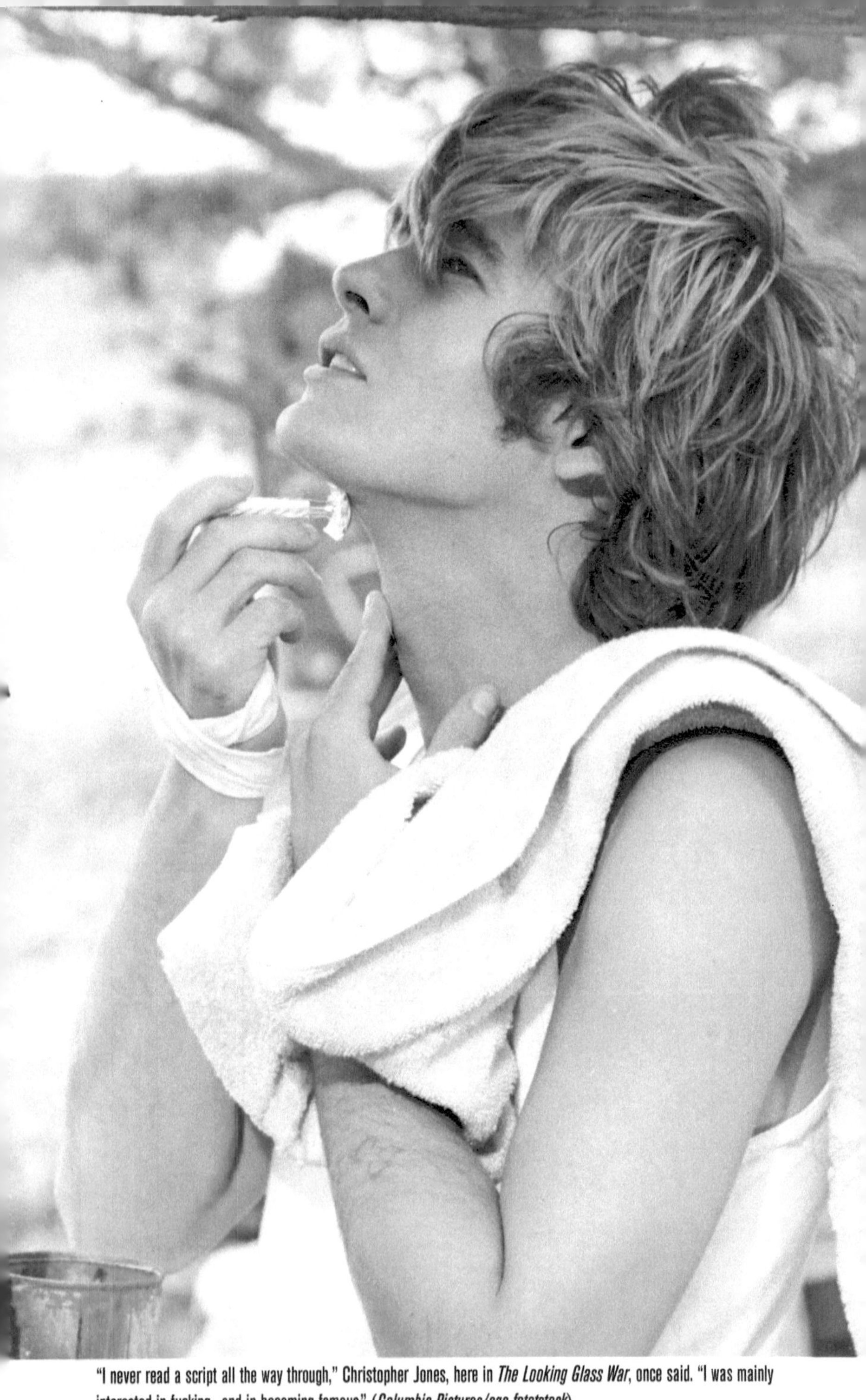

"I never read a script all the way through," Christopher Jones, here in *The Looking Glass War*, once said. "I was mainly interested in fucking—and in becoming famous." (*Columbia Pictures/age fototstock*)

SELECTED BIBLIOGRAPHY

WHEN DINOSAURS RULED THE EARTH

Mailer, Norman. *The Armies of the Night*. New York: New American Library, 1968.

Scanlon, Paul. "George Lucas: The Wizard of 'Star Wars.'" *Rolling Stone*. August 25, 1977.

GOLDEN STATE GIRL

Banner, Lois. *Marilyn: The Passion and the Paradox*. New York: Bloomsbury USA, 2012.

Grissom, James. *Follies of God: Tennessee Williams and the Women of Fog*. New York: Knopf, 2014.

Leaming, Barbara. *Marilyn Monroe*. New York: Crown Publishers, 1998.

Mailer, Norman. *Marilyn*. New York: Grosset & Dunlap, 1973.

Spoto, Donald. *Marilyn Monroe: The Biography*. New York: Cooper Square Press, 2001.

Summers, Anthony. *Goddess: The Secret Lives of Marilyn Monroe*. New York: Macmillan, 1985.

Wills, David. *Marilyn Monroe: Metamorphosis*. New York: It Books, 2011.

NOWHERE MEN

Burrows, Larry. *Vietnam*. New York: Knopf, 2002.

Herr, Michael. *Dispatches*. New York: Knopf, 1977.

Meyers, Jeffrey. *Inherited Risk: Errol and Sean Flynn in Hollywood and Vietnam*. New York: Simon & Schuster, 2002.

Niven, David. *Bring on the Empty Horses*. London: Hamish Hamilton, 1975.

Ray, Michèle, and Abbott, Elisabeth (translator). *The Two Shores of Hell*. New York: David McKay, 1968.

Tucker, Anne Wilkes, and Michels, Will, and Zelt, Nathalie. *War/Photography: Images of Armed Conflict and Its Aftermath*. Museum of Fine Arts, Houston/Yale University Press, 2012.

Young, Perry Deane. *Two of the Missing: Remembering Sean Flynn and Dana Stone.* New York: Coward, McCann & Geoghegan, 1975.

ROOM 32

Babitz, Eve. "Jim Morrison Is Dead and Living in Hollywood." *Esquire.* January 1991.

Butler, Patricia. *Angels Dance and Angels Die: The Tragic Romance of Pamela and Jim Morrison.* New York: Schirmer Trade Books, 1998.

Dalton, David. *Mr. Mojo Risin': Jim Morrison, the Last Holy Fool.* New York: St. Martin's Press, 1991.

Davis, Mike. *City of Quartz: Excavating the Future in Los Angeles.* New York: Verso, 1990.

Davis, Stephen. *Jim Morrison: Life, Death, Legend.* London: Ebury Press, 2004.

The Doors, and Fong-Torres, Ben. *The Doors.* New York: Hyperion, 2006.

Hopkins, Jerry, and Sugerman, Dan. *No One Here Gets Out Alive.* New York: Warner Books, 1980.

Morrison, Jim. *The Lords and the New Creatures.* New York: Touchstone, 1971.

Priore, Dominec. *Riot on Sunset Strip: Rock'n'Roll's Last Stand in Hollywood.* London: Jawbone Press, 2007.

LIFE IN ELIZABETHAN VIRGINIA

Bosworth, Patricia. *Montgomery Clift: A Biography.* New York: Houghton Mifflin Harcourt, 1978.

Scherman, David E. (editor). *Life Goes to the Movies.* New York: Time Life, 1975.

OSWALD HAS BEEN SHOT

Bugliosi, Vincent. *Four Days in November.* New York: W. W. Norton, 2008.

Cox, Alex. *The President and the Provocateur: The Parallel Lives of JFK and Lee Harvey Oswald.* Port Townsend, WA: Feral House, 2013.

Epstein, Edward Jay. *Legend: The Secret World of Lee Harvey Oswald.* New York: McGraw-Hill, 1978.

Friedman, Josh Alan. *When Sex Was Dirty.* Los Angeles: Feral House, 2004.

Loken, John. *Oswald's Trigger Films: The Manchurian Candidate, We Were Strangers, Suddenly?* Ann Arbor, MI: Falcon Books, 2000.

Mailer, Norman. *Oswald's Tale: An American Mystery.* New York: Random House, 1995.

McMillan, Priscilla Johnson. *Marina and Lee.* New York: HarperCollins, 1977.

Morrison, Jim. *The Lords and the New Creatures*. New York: Touchstone, 1971.

Warren Commission. *Report of the President's Commission on the Assassination of President John F. Kennedy*, U.S. Government Printing Office, 1964.

_____. *Warren Commission Hearings*. U.S. Government Printing Office, 1964.

YOU WILL BECOME SHORT OF BREATH

Corman, Roger, and Jerome, Jim. *How I Made a Hundred Movies in Hollywood and Never Lost a Dime*. New York: Random House, 1990.

Gray, Beverly. *Roger Corman: An Unauthorized Biography of the Godfather of Indie Filmmaking*. Los Angeles: Renaissance Books, 2000.

I WANT TO TAKE YOU HIGHER

Uncredited. "Funk legend Sly Stone homeless and living in a van in LA." *New York Post*. September 25, 2011.

Uncredited. "Hildegard Quits Earl Bostic: Earthquake Named as Cause." *Jet*. October 28, 1965.

PLAYBOY IN THE DARK

Acocella, Joan. "The Girls Next Door." *The New Yorker*. March 20, 2006.

Biskind, Peter. *Easy Riders, Raging Bulls*. New York: Simon & Schuster, 1999.

Bogdanovich, Peter. *The Killing of the Unicorn: Dorothy Stratten, 1960-1980*. Now York: William Morrow, 1984.

Carpenter, Teresa. "Death of a Playmate." *The Village Voice*. November 5-11, 1980.

Davis, Mike. *City of Quartz: Excavating the Future in Los Angeles*. New York: Verso, 1990.

DuBois, Larry. "Playboy Interview: Hugh M. Hefner." *Playboy*. January 1974.

Edgren, Gretchen. *The Playboy Book*. Los Angeles: General Publishing Group, 1994.

_____. *Inside the Playboy Mansion*. Los Angeles: General Publishing Group, 1998.

_____. *The Playmate Book*. Los Angeles: General Publishing Group, 1996.

Lisanti, Tom. *Glamour Girls of Sixties Hollywood: Seventy-Five Profiles*. Jefferson, NC: McFarland, 2007.

Miller, Russell. *Bunny: The Real Story of Playboy*. New York: Holt, Rinehart & Winston, 1985.

Polanski, Roman. *Roman by Polanski*. New York: William Morrow, 1984.
St. James, Izabella. *Bunny Tales: Behind Closed Doors at the Playboy Mansion*. Philadelphia: Running Press, 2006.
Talese, Gay. *Thy Neighbor's Wife*. New York: Doubleday, 1980.
Watts, Steven. *Mr. Playboy: Hugh Hefner and the American Dream*. Hoboken, NJ: John Wiley & Sons, 2008.

THE PHANTOM OF THE PUBLIC THEATER
Rich, Frank. "Theater: 'Midsummer Night.'" *The New York Times*. January 13, 1988.

PLUTO IN THE TWELFTH HOUSE
Bloom, Harold (editor). *Sam Shepard (Bloom's Major Dramatists)*. Philadelphia: Chelsea House Publishers, 2002.
Cameron, Julia. "The Twice-Torn Soul of Mark Frechette." *Oui*. March 1975.
Dole, Robert. *Comment réussir sa schizophrénie*. Montréal: VLB Éditeur, 2000.
_____. *What Rough Beast*. London: Austin Macauley, 2017.
Felton, David. "The Lyman Family's Holy Siege of America." *Rolling Stone*. December 23, 1971, and January 6, 1972.
Flatley, Guy. "Antonioni Defends 'Zabriskie Point.'" *The New York Times*. February 22, 1970.
Hamilton, Elizabeth, and Rich, Eric. "Abusive Priest Found In Caribbean Hideaway." *Harford Courant*. August 29, 2002.
_____. "A Predator Blessed with Charm." *Hartford Courant*. September 15, 2002.
Hoberman, J. *The Dream Life: Movies, Media, and the Mythology of the Sixties*. New York: The New Press, 2003.
Kindman, Michael, and Wachsberger, Ken (editor). *My Odyssey Through the Underground Press*. Lansing, MI: Michigan State University Press, 2011.
Lewis, Jon. *Hollywood V. Hard Core: How the Struggle Over Censorship Created the Modern Film Industry*. New York: New York University Press, 2000.
McLellan, Vin, and Avery, Paul. *The Voices of Guns*. New York: Putnam, 1977.
Miles, Barry. *Hippie*. New York: Sterling, 2004.
O'Brian, Dave. "Mark Frechette: A Manipulated Life." *The Boston Phoenix*. October 7, 1975.

Paglia, Camille. *Sexual Personae: Art and Decadence from Nefertiti to Emily Dickinson.* New Haven: Yale University Press, 1991.

People Staff. "In Prison, An Ex-actor Stages the Watergate Tapes." *People.* April 14, 1975.

Pomerance, Murry. *Michelangelo Red Antonioni Blue: Eight Reflections on Cinema.* Berkeley: University of California Press, 2011.

Robbins, Ira. "Where Are They Now: Daria Halprin." *Rolling Stone.* September 12, 1985.

Rosenthal, M. L. (editor). *Selected Poems and Two Plays of William Butler Yeats.* New York: Collier Books, 1962.

Sales, Bob. "Where are the listeners? A journey from Fort Hill to Zabriskie to Cell 104." *The Boston Globe.* September 9, 1973.

Sanders, Ed. "The Squeaky Fromme Story." *Oui.* March 1976.

Winkler, Peter L. *Dennis Hopper: The Wild Ride of a Hollywood Rebel.* Fort Lee, NJ: Barricade Books, 2011.

Winters, John J. *Sam Shepard: A Life.* Berkeley: Counterpoint, 2017.

Wolmuth, Roger. "After Two Oft-Troubled Decades, the Lyman Family Commune Scores a Sweet Song of Success at Last." *People.* September 22, 1986.

WILLIAM DESMOND TAYLOR DIED FOR YOUR SINS

Giroux, Robert. *A Deed of Death: The Story of the Unsolved Murder of Hollywood Director William Desmond Taylor.* New York: Knopf, 1990.

CATCH ME

Adams, Cindy. *Lee Strasberg: The Imperfect Genius of the Actors Studio.* New York: Doubleday, 1980.

Barnes, Mike. "'Ryan's Daughter' Star Christopher Jones Dies at 72." *The Hollywood Reporter.* January 31, 2014.

Brownlow, Kevin. *David Lean: A Biography.* New York: St. Martin's Press, 1996.

Bugliosi, Vincent, and Gentry, Kurt. *Helter Skelter: The True Story of the Manson Murders (25th Anniversary Edition).* New York: W. W. Norton & Company, 1994.

Butler, Patricia. *Angels Dance and Angels Die: The Tragic Romance of Pamela and Jim Morrison.* New York: Schirmer Trade Books, 1998.

Dakota, Bill. *The Gossip Columnist.* Studio "D" Publishing Company, 2010.

Des Barres, Pamela. "The Agony and the Ecstasy." *Movieline.* August 1996.

Kiernan, Thomas. *The Roman Polanski Story.* New York: Grove Press, 1980.

King, Greg. *Sharon Tate and the Manson Murders.* Fort Lee, NJ: Barricade Books, 2000.

Lowe, Skip E. *The Boy with the Betty Grable Legs: A Showbiz Memoir.* Los Angeles: Belle Publishing, 2001.

Miles, Sarah. *Serves Me Right.* London: Macmillan, 1994.

Priore, Dominec. *Riot on Sunset Strip: Rock'n'Roll's Last Stand in Hollywood.* London: Jawbone Press, 2007.

Richardson, John H. "The Wasp Woman Stung." *Premiere.* April 1991.

Strasberg, Susan. *Bittersweet.* New York: G. P. Putnam's Sons, 1980.

Winters, Shelley. *Shelley II: The Middle of My Century.* New York: Simon & Schuster, 1989.

THE END OF COCK RUN

Associated Press. "Guatemala Closes Case of Steve Cochran's Death." *Star Tribune.* July 4, 1965.

Austin, John. *Tales of Hollywood the Bizarre.* New York: S.P.I. Books, 1994.

Cardullo, Bert. *Michelangelo Antonioni: Interviews.* Jackson, MS: University Press of Mississippi, 2008.

Haley, James L. *Wolf: The Lives of Jack London.* New York: Basic Books, 2011.

Hannsberry, Karen Burroughs. *Bad Boys: The Actors of the Film Noir.* Jefferson, NC: McFarland Publishing, 2003.

Keating, Jeanne Markham. "Portrait of a Friend." *The Valley News.* June 29, 1965.

Mann, May. *Jayne Mansfield: A Biography.* New York: Drake Publishers, 1973.

Mayo, Virginia, and Van Savage. L.C. *The Best Years of My Life.* Chesterfield, MO: Beachhouse Books, 2002.

Parfrey, Adam. *It's a Man's World: Men's Adventure Magazines, The Postwar Pulps.* Los Angeles: Feral House, 2003.

Salazar, Ruben. "Actor's Sea Death Tied to Lung Attack." *The Los Angeles Times.* June 28, 1965.

Uncredited. "Policeman's Shot Stops Steve Cochran in Auto." *The Los Angeles Times.* November 9, 1953.

Van Doren, Mamie. *Playing the Field.* New York: Putnam, 1987.

Zimbalist, Efrem, Jr. *My Dinner of Herbs.* New York: Limelight Editions, 2003.

MONSTER BISQUE: HAWKINS AND HANEY TALK FRANKENSTEIN

Heffernan, James A. W. "Looking at the Monster: *Frankenstein* and Film." *Critical Inquiry 24, no.1* Autumn 1997.

Shelley, Mary. *Frankenstein; or The Modern Prometheus.* London: Lackington, Hughes, Harding, Mavor & Jones, 1818.
Skal, David J. *The Monster Show: A Cultural History of Horror.* New York: W.W. Norton, 1993.

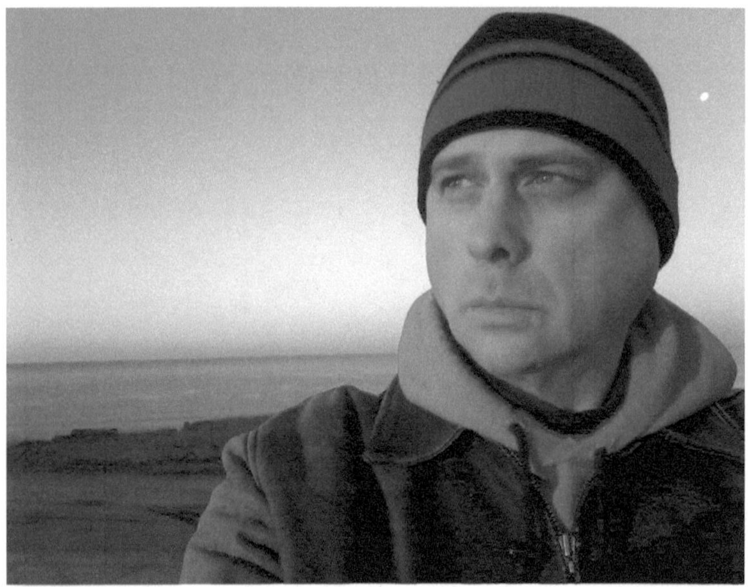

DUKE HANEY, a.k.a. Daryl Haney, has spent most of his adult life working in the movie business, with twenty feature-film credits as an actor and twenty-two as a screenwriter. He used pseudonyms for some of the screenplays and went by "D. R. Haney" as the author of a novel, *Banned for Life*, and an essay collection, *Subversia*. After he was struck by a car in a crosswalk on Sunset Boulevard, a friend claimed he walked like John "Duke" Wayne and gave him the nickname by which most people know him and he has taken belatedly as his pen name. He plans to follow *Death Valley Superstars* with a novel tentatively titled *XXX*.

www.ingramcontent.com/pod-product-compliance
Lightning Source LLC
LaVergne TN
LVHW091110080826
845145LV00008B/1860
9780692172391